"Nagging" Questions

New Feminist Perspectives Series
General Editor: Rosemarie Tong, Davidson College

Claiming Reality: Phenomenology and Women's Experience
   by Louise Levesque-Lopman

Evidence on Her Own Behalf: Women's Narrative as Theological Voice
   by Elizabeth Say

Feminist Jurisprudence: The Difference Debate
   edited by Leslie Friedman Goldstein

Is Women's Philosophy Possible?
   by Nancy J. Holland

Manhood and Politics: A Feminist Reading of Political Theory
   by Wendy L. Brown

"Nagging" Questions: Feminist Ethics in Everyday Life
   edited by Dana E. Bushnell

Rethinking Ethics in the Midst of Violence: A Feminist Approach to Freedom
   by Linda A. Bell

Rethinking Masculinity: Philosophical Explorations in Light of Feminism
   edited by Larry May and Robert A. Strikwerda

Speaking from the Heart: A Feminist Perspective on Ethics
   by Rita C. Manning

Take Back the Light: A Feminist Reclamation of Spirituality and Religion
   by Sheila Ruth

Toward a Feminist Epistemology
   by Jane Duran

Voluptuous Yearnings: A Feminist Theory of the Obscene
   by Mary Caputi

Women, Militarism, and War: Essays in History, Politics, and Social Theory
   edited by Jean Bethke Elshtain and Sheila Tobias

Women, Sex, and the Law
   by Rosemarie Tong

"Nagging" Questions

Feminist Ethics in Everyday Life

Edited by
Dana E. Bushnell

ROWMAN & LITTLEFIELD PUBLISHERS, INC.

ROWMAN & LITTLEFIELD PUBLISHERS, INC.

Published in the United States of America
by Rowman & Littlefield Publishers, Inc.
4720 Boston Way, Lanham, Maryland 20706

3 Henrietta Street
London WC2E 8LU, England

British Cataloging in Publication Information Available

Library of Congress Cataloging-in-Publication Data

"Nagging" questions: feminist ethics in everyday life / edited by
Dana E. Bushnell.
p.   cm. — (New feminist perspectives series)
Includes bibliographical references and index.
1. Feminist ethics. 2. Feminist theory. I. Bushnell, Dana E.,
1958– . II. Series.
BJ1395.N34   1995   170'.82—dc20   94-32590   CIP

ISBN 0–8476–8006–1 (cloth : alk. paper)
ISBN 0–8476–8007–X (pbk. : alk. paper)

Printed in the United States of America

For Brian, Ada Emrys,
and Myrtle Marie

Contents

Part IV
Body and Sexual Images

Acknowledgments

I am grateful for the help of the women who typed and proofread this book, Lisa Drake, Linda Lacny, Cathy Byers, Thelma Pascaran, and Carrie James. I would never have gotten through without their support. I am also extremely grateful for the wonderful and helpful suggestions of Richard Double and Katherine Sotol and to all of the contributors to *"Nagging" Questions.*

I would also like to thank the authors and publishers who allowed us to reprint the following essays:

"Oppression and Victimization: Choice and Responsibility," Susan Wendell, originally appeared in *Hypatia* and is reprinted here by permission of the author.

"Right-Wing Women," from *Journal of Social Philosophy* 24, no. 30 (Winter 1993): 40–61, by permission of the publisher.

"New Reproductive Technologies," Susan Sherwin, from *No Longer Patient: Feminist Ethics and Health Care* (Philadelphia: Temple University Press, 1992), by permission of Temple University Press.

"Markets in Women's Reproductive Labor," Debra Satz, *Philosophy and Public Affairs* 21, no. 2 (Spring 1992) © 1992 by Princeton University Press.

"Privacy and Reproductive Liberty," Anita L. Allen, from *Uneasy Access* by permission of Johns Hopkins University Press.

"Coercing Birth Control," Lenore Kuo, *Biomedical Ethics Reviews* by permission of Humana Press.

"Is IVF Research a Threat to Women's Autonomy?" Mary Anne Warren, from *Embryo Experimentation,* ed. Peter Singer et al. (New York: Cambridge University Press, 1990). Reprinted by permission of Cambridge University Press.

"To Be or Not Be a Woman: Anorexia Nervosa, Normative Gender Roles, and Feminism," Mary Briody Mahowald, *The Journal of Medicine and Philosophy* by permission of Kluwer Academic Publishers.

"Women and the Knife: Cosmetic Surgery and the Colonization of Women's Bodies," Kathryn Pauly Morgan, originally appeared in *Hypatia* and is reprinted here by permission of the author.

"Feminine Masochism and the Politics of Personal Transformation," Sandra Lee Bartky, from *Femininity and Domination: Studies in the Phenomenology of Oppression* (New York: Routledge, 1990), by permission of the publisher.

1

Introduction: Philosophy and Feminism

Dana E. Bushnell

Theory and Practice

Philosophy literally means "love of wisdom." Loving wisdom requires considering difficult problems and searching for reasonable answers. Traditionally, philosophy examines the unanswered questions concerning knowledge, existence, and value (epistemology, metaphysics, and ethics). Philosophy also confronts a multitude of other areas of human thought, including the practical and moral difficulties we face in everyday life. This is where the discipline of feminism and the real-life problems of women lie.

Philosophy is a critical approach to all intellectual disciplines and to life itself. It is bound by reason, thoughtfulness, and logical analysis, and it deals with all sorts of problems, trying to find truth. For example: What is "not logically sound" reasoning? What is "biased" reasoning? Are there any views on an issue that are "absolutely irrational"? If so, what makes a viewpoint "irrational"? In philosophy, no less than in psychology, we wonder what makes people tick. Unlike psychologists, we philosophers try to figure out what makes human actions morally right and wrong. We do not ignore this core of hard questions by saying that we do not make value judgments. Making value judgments is philosophy's business, and making value judgments about the difficulties that women face is one of philosophy's specialties.

At root, the feminist believes, and even insists, that women deserve the same social, political, and economic rights as men. A feminist believes that the oppression of women is morally wrong and, therefore, is necessarily a champion of equality. The chapters in this book are feminist in this sense, and they are also philosophical because they are all critical approaches to issues in feminism. The papers in this book are feminist in this sense. And they are also philosophical because they are all critical approaches to issues in feminism.

Although all feminists share a fundamental belief in the moral necessity of gaining equality for women, there are many differences of opinion about how to reach that goal. Some feminists believe that equality cannot be achieved unless women today are compensated for all of society's past discrimination against women. Other feminists believe that such compensation is not necessary, however much it might be morally justified. Others wonder whether advocating compensation at this time, however justified it might be, is in the best interest of the feminist cause, since this sort of compensation may lead to backlash and dissent even among women. The question of strategy, as these examples show, is an interesting, ongoing debate. It is a *theoretical* debate regarding what is the best *practical* strategy for feminists to adopt.

To an observer of current feminist philosophy, theory may seem to be the most prevalent feature. Feminists address theoretical questions about what femininity is, about whether gender-neutral language is morally obligatory, about whether women's theorizing is fundamentally different from men's, and about whether women's way of knowing differs from the way men know, for example. These are fascinating questions. I applaud the growth in the amount of theorizing being done concerning these questions because most of this theorizing is being done not just *about* women, but *by* women. We are, to some extent, having our own say about our lives and our viewpoints. Although there is nothing inherent in these questions that bars men from speaking about them, it is important that women are the major contributors. Women often have greater experience in these areas and usually have much more at stake.

But there is a second, less theoretical, way of pursuing feminist philosophy. We can apply feminist perspectives to specific problems and dilemmas that trouble feminists today. This is the focus of *"Nagging" Questions*. As an ethicist and a teacher, I decided that this book would focus on concrete ethical issues that uniquely affect the lives of women. The result is a hands-on approach to feminist philosophy: feminist theories are applied to practical problems, the nagging questions that continue to cry out for answers.

This book does not cover all possible positions on every issue concerning women. Nor does it contain challenges of each argument found in the chapters. This task is for the reader. The pieces in this book focus on a variety of current problems concerning women and their places in society, issues I have found particularly stimulating to the undergraduates I have taught in my classes. Several of these chapters confront dilemmas partially caused and intensified by recent technologies. Others focus on new problems generated by old social standards. But all ultimately reflect the difficulties created by social stereotypes that disadvantage women, limiting and impoverishing their lives.

Stereotypes are oversimplified generalizations about groups of things, sometimes accurate, sometimes inaccurate, sometimes favorable, and sometimes unfavorable. For example, a stereotype of a bat is that it is a flying mammal that hangs upside down to sleep. This is an accurate stereotype and there is nothing unfavorable about it. But in an inaccurate and unfavorable sense of ''stereotype,'' which is how the term is usually understood, a stereotype is an untruthful, and often malicious, generalization about a group of persons. In this unfavorable sense, stereotypes often are concocted by persons who harbor biases toward the group they stereotype. The persons who rely upon stereotypes often interpret reality in such a way as to support their biases against the group that is stereotyped. For example, suppose you see a man staggering down the street just past a bar. As you watch this person stagger, you assume that he is drunk. This assumption is your *interpretation* of reality. Such assumptions are not always accurate. The person you believe to be drunk may instead be having a seizure. Other persons, especially the young, may not have preexisting biases against the stereotyped group, but may be influenced by the stereotype through repeated exposure and tacit endorsement. Unless discredited, even stereotypes that deplorably fail to represent objective truth may affect a society that assumes them to be necessary and obvious.

There are many stereotypes of women in American culture and their common themes are not difficult to detect. Most stereotypes of women center on the theme that even typical, healthy women are weaker, less rational, less competent, and more emotional than their male counterparts. Until early in the twentieth century such stereotypes were used to justify denying suffrage to women. In addition, throughout our century these stereotypes supported the denial of educational and job opportunities and then the denial of equal pay for equal work once women were able to get better jobs. The effects of stereotyping on women's lives beyond these obvious cases are often more subtle, although also injurious, as the chapters in the anthology show.

The problems addressed in this book apply to women around the world. In most societies, women and men have different roles. As children, girls and boys are encouraged, subtly or blatantly, to adopt these different roles. In contemporary American culture, the sex of children at birth is accorded great importance: even disposable diapers come in pink and blue. This color typing provides a tangible indicator of the sex of persons at an age when the actual differences between males and females are not great. This tradition announces that the following shall be very important to children in this society: What sex a person is; that each person *knows* what sex she or he is and; that *everyone else* be able to know what sex each person is. Why are these matters thought to be so significant?

The word *sex* refers to classifications of men and women according to their reproductive properties. A person is female or male simply because of her or his body. *Gender*, however, differs from the term *sex*. Gender refers to categories of feminine and masculine, but a female is not necessarily feminine. This would depend on whether she adopts stereotypically feminine characteristics. In our society, someone who is seen as "feminine" may be seen as soft and cuddly. Someone who is seen as "masculine" might be thought of as tough and strong. But most of us have encountered women who are tough or strong and men who are soft or cuddly. The characteristics of femininity and masculinity are really the characteristics that apply to human behavior as a whole.

Pink and blue are arbitrary colors assigned to females and males. But intrinsically, the color of pink or blue has nothing to do with a person's sex. As a culture, we impose these colors onto the sexes. Colors are simply colors, but the message found in these different colors is more intrusive than many realize. This instance of "color coding" reflects the assumption that girls and boys are drastically different from each other. This idea has contributed to the stereotypes that we have encountered all of our lives. And these stereotypes have determined our lives, creating hierarchies of value and limiting our ambitions and our futures. For instance, consider a stereotype that holds that women are created to bear children. If most persons in a society believe this stereotype, then women who do not comply may be ostracized in some way by that society. They may lose job opportunities, be considered egotistic, and be thought of as immoral persons.

The terms *feminist* and *feminism* are considered negative by some people. The reason for this probably lies in stereotyping once more. There are unflattering stereotypes of feminists that revolve around the unanalyzed notion that feminists are too unreasonable, too dogmatic and myopic—in short, that they are irrational. Although there may be individual feminists who warrant some of these descriptions, there is nothing about feminism that requires an irrational approach to moral problem solving. Feminism can be understood as an application of the principles of basic human decency to the problems of women. Feminism also should be understood as holding the desire that women define themselves without having their lives be stamped out by social and cultural stereotypes.

But the case for feminism need not be made on moral grounds alone. There is a compelling argument based on pure common sense to be made as well. Anything that affects the female portion of a society also affects the society as a whole. More than fifty percent of human beings are female. When one large group of persons is frustrated in trying to accomplish its best, the entire society suffers. If person A has a specific talent but is not allowed to work a certain job on the basis of being the "wrong" sex, then not only does A lose, but also society loses. We can now understand how discrimination against women not only hurts women, but also the entire society.

Overview

Each issue considered in this anthology is an *ethical* issue because each concerns how we should act toward other persons. What makes each concern a *feminist* concern is that each pertains to situations where females, as a group and individually, are treated as being less important, less competent, less intelligent, or of lower status. What sort of issues are of special interest to feminists? Some familiar ones include women who are harassed at work, school and in public, date rape, and the battering of women. As philosophers, we must ask questions and ultimately seek answers. How do people get into these situations? What constitutes harassment? What's the difference between harassment and teasing? What is consent? Can a person mean "yes" when she says "no"? Must women take any responsibility for being raped? Should a battering victim who kills the batterer be condemned? Is such an action murder or self-defense? What sort of things could be done to stop oppression? How can women become empowered physically, emotionally, and psychically? What is the best response to these problems?

The papers in this anthology cover a wide range of feminist issues logically analyzed by philosophers. The first of the four sections in *"Nagging" Questions* focuses on the ideas of autonomy and responsibility. The second section pertains to problems encountered by women at work. The authors in section three consider reproductive technology and liberty. And the fourth section concentrates on the body and sexual images.

Autonomy and Responsibility

In ''Feminism and Autonomy,'' John Christman analyzes the idea of autonomy and asks whether it should be an acceptable feminist goal. To understand Christman's chapter, we must understand the notion of autonomy. *Autonomy* can be used in many ways, but in philosophy, it refers to independence in decision making, not relying on others for their ideas on what is right and true. So autonomy is based on reasoning, thinking for oneself. How can we know whether a person is thinking for herself or merely accepting what others have told her? Is it good to believe what others say without verifying it for ourselves? As children, it is probably good to listen, obey, and believe what parents tell you most of the time. The reason for this is that most young children are not yet experienced enough to make informed decisions. For instance, small children do not *know* what may happen if they play with matches. But as we grow and experience our environments, we can take responsibility for checking our beliefs to see if and how they can be justified. In doing this, we are becoming autonomous thinkers. Our patriarchal society rewards autonomy. So, on the face of it, it seems that if women do not think independently, society will not reward them. If this is true, how can a feminist oppose autonomy?

The concept of autonomy extends into Susan Wendell's paper ''Oppression and Victimization: Choice and Responsibility.'' Wendell discusses different viewpoints regarding the victimization of women. For instance, should a rape victim believe that she is to blame for being raped? Should society place blame upon the woman who is raped? Some persons may argue that the clothes victims wear sometimes contribute to, even invite the rape. Can clothes signify that the person wearing them wants to be raped? Consider the case of a woman who is mugged while walking alone late at night. Is she responsible, or partially responsible, for being mugged? We might also ask whether a man walking alone late at night is asking to be mugged. Also, think of women who are battered by their spouses or boyfriends and refuse to leave them. Do these women deserve their fate? Are these women oppressed? Do they have autonomy? Are the batterers also oppressed? Why would a man beat his wife or girlfriend? Wendell, in considering some of these questions in her paper, outlines several perspectives through which women may come to understand their own situations as well as those of others. As a woman gains autonomy, she becomes more responsible for her life.

If some women lack autonomy, can this lack cause these women to adopt the views of the patriarchy? If these views are adopted, should these women be considered entirely responsible for their choices? In other words, can nonautonomous women make free choices? How might they be responsible for their choices? Logically, women could embrace a patriarchal system. The term *patriarchy* neither includes all men nor excludes women. Instead it is a description of a social scheme where most of the people in power are male. This does not mean that all men have an equal amount of power. This also does not say that some women do not have the ability to publicly support a patriarchy. In the last paper in this section, "Right-Wing Women: Causes, Choices, and Blaming the Victim," Anita M. Superson investigates women who seem to have chosen patriarchy as society's proper path. Why might a woman choose not to become a feminist? Is it due to fear? Is it an autonomous choice? Is it a responsible choice? Why would a woman choose to believe in a patriarchal system rather than an egalitarian one? Is there more security in following patriarchy? Are right-wing antifeminists autonomous? Can it be that a woman feels autonomous, yet isn't? Superson's feminist analysis raises some of these questions.

Women at Work

As discussed in Wendell's paper (chapter 3), there are women who endure physical abuse caused by their mates. Women can be oppressed not only physically, but also emotionally. Emotional oppression can affect a person's sense of self-confidence, self-esteem, and feelings of worth. In other words, emotional oppression can cause a loss of the person's autonomy. Imagine walking into a new job feeling confident and professional. As you approach your desk, your immediate supervisor, whom you don't know well, remarks on the shirt you are wearing, saying that he really likes the way it looks on you. You may not consider this inappropriate, but, as the days go by, he continues to mention your clothing, and you feel conspicuous and uncomfortable. What is going on in this situation? Are you being victimized? In such a situation, there are many questions that must be answered before any judgment can be made. Why do you feel uncomfortable about your supervisor's comments? Have you told your supervisor that you would prefer that he stop commenting on your clothing? Harassment is an impediment to a person's livelihood. This issue is a feminist issue, not necessarily because the victim is a woman, but because traditionally, *women* are the people who suffer such indignities. In a business where normally clothing is not of import, commenting on someone's dress on a regular basis may be harassment. Not only is this sort of question feminist, it is also an appropriate philosophical question. It is philosophical when it is considered objectively and rationally. Melinda A. Roberts addresses the issue of workplace sexual harassment in "Sexual Harassment, the Acquiescent Plaintiff and the 'Unwelcomeness' Requirement."

Impediments to a woman's livelihood can be found not only in the workplace but also the military. Traditionally, the military has been a fraternity. Women have been employed in the military, but until recently, have never been thought appropriate for combat. What reasons have been used to justify this position? Some have believed that women are too directed by their emotions to be reliable soldiers. If this is used as a reason to exclude women from the military, does it mean that *all* women are more emotional than *all* men? If this is not true, is it true that *most* women are more emotionally driven than *most* men? If so, is it logically sound to count *all* women unfit for combat? Is having emotions a bad characteristic for a soldier? What does it mean to be "emotional?"

Other people have argued that women do not belong in the military, especially in combat, because women are built for childbirth and mothers should not be fighting in a war. The image of a mother, or even a potential mother, involved in combat, carrying military gear, which may weigh upwards of seventy-five pounds, shooting and killing the "enemy" is repellent to our standard ideas of mothers. In "Women, Equality, and the Military," Judith Wagner DeCew discusses important concerns regarding the inequality between women and men in the military.

Reproductive Technology and Liberty

In her essay, "New Reproductive Technologies," Susan Sherwin focuses on women's reproductive systems. Today as always, many couples who wish to have children find themselves to be infertile. Because of this, science has stepped in to provide alternate reproduction techniques. On the face of it, reproduction technology increases couples' options. This seems to be a social advance. But there are questions to be asked here. Specifically, what are reproductive technologies? How do reproductive technologies affect women as a group? Can they enhance the lives of women or can they limit women's choices? Are they physically dangerous? Can they be compared with any technology appropriate for men? Do scientists benefit more from reproductive technology than the infertile couples?

Debra Satz's essay, "Markets in Women's Reproductive Labor," also analyzes women's reproduction. Satz investigates the idea of surrogate motherhood, which she refers to as *contract pregnancies*. Like any other contract, a contract pregnancy is a legally binding agreement between at least two parties. Specifically, a contract pregnancy includes one woman who offers to bear an infant for another person or couple. The egg for the pregnancy commonly comes from the surrogate, while the sperm is provided by the man. The embryo also could be formed from both gametes of the paying couple. Whichever technique is chosen, the surrogate contracts to carry the fertilized egg to term and surrender the infant at birth. She is paid according to the contract.

Questions about this procedure are widespread. For example, if the surrogate is the biological mother, has bonded with the fetus during pregnancy, and at birth wants to keep the infant, what moral rights does she have? We must remember that she agreed to a contract, ostensibly without coercion. If this is so, keeping the infant would be breaking the contract. Is such a contract morally justifiable? If so, does the surrogate have any rights regarding the infant? Assuming that no one forced her to bear the fetus, is there any other way she might be coerced? Is a contract pregnancy a bad idea? Is it especially unfair to women in general, even those who are not surrogates? How? If it is unfair, why is it unfair when the surrogate is compensated for her labor? Is the labor involved in surrogate motherhood relevantly different from any other paid human labor? Many questions can be asked regarding this topic.

Satz's and Sherwin's papers both center on women who desire or choose to become pregnant. What about those women who do not desire to be pregnant, but are? Nearly everyone today is aware of the "abortion debate." Do fetuses have the same moral standing as adult human beings? Should abortion be legal and easily attainable or should it be considered a form of murder? Obviously there can be no doubt that a human fetus is human, but does being a part of a species necessitate moral status? If the human fetus is living, does this fact give it moral status? Does the concept of privacy have anything to do with abortion? What is privacy? In "Privacy and Reproductive Liberty," Anita L. Allen is particularly interested in the tension between privacy and reproductive liberty in our legal system. A major debate has blossomed in our society regarding the legal and moral questions about abortion and has extended, to some degree, to other types of birth control.

In "Coerced Birth Control and Sexual Discrimination," Lenore Kuo discusses Norplant®, a form of birth control in which a device is surgically inserted under the skin on a woman's arm. Although Norplant is meant to prevent conception and abortion is meant to prevent the birth of a fetus. Both can be used to enhance a woman's choice not to have a child. Kuo, like Allen, looks at birth control in terms of the legal system.

What reasons have been used to justify forcing women to use Norplant? If a woman is on welfare, has five young children, and is pregnant, what justification is there to force birth control on her? In deciding, should we consider the opinions of the majority of the society? If so, would this be reasonable justification? Should we focus entirely on the woman and her children? We can ask whether the children are properly cared for or are neglected or abused. Let's say that the children are neglected. What reasonable questions should be asked at this point? What if the children are not neglected? Should women be *forced* to have surgery or to use birth control? How might the coercion of birth control on a specific woman affect women as a whole? What responsibilities do men have regarding birth control and childcare? Should our society work to provide more birth control measures for men? As a society, are we responsible, to some extent, for mothers on welfare? What places mothers in the welfare system to begin with?

As we have seen, our technological abilities have expanded to the point where new moral dilemmas have been created. Each new technology must be examined for safety and for social approval. In "Is IVF Research a Threat to Women's Autonomy?" Mary Anne Warren writes about in-vitro fertilization (IVF). She asks not whether this specific new technology properly addresses the moral rights of potential "pre-embryos," but whether it properly addresses the autonomous choice of women. Remembering that autonomy includes the ability to make decisions freely, if women know what IVF means and how it is done, how could IVF reduce women's autonomy? Control over one's reproductive powers is only one expression of bodily autonomy. Women's autonomy is also affected by the ways in which society shapes their body images.

Women's Bodies and Sexual Images

Think of anorexia nervosa, a disorder that afflicts a large number of adolescent girls. This condition begins when a teenage female mistakenly believes that she is overweight. The girl then restricts her diet so that she loses weight until she is becoming emaciated, and remains convinced that she is overweight. She literally does not see herself as she truly is. This is a common disease today, but what is its cause? Should we believe the victims of this disease are conforming to a female role or that they are struggling *against* the mature female role? Is anorexia nervosa a form of suicide? If not, what would compel anorexic teenage girls to want to starve themselves? Is society responsible for this? In what way? *Who* is society? Mary Briody Mahowald addresses these questions in her paper, ''To Be or Not Be a Woman: Anorexia Nervosa, Normative Gender Roles, and Feminism.''

Cosmetic surgery brings up a similar issue. Kathryn Pauly Morgan's ''Women and the Knife: Cosmetic Surgery and the Colonization of Women's Bodies'' discusses women's motivations when they choose to have a ''facelift'' or a ''tummy tuck.'' Why do these women choose to have cosmetic surgery? Some patients believe that such surgery will make them feel better about themselves, because they would look ''younger,'' and therefore be more ''attractive.'' But there are several questions to be asked here. First we might ask why, for women, looking younger is equated with being more attractive. Another question is why an adult woman would want to look younger than she is. It is ironic that many grown women want to seem younger, while many young girls ache to be older. Young girls, even young teenage women, often yearn to put on all the accoutrements of older women. Each tries to obtain that ultimately desirable state, but it is not so clear what that state actually is. Why would people go to the extreme of having surgery to correct imagined flaws? If, for example, your society believes that a certain shape of nose is unbecoming on a woman, this does not signify any ultimate truth about that sort of nose. It is merely an opinion. Another society may see this nose as beautiful. The point is that we make judgments about what is beautiful and what is ugly based on other people's opinions. Might we not instead use our own autonomous ability to decide whether society is or is not right?

While both Mahowald and Morgan's chapters focus on the consequences caused by the fact that physical perfection is selected by our culture, we also might consider whether this idea of perfection may be linked to pornography. What counts as pornography? Many famous artworks are of nude women. Is this pornography? If so, is there any difference between ''works of art'' and nude women in men's magazines like *Penthouse, Hustler,* or *Playboy*? What about other men's magazines that cater to more specific tastes, such as bondage and discipline magazines where the woman is portrayed as a bound ''slave'' obeying her male "master?" Should these images be considered art? Does pornography degrade all women or just those who appear in the photographs? Is it degrading at all? Does it degrade those who purchase pornography or the culture that legalizes it? If feminism works to abolish pornography, does this limit women's autonomy, therefore perhaps limiting women's free choices? Is pornographic freedom a way to increase autonomy or destroy it? Edward Johnson answers some of these questions and more in his paper, "Beauty's Punishment: How Feminists Look at Pornography."

And what of sexual tastes themselves? In "Feminine Masochism and the Politics of Personal Transformation," Sandra Lee Bartky discusses the idea of masochistic feminists. *Masochism* refers to the act of a willing person deriving pleasure, usually sexual pleasure, from pain. What might make a woman masochistic? Do women take pleasure in pain? In what ways? Does self-sacrifice in a nonsexual atmosphere count as masochism? Consider the housewife, the mom who puts herself last in the family and takes pleasure from it. She helps everyone else before she helps herself. Does this count as a type of masochism? Why might someone argue that it is masochism? Why might someone argue that it is not masochism? If women are taught to be selfless, would masochism be natural for women's sexual pleasure? Is masochism a good thing? If not, how can this be changed? Should it be changed? Does it foster equality between the sexes? Is equality important? Do conditions that limit autonomy reach so far into our being as to affect our sexual desires?

Conclusion

Whether or not each of these papers in *"Nagging" Questions* definitively answers all of the questions that are asked, the *asking* of questions is critical. The questions about these topics make each paper philosophical and feminist. Perhaps some readers will disagree with different arguments, but in reading thoughtfully and carefully, readers will gain insight into each problem discussed.

Questions

1. What is feminism? Is it inconsistent to be a woman but not a feminist in a society like ours? Explain your answer.

2. What does the concept *patriarchal* mean? What relation does it have with feminism? What is your opinion about these notions?
3. Explain what philosophy is. In what ways can a philosopher interact with feminism? How might a philosopher become interested in feminism?
4. Explain the difference between theoretical feminist philosophy and issue-oriented feminist philosophy.
5. What is a stereotype? From what do stereotypes derive? In what ways are they damaging to society? Can you think of any ways in which they are useful? What sorts of stereotypes damage society or individual members of society?
6. Explain the difference between sex and gender. What do you think is most important about this difference?
7. How does one engage in asking critical questions?

Part I
Autonomy and Responsibility

2

Feminism and Autonomy

John Christman

Feminism can be characterized as the study of, and struggle for, the liberation of women from the oppressive circumstances of patriarchal cultures. Autonomy, both as a personal trait and as a framework for moral thinking, embodies ideals such as independence from manipulation and oppression, self-determination, and authenticity of character. It seems, then, that the connection between these two concepts ought to be a close one. But increasingly in recent years, feminists have been critical of the inclusion of autonomy, in any of its many guises, into the pantheon of goals and values espoused by the movement. The general line of criticism that some feminists wage against autonomy is based on the view that to value autonomy is to embrace an exclusively male ideal, born of an age of inequality and limited privilege and inextricably connected with notions such as individuality, separation, and self-reliance. These ideas refer to values that only privileged males have been disposed and at liberty to attain. Therefore, to value autonomy, some argue, is to denigrate and devalue the experience and psychology of women, a result antithetical to the deepest goals of feminism.

These are powerful criticisms and, like much feminist theory and practice, they strike at one of the most basic elements of the value structure of Western culture.[1] In this chapter, I will examine this charge. I will analyze the notion of autonomy in order to determine whether the incompatibility between that idea and the goals of feminism has indeed been established. What we will discover, I think, is that while the notion of autonomy is more flexible than these arguments have presupposed, the critique nevertheless powerfully challenges defenders of traditional notions to amend their theories. My conclusions, therefore, will turn out to be rather hedged: while arguments concerning some traditional notions of autonomy are indeed very powerful (and must force us to re-

17

think the basic architecture of our moral discourse), they may not support the sweeping conclusion that autonomy must be jettisoned in the framework of moral values to which feminists rightfully aspire.

Feminism and Autonomy: The Basic Concepts

"Feminism" is not a term that is easy to define, and I will make no precise attempt here. It is a movement and a perspective; it is political, intellectual, social, and deeply personal. But despite the wide variety of uses of the term, I take it that "feminisms" of every form have certain common elements, of which these might be mentioned[2]: (1) The fact of patriarchy. It is understood that the structure of past and present societies has instantiated an inequality of privilege and power that favors the position of men, so it is basic to feminism to analyze and further expose these power inequities. (2) The struggle against patriarchy. Almost as an adjunct to the first tenet, feminists claim that the patriarchal structure of personal and social relations must be altered or must evolve into a less repressive, more liberated and egalitarian structure. (3) An insistence that the experiences of women receive greater focus and promotion. Feminism is concerned with highlighting and placing into greater prominence the aspects of female life that patriarchy has served to suppress. Feminists are committed to exposing those aspects of accepted norms that deny, under-represent, or denigrate women's experiences.

There are, of course, many other aspects of this complex phenomenon, and often the central tenets of feminism are as controversial and complex as are questions about the best means of carrying out its aims. What is of crucial importance, however, is whether these entail a rejection of the value of moral and personal autonomy as those notions have traditionally been understood.

As for autonomy, we must make several distinctions concerning this term in order to clarify the issue.[3] There are numerous accounts of this notion, and indeed autonomy functions in a variety of ways in different contexts. In general, the unifying idea behind the various uses of the notion of autonomy is that of "self-government"—being or doing only what one freely, independently, and authentically chooses to be or do. As Gerald Dworkin has pointed out, these ideas reduce in general to two components of autonomy: independence and authenticity.[4]

This is not to suggest that those who defend autonomy as an ideal think that people can fully "create" themselves ex nihilo (though it is no mean trick for many of them to show that their views don't reduce to this[5]). Theorists of autonomy have put forward various conditions that they regard as essential to this sense of self-government, conditions ranging from second-order identification with one's desires to critical competence in decision making to normative competence to historical conditions.[6] In all these cases what theorists are trying to capture is the idea that being autonomous means that one acts or deliberates fully, authentically, and according to one's "true" self.

Further, the idea of autonomy can be used in both a "normative" and a more purely "descriptive" sense. In the normative sense, to say someone is autonomous is to say that they ought to be (or have a right to be) independent and self-governing in the way implied by the concept. The normative use of the notion could also amount to the claim that a person ought to be treated *as if* she or he had that independence and self-government.[7] In a more descriptive sense, being autonomous simply means possessing the psychological or cognitive capacities that independence and self-government involve. This use of the term does not necessarily imply an evaluation of such characteristics.

Finally, one must also distinguish what has been called "moral autonomy" from "personal autonomy." The former, roughly, is the view that moral agency and deliberation does or ought to manifest independent self-legislation. One's choice of what is good or right manifests moral autonomy when the principles embodying the good and the right are, in some sense, self-chosen. Personal autonomy has more general scope and refers to a state in which a person is able to live an independent and self-governing life. While moral autonomy functions as an ideal for the self-imposition of moral principles and values, personal autonomy is an aspect of a person's general psychological and material circumstances that allow her or him to live free of manipulative and heteronomous influences. (This distinction cuts across the "normative/descriptive" split just mentioned.)

But for both of these ideas, the charge has been made that raising them as standards for the fully moral and ideally fulfilling life reflects the perspective and interests of (exclusively) men as members of societies that systematically denigrate and oppress women. As we will see, many argue that seeing autonomy as the height of moral development indicates a devaluing of the "female" perspective that values connection, care, and interdependence.

The Feminist Critique of Moral Autonomy

Central to the feminist critique of autonomy is the suspicion that having autonomy means being able to assume an impartial and independent perspective from which one judges and justifies normative arrangements, a perspective that critics charge is essential to moral autonomy in its traditional sense. Many feminists object to the claim that such an objective impartiality is faithful to the experience and psychology of women, or they are doubtful that such an objectivity is achievable or reliable for pointing out the deep roots of sexism and patriarchy. Impartial and objective thinking is always a mask behind which hides exclusionary and inegalitarian principles, some feminists claim.

In considering such a criticism, it is necessary to look more broadly at the general tradition out of which the notion of autonomy grows. That tradition comes to fruition with the work of Immanuel Kant, whose views I will discuss in more detail below. The essential idea in Kant's thinking, however, was his view that feelings and desires are part of a person's "pathological nature," indicating an aspect of the person that is wholly accidental (that is, contingent) and totally outside of the reflective control that is the seat of moral responsibility.[8] To be autonomous—and so to be responsible in this sense—is to be motivated to act totally independently of one's pathological feelings and desires. Kant coupled this view with a disparaging opinion of the high degree to which women were essentially motivated by their emotions. Hence it followed from these two sets of views (that moral responsibility could never reside in feelings and that women were preponderantly moved by feelings over reason) that women were not included in the scope of moral agency in his theory. Feminists, as one might expect, are highly critical of this view.

But interestingly, this can be criticized in one of two importantly distinct manners. Either one can claim that reason should *not* be regarded as the sole source of moral justification and responsibility, and hence even if women (or whoever) are more often moved by feeling than by reason, this does not affect their status as moral agents; or one can accept the claim that reason ought to be the final arbiter of moral judgment but that it is an archaic myth (born of and fostered by patriarchy) that women are by nature more emotional than men. The latter would certainly have been the tack taken by the feminism of the 1950s and 1960s, but it is the former that has more recently become the focal point of feminist resistance to autonomy as a model of moral reasoning.[9]

The force of this criticism is directed at the use of the notion of moral autonomy to represent the highest level of cognitive development a person is able to achieve. This psychological model has been the focus of some of the most intense criticism by feminist scholars. Indeed, what might be thought of as the flashpoint of feminist criticism of these values occurred with the work of Carol Gilligan and her description of the "different voice" purportedly used by women to express their own moral thinking.

Gilligan brought into question the traditional view of development that rested on the work of Lawrence Kohlberg and his theory of moral and psychological growth.[10] Kohlberg constructed his model of moral maturation based on research almost exclusively involving male subjects and in typically male situations. Kohlberg used schoolboys to develop his model of six stages (three major levels) of moral development. At the highest stage of development, according to Kohlberg's theory, agents follow universal ethical principles that accord with self-chosen, consistent principles of justice and right. This last stage (which is seen in some studies as merely of theoretical interest since so few subjects display this behavior) manifests the fully autonomous moral agent who adopts the perspective of "justice" akin to the moral theories of Plato and Kant.

Gilligan criticized this model as male biased, since, she argued, women tended to reach only "intermediate" stages of Kohlberg's hierarchy of moral development, ones where agents tend to respond primarily to group and social needs. This manifests the tendency on the part of women to value "care" (protection of relationships, obligations toward nurturing, and connectedness with others) as opposed to taking on the perspective of justice (obedience to abstract and impersonal rules of universal morality). In terms of the conditions of autonomy, the claim is that many women see themselves as intimately interwoven in established relationships whose maintenance is of primary importance to their moral deliberations, while men have the opportunity and impetus to separate themselves from such connections and reason as "independent" moral individuals. Gilligan then generated a replacement scale of development that, she claimed, better mirrored the female experience. The alternative model put the notion of "care" at the apex of moral maturity, in contrast to "justice" at the top of the Kohlberg hierarchy.

There are two ways to understand Gilligan's departure from the Kohlberg model. The first, which is the lesson that most have drawn from her data, is that she has shown that women and men have distinctly and significantly different orientations toward moral thinking, corresponding to the "care" and "justice" perspectives, respectively. The second is more complex: one could see her work as pointing out the *limitations* of the male-based Kohlberg model by showing that some or many women (who were neglected in the original data base for the model and traditionally have been "silenced" in Western moral theories) think in ways that ought to be given greater prominence in theories of moral maturity. This second interpretation amounts to a criticism and a call for a richer model, not necessarily a claim of significant sex differences in moral thinking.

Gilligan has clearly been interpreted in the former way. This is despite her explicit expressions, both in *In a Different Voice* and in later work,[11] that the empirical hypothesis that men and women think differently about moral questions has not been established. The question at issue is simply whether the preponderance of males and females (in the United States, say) exhibit statistically significantly deliberation patterns for moral problems. Gilligan's original research could hardly be understood as establishing such a difference since the bulk of her conclusions were based on interviews only with women and in uniquely female moral difficulties (the decision of whether to have an abortion, for example). To establish a difference one must make controlled and consistent comparisons.[12]

In the years since Gilligan's original work, much research has indeed been done on this empirical question, and all one can say at this point is that the jury is still out. Or, less guardedly, one could say that the claim that men and women tend to reason differently (in similar situations) has not been established with certainty.[13]

So one must be careful not to simply *assume* that women and men display significantly disparate patterns of moral deliberation when constructing arguments concerning the ideal of autonomy. Also, even if such a differential pattern were noted, it remains a complicated and contentious issue just how such a social "fact" should be interpreted. Certainly one could argue that the tendency on the part of women to exhibit care and men justice is nothing more than the remnant of the dichotomous role assignments that exist in patriarchal culture. Men, having been assigned more impersonal and public social roles, might well tend to embody the detached and generalizable moral perspective characterized by justice. And women's proclivity toward care might be an outgrowth of maternal and domestic social roles. In such a case, the discovery of these social tendencies should not be seen as sufficient reason to embrace or reject either of the moral perspectives that people have been socialized to adopt under patriarchal cultures.

But most importantly, it is crucial that the argument for the rejection of autonomy as an ideal should not rest simply on the claim of psychological difference. For if the only reason to resist ethics centering on autonomy is based on the factual claim that men and women think fundamentally differently, then that criticism founders on the disputability of that very claim.

However, the specifically empirical claim that men and women think differently is not the only basis upon which to rest skepticism about an ethic of autonomy and (impersonal) justice. It cannot be denied that, traditionally, obligations to protect relationships, nurture those around one, and focus on the particular and private effects of one's actions rather than their conformity to public rules of justice are a moral focus that is closely *associated* with women's roles. As I mentioned at the outset, one of the undisputed aims of feminism is to validate, highlight, and put into greater prominence the roles and attitudes associated with the female. For this reason, autonomy-based ethics could be criticized for reflecting social roles and personal situations—ones that are public, rule-bound and impersonal—that have been considered to be the purview exclusively of men (until very recently).[14]

So part of the feminist critique of the ideal of moral autonomy is the claim, first, that such an ideal has no place in the framework of moral reasoning it presents for empathy, care, nurturance, and the emotions—aspects of character associated with women. Second, the objective and detached process of justification that such an ideal involves (to reason according to universal laws that transcend one's particular situation and relations with others) is unfaithful to those more connected and embedded individuals (many of whom are women) who do not reason in this manner in moral situations. A criticism that this leads to and one we will soon consider is that the presupposition of the detached, unembedded self is a dangerous fiction that this model presupposes and exploits. Moreover, the corresponding ideal of abstract, objective reasoning that moral autonomy presupposes denigrates the particular in favor of the general or universal, hence undervaluing those people who respond to the concrete details of moral relations—who care more for protecting the individual attachment of those involved than they do for abstract universal principle.

As I will discuss in more detail below, these lines of criticism of the ideal of moral autonomy are powerful ones, especially if it can be argued that the perspective of care is ignored *because* of its association with women's experience. Also, if it is the case that theories that place autonomy at the apex of developed moral thinking systematically undervalue and ignore the kinds of psychological impulses and reasoning techniques associated with women, then feminists have good reason to resist the valorization of moral autonomy.

It is clear, however, that we have moved from the descriptive realm of psychological theories to the straightforwardly normative area of moral principles. That is, the question that our discussion of Gilligan has led us to is whether the ideal of moral autonomy ought to be resisted by the basic principles of feminism, especially in light of its alleged exclusion of values associated with the feminine. But to fully analyze this issue, a slight digression is necessary. As I mentioned above, the feminist critique of moral autonomy finds its most definitive (and notorious) adversary in Kant. Therefore, a fuller discussion of Kant's own views is called for.

The Feminist Critique of the Kantian Model

Kant placed autonomy at the center of his ethical framework. For Kant, the structure of practical reason itself implied and presupposed the possibility of a will giving the moral law "unto itself" as an expression of both the necessity of moral truth and the freedom of moral agency, both of which are necessary to make personal responsibility possible.[15] And as I mentioned above, Kant was adamant in his exclusion of affective elements of individual psychology in his conception of moral autonomy. Since such aspects of the self were part of "nature," and morality necessarily must reside in the realm of "freedom," such parts of the person could never enter in the final grounding (justification) of moral rules.

As I also said, Kant was unabashed in his claims for the complete exclusion of women from the realm of full moral responsibility. In Kant's view, women are too moved by their sensual natures, too guided by "sense" over reason, to be amenable to the requirements of the laws of pure practical reason.[16] Rejection of the Kantian conception of autonomy (and hence morality generally) has been spurred by these aspects of his views.

The general charge that interests us here, however, is that the conception of moral autonomy that prizes pure reason over feeling is a sexist conception. To investigate this charge fully one need not limit oneself to the skewed presentation of this view made by Kant himself (since his arguments are laced with an obviously distorted anthropology and manifest inconsistencies). One should look at the best version of the general arguments for such a conception. What reasons other than the relative devaluing of characteristics considered to be feminine could be offered in favor of a view of morality like Kant's?

   The question at issue is whether, contrary to the requirements of Kantian moral autonomy, moral judgments and actions could be justified with reference to a person's emotions and affective responses rather than on the basis of pure, practical reason. There are two questions that could be raised about trying to justify a particular act on the basis of feeling, one has to do with the accidental nature of emotion and the other with the supposed distinction between facts and values. If I want to claim that what I am about to do is absolutely, all things considered, the right thing to do, and I rest this judgment on a particular feeling I have, then two questions arise: First, I may well not have had this feeling. This is what is meant by the "accidental" nature of the feeling. I didn't choose to have it, or if I did, then it is that choice (and the reasons for it) that is the basic justification for my act, not the feeling. Furthermore, the question must always arise, why *should* I have that particular feeling? Is it just a fact about me? If so, then the first difficulty arises. Or is it based on other feelings and unchosen aspects of my character (like my deeper nature, or my personality as a whole)? If that is so, then the question merely moves back one step and focuses on those things, raising the same questions anew.

   Clearly what is at issue here is the notion of a *final* (that is, absolute, all things considered) justification of moral action. The specifically Kantian tradition of rigoristic morality that places a reason-dominated conception of moral autonomy at its center presupposes that such a final justification is necessary to establish that an action has moral worth. Furthermore, such a justification must have the status of a necessary truth: such truths must be based (at some level) on self-evident reasoning. What is questioned by critics of this tradition may well be this very requirement. It is claimed that since we cannot be severed from our empirical selves, and being such we must make judgments that are ultimately based on those (contingent and accidental) selves, then it is implausible to believe that we can achieve the final justification demanded in this tradition.[17]

   On the other hand, it is difficult to dismiss the force of the requirement of a final justification. To test our intuitions on this issue, we should consider cases where we think an action is unwise or immoral and the person proposing to do the action claims that it is indeed wise or justified "because that's just the way I feel." In any number of situations we can imagine considering such a response and simply being compelled to reply: "but you *shouldn't* feel that way" (or act on that feeling). Now we may say or think this only after probing more deeply into the (perhaps submerged or repressed) reasons and feelings lying behind the affect in question; but we wouldn't, in such cases, accept the response as a justification on its face.

The kind of case of this sort that seems most powerful to me is, for example, a man who commits acts of violence toward women out of feelings of anger and jealousy. We would need reasons (presumably non-feeling-based reasons) for the person to counter our obvious reaction that such feelings do not come close to an acceptable justification. In other words, the deeply felt emotion that a person finds him or herself with is exactly what must be reexamined from a point of view not enmeshed in that emotion (if that is psychologically possible).

Furthermore, doing this in no way entails taking the totally disembodied and coldly calculating stance of "objective reasoning" that traditional ethics sometimes seems to demand. There are many situations where one must ask whether it is good or appropriate to feel a certain way, or whether it is good or appropriate to act on the basis of certain feelings one has. This, I would suggest, is the chief insight upon which the Kantian conception of moral justification, and hence moral autonomy, rests. Namely, at some point in the process of providing a true justification for our actions, we must appeal to principles or values that are not simply reducible to facts about our current natures (as is often the case with emotions).

This suggests that perhaps a conception of moral autonomy that is clearly in the Kantian tradition but that is shorn of the misogynistic trappings of the original model could be articulated. A major sticking point here is that the traditional Kantian framework demands that a perspective of detached, impartial reflection (pure, practical reason) must be the *ground* of our moral motivation (where "ground" is taken in a quasi-causal way: the "determining ground").[18] The main charge is that such detached, impartial reflection is not something associated with the perspective of women, and hence demanding such reflection in the principles of moral justification improperly valorizes the perspective of men. But perhaps an alternative interpretation (or a shift in position, depending on how one understands *der Grund*) might be constructed where motivations and proximate reasons for action are allowed to be comprised of feeling, connections with others, empathy, and sentiment. The view would be that for such actions to exhibit true moral worth expressed by moral autonomy, they must be such that they *could* be approved of from a (perhaps hypothetical) perspective of reflection. That perspective need not be the unrealistic, disembodied, neumenal self of Kantian tradition, but it must be a perspective that is not infused with the very connections and emotions it is involved in evaluating.

In this view, I can be autonomous while being thoroughly emotional, connected, and empathic as long as that emotion, those connections, and that empathy are things I would approve of from a position of reflection. This is true, I think, whether or not I am currently reflecting or if I ever actually reflect on those aspects of myself. If my motives *would not* pass such a test of approval, it then seems deeply problematic to say I am being "my own person," truly and deeply free, or any of the things the objective of liberation is meant to underscore. If I could not in principle approve of my character in this way, then it is not clear how we could ever declare that such a character is a good thing to have. There would be no difference, in regard to moral goodness, between a deeply committed caring person and someone in the throws of a passionate rage.

Recall that Kant's rejection of feeling and emotion as a possible basis for moral worth stemmed essentially from his metaphysics: morality must reside in a realm that exists outside the rigid and strictly deterministic world of nature, namely in the "neumenal" world of free agency. But there is also an anthropological component to Kant's view that emotion cannot enter into the basic contours of the justification process: this was Kant's extreme pessimism that people's natural inclinations (their feelings and desires) could ever be brought under sufficient habitual control for a life moved by feeling to conform to reason and the moral law. But as we know, Kant systematically undervalued and ignored the arena of people's lives where empathy, nurturance, and compassion were overwhelming and consistent motives, in particular the world of females and families. If we hold on to the "Kantian insight" that moral action must be amenable to a full justification, but we reject his myopic pessimism about the human capacity to be moved by feeling toward good ends, then a Kant-inspired view that allows a significant place for human emotions may be possible.

Now this revised Kantian picture may, when it is more fully spelled out, face any number of difficulties. Indeed, it still represents a framework of moral justification that is diametrically opposed to well-discussed and well-defended moral theories (such as that inspired by David Hume[19]). But it is not clear that *feminism*, given its commitments as outlined at the outset, must take a particular position on this deep and ongoing debate. As long as those aspects of social life, individual psychology, and moral reasoning that have traditionally been labeled (and denigrated) as "female" find a central place in the principle components of a moral theory, feminism should not automatically take a critical stance in its regard.

The Postmodern Critique

One final line of criticism of the ideal of moral autonomy takes a much more sweeping tack. What might be called the "postmodern" feminist critique of autonomy could be understood as claiming that feminism is a movement of social resistance that must cut deeply into the foundations of epistemological and ethical frameworks for it to be faithful to the radical impulses by which it is motivated. That is, patriarchy, it is claimed, is directly interconnected with the assumptions of "modernism," according to which the unbridled, dispassionate, and objective thinker, who is detached from his emotional personality and personal connections, represents the idealized perspective from which to judge questions of fact or value. In the modern era—from Descartes to Kant and beyond—the assumption has been that objectivity, defined in a way that shows direct links to the notion of autonomy, is the sole criterion according to which correct judgment can occur. But critics claim that it is this presupposition that made it possible to rationalize the oppressive social conditions of the modern patriarchy and hence this set of beliefs that must be resisted.

Applied to autonomy, this criticism goes like this: the idea of moral autonomy implies that the true moral agent makes judgments from a perspective of a separated, dispassionate, and impartial self, one disencumbered by any aspects of the person herself that are not considered reliable guides to truth and valid principle. But such a detached perspective is a dangerous illusion that has systematically served as a rationalization for oppression; and so it must be jettisoned as an ideal.

Iris Young has put the point this way:

> The ideal of impartiality is an idealist fiction. It is impossible to adopt an unsituated moral point of view, and if a point of view is situated, then it cannot be universal, it cannot stand apart from and understand all points of view. It is impossible to reason about substantive moral issues without social and historical context; and one has no motive for making moral judgments and resolving moral dilemmas unless the outcome matters, unless one has a particular and passionate interest in the outcome.[20]

There are two charges here: one is that impartiality implies universality, which implies being "unsituated," and that this is impossible; the second is that one would not be *motivated* to act on reasons that are not tied to particular outcomes about which one cares. The latter charge is an old one and does not really touch those conceptions of autonomy that do not claim that reason must itself motivate for a person to be autonomous (this harks back to the ambiguity of "ground" in the Kantian picture). Rather, reason (or simply reflection) must "mediate" one's motivations in the sense that one must be in a position to reflect upon and not reject the affects that undergird one's actions, from a point of view independent of those affects, for one to be autonomous.

As for the first charge, it raises the question of the idea of impartiality. Young's view is that impartiality essentially commits one to a "totalizing" view—a commitment to principles that apply universally to all agents and that utilizes the "logic of identity" in equating all agents' points of view on the matter.[21] But a distinction must be made between a "totalizing," universal principle of action and merely a "general" principle. The former refers to principles that apply to all agents everywhere, treating all agents as indistinguishable. But the latter simply abstracts from *some* aspects of the particular situation and applies to other situations that share *those* aspects. General principles carry with them no necessary inference from the particular case to *every* case in all possible worlds.[22]

And indeed, I would argue that the very idea of "normativity"—of recommending or rejecting actions or principles—involves a commitment to minimal generality. If one thinks that action A is a good or right or caring or appropriate thing to do, then one is committed (trivially?) to thinking that actions sufficiently similar to A *in the relevant respects* will also be good, right, etc. (if indeed there are any other such cases, for A may be unique). This in no way blinds one to the particularity or concreteness of the situation or the person(s) with whom one interacts. In fact it is just that particularity—the fact that the person is one's sister or one's lover or one's friend—that may ground a judgment one way or the other.

Driven to the extreme, reflection based on *pure* particularity would never count as reflection (or justification) at all: to say "I think treating Jenny this way is correct because, simply, she is Jenny and I am me" (where one is not submerging complex generalizable characterizations in those phrases) is to *fail* to answer the question "why did you do that?" So the very idea of normativity implies the minimally general judgment that the same normative view would obtain in similar circumstances.

Young, in effect, agrees with this since she later claims that reflection of some sort is indeed called for:

> Moral reason certainly does require reflection, an ability to take some distance from one's immediate impulses, intuitions, desires, and interests

in order to consider their relation to the demands of others, their consequences if acted upon, and so on. This process of reflection, however, does not require that one adopt a point of view emptied of particularity, a point of view that is the same for everyone.[23]

This is essentially the point I want to make. But doing so in no way involves a significant departure from the tradition of moral autonomy we are discussing here.

So moral autonomy may well not be an ideal that feminists will adopt in the framework of moral thinking that they favor. But it is not a conception that must be *rejected* by feminism in all of the ways that it (moral autonomy) can be understood. I have tried to give a brief outline of some of the ways that a (though perhaps not "the") notion of moral autonomy could be consistent with the values and goals of feminism, though it is certainly an ideal that is reshaped and molded by those values and goals.

We will now turn to the more general concept of personal autonomy and see if a feminist-inspired criticism of that ideal again forces us to rethink the components of the concept.

The Feminist Critique of Personal Autonomy

Many of the same themes that arise in the criticisms of moral autonomy apply here as well. Recall that personal autonomy refers to the psychological, social, and cognitive ability of people to be independent and self-governing. "Women's liberation" could be seen, in retrospect, as attempting to establish the provision of those resources necessary for the achievement of this capacity for women. This could be seen as a response to the position of women whose place in society, self-definitions, and relations to others had traditionally been marked by dependence, oppression, denial, and silence. It would be natural, then, to connect the ideal of the fully autonomous person, one who runs her or his own life without manipulation and interference from oppressive circumstances, with the ideals of liberation espoused by feminism.

But for many feminists, the ideal of a separated, self-governing self is nothing but a cover for an egoistic, detached, single-minded person unencumbered by obligations to others or constitutive relations with families, partners, and communities.[24] There are, I think, many separable lines of criticism contained in these claims. One is that personal autonomy involves a kind of selfishness or egoism, hence valuing such autonomy surreptitiously (or explicitly) implies valuing the rational, economically self-interested man of capitalist social theory.[25] Second, some argue that the value of personal autonomy presupposes the impossible and dangerous goal of becoming a detached and unconnected individual; such a model of individuals, it is claimed, denies the constitutive connection that we all have (and women have in a more pronounced way perhaps) to our families, children, communities, and histories. Finally, autonomy has been questioned by virtue of its alleged presupposition of a unified and self-revealing mental self. This in turn implies a denial of unconscious and hidden aspects of the self, characteristics that may lie beyond (or below) the reasoned, self-aware, and dispassionate perspective that models of autonomous thinking have valorized. As we can see, we touched upon this ground above.

Jean Grimshaw discusses the first charge in her consideration of the views of various feminists who have both embraced and criticized the ideal of personal autonomy. Feminist writers of the 1960s and 70s such as Mary Daly, Marilyn Frye, and Kate Millet rallied around the goal of liberation from the oppressive familial and social relationships in which women found themselves.[26] At times inspired by individualist self-actualizing schools of psychology (such as that developed by Abraham Maslow), these feminists argued for and presupposed an ideal of personal liberation to which individual independence and autonomy was central. But these writers went too far, Grimshaw argues, in praising the life of independent self-determination for women in that they implied, to varying degrees, that a unified, self-aware, and particularly feminist self lay lurking in the psyches of all oppressed women and that the liberation movements of the day would free this autonomous self from its shackles. Grimshaw argues convincingly that the true self lurking inside many women may well be somewhat fractured, complex, self-deceived, and deeply connected to the others around her. Hence the ideal of a fully individualist notion of autonomy is a false (or misleading) one for the feminist struggle to embrace.

In the other direction, however, Grimshaw takes issue with the critics of autonomy such as Naomi Schemann who argue that such an ideal implies egoism and individualism as well as an implausibly individualistic conception of the self. Schemann claims that the mental states that partially define all individuals can only be specified in social terms (to be "in love" is to be in love "with someone"). Schemann then infers that selves are essentially social and any individualist ethic that postulates an individualism of interests is implausible (such as traditional liberalism for example).[27] The feminist lesson in this argument comes by way of developmental psychology (and the work of such thinkers as Nancy Chodorow), which stresses the greater connectedness and empathy of female psychological development.[28]

Grimshaw argues that it may well be correct to reject such things as egoism (that everyone will or ought to pursue only their own self-interest) or abstract individualism (that a person's psychological states, preferences, and values can all be specified without essential reference to social relations). But this in no way implies the more radical view that a person cannot even be *identified* without reference to others. Indeed, some of the most extreme examples of a fully "connected" self—a person who cannot differentiate her own wishes, plans, and desires from those of others—are those people who suffer from mental illnesses such as schizophrenia. That is, the idea of being "fully connected" is ambiguous: it may mean (quite plausibly) that a person's values and desires essentially involve others or it may mean (quite implausibly) that a person cannot even identify her or his *self* separately from others. Feminism should certainly not commit itself to the latter idea (and it does not follow from the former) for the simple reason that it is a misdescription of human thinking; but moreover, it is women especially, who have traditionally been dependent upon others and had feelings of overwhelming obligation toward others, who have been particularly oppressed by the denial of individual needs.

Hence, one need not accept that rejecting one type of individualism (that individual interests can be separately described) entails accepting another kind, "ontological" individualism (that individual *people* cannot be described, even to themselves, without reference to others). But does autonomy as a personal characteristic imply either of these? Does it imply the egoistic view that all people are or should be selfish and driven individualists? Grimshaw's arguments provide a strong initial case that it does not. But the real test of whether autonomy is normatively or conceptually tied to these other views must involve a closer examination of the very concept of personal autonomy and, in particular, what varying conceptions of autonomy have implied or presupposed about these issues.

Some traditional notions of autonomy have certainly carried the implications of individualism and egoism. But recently there has appeared a spate of new analyses of the concept of autonomy, and although a variety of positions concerning its essential nature have been taken, all of these recent theorists have taken the view that autonomy is consistent with any number of life plans, personality types, and value systems. This "content neutral" approach to autonomy markedly deflates the charge that the characteristic of individual autonomy necessarily implies that one is selfish and asocial.[29]

Recent attempts to define autonomy can be divided, I think, into those that stress some kind of self-reflection and/or approval and those that ignore that condition (or downplay it) in favor of various kinds of internal integration or competence of critical reasoning abilities.[30] In none of these cases is it implied, suggested, or presupposed that the only way to be autonomous is to pursue one's own interests and desires while ignoring others or even to *define* one's needs and desires apart from others. In what remains of this discussion, I want to consider how a conception of autonomy could be fashioned that avoids the untoward implications described by that notion's critics.

A charge often made about the conception of the autonomous person in the "liberal" tradition of political and moral philosophy is that it presupposes that such people can be conceived of independently of their particular *histories*. It is pointed out that people are a product of their particular (and by extension their social) pasts and any conception of a "self" should make reference to this. Therefore, one's conception of autonomy should make essential reference to this fact as well.

Therefore, an adequate notion of autonomy must take history directly into account. Consider, then, a model of autonomy that makes the agent's history and embeddedness its centerpiece: A person is autonomous (relative to some desire, value, or aspect of him or herself) if the person did not or would not resist the development of the desire (value, etc.) when attending to this process of development; also, this lack of resistance to the development of the desire did not take place (or would not have) under the influence of factors that inhibit self-reflection itself; and this lack of rejection was "minimally rational" in the sense that no manifest contradictions in beliefs or desires were involved in it.[31]

This view of autonomy demands that a person be able to accept the way that she became the person she is, and to do so from a perspective that allows an unclouded view of herself and her relation to factors in her environment with which she is intimately connected. And being "minimally" rational in no way demands that a person be moved by reason alone (or by reason at all at the base level of action) or that she or he has fully calculated all aspects of the situation from a universal point of view. It only demands that the person not be engaging in such obviously contradictory inference patterns that she herself could not embrace her own full set of beliefs and desires (this is what is meant by "manifest" contradictions).

I put forward this approach to autonomy by way of example (there could be many others).[32] The point here is that not only is it possible for a conception of the autonomous person to avoid being silent on the contextual nature of the self, but also that models such as this one make that context an essential component of their conditions.

Also, autonomy conceived this way does not imply that a person must lead a life separated from others, devoid of care and connection, in egoistic pursuit of self-interest, or characterized only by public, masculine habits. The main idea of the view is that a person is autonomous if she or he can, from some point of view not consumed by factors that restrict her ability to reflect, approve of the way that she is in light of the way she came to be that way.

I mentioned above the criticism of the ideal of autonomy that claimed that the notion of a unified and consistent perspective from which a person can judge both external circumstance and internal relations is a dangerous and powerful myth. This myth is revealed by critical analysis of the power structure of institutions, greater understanding of the unconscious forces of our personality, and the historical embeddedness of our natures. The "myth of the enduring subject" belies any belief in a unified and encumbered point of view that the ideal of personal autonomy seems to presuppose. In a word, people are more complex than autonomy implies.

This line of argument can only be adequately considered by way of a detailed analysis of its rich theoretical underpinnings, an undertaking outside the scope of this essay. What we can say here, however, is that the ideal of personal autonomy would run afoul of the complex nature of human subjectivity only if the conditions of autonomy presupposed an enduring and unified "self" somehow detached from the real historical forces under which it reasons and judges. But the model of autonomy I sketched just now need make no such presupposition. For a person can be autonomous in regard to a single *aspect* of herself while not presupposing that every other aspect or characteristic has passed the test. This is why the view is spelled out as autonomy "relative" to a desire, value, or the like. Autonomy becomes a piecemeal process of self-evaluation, no part of which requires a separated, unified, and detached perspective. "Full" autonomy, then, is simply an ideal, characterized by the completion of the piecemeal process: if I can say, seriatim, of every important aspect of myself, that I do not reject the way I came to be that way, then I am fully autonomous but not in a way that presupposes a single unified subjectivity or a complete abstraction from the whole of my being.[33]

Nor does this view assume that the "true" self that resides inside all of us is some well-defined, fully rational, and omniscient personality. As long as I can be minimally rational (that is, not engage in *manifestly* contradictory inferences and belief patterns), then my autonomous self could be as fractured or complex as one can imagine. In fact, many external life situations display such contradictory and confusing charac- teristics that one's very survival may demand at least a partially con- flicting set of desires and values.[34]

While many will find flaws in this way of describing autonomy, I present it here as an illustration of how autonomy can be conceptualized in a way that avoids some of the most powerful objections that feminists have brought out. Therefore, feminism, as defined in the broad manner I described at the beginning of this chapter, need not see autonomy as a value that is antithetical to its central goals and tenets. Indeed, the kind of self-awareness, independence, and authenticity required by au- tonomy (in a way that is sensitive to one's context and history) is a characteristic that has been systematically denied to women (and in a different way to men) by the structure of a patriarchal culture. To have a character that one would not reject if brought into the light of self- awareness, in view of its genesis and formation, is to be allowed to achieve one of the most basic components of liberation and freedom. Hence, feminism should not reject a sufficiently nuanced notion of the ideal of autonomy, it should positively embrace it as a goal and a value.

Conclusion

We can see, then, that it may indeed be possible to understand both moral autonomy and personal autonomy in a way that takes full account of those aspects of the human experience that feminists have rightly argued were adumbrated in traditional theories. If "full justification" remains a standard of moral self-appraisal, then this can be achieved while affording a full motivational role for those aspects of character that have been traditionally associated with the "feminine." Similarly, connectedness, context, and history can also be accounted for by no- tions of personal autonomy that do not carry with them the implications of egoism and individualism rightly questioned by many feminists.

It should be remembered that these questions concerning the value of autonomy in its various guises have been taken up, in some form, en- tirely *within* the framework of feminism. Indeed, many of the positions I have described, on either side of the question, have been taken by feminists themselves. My goal here was to spell out some of the most powerful aspects of the feminist critique of traditional notions and theories and to suggest ways that those theories can respond to those critiques. And I have suggested, in particular, that while autonomy must be fundamentally altered and shaped by the normative concerns of feminism, it should nevertheless be included among the full array of values and ideals such concerns motivate.

Notes

1. The view that autonomous deliberation and agency is at the apex of moral ideals has dominated moral theorizing at least since Kant, and arguably since much earlier. And even utilitarians such as John Stuart Mill include the ideal of "individuality" (as one of the elements of well-being) in descriptions of the basic aspects of a free society. For discussion, see Richard Lindley, *Autonomy* (Atlantic Highlands, N.J.: Humanities Press International, 1986), Part I.

2. Cf., Karen Offen, "Feminism and Sexual Difference in Historical Perspective," in *Theoretical Perspectives on Sexual Difference,* ed. Deborah L. Rhode (New Haven, Conn.: Yale University Press, 1990), 13–20, who also identifies some unifying ideas central to feminism: cf. p. 15, n. 3.

3. For a similar laying out of distinctions see Thomas Hill Jr., "The Importance of Autonomy," in *Women and Moral Theory,* ed. Eva Feder Kittay and Diana T. Meyers (Totowa, N.J.: Rowman & Littlefield, 1987), 129–38. For a survey of the various notions of autonomy see my "Constructing the Inner Citadel," *Ethics* 99, no. 1 (Fall 1988): 109–24.

4. Gerald Dworkin, *The Theory and Practice of Autonomy* (Cambridge: Cambridge University Press, 1988), chapter 1.

5. See my introduction to *The Inner Citadel: Essays on Individual Autonomy* (New York: Oxford University Press, 1989), 6–12.

6. See Robert Young, *Personal Autonomy: Beyond Negative and Positive Liberty* (New York: St. Martin's Press, 1986); Diana T. Meyers, *Self, Society and Personal Choice* (New York: Columbia University Press, 1989); Lawrence Haworth, *Autonomy: An Essay in Philosophical Psychology and Ethics* (New Haven, Conn.: Yale University Press, 1986); Gerald Dworkin, "The Concept of Autonomy," chapter 1 of *The Theory and Practice of Autonomy*; and John Christman, "Autonomy and Personal History," *Canadian Journal of Philosophy* 21, no. 1 (March 1991): 1–24.

7. For discussion, see introduction to *The Inner Citadel.* Cf. also Thomas Hill Jr., "The Importance of Autonomy."

8. For Kant's pessimism about Reason's ability to shape emotions, see *Grounding for the Metaphysics of Morals,* AK 407f.

9. A third possibility is to claim that Kant is right on both counts, but that women's failure to develop psychological profiles that enable them to achieve

the highest levels of autonomy is a direct result of patriarchal oppression. This is essentially the tack taken by Simone de Beauvoir; see *The Second Sex*, trans. H. M. Parshley (New York: Alfred A. Knopf, 1952). For discussion of this position, see Diana T. Meyers, *Self, Society and Personal Choice*, 142–60.

10. See Carol Gilligan, *In a Different Voice* (Cambridge, Mass.: Harvard University Press, 1982).

11. See, for example, "Moral Orientation and Moral Development," in *Women and Moral Theory*, 19–33.

12. Gilligan's more recent discussions have moved away from even suggesting significant differences, preferring to liken the dichotomy to a "duck-rabbit" picture, where within a particular individual (male or female) there may well be shifts in moral framework from justice to care and back again, depending on the situation and question asked. See "Moral Orientation and Moral Development." For a bibliography of discussions of Gilligan's work, see *APA Newsletter on Feminism* 90, no. 2 (Winter 1991): 103–8.

13. There is voluminous work on this question. For a bibliography, see *APA Newsletter on Feminism* 90, no. 2 (Winter 1991): 103–9. For two examples of the empirical debate, see L. J. Walker, "In a Different Voice: Cryptoseparatist Analysis of Female Moral Development," *Social Research* 50 (1983): 665–95 and "Sex Differences in the Development of Moral Reasoning: A Critical Review," *Child Development* 55 (1984): 677–91. For criticism of Walker, see Diane Baumrind, "Sex Differences in Moral Reasoning: Response to Walker's (1984) Conclusion That There Are None," *Child Development* 57 (1986): 511–21.

14. In that very spirit, Nell Noddings rejects what she calls an ethic based on "Logos, the masculine spirit" in favor of a "feminine" ethic (caring), one that is feminine "in the deep classical sense—rooted in receptivity, relatedness, and responsiveness." See Nell Noddings, *Caring: A Feminine Approach to Ethics and Moral Education* (Berkeley: University of California Press, 1984), 1–2. She goes on to say that this new ethic

does not imply either that logic is to be discarded or that logic is alien to women. It represents an alternative to present views, one that begins with the moral attitude or longing for goodness and not with moral reasoning. It may indeed be the case that such an approach is more typical of women than of men, but this is an empirical question I shall not attempt to answer (p. 2).

It is also the case that Noddings does not rest her case for an ethic of care on the rejection of autonomy as an ideal but rather as a possible alternative.

15. See Kant, *Grounding for the Metaphysics of Morals*, in *Kant's Ethical Philosophy*, trans. James Ellington (Indianapolis, Ind.: Hackett Publishing Co., 1983).

16. See, e.g., his "Observations on the Beautiful and Sublime" and the *Metaphysical Elements of Justice*, trans. John Ladd (New York: Macmillan, 1965). For discussion, see Sally Sedgwick, "Can Kant's Ethics Survive the

Feminist Critique?'' *Pacific Philosophical Quarterly* 71 (1990): 60–79. Here is a case where Kant's sexism simply overwhelms the internal structure of his own theory. For according to Kant's view of moral obligation, contingent aspects of anthropology (which enter directly into the foundation of the moral law) moral principle applies to rational beings *as such*, not to humans in particular, and contingent facts about the situation—one's psychology or one's natural attributes—are not relevant to moral justification.

17. For powerful arguments against the Kantian approach which many feminists have embraced, see Lawrence A. Blum, *Friendship, Altruism and Morality* (London: Routledge and Kegan Paul, 1980), chapter 1.

18. Though as Larry Krasnoff has reminded me, this can in no way be ''causal'' in the way that Kant uses that term.

19. See Annette Baier, ''Hume, the Women's Moral Theorist?'' in *Women and Moral Theory*, 37–56.

20. *Justice and the Politics of Difference* (Princeton, N.J.: Princeton University Press, 1990), 104.

21. Young, *Justice and the Politics of Difference*, 98–99.

22. For a similar argument distinguishing ''idealizing'' principles from ''abstracting'' ones, see Onora O'Neill, ''Justice, Gender, and International Boundaries,'' in *The Quality of Life*, ed. M. Nussbaum and A. Sen (Oxford: Clarendon Press, 1993), 303–23.

23. *Justice and the Politics of Difference*, 105.

24. Cf., e.g., Alison Jaggar, *Feminist Politics and Human Nature* (Totowa, N.J.: Rowman and Allanheld, 1983); Caroline Whitbeck, ''A Different Reality: Feminist Ontology,'' in *Women, Knowledge, and Reality: Explorations in Feminist Philosophy*, ed. Ann Garry and Marilyn Pearsall (Boston: Unwin Hyman, 1989); Loraine Code, ''Second Persons,'' in *Science, Morality and Feminist Theory*, ed. Marsha Hanen and Kai Nielsen (Calgary: University of Calgary Press, 1979); and Virginia Held, ''Noncontractual Society: A Feminist View,'' in *Science, Morality and Feminist Theory*.

25. Alison Jaggar says that socialist feminism sees autonomy ''as characteristically masculine and characteristically capitalist.'' (*Feminist Politics and Human Nature* [Totowa, N.J.: Rowman and Allanheld, 1983] 131).

26. See Jean Grimshaw, ''Autonomy and Identity in Feminist Thinking,'' *Feminist Perspectives in Philosophy*, ed. M. Griffiths and Margaret Whitford (Indianapolis, Ind.: Indiana University Press, 1988), 90–108. Cf. also her *Philosophy and Feminist Thinking* (Minneapolis: University of Minnesota Press, 1986).

27. See ''Individualism and the Objects of Psychology,'' *Discovering Reality*, ed. S. Harding and M. Hintikka (Dordrecht, Holland: D. Reidel, 1983).

28. See, for example, Chodorow, *Feminism and Psychoanalytic Theory* (New Haven, Conn.: Yale University Press, 1989).

29. Cf. Gerald Dworkin, *The Theory and Practice of Autonomy*, 8–9. The term ''content neutrality'' is explained in my introduction to *The Inner Citadel*, 14–15.

30. Examples of the former are Harry Frankfurt, "Freedom of the Will and the Concept of the Person," *The Journal of Philosophy* 68 (1971): 829–39; Gerald Dworkin, *The Theory and Practice of Autonomy*; and John Christman, "Autonomy and Personal History." The latter approach is pursued by Haworth, *Autonomy: An Essay in Philosophical Psychology and Ethics*; Paul Benson, "Freedom and Value," *Journal of Philosophy* 84, no. 9 (1987): 465–87; Diana T. Meyers, *Self, Society and Personal Choice*; and Marilyn Friedman, "Autonomy and the Split-Level Self," *Southern Journal of Philosophy* 24, no. 1 (1986): 19–35.

31. A fuller articulation of such a view would have to add, at least, the condition that the person is minimally rational concurrently with respect to the desire (that is, she is not presently moved by manifestly contradictory beliefs or desires that are not themselves subsumed under some otherwise rational plan of action). I defend a version of this view in "Autonomy and Personal History." What I put forward here is a revision of my earlier view discussed in "Defending Historical Autonomy: A Reply to Professor Mele," *Canadian Journal of Philosophy* 23, no. 2 (June 1993): 281–90.

32. For a discussion of autonomy that directly responds to the feminist critiques of that notion, see, e.g., Diana T. Meyers, *Self, Society and Personal Choice*.

33. For a similar claim, see Marilyn Friedman, "The Social Self and the Plurality Debates," in *Feminist Ethics*, ed. Claudia Card (Lawrence, Kans.: University Press of Kansas, 1991), 161–79, esp. 168–73.

34. Cf., Jean Grimshaw, "Autonomy and Identity in Feminist Thinking." Many will not be satisfied with this manner of reply, for their view is that *any* postulation of a conscious and identifiable subjective perspective is unwarranted. I have so far claimed that such views are indeed not inconsistent with the ideal of autonomy. In the end, however, I would resist the total denial of an enduring identity for the subjective self.

Questions

1. According to Christman, what is autonomy? What is the difference between independence and authenticity, the components of autonomy? Can you give an example that explains their meanings? In what ways are you autonomous? Are there any ways you believe you are not autonomous?
2. Why would feminists argue that autonomy should not be the foundation of a woman's liberation from patriarchal oppression?
3. What is the difference between moral and personal autonomy?
4. Why are feminists highly critical of Kant's view of moral responsibility?
5. To what does Carol Gilligan object in Kohlberg's model of moral maturation? Do you agree with her? Why or why not? If she is correct, do you suppose that females are born with different values than males? Can you think of any evidence that shows that this is true? How could this be tested?

3

Oppression and Victimization: Choice and Responsibility

Susan Wendell

Feminists have always sought to understand the social causes of women's unhappiness and lack of freedom. One consequence of increasing our knowledge of the power and pervasiveness of the social forces acting on women is that we tend to focus upon women's victimization. This enables us to see that the causes of much of our own and other women's suffering, and of many of our bad choices, have not been ultimately within our control, and that no one could reasonably expect us to have avoided them. It frees us from the power of other people's blame and from our own feelings of guilt, personal failure, and inadequacy. It also prevents us from blaming other women for not making better lives for themselves. In short, it enables us to look upon the past and present with more compassion for ourselves and other women.

Our sense of the future may not fare as well. It sometimes seems that the better we understand the social forces that caused much of our unhappiness and frustration and that could cause them again, the more difficult it is to maintain a sense of our own power to affect the future. Yet in order to act with any hope, and certainly to act with the kind of sustained energy and discipline needed to oppose oppression, we need to think of ourselves and other women as unfinished, capable of change, and capable of gaining power to direct our lives. In addition, unless we believe we have some power in our lives, it makes no sense to think of ourselves as responsible for our own welfare.

The radical feminist philosopher Marilyn Frye raised this issue, which she characterized as the problem of reconciling responsibility and history, in a short essay published in 1985. She wrote:

> As some brand of radical feminist, I am committed to the view that the
> oppression of women is something women do not choose. Those of our

41

activities and attitudes which play into women's oppression are themselves strategies we are forced into by the circumstances of oppression we live with. A woman may continue to live with the man who batters her, but the choice to remain is not a free one; it is a choice among evils in a severely constrained situation, and she has not chosen that situation. The oppression of women is something consisting of and accomplished by a network of institutions and material and ideological forces which press women into the service of men. Women are not simply free to walk away from this servitude at will. But also, it is clear that there has always been resistance to female servitude, taking different shapes in different places and times. The question of responsibility, or rather, *one* important question, is this: Can we hold ourselves, and is it proper to hold each other, *responsible* for resistance? Or is it necessarily both stupid cruelty and a case of "blaming the victim" to add yet one more pressure in our lives, in each others' lives, by expecting, demanding, requiring, encouraging, inviting acts and patterns of resistance and reconstruction which are not spontaneously forthcoming?[1]

The problem Frye so eloquently described has not often been discussed in the literature of feminism.[2] It is part of a cluster of problems for feminist theory and practice that concern responsibility and choice under conditions of oppression. In this cluster, philosophical, psychological, and political issues come together. I will begin by sorting out and describing the problems as they confront us specifically as feminists. Then I will characterize four major perspectives from which situations of oppression or victimization can be seen and questions about choice and responsibility can be answered. I will compare their strengths and weaknesses and discuss their compatibility with one another. Finally, I will discuss how both recognizing these possible perspectives and making use of them can help to solve the problems I have described.

Three of the perspectives I will characterize are potentially feminist. I shall argue that we should not expect to find a single feminist perspective on responsibility that meets all our philosophical, psychological, and political needs, and that if we cultivate more than one perspective, we can have some choice about which one to take at various times and in various situations.

The Problems

1. The causal picture and the agency picture—
are they compatible?

The most abstract of the problems about choice and responsibility concerns the compatibility of two different pictures of human actions, which I shall call the causal picture and the agency picture. In the causal picture, we see people (including ourselves) and their actions as part of a larger social system of causes and effects, which includes women's oppression. We can, to some extent, explain and predict people's actions on the basis of our knowledge of this system and of people's positions in it. In the agency picture, we see ourselves and others as capable of change, capable of gaining power in our lives and of choosing the future, which is open and undecided. Many people believe that these two pictures are incompatible and that they must choose between them. For example, the psychotherapist Cerise Morris, in an essay entitled, ''Against Determinism: The Case for Women's Liberation,'' suggests that just such a choice is necessary: ''I contend that positivistic and deterministic accounts of our situation as women deny the primacy of our personal experience, ignore our active participation in shaping our reality and question our capacity to make meaningful choices about our lives.''[3]

Concerns about the compatibility of the causal picture and the agency picture of human actions are not new. People have long been aware of an apparent conflict between, on the one hand, our belief that at least sometimes we choose freely and that we are often responsible for our actions and, on the other hand, our belief that human choices and actions have causes. From this point of view, oppression is only a particular kind of cause of human actions, though it is one that presents the apparent conflict in a vivid and pressing way.

2. Does patriarchy make it impossible for women to choose freely and responsibly?

Even if we take the philosophical position that the causal picture and the agency picture are *in general* compatible, we might well ask whether the particular causes at work in women's oppression leave women free enough to make full-fledged responsible choices. We know that women's choices are circumscribed under patriarchy and that a patriarchal society exercises illegitimate influences over women's fears and desires, causing us to internalize our oppression.[4] Much of what women appear to do freely is chosen in very limiting circumstances, where there are few choices left to us. Even where the circumstances present many choices, it is often the case that our knowledge, our ability to judge, and our desires have been so distorted and manipulated by social influences as to make a mockery of the idea that we choose freely.

These sorts of considerations have prompted some feminist theorists to expand the concept of coercion, especially in the area of sexuality. They imply that women cannot make responsible choices under our present oppression, that all our choices are coerced, and that we cannot give meaningful consent.[5] Although we may appreciate the theoretical reasons for taking this position, many feminists fear that the psychological and political consequences of undermining the importance of consent in practice would be appalling. For example, it would effectively erase the distinction between rape and lovemaking; this may be plausible to some women, but it violates many women's experience and invites men to ignore women's desires. Furthermore, if we claimed that all women's choices are coerced, then on what basis, under patriarchy, could we demand to participate in decisions that affect our lives?

On the other hand, if we claim that women sometimes make significantly free and responsible choices even under patriarchal oppression, we must give an account of the conditions that make this possible, and our account must consider fully the effects of internalized oppression on women's freedom and responsibility.

3. How should we interpret exceptional women?

When we realize the strength and pervasiveness of social limitations and influences on women's choices, we can better understand why so many women have chosen and go on choosing situations that make them suffer and reduce their freedom. But then how should we interpret the exceptions—women who have lived happy, creative, and unconventional lives because they fought for themselves; women who have developed talents in spite of other people's discouragement and disapproval and a daunting lack of resources; women who have accomplished things almost universally considered both impossible for and unsuitable for a woman? There have been many such exceptional women, and it is useless to try to explain it by claiming that they must have had exceptional material or social advantages, for dozens, even hundreds, could be named for whom that was not true. Consider only Emma Goldman, Sojourner Truth, Gloria Steinem, and Alice Walker.

On the one hand, we do not want to underestimate the power of oppression. To deny that we are harmed and weakened by social conditions is to deny that we are oppressed. Clearly, oppression reaches into our psyches and undermines our ability and our very desire to oppose it. It can blind us to the choices that remain to us and to our own strength to make them. To say of the exceptional woman, "If she can do it, you (or I) can do it," is simply false. No two people have faced exactly the same social forces with the same body and mind, and thus no two of us have the same inner or outer resources with which to live our lives.

On the other hand, we do not want to overestimate the power of oppression. We do not have to believe that the individual can transcend her circumstances totally to acknowledge that some people have fought oppression, even within themselves, and (to varying degrees) won. In fact, most of us have won battles against it. Yet this philosophical dilemma is raised for us repeatedly by our experience, because the more we fight oppression, the more we learn about its many aspects and how they affect us personally, and the more pervasive and powerful it looks.

4. When should we hold ourselves and others responsible, and for what?

As Marilyn Frye asked, should we ever hold individual women, including ourselves, responsible for resisting oppression?[6] How can we decide whom to hold responsible and for what? Responsibility is hard to assign in the best of circumstances. It is always relative to a person's knowledge and choices, which are always limited. Therefore, responsibility is a matter of degree. It lies on a continuum between knowledgeably and freely choosing among a wide range of possibilities and ignorantly and fearfully choosing between two evils.[7] We hold ourselves and others responsible for various purposes, and different degrees of responsibility are relevant to different purposes. The appropriate degree of responsibility for holding some *legally* responsible is usually specified in a law or a courtroom. In most other situations, it is implicit and it may not be agreed upon.

Thus, people may have very different intuitions about such questions as whether a woman is responsible for staying with an abusive husband, not only because they have different pictures of the facts, but also because they differ about how responsible she must be in the situation to be held responsible. They may also disagree because they have different purposes in determining whether she is responsible. Some people may be wondering if they should try to persuade her to leave him; other may be asking if it is appropriate to blame her for contributing to his violence. In addition, the question of what future actions to hold people responsible for is different from the question of what to hold them responsible for after they have acted. In matters of responsibility, the viewpoint on the future is different from that on the past, because holding people responsible before they act can influence what they do, when they know that we hold them responsible.[8]

Judgments of responsibility are thus relative to their contexts and the purposes for which they are made. They may also be quite complex, especially since more than one person, indeed millions of people, may be responsible, in some degree, for a situation. To these difficulties inherent in determining our responsibilities are added the mystifications of responsibility, including those that have come to be known as "blaming the victim."

5. How can we avoid blaming the victim without denying that women have power to resist or escape victimization?

As Marilyn Frye noted, questions about whom to hold responsible for what raise concerns about not blaming the victim. Blaming the victim may involve one or more of the following:

(a) Blaming or punishing someone for a situation in which s/he was harmed and over which s/he had no control.

(b) Focusing concern on whether victims provoked or encouraged actions that harmed them when those actions would be illegal and/or immoral even if there *were* some sort of provocation or encouragement.

(c) When judging responsibility, stressing the importance of the choices the victim had in a situation (e.g., fighting or submitting to the demands of a man with a knife) rather than the limitations of choice imposed by the person who hurt or threatened the victim.

(d) And finally, seeking causes of oppressive actions and situations in those who are oppressed by them. It does not necessarily involve blaming or even assigning responsibility to victims. It does focus attention on characteristics of the victims and away from other people's responsibilities, such as the oppressive actions of individuals who are harming them or the more general social causes of the victims' oppression, including institutions, laws, or economic conditions. For example, studying the IQ scores of disadvantaged racial groups and attempting to measure girls' fear of success have been called "blaming the victim" in this sense.

Feminists have been especially concerned to expose and oppose all forms of blaming the victim, since women are so frequently the victims in question. The various ways of blaming the victim not only interfere with victims' obtaining justice, help, and sympathy when they have been harmed, but also add to their harm by creating confusion and feelings of guilt about their own responsibility for their suffering. Some victims are forced or led to relive their victimization again and again in an effort to find their alleged "contribution" to it.

Not all concern about victims' actions, choices, and characteristics tends to blame them, unfairly assign responsibility to them, or otherwise act to their disadvantage. For example, research into the effects of victims' behavior on aggressors could be important in reducing and preventing victimization, and knowing that they have certain choices in frightening situations will sometimes enable victims to prevent themselves from coming to worse harm, even to save their lives. However, supporting actual victims requires that we guard against the tendency to shift too much responsibility onto potential victims and away from aggressors and the rest of society.

Nevertheless, problems are created when feminists' efforts not to blame the victims lead us to deny or ignore two vitally important truths: first, that women do sometimes contribute, by the choices we make, to our own oppression and that of other women; second (and this is not at all the same thing), that women do have some power to avoid victimization and to end our own oppression and that of other women. Although these truths have often been distorted and misused in defense of sexist conservatism, they are vitally important to women's liberation. We must somehow balance recognition of them with our concern not to blame the victims and the oppressed.

Introduction to the Perspectives

I shall describe four major perspectives on choice and responsibility. Each perspective is a pattern of thought, but also of emotion, perception, expectation, and motivation. This reflects my own belief that how we feel about a situation permeates our thoughts about it and *vice versa,* and that what we can perceive about a situation, what we expect, and what we want all interact with and transform each other and our thoughts and feelings. Sometimes these complex processes of interaction form ways of approaching situations that we can recognize as patterns in ourselves and other people. The perspectives on choice and responsibility that I shall discuss are examples of such patterns. They affect profoundly how we understand and interpret events, situations, ourselves, and other people. In that they affect what we can know, they are epistemic. They are also moral perspectives, since they affect our moral judgments and the choices we make. In addition, the perspectives we take on choice and responsibility affect our own degree of moral responsibility, since they influence both what we have the power to do and how well we know our choices.

The perspectives I shall describe are not perspectives *on everything,* i.e., they are not world views. These are perspectives on situations of choice and responsibility. I do not call them "standpoints," although they have similarities to the epistemic "standpoints" described in the recent literature of feminist theory.[9] The "standpoints" described by other feminist theorists are epistemic positions from which a person could know (or have beliefs about) anything or everything. Nevertheless, it may help to orient the reader if I describe briefly how my concept of a perspective stands in relation to some major issues on the nature of standpoints.

I do not think that there is a single perspective of women or even a single perspective of feminists on the questions of choice and responsibility under oppression. In this respect, I agree with Dorothy Smith and Jane Flax, both of whom assert that there will be many different feminist versions of reality, and I disagree with Nancy Hartsock, who describes *"the* feminist standpoint" as an ideal type.[10] The concept of a perspective that I am using here is like Hartsock's concept of a standpoint in some other respects, however. For Hartsock, a feminist standpoint is not a straightforward consequence of the experience of being a woman in an oppressive society. "A feminist standpoint picks out and amplifies the liberatory possibilities contained in that experience" (232), and is thus achieved within, rather than simply given by, the oppressive conditions of one's life. The three potentially feminist perspectives I describe must also be achieved and so are not necessarily created by any given set of life circumstances. Moreover, these perspectives are not what the philosopher Terry Winant recently described as emancipatory standpoints, "acquired by acknowledging one's commitments to projects for political and cultural transformation."[11] Complex psychological processes, both conscious and unconscious, influence our adoption of the perspectives I shall describe; they cannot always be achieved by making political commitments, they do not always include conscious political commitments, and the same political commitments are compatible with different perspectives on responsibility and choice.

Only people who have had certain kinds of experiences will be likely to adopt any one of the perspectives I shall describe, but a perspective is not guaranteed by any given set of life circumstances. For example, what I shall describe as the perspective of the victim requires either identifying oneself as a victim and feeling outrage and sorrow on one's own behalf or identifying sufficiently with someone who is a victim that one experiences outrage and sorrow on the victim's behalf. However, *being* a victim or being well-acquainted with victims does not guarantee that a person will ever reach the perspective of the victim. In those circumstances one can still identify with the oppressor(s), perceiving victims (including oneself) as responsible for their own victimization.

As I understand these perspectives, taking one of them may sometimes be as voluntary as choosing to see something from a certain point of view. Yet even when it is voluntary, taking a new perspective is not always easy. For example, the appropriate feelings do not always come with a change in beliefs; I may continue to feel guilty for being victimized even when I know that I am not at fault. An important difficulty is that some components of a perspective may be held unconsciously (e.g., I may feel, without realizing it, that my victimization was my fault), so that changing perspectives may require becoming conscious of and changing feelings, beliefs, expectations and motivations I didn't know I had.

Having a particular perspective may also be completely involuntary. It may be a consequence of never having been exposed to any other perspective, or it may be a consequence of having one's ability to know so damaged or denigrated that one doesn't have the self-confidence to think, perceive, feel, or want anything but what one is told to think, perceive, feel, or want.[12] Since taking a perspective can be more or less voluntary, we can be more or less responsible for having a particular perspective.

Nancy Hartsock argues that not all epistemic standpoints are created equal; some have more access to reality or perceive deeper levels of reality than others. I think she is right about this. With regard to the four perspectives on responsibility and choice, I shall contend not only that the potentially feminist perspectives are epistemically and morally superior to the nonfeminist perspective, but also that some of the potentially feminist perspectives are epistemically and morally better than others.

Finally, some cautions about the perspectives: They are a framework for thinking about how we think, feel, perceive, expect, and act about responsibility and choice in situations of oppression. My descriptions are outlines of patterns. Not everyone with a particular perspective will have the same thoughts, feelings, perceptions, expectations, or motivations, either consciously or unconsciously, but they will share a pattern I shall try to describe. In addition, because people are always changing, one person may take different perspectives in different situations or in similar situations at different times; therefore, at any given time many of us are in transition between perspectives, subscribing to some components of one perspective and some components of another.

The Perspective of the Oppressor

This is the only one of the perspectives I shall be describing that is not compatible with feminism. The perspective of the oppressor always assigns responsibility and blame to the victims of oppression. It always involves mystification of the oppressor's responsibility and of the distribution of power. I call it the perspective of the oppressor because it tends to work to the benefit of oppressors and because members of oppressing groups and perpetrators of violent or coercive actions against others often (perhaps usually) take this perspective. Nevertheless, people not directly involved in oppressive situations and even victims of oppression can take the perspective of the oppressor.

An oppressor imposes unjust constraints on the freedom of individuals or groups[13] and/or inflicts unjust suffering on them. "The oppressor" in a situation is not necessarily an individual person. Sometimes it is a group of people, a system of organization, or even an abstraction, such as the concept of a cruel and vengeful God who must be appeased. The oppressor may also be an aspect of a person's psyche. For example, in her descriptions of the oppression of children, the psychoanalyst Alice Miller depicts very vividly adults' attempts to control, dominate, and use children, and it seems at first that she sees the parents as the oppressors.[14] Then it emerges that Miller believes parents often try to control and dominate children out of fear of identifying with them and thereby experiencing the pain of their own oppression as children. In other words, their own victimization created the oppressors within the parents, but victims continue to exist side-by-side with the oppressors in their psyches.

When violent or coercive individuals or members of oppressing groups take the perspective of the oppressor, they work hard to keep themselves and others from seeing them as responsible, wrong, cruel, or even as simply advantaged in the oppressive situation. Sometimes they do this straight-forwardly to escape retaliation, punishment, or feelings of guilt. Frequently, they also want the victims of oppression to believe that they are themselves responsible for their own victimization and that they deserve it. This has definite political advantages in conditions of social oppression; Elizabeth Janeway has described these advantages with great clarity in *Powers of the Weak*.[15] Oppressing groups use their social and economic power to make their perspective the perspective of the whole society. Insofar as they succeed, the perspective of the oppressor is embodied in social institutions, such as the law, and represented as the truth throughout the culture.

Alice Miller points out that blaming the victims can be an important psychological strategy for violent and coercive individuals who were themselves victimized in the past. They are afraid of seeing that they were not responsible for the victimization they suffered; if they saw their past innocence clearly, they would have to experience the rage, grief, and humiliation they felt at being victimized. So, like their oppressors, they project responsibility for their violence and coercion onto their victims, forbidding the victims to see the perpetrators' responsibility. This is a self-perpetuating pattern of behavior, passed on from generation to generation. In her writings, Miller applies this analysis primarily to the abuse of children, but I think it has potential for explaining many patterns in which people "pass on" their own suffering to others.

Victims can and frequently do take the perspective of the oppressor. The victim with this perspective usually feels guilty for her/his victimization and takes all or most of the responsibility for it. "I must have done something wrong," or, "There must be something I could do to make it better," are frequent responses of victims from this perspective.[16] Victims with the perspective of the oppressor do not necessarily identify with the oppressor, but they do protect the oppressor from blame and responsibility, and they protect *themselves* from feelings of helplessness, anger, and grief and from the awareness that they are not in control of situations that could hurt them. Janeway describes victims who "choose" to do what they believe they will be forced to do, thus preserving the illusion of choice and avoiding overt and shameful defeat.[17] In an article on victims of discrimination, Kristin Bumiller describes their psychological resistance to acknowledging their victimization:

> In order for an individual to press a claim that unfavorable treatment stems from discriminatory practices she must assume the role of the victim. This transforms a social conflict into a psychological contest to reconcile a positive self-image with the image of the victim as powerless and defeated. Deciding whether or not to make a public claim of discrimination thus becomes intertwined with the process of reconciling these self-images.[18]

If the victim is to any degree responsible for her/his victimization, this will be impossible to disentangle from the mystifications of responsibility of this perspective. No one with the perspective of the oppressor can see the truth about an oppressive situation; that requires finding a new perspective.

Victims who give up the perspective of the oppressor usually do so by gaining what I shall call the perspective of the victim. They often make this change when they meet or learn about other victims and realize that their own experience is not unique. For example, often a woman who has been sexually harassed by her boss at work feels that she is responsible for his behavior and tries to determine how she encouraged it. Then, when she discovers that other women who held her position were treated the same way by the same man, she begins to change her perspective; she sees that she was victimized and that he is responsible for it. Changing perspectives is not usually easy. It requires victims to feel at least some of the pain, anger, and helplessness of having been victimized. It may also require them to oppose a tide of victim-blaming expressed by their families, their communities, and the media. Understandably, some victims resist doing all this, even when they know they are not alone in their victimization; they prefer to blame themselves and other victims. Nevertheless, changing perspectives offers victims many benefits, including opportunities to shed their burden of unjustified guilt and to experience solidarity with other victims.

Violent and coercive people and members of oppressing groups sometimes relinquish the perspective of the oppressor, but their investment in maintaining it is greater than other people's. Experiencing some form of victimization themselves may lead them to take the perspective of the victim. (For example, people who believe that the poor bring their poverty on themselves may change that perspective when they lose their own jobs, although they may return to it if they become prosperous again.) Experiences of empathizing with victims' suffering through a close relationship with a victim or by means of a work of art may also open their eyes. Changing perspectives will usually require them to acknowledge their guilt and feel remorse, not only for blaming those who did not deserve it and for closing their hearts to other people's suffering, but also for any part they may have played in causing that suffering. The rewards of changing perspectives for violent and coercive people and for members of oppressing groups are not as obvious as they are for victims; they include reducing both their need for self-deception and their alienation from victimized people (who may include themselves).

The Perspective of the Victim

This is a feminist perspective, but not the only feminist perspective. The perspective of the victim recognizes the oppressor's responsibility and assigns blame to the oppressor. I call it the perspective of the victim because it tends to work to the advantage of victims and because it is the perspective taken by victims when they are most acutely aware of their victimization and by people who identify with or empathize with victims. This perspective recognizes little or no responsibility of the victim for her/his victimization. This is sometimes an accurate representation of the situation and sometimes a falsification of it. If the victim is contributing in any way to the oppressive situation, that contribution will be difficult to see from this perspective.

The perspective of the victim is probably the best perspective for someone who has recently been victimized. Most people find it difficult to avoid blaming themselves for their victimization unless they see clearly that someone or something else is responsible. Gaining this perspective is also the easiest way for victims to give up the perspective of the oppressor, and it offers an opportunity to heal the psychological damage caused by that perspective. The victim who gains this perspective stops feeling guilty for her/his victimization, sees the power and responsibility of the oppressor, and blames the oppressor. Thus, this perspective is more realistic than the perspective of the oppressor, in that it places more (and in some cases all) responsibility where it belongs. Because it thus reduces mystification, reaching this perspective is often a great relief to the victims of oppression, as though a fog has cleared and they can, at last, see what is really going on. It also relieves victims of the guilt they may feel for their own suffering and the burden of seeking ways to improve the oppressor's behavior toward them by changing their own behavior. Their feelings of guilt are often transformed into anger toward the oppressor. Sometimes this anger is turned effectively to opposing oppression.

Sandra Bartky has written: "Feminist consciousness is consciousness of victimization."[19] From the perspective of the victim, people usually realize that they are not alone in their victimization. In fact, as we have seen, this perspective is often achieved when someone realizes s/he is one among many who have undergone a similar pattern of victimization. This realization in turn fosters solidarity among victims and motivates cooperative political action against oppression. In addition, for feminists to see other women as sister-victims of sexist society tends to make us more compassionate toward them, even when they seem to be contributing to our oppression by denying the reality of sexism or aligning themselves with sexist men.

Thus, the perspective of the victim has many advantages over the perspective of the oppressor—epistemic, psychological, moral, and political. However, it has a major disadvantage: Because it focuses primarily on past and present victimization and the responsibility of the oppressor, it can easily obscure the actual or potential power and choices of victims. Feminists are increasingly concerned about the negative consequences of identifying ourselves and others as victims of oppression. Jane Flax says:

> Developing a "feminist" consciousness of oneself as another link in the infinitely long chain of passive victims is more likely to induce a sense of hopelessness than a passionate need for a new self-definition. A woman who so totally lacks a sense of agency cannot take responsibility for herself or analyze her complicity with her own and other women's oppression.[20]

Of the negative effects of identifying others as victims, Kathleen Barry says:

> The assigned label of "victim," which initially was meant to call awareness to the experience of sexual violence, becomes a term that expresses that person's identity. . . . Victimism is an objectification which establishes new standards for defining experience; those standards dismiss any question of will, and deny that the woman even while enduring sexual violence is a living, changing, growing, interactive person.[21]

In the previous section, we noted some sources of resistance to identifying oneself as a victim. Nevertheless, it also holds a number of temptations. It is not always pleasant to have choices. Often when we have to make a difficult decision, we hope that events will take it out of our hands, and we can more easily prevent ourselves from having to make important choices, or convince ourselves that we do not have to make them, when we see ourselves as victims. Responsibility is a burden that increases with freedom; freedom brings not only the possibility of making the wrong choice for ourselves but also the possibility of doing moral wrong to others, and powerless victims have at least the consolation of their own blamelessness.[22]

There are also external pressures that motivate people to continue identifying themselves as victims. All around us we see the opposition people encounter when they resist oppression. We know that those who feel their own power and authority threatened cannot be expected to like it, and even men who are protective and kind to apparently weak women do not necessarily support their efforts to become strong. A woman who is tired of the consequences of not fighting for herself may not be ready to enter a battle for her rights, and she may know that refusing to see herself as a victim is the first move in such a battle.

For feminists to perceive other women as victims may encourage them to identify themselves as victims, and this is not always a good thing. Thus, for example, women who get together to share our problems concerning sexism at work and at home may enjoy the sympathy and understanding we can give one another but leave feeling depressed, because the power of oppression and our own relative helplessness have been confirmed. In addition, feminists are sometimes in danger of infantilizing other, especially nonfeminist, women, thinking of them as helpless victims of both oppressive conditions and false consciousness.

On the one hand, victimization is very real and all around us, and to deny or underestimate it is to deny the truth that victims desperately need to have affirmed and to deny ourselves and other women the support and understanding we need when we are victimized. On the other hand, identifying oneself and others as victims carries with it grave dangers, not the least of which is relinquishing choices and responsibility. Fortunately, not everyone who benefits from taking the perspective of the victim gets stuck with that perspective.

People who give up the perspective of the victim usually do so by taking the perspective of the responsible actor, which I will describe in the next section. Since the perspective of the victim is focused primarily on past and present victimization, moving beyond it requires increasing one's concern about the future and focusing upon choices and taking responsibility. A different perspective on the past may help to bring this about. If victims with the perspective of the victim recognize and take credit for the actions they took to survive under oppressive conditions, they may more easily make the transition to the perspective of the responsible actor.[23] Some victims may need to recognize how their own past choices contributed to their victimization, in order to see how they could avoid being victimized in the future. In addition, in order to relinquish the perspective of the victim, we may sometimes need to change our attitude toward the oppressor.

The perspective of the victim blames the oppressor. Anger toward the oppressor is psychologically healing for people who once blamed themselves (or were blamed by others) for their own victimization, and anger can fuel personal and political action. Nevertheless, victims' anger is not *effective* unless they can see the power they have to oppose their oppression and to prevent their victimization in the future. Blame can interfere with seeing this, because it focuses on the power and choices of the one who is blamed rather than the power and choices of the blamer. Blame can immobilize a victim by making the oppressor power appear absolute and the victim's power insignificant. Susan Griffin describes this danger:

> I can be angry. I can hate. I can rage. But the moment I have defined another being as my enemy, I lose part of myself, the complexity and subtlety of my vision. I begin to exist in a closed system. When anything goes wrong, I blame my enemy. . . . Slowly all the power in my life begins to be located outside, and my whole being is defined in relation to this outside force, which becomes daily more monstrous, more evil, more laden with all the qualities in myself I no longer wish to own. The quality of my thought then is diminished. My imagination grows small. My self seems meager. For my enemy has stolen all these.[24]

Ironically, in order to take back power from those who contribute to our oppression, we may have to take a more practical, forward-looking view of them than is offered by the perspective of the victim. This does not mean reducing our anger about the oppression, but it may mean changing the role of blame in our lives. Blame *can* contribute to ending oppression because it has an important change-oriented function: Blaming people, especially publicly, conveys our moral standards and can influence people's behavior.[25] On the other hand, indulging in too much blame obscures the blamer's choices and exposes her/him to the worst dangers of the perspective of the victim.

A passage from Margaret Atwood's novel *Surfacing* describes a conversion from the perspective of the victim to the perspective of the responsible actor: "This above all, to refuse to be a victim. Unless I can do that I can do nothing. I have to recant, give up the old belief that I am powerless and because of it nothing I can do will ever hurt anyone. A lie which was always more disastrous than the truth would have been."[26]

People with the perspective of the victim may come to take the perspective of the responsible actor when the desire to take power in their lives becomes very strong or when, because of a change of external circumstances or an increase in their knowledge, their *actual* power to direct their lives increases. For example, someone may show us choices we didn't know we had, or new opportunities for action may arise. We may learn of an organized effort to change the situations that victimize or oppress us.[27] Anything that empowers victims can help them see themselves as responsible actors with choices.

The Perspective of the Responsible Actor

This is another perspective that feminists can take. This perspective is forward-looking: interested in the past as a guide to the present and the future, interested in the present for the choices it offers. I call it the perspective of the responsible actor because its guiding questions are: What shall I do? What shall I take responsibility for? What shall I hold others responsible for? Willingness to take responsibility and risks is essential to it.

There is no mystification of responsibility in this perspective, and no ignorance or self-deception is necessary for a person to have it. Unlike the previous two perspectives, this perspective never obscures who or what is responsible for any restriction of choices or how much responsibility one can realistically take for events. It does not, however, guarantee that one will know these things; one has to work to learn them. People with this perspective seek knowledge because they place a high value on realistic assessment of choices and responsibility, of possible actions and their probable consequences. The more they know, the more responsibly they can act. Nevertheless, one can take this perspective even in situations where one is not well-informed.

It is also important to note that a person does not have to have a lot of choices to take the perspective of the responsible actor; it is not a perspective of the privileged. Situations are rare in which a person has no choice. One can take this perspective even when the choices are few, focusing on the remaining possibilities for action.

In order to illustrate the advantages of the perspective of the responsible actor, let us look at a more complex example than any we have considered so far: A woman becomes pregnant when her contraceptive method fails. Her boyfriend leaves her as soon as he finds out that she is not having an abortion. When she can no longer perform to her usual standard at work because of the pregnancy, she loses her job and has to go on welfare. At first she takes the perspective of the oppressor. She blames herself for taking a chance of getting pregnant with a man who was not clearly committed to her well-being. She blames herself for losing her job because she considers it her fault that she became pregnant.

If this woman gains the perspective of the victim, she will see her situation as *not* her fault and herself as a victim of social conditions and of individuals who contribute by their actions to her oppression. She may realize that her boyfriend is responsible for taking a chance of getting her pregnant when he was unwilling to help her live with the consequences, and/or that the company she works for is responsible for not having a pregnancy-leave policy that would allow her to keep her job and support her child. She may develop a broader social analysis that explains why better methods of contraception were not available to her, why her boyfriend feels free, and *is* free, to shirk his responsibility for their child, why her company can get away with not having pregnancy leave with job protection, why a society that expects and encourages women to become mothers allows welfare to be her only alternative to abortion, and so on. She will no longer blame herself for her situation; she will realize that she is not alone in the pattern of oppression she has suffered. She may become politically active on behalf of welfare mothers, universal pregnancy leave, or better contraceptive research, or she may feel so overwhelmed by the circumstances and people who victimized her that she accepts her situation as the inevitable fate of women in her society. In any case, while she continues to have the perspective of the victim, she will probably not see how she can act to avoid being victimized in the future, since it is unlikely that she will recognize how (if at all) her choices contributed to her victimization. Furthermore, with the perspective of the victim, her awareness of her own power will be vague and distant at best.

To face the future with a sense of choice, responsibility, and purpose, she needs the perspective of the responsible actor. With this perspective, she will be able to acknowledge choices she made (if any) that contributed to her victimization, such as choosing to hope that her boyfriend cared about her well-being instead of trying to find out if he really did, or ignoring fellow workers' concerns about the lack of company benefits.[28] She will also be able to recognize and take credit for the choices she made (if any) that contributed to her own well-being and self-respect, such as refusing to have an abortion she didn't want, or working as long as she could and forcing the company to fire her instead of quitting. This perspective will make it possible for her to see the choices she has *now,* to discover her power by taking good risks, and to continue learning how to improve her choices.

The perspective of the responsible actor will also be important in helping her take care of her child. It is from this perspective that we can best form relationships and take account of other people's interests while planning the future. The perspective of the oppressor and that of the victim both focus attention on the relation between victim and oppressor, often at the expense of other relationships. Also, while the woman I have described has those perspectives, her guilt and regret about becoming pregnant or her resentment about her victimization are more likely to poison her relationship with her child.

Reaching the perspective of the responsible actor is not a solution to problems about what to take responsibility for; it simply removes some obstacles to solving the problems. Women with this perspective will still have to struggle to recognize their real choices. Although they will not systematically over—or under—estimate them in the patterns of the perspective of the oppressor or the perspective of the victim, they will still be subject to ordinary self-deception about choices, caused by wishes and fears, and to the deceptions of a world that often misrepresents women's choices as narrower or wider than they really are. In addition, deciding what to take responsibility for requires assessing what they can expect to accomplish, and a sexist society tends to make that difficult for women to do realistically.[29]

We do not always choose our responsibilities fully or directly. Sometimes our caring for individuals or our commitments to groups, projects, and values lead us to take responsibility for all sorts of things we might not choose to undertake without the caring or commitments. For example, a woman is often shocked when she has her first child to discover how many unwanted responsibilities it brings. She intended to care for the child, but she didn't realize what that intention entailed. Sometimes too, other people's holding us responsible pressures us to take responsibilities we would otherwise reject. People may hold me responsible for a young friend's actions because they believe I can influence her; I may reluctantly agree to try. Thus, there is a large realm of partially chosen responsibilities we become involved in when we take the perspective of the responsible actor.

In addition to making decisions about what to take responsibility for, we have to decide when to hold other people responsible for taking future action. Ideally, from the perspective of the responsible actor, we would consider what choices they have, how much they know about their choices, how good they are at making choices, how likely it is that they can carry out their intentions in the situation, and whether they are likely to be overwhelmed by unrealistic fears or compulsive desires. We would also consider how people will respond to knowing they are held responsible for something. Sometimes they will respond by taking responsibility; as a result, they may become energetic, resourceful, and conscientious. Sometimes they will respond by becoming passive or anxious, even by breaking down, or they may refuse outright to take the responsibility.

When deciding whether to hold someone responsible for the future or the past, we should also take account of the effects on other people. This is especially important when moral or contractual obligations are involved, since whether someone is held to a moral or contractual obligation affects the seriousness of her/his own and other people's commitments in the future.

For the person with the perspective of the responsible actor, considering the consequences of holding people responsible is generally more important than making judgments about their responsibility for past events. Thus, blaming someone for past conduct is important from this perspective only insofar as it may affect people's future behavior. Blame, even for that utilitarian purpose, must be used sparingly by people with this perspective, since indulging in excessive blame has a tendency to move the blamer to the perspective of the victim; for someone who has struggled to overcome the sense of powerlessness of the victim's perspective, this would be a regression. Likewise, although everyone needs to acknowledge, understand, and regret her/his mistakes and failures in order to learn from them, victims who engage in too much self-blame may begin to take the perspective of the oppressor about their own victimization. The perspective of the responsible actor requires the ability to forgive ourselves and others in order to make room for the future. Nevertheless, anger about oppression and victimization is just as important here as it is from the perspective of the victim, and the determination to end oppression and prevent victimization is stronger and more effective.

The perspective of the responsible actor empowers people to act responsibly. Its strength is that it is action-oriented, but this is also the source of its only weakness. The demands of action do not always create good conditions for understanding. For those, we need the perspective of the observer/philosopher.

The Perspective of the Observer/Philosopher

This is another perspective with which one can be a feminist. People with this perspective seek understanding; the understanding they seek includes a causal picture of some portion or aspect of the universe. I call it the perspective of the observer because it is oriented toward observing and understanding, rather than taking responsibility and acting. I call it the perspective of the philosopher because it includes critical and self-critical thought about *how* we observe and understand the world. It is not, however, the province solely of professional philosophers; it is accessible to anyone who seeks to understand, to overcome self-deception, and to know the limitations of her/his understanding.[30] There are no mystifications of power or responsibility necessary to the perspective of the observer/philosopher, and therefore it cannot exclude feminist understandings of society. In addition, people with this perspective make an honest effort to be aware of how their own positions in the world, such as whether they are members of the privileged sex or the oppressed sex, a privileged race or an oppressed race, might affect their observations and understanding.

The perspective of the observer/philosopher is not an *objective* perspective on the world, if by "objective" we mean free from the influence of the observer's experiences, emotions, expectations, and motivations and free from the limitations of her/his position in the world. No one can create a causal picture completely free of such influences. Nevertheless, it is with the perspective of the observer/philosopher that we can attain the most objectivity we are capable of: that which comes from an honest and intelligent effort to know ourselves and our limitations and to extend our understanding beyond them.[31] Thus, two people from extremely diverse experiences and positions in the world can both have the perspective of the observer/philosopher because they both seek to *understand* and to extend their understanding as far as possible, and not because they can "step out" of their experiences and positions.

The perspective of the observer/philosopher is the perspective of most feminist theorists when they are theorizing. They seek to understand everything about how oppression works and how it affects women, and they have feminist commitments to ending oppression. From this perspective, one can see causes of both the oppressor's behavior and the victim's. One can also see the mystifications of responsibility and power and need not be deceived by them. However, having this perspective does not imply that one has some particular feminist theory rather than another. The perspective accommodates a number of competing feminist theories of society. Indeed, we should not expect it to produce "the one true picture" of anything. People's best efforts to understand may converge on a single theory or causal picture of a situation, but they may not. Having this perspective implies only that they seek a causal understanding of the world with as much honesty and awareness of their own limitations as possible.

The perspective of the observer/philosopher is primarily backward-looking, since most people can best understand conditions and events that have already occurred. It is harder to understand the present moment, which is the moment of decision and action, though of course this sometimes does occur. People taking this perspective are motivated primarily by the desire to understand rather than to act. In general, while taking this perspective they are not involved in acting to change what they observe, because it is difficult to be involved in acting while observing it all, including one's own actions, with the desire to understand. Immediate concern with action can also interfere with seeking knowledge. For example, focusing on the demands of political action has tended to steer feminists away from efforts to understand how women cooperate with or even contribute to our oppression. Although understanding cannot and should not be divorced from action, too much concern for the practical consequences of seeking knowledge can make it difficult to discover anything unexpected or unwelcome. Our intentions to act come from what we already know; if they govern our inquiries too closely, they interfere with our learning anything new or accepting any truth that might change our plans. The perspective of the observer/philosopher offers room for gaining knowledge that can later inform our actions.

Consider again the woman who became pregnant and lost her job. If she reaches the perspective of the responsible actor, she wants and needs to know whatever will be useful to her, and nothing about that perspective *prevents* her from knowing anything; but the demands of action, the concern to make decisions and take on responsibilities, may make it hard to reflect on her situation and discover everything she could learn from it. For example, if someone points out that she did a lot of wishful thinking about her boyfriend and didn't see him as he really was, she may recognize that as true and even draw conclusions from it and make resolutions about the future. However, if no one points it out to her and she never reflects on the past from the perspective of the observer/philosopher—i.e., seeking to understand her situation, her own part in it, her motivations, and the parts played by others and their motivations—she may never gain this discomforting but important piece of information.

The desire to understand is usually, especially for feminists, motivated by some drive stronger than curiosity. We feel we *need* to understand. We need to find a way out of the false and mystifying views given to us by patriarchal society. While the major motivation of the perspective of the observer/philosopher is the need to understand, the major emotion it creates is compassion, which is evoked when we see why people are doing the things they do, why they did the things they did, the larger social forces acting on their lives, how much of what determined their choices was ultimately beyond their control, and how they suffer.

From this perspective, we assume that all human actions have causes and we look for them. Is this assumption compatible with the idea that people are at least sometimes responsible for their actions? I think that it is. In the picture of responsibility I want to offer, our responsibility for any of our actions, which is a matter of degree, depends upon the following conditions:[32] how large our range of choices was; how well we knew what our choices were and their probable consequences; how successful we were in doing what we intended to do; how good our general ability to make choices was (at the time we acted); and whether and to what extent our fears and desires relevant to the situation were based on unrealistic or needlessly limiting associations. The first three conditions are fairly straightforward, but some clarification of the last two might be helpful.

Our general ability to make choices involves trust in our own perceptions, judgments, abilities, and desires, as well as the ability to make accurate judgments and the ability to make appropriate evaluations. These are all matters of degree. No sane person's confidence is absolute, and we all make mistakes in judgment, and, of course, evaluate things differently from one another. We can most easily see how important these abilities are to responsibility when we look at extreme cases. Consider someone who was afraid to make all but very minor decisions on his own (lack of self-trust), and someone else who falsely believed that everyone had malicious intentions towards her (bad judgment). Do we want to say that these two were fully responsible for their actions, even when all the other conditions for their being responsible were very good? I do not. Their abilities to make choices were impaired, and that reduced their responsibility for the actions they took. There are many ways and degrees to which the general ability to make choices can be damaged by the accidents of life and the influences of individuals or social forces. Our self-confidence can be undermined; tendencies can be produced in us to make certain kinds of errors in judgment and certain kinds of inappropriate evaluations. Damage to our ability to choose reduces our responsibility for our actions.

Influence on fears and desires[33] can also reduce responsibility. The accidents of life, the conscious or not-so-conscious actions of individuals, and social forces produce a multitude of associations in our minds between things we already fear or want and other things, creating new fears and desires. Some of the associations that are produced are realistic, in that they correspond substantially to the usual causal connections between things or events. For example, when we punish small children for running out into the street, we produce realistic associations between that behavior and danger (at far less cost than an encounter with a car). Other associations produced are unrealistic; these often lead to bad consequences when the people who have them meet new circumstances with inappropriate behavior. For example, if we reward little girls with expressions of approval for timid behavior, we do not prepare them well for later life, which holds few rewards for timid adult women besides the approval of people who like women to be timid. Finally, some associations are realistic but importantly both unnecessary and limiting. We often create them in children, out of habit or unthinking obedience to convention, and frequently the resulting desires lead people to choose to do what will fit them into the social roles they are generally expected to fill. When the available social roles are unnecessarily narrow, we have shaped people's desires, and their choices, and needlessly limiting associations, even though they may be realistic associations, given the present state of society. For example, parents, teachers, and peers may punish and ridicule physical assertiveness in little girls, and society may punish and ridicule physical assertiveness in adult women. Thus, the girl is prepared for adult reality, but this adult reality serves no purpose important to her survival and well-being (and, in this case, may work against it). Such associations limit the range of people's desires and choices in ways that fail to benefit them.

We could hardly hope to prevent or correct all the unrealistic and needlessly limiting associations people form. Yet these associations do, to greater or lesser degrees, affect our responsibility for our actions. We readily recognize this when people have associations that restrict their lives in dramatic ways, such as agoraphobia, or associations that affect some very specific type of action, such as those that cause a fear of showing anger. I do not want to say that fears and desires based on unrealistic or needlessly limiting associations always *absolve* a person of responsibility for actions related to them; sometimes these fears and desires, though present, play only a small part in motivating an action, and sometimes, especially when we are aware of the nature of the associations behind our actions, it is reasonable to expect us to struggle with them and act against them. I do want to say that people's responsibility is *greater* to the extent that their fears and desires are based on realistic associations formed in an atmosphere of diverse opportunities for experience and of social tolerance for actions that do not harm others.

It is easy to see that in my picture of responsibility oppression tends to reduce the responsibility of the oppressed for many of their actions. It reduces their choices, it misinforms and mystifies them about the choices they do have and their consequences, it damages their general ability to choose, and it ensures that unrealistic and needlessly limiting associations are created in them, both by direct manipulation and by the unintentional influence of others.

Not everyone who contemplates responsibility from the perspective of the observer/philosopher will agree with my analysis of it. Nevertheless, I think that the perspective of the observer/philosopher is the best perspective from which to make judgments about responsibility for *past* actions or situations, since with this perspective we are in the best position to understand the conditions under which choices were made and actions taken. When we make such judgments from this perspective, our concern is to understand the causes of events, including the extent to which people's responsible choices contributed to them. This can have important practical applications, in that it helps us to determine *whose* motivations have to be changed in order to change some pattern of oppression or victimization, and perhaps to determine what methods of changing motivations would be most effective.

Comparing the Perspectives

The perspective of the oppressor and the perspective of the victim *require* incomplete knowledge. In order to take them, we must remain ignorant of certain facts or ignorant of the relevance of those facts to our beliefs. Maintaining this ignorance sometimes requires self-deception, and we may be completely unaware that we are deceiving ourselves. Ignorance and self-deception usually reduce our choices and adversely affect the other conditions that determine our responsibility for our actions. Thus, the first two perspectives are not only epistemically limiting, but also morally limiting, insofar as they reduce our freedom and responsibility. Because the perspective of the victim requires less ignorance than the perspective of the oppressor, it is less limiting. The perspective of the responsible actor and the perspective of the observer/philosopher do not require any ignorance. Of course, no perspective confers complete knowledge; people with any perspective may be epistemically and morally limited.

I believe we can start out with any perspective and move to any other. To move from the perspective of the oppressor to the perspective of the victim to the perspective of the responsible actor *or* the perspective of the observer/philosopher is epistemically and morally progressive.[34] Nevertheless, it is important to remember that, however we progress, few of us reach a single perspective and remain there. For one thing, most of us want and need to move between the perspective of the responsible actor and the perspective of the observer/philosopher. For another, events can cause us to take a new perspective. For example, most of us can be plunged into taking the perspective of the victim or even the perspective of the oppressor if we suffer some catastrophe, especially an act of violence against ourselves.[35] Furthermore, as I cautioned at the beginning, these perspectives are only a framework for thinking about how we think, feel, perceive, expect, and act. In reality, people's perspectives on choice and responsibility do not conform rigidly to the descriptions I have given. Many of us are in transition between perspectives, subscribing to some components of one and some components of another.

I have said that most of us want and need both the perspective of the responsible actor and that of the observer/philosopher; but are these two perspectives compatible? We might wonder whether assuming that everyone's choices and actions, including our own, have causes, and trying to understand the sources of our own and other people's behavior, would interfere with our ability to take the perspective of the responsible actor, in which we must choose and act. With regard to the future, knowing that our own choices and actions have causes does not remove the need to decide, nor does it hinder us in deciding what to do, since we have neither enough information nor enough science to predict our own choices and actions. There might be a philosophical conflict between predicting and deciding our own actions,[36] but it will not be a practical conflict unless we have the knowledge to predict people's actions very accurately; without that knowledge, claims to be predicting what we ourselves will do are disguised decisions to do what we predict. Of course, we often know enough about certain causes of our actions to help us make decisions. For example, I know that I will find it very hard to resist certain temptations; I do not *know* that I *won't* resist them in particular circumstances, but I know it is safer not to put myself in their way.

Our ability to predict other people's actions is not much better than our ability to predict our own, although we can often see their motives and the direction of their lives more clearly. We are forced to rely quite heavily on our predictions of other people's behavior, but we can also influence other people, and this adds not just another element of uncertainty to the prediction, but another area of decision for us. If we settle for merely predicting other people's behavior when it is open to us to try to influence it, we have in effect decided not to influence it. The knowledge we do have of the causes of people's choices and actions can help us determine how to interact with them. Thus, what we learn from the perspective of the observer/philosopher is useful when we take the perspective of the responsible actor, and there is no reason for it to undermine our sense of choice.

Another kind of concern about the compatibility of the two perspectives arises when we consider the range of emotions characteristic of each. The philosopher P. F. Strawson has argued that certain kinds of reactive attitudes towards other people, especially resentment and gratitude, forgiveness, and a particular type of personal love, are incompatible with what he calls the "objective" attitude we take when we try to understand people for practical purposes such as deciding social policy or out of intellectual curiosity.[37] On the whole, I think he is right. I would put it that reactive attitudes are usually formed from the perspective of the responsible actor, and while strong personal reaction of the kind he describes can motivate us to seek understanding, it is usually incompatible with being in the frame of mind that contemplates the causal picture of the past and present, i.e., taking the perspective of the observer/philosopher. It is not that we cannot have emotions while taking the perspective of the observer/philosopher, but that with this perspective our emotions are different and our relationship to our emotions is often different. For example, while resentment does not necessarily disappear when I honestly try to understand why a friend did something to hurt me, my resentment is changed (at least muted, at most transformed into another feeling) during my effort to understand; I cannot be absorbed in resentment toward someone while I honestly try to understand her, because I need to try to put myself in her position. In addition, honestly seeking to understand often requires us to be self-consciously aware of our emotions in a way that precludes identifying with them or being fully absorbed in them, just as it often requires us to be self-consciously aware of the limitations of our positions and of our interests in the outcome of our investigations. This difference in the range of emotions is one of the reasons we cannot usually take both the perspective of the responsible actor and the perspective of the observer/philosopher at the same time. The other reason is that the perspective of the responsible actor is primarily forward-looking, and the perspective of the observer/philosopher is primarily backward-looking.

Although we cannot usually take both perspectives at once, we can *have access* to both perspectives at any given time. This is like being able to play table tennis *and* knowing the physical laws that govern the movements of the ball. Notice that there can be some mixture of the two perspectives, in that knowing the physical laws can help roughly in aiming the ball. Nevertheless, it is not ordinarily possible to look at the game from the perspective of the physicist while playing it. Likewise, knowing something about the causes of people's actions can help us roughly in deciding what to do, but attempting to understand their actions fully and to predict them while they and we are acting is usually futile.[38] The causal picture is *primarily* backward-looking because most situations and processes are too complex for us to understand while they are occurring. It *can* generate predictions of the future by applying knowledge of the past to new conditions, but detailed prediction of specific events in either the physical or psychological realms would require thorough knowledge of the present situation while it is occurring and, unless we are in complete control of them, most situations are too complex to allow this. When we act we have to rely on the understanding we *already* have (including rough generalizations about what to expect), applying it to our limited knowledge of the circumstance in which we are acting.

The usual impossibility of taking the perspective of the observer/philosopher and the perspective of the responsible actor at the same time explains why feminist theory itself, and not just the perspective of the victim, may undermine our sense of agency. Just because it attempts to paint a large causal picture including a picture of our own internalized oppression, feminist theory places us in a backward-looking perspective. Yet, by increasing our understanding, it also informs and supports our actions. When we take, as we must, the perspective of the responsible actor, feminist theory can help us see what needs changing, what we can realistically hope to change by our own actions, and what strategies are most likely to work.

Looking Back at the Problems

1. The causal picture and the agency picture

Two concerns about the compatibility of the causal picture and the agency picture of human actions can be understood as questions about the compatibility of the perspective of the responsible actor and the perspective of the observer/philosopher. In that context, I have already discussed both the compatibility of predicting our own actions with deciding what to do, and the compatibility of some emotional responses with the attitudes we take when we try to understand people.

In addition, philosophers have long worried that our actions cannot be free, and therefore cannot be responsible, if what we do has been determined by causes that are ultimately beyond our control. Other philosophers have said that we are responsible insofar as conditions allow us to choose our actions, but this has raised another problem: Can we be responsible for our actions if what we want, and therefore what we choose, has been determined by causes beyond our control? In the picture of responsibility that I have sketched, our abilities to choose, in general and in the particular situation, are very important, but so are the causes of what we want when we choose. Some such causes diminish our responsibility; they are the ones that produce in us fears and desires based upon unrealistic or needlessly limiting associations. In juggling the causal picture and the agency picture of human actions, the major concern for feminists, *as* feminists, is to understand exactly how sexist society limits our choices, damages our abilities to choose, and creates fears and desires based on unrealistic or needlessly limiting associations.

2. Does patriarchy make it impossible for women to choose freely and responsibly?

This question has to be answered for each individual woman in the circumstances of her life at any particular moment. It can be answered from either the perspective of the observer/philosopher or the perspective of the responsible actor. From the perspective of the observer/philosopher, we can realize that oppression tends to reduce the responsibility of the oppressed for many of their actions, because it adversely affects all the conditions that determine responsibility. Nevertheless, women are not always acting in circumstances of drastically reduced choices, and we are not always misinformed or mystified about our choices and their consequences; we sometimes have excellent general abilities to make choices, and we are not always acting from fears or desires created by unrealistic or needlessly limiting associations. Many women have worked hard to understand and overcome internalized oppression and have, to a great extent, freed themselves. Freedom and responsibility are always matters of degree, but in the view of responsible action I have offered, women are at least sometimes in a position to choose relatively responsibly, even under patriarchy.

From the perspective of the responsible actor, many women would be insulted by the suggestion that they cannot choose responsibly, since they are deeply concerned with making good choices and taking responsibility. This perspective must not be neglected when we consider such legal/ethical proposals as expanding the concept of coercion. We must ask how it would affect women's actions and their abilities to *take* responsibility if we tell them that it is not possible for a woman to voluntarily consent to anything in a patriarchal society. Also, and equally important, we must ask how it would affect men's actions to hear that there is no such thing as a woman's consent; how would this differ in practice from the old lie that ''no'' means ''yes?'' The perspective of the responsible actor keeps us in touch with the practical problems of what to take responsibility for and what to hold others responsible for.

3. How should we interpret exceptional women?

Each of the perspectives I have described treats exceptional women differently. From the perspective of the oppressor, the examples of exceptional women who resisted oppression or victimization successfully are often used against the victims, and victims with this perspective turn such examples against themselves. The exceptions are supposed to prove that any woman can achieve what she wants if only she wants it enough, is willing to work hard, and has the talent to accomplish it. The oppressor with this perspective feels complacent when he contemplates exceptional women; to him they prove that victims are responsible for their own victimization. (We might speculate that token women and token members of oppressed races are allowed to succeed in part because they fulfill this psychological function for oppressors.) The victim with the perspective of the oppressor, instead of being heartened or inspired by the example of exceptional women, feels diminished by comparison to them.

Women with the perspective of the victim tend to ignore exceptional women or to categorize them as male-identified or privileged and dismiss them. From this perspective, a woman finds it difficult to identify with women who resisted oppression successfully, because she is focused on oppressive forces that she cannot control and not on her own potential sources of power. It is hard for her to see that many exceptional women rose from backgrounds of conspicuous lack of privilege and from victimization. She will also tend to ignore or minimize the many ways that ordinary women also resist oppression successfully in their daily lives.

Knowledge of exceptional women who resisted oppression successfully, some of them from severely underprivileged or victimized positions, is a source of inspiration and hope for women with the perspective of the responsible actor. They want to know about such women, are hungry for the details of their lives, and speak proudly of them. They are able to identify with them and want to learn their tactics and strategies.

A woman with the perspective of the observer/philosopher will be interested in the causal histories of exceptional women. Such histories can tell her something about how oppression works, what pushes people to oppose it, and what circumstances enable them to do so. Any adequate feminist theory must ultimately be able to give an account of what causes some people to fight women's oppression, others to live within its limitations, and still others to be crushed by it.

4. When should we hold others responsible, and for what?

The best perspectives, morally, politically, and epistemically, from which to answer these questions are the perspective of the responsible actor and the perspective of the observer/philosopher, and both are important in deciding when to hold others responsible. When considering whether to hold people responsible for taking future action, we should take account of the factors I already outlined in the description of the responsible actor's perspective. The perspective of the observer/philosopher is the best perspective from which to judge people's responsibility for *past* events, because it enables us to understand the parts they played in those events. Such understanding is essential to making just decisions about whether to hold them responsible for what has occurred. Nevertheless, we need the perspective of the responsible actor here, too, since from that perspective we will be especially concerned with the consequences of assigning responsibility, i.e., with holding people responsible as an action that affects the future.

5. How can we avoid blaming the victim without denying that women have power to resist or escape victimization?

Blaming the victim arises from the perspective of the oppressor, in which the oppressor's responsibility and the distribution of power are not seen clearly and the victim is seen as primarily or solely responsible for her/his victimization. We can avoid blaming the victim by making sure that we are not identified with or protecting the oppressor. It is legitimate to be concerned about the victim's contribution to her/his victimization, but only when the oppressor's contribution has been thoroughly and honestly examined and described. Understanding the victim's contribution to oppression, if any, is necessary in order to move beyond the perspective of the victim, which in turn enables us to see the power we have to resist or escape victimization. The perspective of the observer/philosopher is the best perspective from which to see the full distribution of power and responsibility in an oppressive situation. The perspective of the responsible actor is the best one from which to act to end oppression.

Notes

1. Marilyn Frye, "History and Responsibility," Women's Studies International Forum—*Hypatia* 8(3) (1985): 215–216.
2. Recently, this problem was raised by the debate over the Joel Steinberg murder. Feminists asked whether Hedda Nussbaum, Steinberg's battered companion, should be held responsible for not doing more to prevent Steinberg from beating the child who lived with them to death. See *Ms.* "The Hedda Nussbaum Conundrum," (April 1989): 54–67.
3. Cerise Morris, "Against Determinism: The Case for Women's Liberation," in *Women and Men: Interdisciplinary Readings on Gender,* Greta Hoffman Nemiroff, ed. (Canada: Fitzhenry and Whiteside, 1987).
4. On the internalization of oppression, see Sandra Lee Bartky, "Toward a Phenomenology of Feminist Consciousness," in *Philosophy and Women,* Sharon Bishop and Marjorie Weinzweig, eds. (Belmont: Wadsworth, 1979) and "Feminine Masochism and the Politics of Personal Transformation," Women's Studies International Forum—*Hypatia* 7(5) (1984): 323–334; Catherine Itzin, "Margaret Thatcher Is My Sister: Counseling on Divisions Between Women," *Women's Studies International Forum* 8(1) (1985): 73–83; and Gail Pheterson "Alliances Between Women: Overcoming Internalized Oppression and Internalized Domination," *Signs: Journal of Women in Culture and Society* 12(1) (1987): 146–160.
5. This is a frequently heard and, I think, plausible interpretation of Catherine MacKinnon's views. See Catherine A. MacKinnon, "Feminism, Marxism, Method and the State: Toward Feminist Jurisprudence," *Signs: Journal of Women in Culture and Society* 8(4) (1983): 635–658.
6. To this question, I would like to add another, equally important one: Should we hold individual men responsible for ending women's oppression? If women contribute to our own oppression, this fact does not in itself diminish men's responsibility for it, nor does men's responsibility necessarily diminish women's responsibility to resist. Responsibility is not a fixed quantity in most situations; it is not like a pie, to be divided among the actors. But men's responsibility for ending women's oppression is too big a subject to discuss here; it is a subject for another essay. For a discussion of this issue, see Cheshire Calhoun, "Responsibility and Reproach," *Ethics* 99, no. 2 (1989): 389–406.
7. When we say, flat out, "A is responsible for x," we make this declaration in a context of holding someone responsible *for some purpose.* The appropriate *degree* of responsibility for making the assertion true (the degree appropriate for the purpose) is implicit or explicit in the context. Absolute or unlimited

responsibility could only derive from unlimited knowledge *plus* unlimited choice. Thus, "She is responsible for the bad atmosphere in the class" does not imply absolute or unlimited responsibility, only sufficient responsibility to assign blame, justify correcting her, or whatever the purpose of determining responsibility is in the context.

8. Patricia Greenspan discusses this latter difference in "Unfreedom and Responsibility," in *Responsibility, Character, and the Emotions: New Essays in Moral Psychology*, Ferdinand Schoeman, ed. (Cambridge: Cambridge University Press, 1987).

9. For a good overview of standpoint epistemologies, see chapter 6 in Sandra Harding, *The Science Question in Feminism*, (Ithaca: Cornell University Press, 1986).

10. See Dorothy Smith, "A Sociology for Women," in *The Prism of Sex: Essays in the Sociology of Knowledge*, J. Sherman and E. T. Beck, eds. (Madison: University of Wisconsin Press, 1979) and "The Experienced World as Problematic: A Feminist Method," *Sorokin Lecture No. 12* (Saskatoon: University of Saskatchewan, 1981); Jane Flax, "Review of 'Bound by Love: The Sweet Trap of Daughterhood,' " *Signs: Journal of Women in Culture and Society* 8(4) (1983): 710–712 and "Gender as a Social Problem: In and For Feminist Theory," *American Studies/Amerika Studien* (see Harding 1986.); and Nancy C. M. Hartsock, *Money, Sex and Power* (Boston: Northeastern University Press, 1983).

11. Terry Winant, "The Feminist Standpoint: A Matter of Language," *Hypatia: A Journal of Femininst Philosophy* 2(1) (1987): 123–148.

12. This latter condition is movingly described in May Field Belenky, Blythe McVicker Clinchy, Nancy Rule Goldberger, and Jill Mattuck Tarule, *Women's Ways of Knowing: The Development of Self, Voice and Mind* (New York: Basic Books, 1986), esp. chapters 1 and 2.

13. See Alison Jaggar, *Feminist Politics and Human Nature* (Totowa: Rowman and Allanheld, 1983).

14. Alice Miller, *Thou Shalt Not Be Aware: Society's Betrayal of the Child*, Hildegarde Hannum and Hunter Hannum, trans. (New York and Scarborough, Ontario: Meridian, New American Library, 1986).

15. Elizabeth Janeway, *Powers of the Weak* (New York: Morrow Quill Paperbacks, 1981), esp. chapters 5, 6, and 10.

16. The literature on wife abuse abounds with victim responses such as these. See, for example: *Wife Assault Information Kit* (Ministry of the Attorney General, Province of British Columbia, 1986) and *Wife Assault/Victim Support Worker Handbook* (Justice Institute of British Columbia, 1987).

17. Janeway, *Powers of the Weak*, 62.

18. Kristin Bumiller, "Victims in the Shadow of the Law: A Critique of the Model of Legal Protection," *Signs: Journal of Women in Culture and Society* 12(3): 433.

19. Sandra Lee Bartky, "Toward a Phenomenology of Feminist Conscious-

ness,'' in *Philosophy and Women*, Sharon Bishop and Marjorie Weinzweig, eds. (Belmont: Wadsworth, 1979), 254.

20. Jane Flax, ''Review of 'Bound by Love: The Sweet Trap of Daughterhood,' '' *Signs: Journal of Women in Culture and Society* 8(4) (1983): 712.

21. Kathleen Barry, *Female Sexual Slavery* (New York: Avon, 1979).

22. See Simone de Beauvoir's discussion of the temptation to forgo liberty. *The Second Sex* (New York: Alfred A. Knopf, 1952), xx–xxi.

23. This point was made to me in discussion with feminist therapists at the Canadian Psychological Association Section on Women and Psychology meetings in Vancouver, June 1987.

24. Susan Griffin, ''The Way of All Ideology,'' *Signs: Journal of Women in Culture and Society* 8(3) (1982): 657.

25. See Calhoun, ''Responsibility and Reproach.''

26. Margaret Atwood, *Surfacing* (Don Mills, Ontario: Paper Jacks, 1972). In her book about Canadian literature, *Survival,* Atwood also provides an analysis of responses to victimization. It consists of four ''Basic Victim Positions'' that divide psychological experiences and attitudes quite differently from the analysis I offer here; Atwood's is, as she says, designed primarily as a model for making sense of Canadian literature.

27. Liberation movements do not always foster this change to the perspective of the responsible actor in their members. As I have pointed out, organizations are not immune to the pitfalls of the perspective of the victim.

28. These are just examples of possible contributing choices. Not everyone who is victimized contributes to it by her/his choices.

29. For example, psychologists find that girls tend to underestimate their abilities to perform tasks. See V. C. Crandall, ''Sex Differences in Expectancy of Intellectual and Academic Reinforcement,'' in *Achievement Related Motives in Children*, C. P. Smith, ed. (New York: Russell Sage, 1969); E. Lenney, ''Women's Self-Confidence I Achievement Settings,'' *Psychological Bulletin* 84 (1977): 1–13; and M. Kimball and V. Gray, ''Feedback and Performance Expectancies in an Academic Setting,'' *Sex Roles* 8(9) 1982: 999–1007.

30. By using the term ''philosopher'' here, I want to affirm the possibility for all women to be philosophical in the sense that Elizabeth Young-Bruehl speaks of ''the education of women as philosophers'' (*Signs: Journal of Women in Culture and Society* 12 no. 2 [1987]: 207–221).

31. For valuable discussions of this issue from two different points of view, see Evelyn Fox Keller, *Reflections on Gender and Science* (New Haven, Connecticut: Yale University Press, 1985) and Thomas Nagel, *The View from Nowhere* (New York: Oxford University Press, 1986).

32. Although responsibility and freedom are clearly related, the conditions of responsibility are not necessarily the same as the conditions of freedom. For example, it can be very important to my freedom that I not have certain desires, such as the desire to drink alcohol excessively, but having a desire for something, even wanting it *very much*, does not necessarily decrease my responsibil-

ity for choosing it, depending (as I claim) on the origin of my desire. Thus, in order to avoid questions that are too complex to discuss here, I prefer to discuss responsibility in terms of choices and desires rather than in terms of freedom.

33. Influences on desires have been extensively discussed by philosophers who are concerned with their effects on freedom and responsibility. (Fears are discussed under the rubric of desires, on the grounds that they create desires.) See, for example, Jonathan Glover, *Responsibility* (London: Routledge and Kegan Paul, 1970); Sharon Bishop Hill, "Autonomy and Self-Determination," in *Philosophy and Women*, Sharon Bishop and Marjorie Weinzweig, eds. (Belmont: Wadsworth, 1979); and Janet Radcliffe Richards, *The Skeptical Feminist* (Middlesex: Penguin, 1980), esp. chapter 3.

34. There may be intermediate perspectives that facilitate this progress. For example, there are distinctive perspectives of the victim's counselor and the oppressor's counselor, which help people to move beyond the perspective of the victim and that of the oppressor, respectively. I regret that there is not room here to describe these in detail. They are interesting, in that the counselors focus upon the needs, motivations, and responsibilities of individuals whose perspectives they do not share. They must nurture their clients' abilities to move to less limited perspectives, while maintaining their own understandings of the clients' perspectives and remaining the clients' advocates.

35. Even a catastrophic illness, where there is no identifiable "oppressor," can do this. We can take the perspective of people who blame us for being ill, and then we look for how we "made ourselves ill" and expect to "make ourselves better" with the "right attitude" toward the illness. On the other hand, we can take the perspective of the victim, and then we feel powerless in relation to the illness.

36. On this question, see, for example: A. I. Melden, *Free Action* (London: Routledge and Kegan Paul, 1961) and Richard Taylor, "Deliberation and Foreknowledge," *American Philosophical Quarterly* 1(1) (1964): 73–80.

37. P. F. Strawson, "Freedom and Resentment," *Proceedings of the British Academy*, May 1962: 187–211.

38. I say "usually" because I think that sometimes people may manage to combine these two perspectives. Déjà vu gives a brief impression of combining them, and mystics describe more prolonged experiences of a similar kind. See William James, *The Varieties of Religious Experience* (New York: Modern Library: 1902).

Questions

1. To be capable of gaining power to direct our lives, what does Wendell believe is necessary? What benefit is there in gaining power to direct our own lives? Might there be disadvantages in having such power?
2. How might Wendell's perspectives be applied to the case of a battered

woman? Which perspective does Wendell think is the best perspective? Why? Would any of these perspectives be useful for other women, perhaps anorexic teenagers? Explain.

3. In what sense, if any, might a woman be responsible for her victimization? What might cause a woman to believe she deserves to be punished by her husband or boyfriend?
4. Some women date men who are violent and abusive to them. What kinds of motivations would women have to continue dating these men? Why would women marry these men?
5. Why might men become batterers?
6. How does Wendell explain the notion of blaming the victim? What is the difference between *blaming* a victim and holding that same victim *responsible* for her victimization?

4

Right-Wing Women: Causes, Choices, and Blaming the Victim

Anita M. Superson

Much philosophical discussion in feminism focuses on the harm men as a group cause women as a group. Not much attention is paid to the harm that some women cause women as a group. Borrowing an expression from Andrea Dworkin,[1] I will refer to these women as "right-wing women." It is undoubtedly true that men harm women as a group. I believe that the harm right-wing women cause all women is at least as severe as the harm men cause. The question is whether the appropriate response is to blame these women in the way men are blamed, or whether blaming them is an instance of wrongful blaming of the victim. The recent debate between Marilyn Friedman and Christina Sommers serves as a stark reminder of the issue. Sommers claims that feminists such as Friedman inappropriately denigrate the roles that most women (freely) choose (being mothers, marrying good providers, enjoying clothes that render them sex objects, etc.).[2] Feminism makes right-wing women feel guilty for choosing the lifestyle they want, and by doing so, aims to restrict their choices.

In this paper I argue that the appropriate response of feminists to right-wing women is *not* to blame them. I offer an analysis of the behavior of right-wing women, concluding that their choice of lifestyle, and the values and beliefs accompanying it, in the ordinary case takes place in the context of severe restrictions of their freedom caused mainly by patriarchy. Their lifestyle, in turn, significantly limits their choices further. To blame them is to say they ought not to act the way they do, in other words that they have an obligation to change. But to impose such an obligation on them is to expect them to act in ways that restrict their choices even further.

Harm to Women

The notion of harm is central to the notion of victim. Joel Feinberg
has traced the etymology of the word "victim," citing one of the later
definitions as "a person who suffers any kind of serious misfortune
(and not just death or physical injury), whether through cruel or oppressive treatment by other persons, or from any kind of hard circumstances."[3] For purposes of this paper, I will use the term in this broad
sense, as doing so allows us to make sense of one's being a victim of a
tornado or being a victim of one's own stupidity.

Sexism harms women; it makes them victims. It harms them individually, as when, for example, a woman is raped or sexually harassed on
the job. But sexism causes a more subtle harm, namely, the group harm
it causes all women, and I believe it is this kind of harm that right-wing
women cause.[4] Sexist behavior may be directed at a particular woman,
but its message is meant for all women. The particular woman is singled
out merely because she has in common one property with all women,
namely, her sex. Since any single instance of sexism has as its target
the group of all women, it is this group that suffers harm as a result of
the behavior.[5]

The harm is integrally related to sex roles. Sexist attitudes reflected
in sexist behavior express and perpetuate the stereotype that women are
fit to occupy only certain roles because of their sex. These roles are
associated with "body" (versus mind) and "emotions" (versus reason). They include being sex objects, mothers, nurturers, sympathizers,
etc. One of the primary harms associated with assigning women to these
sex roles is that it significantly restricts their choices regarding how
they live their lives. No matter what a particular woman may accomplish, all women are seen as being best suited for roles emphasizing
body and emotions. They are denied opportunities in education and the
workplace, are forced to bear the brunt of childrearing, are expected to
be ready to give emotional support to their mates, are expected to dress
in uncomfortable and restricting ways to catch and keep a man, and so
on. Once they come to occupy the sex roles determined for them, the
view that they can occupy only these roles gets reinforced. The restriction of choices is cyclical, seemingly with no way out. It denies wom-
en's autonomy, as they cannot do what they prefer, or *would* prefer
were it not for patriarchy's powerful influence on their beliefs, desires,
and values.

Women are victims because they are harmed in serious ways. They
are victims of men's oppression. But they are also harmed by members

of their own group, right-wing women who perpetuate sexism in much the same way men do. Right-wing women accept—even endorse whole-heartedly—the roles men impose on them, and by doing so cause group harm to all women. Examples range from the seemingly innocent, such as women who wear makeup and revealing yet uncomfortable clothes in order to make themselves attractive to men, to much more damaging ones, such as women who engage in pornography and prostitution[6] and those who vigorously fight for the pro-life cause, blockading entrances to clinics and denigrating those women who chose to have abortions. Still others cause harm by living out traditional family roles, by staying with men who abuse them, and by acting in "feminine" ways such as being demure and submissive because they think they *ought* to do these things.

I will take right-wing women to be women whose lifestyles by and large reflect right-wing values, for the reason that they believe women *belong* in stereotypical roles. Right-wing women possess the same attitudes about women as do sexist men. Thus, we cannot detect right-wing women just by observing lifestyles—a woman can be rich and powerful but right-wing, or she can be a feminist and in a traditional role. My definition of right-wing women excludes women who on occasion engage in right-wing behavior, for reasons other than because they believe women ought to adopt stereotypical roles (e.g., women who are mothers because they like children, women who work in servile, low-paying jobs because they have no other skills, etc.). To the extent that a person can be sexist on some issues but not on others, the property of being right-wing comes in degrees. I believe that those who are sexist even on only some issues do not fully understand feminism and have inconsistent beliefs. The more they come to grasp feminism, the greater the likelihood that their beliefs will change and that their beliefs and attitudes will form a coherent picture. I include in the class of right-wing women any woman who in any way endorses patriarchal attitudes, and the question is whether we should blame them for those particular behaviors that reflect those attitudes. By endorsing and thus perpetuating sexist stereotypes, right-wing women restrict the choices of all women.

Arguably, right-wing women cause *more* harm to women as a group than men do. By engaging in sexist behavior they create the belief that women really do not mind having their choices restricted or, even worse, that they like the sex roles men have designated for them. This imposes an additional burden on feminists who are striving to change sexist attitudes and to obtain personal freedom. The burden is felt when, for instance, after teaching feminist philosophy courses all day a professor turns on the television and sees a commercial in which a young, seductive woman named "Misty" encourages male viewers to call a "1–900" number for phone sex.

Feminists are quick to blame men as a group for sexism, and rightly so. Cheshire Calhoun has argued that in "normal moral contexts," that is when an individual has generally good moral reasoning skills and can for the most part figure out which actions are right, wrong, or controversial, his claims of moral ignorance should not be used to excuse him.[7] Excusing has a sanctioning force, giving the action an implicit legitimacy: "[the] excuse can be repeated for ongoing resistance to seeing that there is anything wrong with what one is doing."[8] Ordinary men are capable of taking the moral point of view and seeing what is wrong with their behavior; thus, they are blameworthy for their sexist behavior. Moral reproach, according to Calhoun, serves three functions: it teaches us that certain actions are morally wrong; it motivates us to change the way we act; and in labeling us, it confirms our identities as moral agents.[9]

But if Calhoun is right, these same points about blameworthiness and reproach might be made about right-wing women. We are faced with a dilemma. If we do not blame right-wing women, we need to show why it is legitimate to blame men, given that they both engage in the same behavior. If we are unable to do so, we ought not to blame men for sexism. The problem is that sexist behavior then gets sanctioned: we risk its continuation, resulting in serious harm to all women. On the other hand, blaming right-wing women seems to blame the victim. As many feminists have suggested, this unfairly places an additional burden on women. It has been argued more strongly that blaming these women only divides women and prevents them from uniting against a common foe: the oppression of patriarchy.[10]

The place to start in attempting to solve the dilemma is to seek an explanation for the behavior of right-wing women.

Right-Wing Women: Causes and Choices

Obviously there are quite a few reasons why some women are right-wing. Detailed psychological profiles are unnecessary for the purposes of this essay.[11] Instead, my analysis draws upon what I consider to be the most pertinent and important literature, which in some cases relies on sociological data, and which gives a sufficient overview for revealing the primary causes of "right-wingness."

The literature reveals that there are two main reasons why some women are right-wing. One is that some women are reared within or later become associated with a religious tradition that strongly supports and emphasizes right-wing values. These values come to form an integral part of their personal identity. They become blinded by such values and feel their identity and personal worth severely threatened by feminist values. As a result they find that a life sustaining "traditional" values is their only option.

A second reason that some women are right-wing is that they believe a "traditional" lifestyle is their best (i.e., utility-maximizing) option: they feel constrained by the options made available to women in a patriarchal society.[12] Once they choose this lifestyle they are likely to adopt the values it endorses. Again, these values form an integral part of their identity, and feminism threatens their personal worth. They firmly believe that a traditional lifestyle is their best option, and so are averse to adopting feminist values. In the end, I shall argue that in either case the choices of right-wing women are severely limited by some form of patriarchy, and for that reason it is wrong to limit their choices even further.

Religious Reasons

In her recent book, *Abortion and the Politics of Motherhood*,[13] Kristin Luker offers a revealing profile of pro-life women, or as I shall call them, anti-choice women. Since most right-wing women are anti-choice, her findings are relevant to my purposes here. Almost half of all anti-choice women in Luker's survey reported an income of less than $20,000 a year, most earning only between $5,000 and $10,000 a year. Sixty-three percent of them did not work in the paid labor force, and almost all of those who did were single. Ten percent of them had a high school education or less, 30 percent never finished college, and only 6 percent had an advanced degree. Most of them were housewives, or if they worked in the paid labor force, held jobs that are traditionally female. Only 16 percent of them never married, and only 5 percent had been divorced. Their families had an average of about 3 children, and 23 percent had 5 or more children. Most significantly, almost 80 percent of them were Catholics, and another 9 percent Protestant. Fifty-eight percent said they were raised Catholic and 15 percent were raised Protestant, so there were a number of converts. Sixty-nine percent said religion was important in their lives, and another 22 percent said it was very important. Only 2 percent of anti-choice advocates surveyed said they never attended church.

According to the same survey, almost all pro-choice women worked in the paid labor force, and over half of them had incomes in the top 10 percent of all women in the country. If they were married, their husbands usually had good incomes as well. In general, they had much more education than anti-choice women, with 37 percent having some graduate school work. They tended to be in the major professions, to own small businesses, or to hold executive positions in large businesses. Twenty-three percent of them never married, and if they did their families had only 1 or 2 children. Most notably, 63 percent of them said they had no religion, and not one surveyed claimed to be Catholic. Twenty percent were raised Catholic, 42 percent Protestant, so unlike many anti-choice believers who were converts, many had chosen to abandon their religion. As Luker points out, the most dramatic difference between anti-choice and pro-choice women is the role religion plays in their lives. Almost 75 percent of pro-choice people surveyed said that religion was either unimportant or completely irrelevant to them, and only 25 percent of them said they ever attended church.

The statistics on the role that religion plays in the lives of anti-choice people—women in particular—are astonishing and revealing.[14] Women who were raised in the Christian faith (particularly in Catholicism) and remained believers, or those who for whatever reason converted to Christianity, were likely to endorse Christian values that became central to their lives. Indeed, Christians are notorious for the strict upbringing of their children, including their indoctrination into the beliefs of the church and, insofar as these beliefs are sexist, their indoctrination into the tenets of patriarchy. Being reared in a strict, Christian household makes it likely that these women will acquire the values of the church.

Central among these is the value of life, including the life of a fetus. Catholics believe that life begins at conception, at which point a soul is infused into the embryo. Whether Catholic or not, all the anti-choice people in Luker's survey grew up believing that the embryo is a baby deserving all of the rights any rational human adult has.[15] The Catholic Church's position is that all (innocent) life, including the life of the unborn, is sacred, and abortion breaks the divine law "Thou shalt not kill." According to the Catholic Church, pregnancy is an exalted state and abortion is murder; motherhood is sacred. The belief instilled by the Catholic Church is that all married people should at least be willing to be parents: sex is sacred, and to be engaged in only for purposes of procreation. "Unnatural" birth control methods are not supported by the church. Given the ban on both abortion and the most reliable methods of birth control, the traditional family is endorsed by the church. For women, participation in the paid workforce is secondary to motherhood, if undertaken at all. Indeed, the New Right preachers who felt threatened by the force of feminism often quoted the Bible passage; "The husband is the head of the wife, even as Christ is head of the church."[16] One minister even attributed the rise of wife-beating to the fact that men are no longer leaders in their homes, suggesting that women should be more submissive.[17]

Such views of the Catholic and other fundamentalist Christian churches are adopted by their followers, and the values their church endorses become central to the followers' world view. The anti-choice world view is one that centers around God. According to Luker, one important consequence is that anti-choice people are skeptical about our ability to understand and control events in the world, including procreation and, I would add, stereotypical gender roles. Most anti-choice people believe that men and women are different and have different roles in life, and that women should be wives and mothers first.[18]

Anti-choice women's skepticism about understanding and controlling events in the world might explain why they accept their role in life as homemakers and mothers, why they let their husbands make important decisions about their lives, and why they would not consider birth control or abortion as options. They believe their lot in life is out of their control, and governed by God's will as part of His plan. Right-wing women are taught by their religion to accept and bear their crosses in life. They object to pro-choice women's attempts to control their own lives on the ground that doing so interferes with God's plan, which should not be tampered with. Indeed, since feminism opposes much of what God decrees, it must be wrong. Their belief in God essentially leaves them with no choice of lifestyle.

The values anti-choice women adopt become central to their identity and personal worth. Feminism, since it threatens these values, threatens their identity. Sandra Bartky offers the following analysis of why not all women are feminists, and I believe it is correct. A person internalizes a sense of self as a distinct individual that is tied to what she knows and especially what she knows how to do. Women, like men, have a stake in the perpetuation of their skills, and feminism threatens them with deskilling.[19] Feminism supports a world view that deemphasizes and therefore downgrades the traditional roles of men and women.[20]

The Supreme Court's decision in *Roe v. Wade* threatened the personal worth of women who made pregnancy central to their lives by making motherhood less sacred. Luker puts it best: "When pregnancy is discretionary—when people are allowed to put anything else they value in front of it—then motherhood has been demoted from a sacred calling to a job."[21] Beverly LaHaye, founder of Concerned Women for America, is reported as saying that "the women's liberation movement is destroying the family and threatening the survival of our nation"[22] and "[f]eminism really blotted out motherhood family must come first for a woman; it's just not natural any other way."[23] Insofar as feminism promotes the view that women's most meaningful work is in the man's world, it fills anti-choice women with resentment as it allegedly diminishes the worth of women who choose to stay home and rear children.[24] Feminism threatens their most basic, self-defining skills, namely, those of being homemaker and mother. When feminism strikes that close, change is unlikely. Indeed, once entrenched in the Christian tradition, right-wing women are unlikely even to consider the alternatives. Luker's study shows that only four of the anti-choice activists interviewed had ever considered any other view about abortion than the anti-choice position.[25]

In sum, religious right-wing women are restricted in their choice of lifestyle. Once they adopt the values associated with this lifestyle, they feel threatened by feminism and see a religious lifestyle as their only option.

Secular Reasons

Many women do not make religion central to their lives, but have what they consider to be good secular reasons for adopting nonfeminist lifestyles. Primary among these is survival.

First is economic survival. Susan Faludi reports that in 1986, full-time female workers earned only 64 cents to a man's dollar, the same wage gap that existed in 1955.[26] Given these figures, worries about economic thriving for some women turn into worries about economic surviving for women in low-paying jobs. Many women believe that marriage is the solution to economic thriving or survival. Andrea Dworkin describes right-wing women as fully aware that women are economically disabled under patriarchy, and as a result believing they must play sex games with men, agreeing to "privatized male ownership" of their bodies (or, in the case of prostitutes, selling to hundreds of men).[27]

The disparity in income for men and women is exacerbated by the hardships women are faced with when they do secure jobs. The story of Betty Riggs, who worked at American Cyanamid, is poignant. Riggs was a victim of sex discrimination and sexual harassment from male coworkers and supervisors who resented women entering their territory. She finally suffered the grievous harm of essentially being forced to get sterilized because the company said that chemicals present in her working environment posed a possible risk to women's reproductive organs.[28] Riggs is not alone: one study reports that as many as 88 percent of women are faced with sexual harassment and sex discrimination on the job.[29] Women are even raped on the job, as in the case of Mechelle Vinson who reportedly had sexual relations with (was raped by?) her supervisor forty to fifty times and was forcibly raped several times.[30] Faced with such serious risks to their bodies and their integrity, it is easy to see why traditional marriage seems to be the best option for many women.

Women fear men, and not just in the workplace. They fear physical violence on the streets. They quietly accept catcalls and innuendoes from men because they take them to be warnings or threats from men who are angry at women as a group. Dworkin puts it best:

Calling a woman a name temporarily brands her; it molds social perceptions of her in a way that upholds her social inferiority; it frequently comes before the fist or before the fuck, and so women learn to associate it with uses of themselves that they abhor, hostile uses of themselves . . . it expresses a serious, not a frivolous, hatred—the hatred of women.[31]

Women believe a husband or lover will protect them from such abuse, allowing them to walk down the street freely. George Gilder warns women: ''You have no choice—wed or prepare to die. . . . Better to march down the aisle with them—than to meet them in a dark alley.''[32] Even if Gilder's warning is a bit exaggerated, the fact remains that women are paid less than men for equal work in many fields, that equal work is not in reality always available, and that sexism on the job is alive and well.

If marriage promises protection from men, pregnancy promises control over men. Right-wing women take abortion to be linked to the sexual degradation of women. Access to abortion for women translates into easy access to sex for men without having to bear the burden of any consequences. Secular right-wing women oppose abortion and birth control for the same reason: ''pregnancy is the only consequence of sex that makes men accountable to women for what men do to women. Deprived of pregnancy as an inevitability, a woman is deprived of her strongest reason not to have intercourse.''[33]

Dworkin describes right-wing women as smart and fully aware of their oppression. I believe they are aware of some of the harms they suffer as individuals, but I believe they do not fully understand the notion of oppression or the group harm women suffer. Unlike religious right-wing women, secular right-wing women buy into the system not because they believe it is the way things should be, as part of God's plan, but because they believe things are unalterable[34] and that it is their best option. They are socialized from an early age to believe this by the numerous elements of patriarchy present in society. To different degrees, right-wing women actually change their values, coming to believe that the patriarchal system is really the way things *should* be. This can easily happen, given the pervasiveness of sexism.

The traditional lifestyle shapes and defines the identity of right-wing women and its values become central to their integrity. They need the traditional lifestyle (or, in the case of prostitutes and pornographic models, nontraditional but sexist lifestyle) to survive. Feminism threatens their integrity because not only does it go against right-wing values of marriage and family, but it also threatens to leave them unprotected and without any control over men. In short, it threatens their survival.

Like religious right-wing women, secular right-wing women have severely restricted choices. Their choice of lifestyle is restricted by the forms oppression takes politically, economically, and socially. They know no other world (nor can they conceive of the possibility of one in their lifetime) than the patriarchal one they inhabit. Once entrenched in a right-wing lifestyle, they adopt its values, and, just like their religious counterparts, are likely to be blinded to alternatives. This, coupled with the fact that feminism threatens them, makes them resistant to change.

Shortsighted—Not Self-Interested—Reasons

Where both kinds of right-wing women go wrong is in their choice of lifestyle. Biased values and beliefs, together with the lack of a complete understanding of feminism, forces them to believe wrongly that the traditional lifestyle is their best option.

Religious right-wing women live the lifestyle that they believe God has chosen for them. It is not a feminist one, and arguably it even blinds them to feminist concerns. Since their time is taken up with family matters, they do not participate in community activities and as a result are not exposed to women with different lifestyles, such as poor women whose only real option when faced with pregnancy is abortion.[35] Indeed, Luker's study shows that many of them would end a friendship if the person had an opposing view on abortion.[36] They do not see discrimination as being relevant to them because they do not work in the paid labor force.[37] In short, they do not understand feminism because they do not have to.

Secular right-wing women also do not fully understand feminism, believing that it will leave them worse off than they are now which, in general, is false. At the root of their belief is their view that oppression is unchangeable.[38] They see feminists as women who are in the same position they are: powerless under men. So long as men retain the power they have—and right-wing women believe they will—feminism is futile. Instead of religion standing in their way, it is the infusion of sexism in all realms of political, social, and economic spheres of society that stands in the way of their fully understanding feminism.

Right-wing women in most cases are mistaken about their choice of lifestyle. They turn to marriage for protection from men, yet the home turns out to be the worst place for them: "the home is the most dangerous place for a woman to be, the place she is most likely to be murdered, raped, beaten, certainly the place where she is robbed of the value of her labor."[39] Right-wing women wrongly believe that abortion oppresses them: they believe it disrupts traditional sex roles by diminishing male decision-making power and responsibility and takes away women's only power over men. Religious right-wing women believe fetuses have souls and abortion is murder, a view that is disputable. Right-wing women wrongly believe that feminists are a burden or at least unnecessary for improving their lives. Because they do not fully understand feminism, they turn against the oppressed instead of the oppressors. They believe women are treated favorably when exempt from doing heavy work on the job, when exempt from the draft, when put on a pedestal, and when free to stay home to raise children. They believe that victimization is a woman's choice, and that speaking out against oppression is "wallowing in the victim-state."[40] Feminists are seen as troublemakers. The few women who make it through the system and get good positions wonder what all the fuss is about—if they made it, why can't other women?

Right-wing women fail to realize that leading a right-wing lifestyle limits their choices even further. Valuing fetal life means abortion is not an option; valuing traditional sex roles endorsed by the Catholic Church means being the head of the household is not an option; and valuing the traditional family means, at the very least, a lessening of economic power. Buying into the system means they can expect to suffer all the harms of sexism, including degradation, violence, and being forced to occupy certain sex roles. They must spend time catering to husbands and children and spend money on dressing up to attract a man instead of spending time and money on education, development of skills, and job experience that would increase their chances of breaking out of the traditional lifestyle they have adopted.

Removed from their oppression, right-wing women will have many more and better choices even as individuals under a system that is predominantly patriarchal. But right-wing women cannot appreciate how feminism can free them. It is not self-interest that stands in their way. They do not reject the long-term benefits of feminism for all women including themselves because these are too difficult to achieve by making changes at the individual level. The prostitute, for example, does not reject a feminist lifestyle because she can make more money selling her body than she could if she adopted a non-sexist lifestyle. Rather, right-wing women, if the above analysis is correct, cannot adequately weigh short-term against long-term interests because they do not fully understand the latter. Blinded by their beliefs and values, they do not grasp the benefits they can expect living a feminist lifestyle rather than one that endorses patriarchy. They cannot break out of the system because they are shortsighted. They suffer from false consciousness.[41]

It has been objected that at least some right-wing women are rational, informed, and fully free and act out of self-interest in adopting their lifestyle and thus ought to be blamed.[42] There is a lot to be said on this issue.

First, we need to distinguish between being right-wing and living a right-wing lifestyle, or at least living a lifestyle that has right-wing elements. Though there are trends in the lifestyles of both right-wing women and of feminists, we cannot judge conclusively what a person's ideology is from observing her lifestyle or elements thereof. There are women who are wealthy and powerful, and so not economically dependent on men, and yet who count as right-wing women in my analysis—Phyllis Schlafly, Margaret Thatcher, and Beverly LaHaye come to mind.[43] By the same token, there are feminists who engage in seemingly right-wing behavior—consider the feminist who waitresses to get through college or the feminist who sports lots of makeup and sexy clothes to ridicule patriarchy and to affirm the belief that she can dress any way she wants. It is their attitudes toward women that distinguish feminists from right-wing women. But right-wing women characteristically engage in right-wing behavior, and it is this, together with the attitudes, that harms all women.

Thus, there are different categories of women that ought not to be confused in the objection. If the objection is addressed to women who merely engage in right-wing behavior, I believe it can be answered, since most if not all of these women are not fully free and do not understand feminism. Moreover, in most cases, it is *not* in a woman's self-interest to *be* a right-wing woman instead of a feminist. To believe otherwise is to overlook the individual benefits she can obtain even under patriarchy where few others are feminists.

It is noteworthy that in my definition it is impossible for a woman to be *both* a feminist *and* a right-wing woman, since these positions are inconsistent. Yet there are women who are feminist, or who at least are not right-wing, but who adopt a right-wing lifestyle at least in certain respects (e.g., they might still vote for pro-choice candidates). Women working in dead-end, low-paying, clerical positions who take time off (as allowed by their employers) to fulfill family responsibilities fall into this class,[44] as does the feminist college student waitress. It may be in their self-interest to act in these ways. Even though such women "milk the system" or seem to perpetuate it on the surface, they are not right-wing women as I have described them because they lack the sexist attitudes. Without the attitudes, it is not clear to me that they *harm* women. Mothers who stay home with their children, though seemingly living a traditional lifestyle, do not harm women. Feminism, after all, does not mean a rejection of motherhood and its associated joys. It is the attitudes together with the behavior that harms women. If these women do not harm women as a group, we do not have to worry about whether to blame them.

Of course, the worry is that just by virtue of their behavior, right-wing women do harm women as a group. Certainly feminists are not threatened by them. But others who observe their behavior and do not know (or understand) their attitudes might have their sexist beliefs reinforced, and so indirectly such women may harm all women after all. Though this may be true, I do not believe we should blame these women because it is quite likely that either they are doing the best they can under patriarchy (and I believe most of these women fall into this category), their behavior is not inherently antifeminist (e.g., mothers staying home with children), or they take themselves to be making fun of patriarchy or something like that (e.g., the feminist who wears makeup and sexy clothes). I believe the latter cases are so rare (and usually the person is careful to do these things in the right context where her behavior will not be misinterpreted) that they do not send a sexist message and so are unproblematic.

Finally, there is the woman who I think provides the biggest threat to my view: one who *understands* feminism but still rejects it. Rejecting feminism implies that she has sexist attitudes towards women. Internalists believe that if a person recognizes and/or assents to having a reason to act (in feminist ways), she necessarily has a motive to do so and (under the right conditions) will do so. Since I am not this kind of internalist, I think it is *possible* for there to be such women. Yet I believe it is highly unlikely. Women who come fully to understand feminism see the benefits it can provide them and all women, whether or not patriarchy continues. Part of what is involved in coming to understand feminism is coming to rid oneself of sexist attitudes toward women. Rare is the woman who fully understands feminism and remains a right-wing woman. Even if such women exist, blaming them, as I will show in the remainder of this essay, is wrong because their choices are still made within the context of patriarchy and thus restricted.

Wrongful Blaming of the Victim

To blame right-wing women is to say they have an obligation—either to themselves or to other women—to change.[45] The view that they are to blame is compelling because they do harm—indeed, seriously harm—all women. The idea is that blaming them will change their behavior, which will ultimately aid in eradicating sexism. Blaming them does not mean forcing them to act a certain way, but it means more than merely saying they ought to act that way. Blaming creates an expectation of action, just as my saying to you, "You ought not to kill," creates an expectation that you will not kill. It involves judging as morally remiss those who fail to fulfill their obligation. The question is, is it wrong to blame right-wing women?

My opponent[46] might offer the following argument. We have a choice to blame or not to blame right-wing women. If we blame them, there will be bad results (e.g., we will be forcing feminist values on them, which threatens their self-identity, we will be making them feel guilty for their situation, etc.). but there will be good results, too, namely, at least partial elimination of sexism, the promotion of feminist values, and the eradication of the view that women like sexist treatment or at least are willing to put up with it (assuming, of course, that they successfully fulfill their obligation). On the other hand, if we do not blame right-wing women, sexism will continue. Given the options, it is better to blame right-wing women.

In response, first, I believe that at least in some cases it is not true that the best option is to blame right-wing women. Consider, for instance, a young women who has turned to prostitution because she has no other means of support and has run away from an abusive home situation. Prostitution might very well be her only means of survival. It is unnecessarily callous to blame her, though perhaps blaming right-wing women in general does not pose this problem since in general right-wing women are better off changing their lifestyle than living in a way that endorses patriarchy.

But second, the argument invokes the false belief that stamping out right-wing women's endorsement of sexism will stamp out sexism, in whole or in part. For suppose that all women give up a right-wing lifestyle. It is still conceivable, and perhaps even likely, that sexist practices will continue. For example, men may still rape women, sexually harass them, discriminate against them on the job, and so on. Eliminating right-wing behavior in women by blaming them is neither a necessary nor a sufficient condition for eradicating sexism. It might not even help. Perhaps eliminating right-wing women's endorsement of sexism will make it *more likely* that sexism will end. I think this is true, yet I do not think this is an argument for *blaming* right-wing women. Blaming them entails that we judge them as being morally remiss. Instead, I believe this is an argument for trying to convince them by way of rational argument that feminism will make women in general better off than they are now.

Third, and most important, to think that blaming right-wing women will aid in stamping out sexism implies that women are the *cause* of sexism. But this parallels the case of blaming a rape victim because of the way she dresses. Had the victim dressed differently the day of the attack, the argument goes, she would not have been attacked, perhaps, because the rapist would not have found her attractive. In other words, the victim is the cause of the harm. But in truth, it is the rapist alone who is at fault in the latter case, just as it is those men who ''oil the gears'' of patriarchy in order to profit who are at fault in the former case. Right-wing women are victims; patriarchy and its beneficiaries are the cause. To focus on *women's* contribution to the perpetuation of sexism is wrong in both cases because it is sexist.

In response, my opponent might argue that blaming the victim is wrong only when the victim is in no way responsible for the harm that occurs.[47] Some victims are responsible. Suppose I decide while sober that I am going to drink alone in a wheatfield far enough away from home that I would need to drive. If I drive home after drinking too much and crash, injuring myself, even though I am a victim it does not seem wrong to blame me for my behavior. I am a victim of my own bad judgment and am responsible for making the decision while sober that could cause me harm.

My opponent would need to show that right-wing women are to some extent responsible for the harm their actions cause women as a group. To refute the opponent, I would need to show that they are not responsible. This might be because (1) they lack full knowledge or understanding of their position and of what feminism can offer them; (2) they cannot change; or (3) they lack freedom to choose their lifestyle.

Consider the reason that right-wing women lack full knowledge or understanding of their own oppression and of how feminism can help them out of it. I have already shown that both kinds of right-wing women do lack a complete understanding of feminism because their values and beliefs stand in the way. Deciding whether the failure to understand frees a person from responsibility for the harm she causes in the usual case turns on whether the person can be *expected* to know/understand her position and how it harms others. This is a difficult issue because many right-wing women simply are not exposed to feminism or enlightened about their oppression. Many have not gone to college and many were raised and continue to live in remote rural areas, and so are unlikely to be exposed to feminist ideas. On the other hand, various television shows, such as talk shows and educational programs, provide some exposure to feminism. And, of course, many right-wing women *have* some idea of what feminism is: they just resist it, at least in part because they do not fully understand it.

One way to settle the issue is to point out that many *men* lack a full understanding of what feminism is. If we are to let right-wing women off the hook and not blame them because they lack understanding and thus responsibility, the same must be said for men (even though they are not themselves victims). Yet we do blame men for sexist behavior and feel justified in doing so. So pointing to right-wing women's lack of understanding will not establish that they lack responsibility for the harm they cause.

Perhaps the second route will fare better: right-wing women are not to blame for their behavior because they cannot change the way they are. The argument relies on the dictum, " 'Ought' implies 'can'." If one cannot change, then we cannot say that one has an obligation to change, and so it is wrong to blame one if one causes harm.

Can right-wing women change? It will undoubtedly be very difficult in many cases, since right-wing values are instilled at a very young age and continue to be reinforced as life goes on. Asking them to change would threaten their personal identity and integrity as they have made right-wing values central to their lives. Yet I believe they can change. They have to come to see oppression for what it is and give up their belief that there is no way out of patriarchy. Or, they have to give up their religious beliefs and values or at least decide not to impose them on other women. Marilyn Frye has pointed out that if we believe that women cannot change and we do not demand a profound redefinition of their selves there is no hope, that is, no escaping women's oppression.[48] Since consciousness-raising has been successful for even some of the most stubborn right-wing women, I think there is hope.

Moreover, since many *men* are raised in the same way as right-wing women, with the same sexist beliefs and values, they can invoke a similar argument (though, again, they are not victims) and be free from blame. "I can't help myself," the harasser might claim, "I have been raised to act this way." Yet since we blame men, and feel justified in doing so, this reason cannot be used to absolve right-wing women from responsibility.

So, third, perhaps right-wing women are not responsible, and so not to blame, because they are not free to choose their lifestyle. In one sense this is false. There is nothing about *them* that is not free.[49] Their ability to choose a lifestyle is not impaired.

Since right-wing women can, perhaps with a lot of effort, understand their position, can change their behavior, and have the ability to choose a different lifestyle, I believe they *are* in part responsible for their choices and actions. Yet I still want to say we should not blame them.[50]

There is a sense in which it is true that right-wing women are not free: their *choices* are severely restricted. Religious right-wing women have no choice. Their religious beliefs offer them only one option, that of a traditional lifestyle. Secular women living under patriarchy are severely limited in their choices. They must choose between a traditional lifestyle that (they believe) promises security and survival and one that seems to threaten their own survival.

Yet it is not the restriction of choices in itself that makes it wrong to blame right-wing women but the way in which their choices get restricted, namely, by a system that is patriarchal through and through. Right-wing women are raised in a system that is entrenched with patriarchal ideology, whether in its religious or secular form. Acting out of that system, they choose sexist lifestyles and adopt the sexist values and beliefs associated with them. Since their choices of lifestyle, and of the values and beliefs associated with it, are severely restricted because they are made within the context of patriarchy, it is wrong to blame right-wing women. Blaming them limits their choices even further because it means they ought or ought not to act in certain ways, and as such, makes them victims twice.[51]

Compare the case of right-wing women to the case of blacks who were born in the South before the Civil War. Their choice of lifestyle, and of the values and beliefs associated with it, though in some sense freely made, was severely restricted. A life outside of slavery was not really an option, since they could not expect to get a formal education, let alone a job that paid enough to ensure survival. Some slaves, like some right-wing women, even claimed to like their position. They said they were well-fed and well-treated by their masters, and believed that was the best they could expect in a racist world. They lacked the understanding of their position in the same way that right-wing women do. To blame the slaves for not breaking out of their lifestyle because living life as a slave harms other blacks by perpetuating the system is wrong because it restricts the choices of those whose choices have already been restricted by a profoundly racist system.

Notice that the argument about the wrongful restriction of choices, unlike the earlier arguments about responsibility, does not render men free from blame for their sexist behavior. The reason is that right-wing women's lifestyle itself limits their choices significantly while men benefit from sexist practices by having their choices expanded (e.g., they have more jobs to choose from, can choose to devote their lives to careers without worrying about mundane tasks that a wife can take care of, etc.). Blaming men for sexist behavior, and thus restricting their choices, does not make them victims twice because they are not victims to begin with.

An opponent might advance one further argument.[52] One reason to blame right-wing women is that they are forcing their beliefs upon all women. This is seen most clearly in their attempt to legislate the anti-choice position on abortion.[53] Right-wing women limit the choices of other women, which is wrong. Indeed, by my own argument, it would be wrong *not* to blame right-wing women because other women's choices are already limited by patriarchy. They would be victims twice: once at the hands of patriarchy and again at the hands of right-wing women.

First, it is true that some right-wing women *are* guilty of forcing their beliefs on other women, but they do this because they take their beliefs to be true. They are no different from those who believe that killing nonhuman animals is morally wrong and who try to prevent this behavior or from those who believe sexist behavior is morally wrong and who try to stamp it out, perhaps in part by making it illegal. Of course, right-wing women who try to restrict abortion rights might be mistaken about their position, as their beliefs in most cases ultimately rely on their controversial belief in a Christian God. But what all of these advocates have in common is that their beliefs are firmly held and taken to be true. Moreover, in all cases, enforcement of the beliefs in question results in a restriction of choices for those the beliefs are forced upon (e.g., animal rights activists want others not to eat meat or wear furs). The best way to make the case against right-wing women but not the others is to argue that it is wrong for them to force their *religious* beliefs upon others who do not necessarily share those beliefs. But then this is not an argument against the enforcement of sexist values *per se*, so any right-wing behavior that was not the result of religious beliefs could not be prohibited.

Second, ideally we want right-wing women to change their behavior. Blaming them does not help them rid themselves of their unfreely chosen desires and beliefs and the subsequent enforcement of these on all women. Instead, blaming them only perpetuates the system by making them feel they have caused their own oppression and deserve it. It does just what blaming the rape victim for the crime committed against her does when judgment is passed on the way she was dressed. Blaming the rape victim does not stop rape; we cannot expect blaming right-wing women to stop sexism. Blaming in either case makes the victim a victim twice, but does not change her. Our focus instead ought to be on changing the system so that right-wing women do not select the values and beliefs they do, and therefore do not want to limit the choices of all women. Persuasion by rational argument should accompany changing the system. This will make right-wing women understand their position and the alternatives, and it will respect their autonomy by letting them make their own choice of a better lifestyle.

Concluding Remarks

Our goal is to end women's oppression. If we do not blame right-wing women, and so permit them to act as they choose, do we allow them to perpetuate the system? The recent debate between Friedman and Sommers brings to light this issue. Sommers suggests that right-wing women should be allowed to act the way they want. On this point she is correct if she means that we should not try to prohibit their behavior by blaming them. But what she fails to recognize is that their choices are so severely restricted that it can hardly be claimed that they are doing what they want.[54] I do not take her critic, Friedman, to be saying that we must restrict women's choices if we are to end oppression. Friedman suggests instead that we direct our criticism to the circumstances under which women live and make choices about their lifestyle.[55] On this point she is correct. If we change the system that creates right-wing women they will not have the desires they now have.

But there is a tension between, on the one hand, allowing right-wing women to act the way they choose and, on the other hand, changing the circumstances under which women make their choices. For instance, changing the system by making illegal certain practices such as prostitution and pornography limits the choices of some women. In effect, women who would have chosen these professions before patriarchy has been sufficiently eliminated will be out of work, perhaps forced on the street to an even worse existence.

Part of the solution is to turn the blame away from women and onto those who use them, by punishing pimps, johns, and pornographers instead of prostitutes and pornographic models. At the same time, programs offering women better options should be instituted. Working conditions must be improved by strict enforcement of better laws against sexual harassment and discrimination so that women have a real choice in the workforce. Tax breaks could be given to women who choose lifestyles other than traditional ones (assuming the right people are in office to institute this!). These are just a few suggestions for attempting to solve a very complex problem. The important point is that we must recognize that any changes in the system that eliminate sexist practices on the part of women, though they appear to limit the freedom of right-wing women, in reality *open* their choices, and the choices of all women. For it is only when the choices are as good and as plentiful as those offered to men that we can say the oppression of women is on its way out.

Notes

I thank Joan Callahan for directing me to the relevant literature on this subject, and for suggestions about the initial direction of the paper. I also thank Ann Cudd for very helpful suggestions on this paper.

1. Andrea Dworkin, *Right-Wing Women* (New York: Coward-McCann, 1983).
2. Marilyn Friedman, " 'They Lived Happily Ever After': Sommers on

Women and Marriage," *Journal of Social Philosophy* 21, 2 (Fall 1990): 57–65, esp. p. 57, citing Sommers. See also Christina Sommers, "Do These Feminists Like Women?," *Journal of Social Philosophy* 21, 2 (Fall 1990): 66–74, esp. pp. 68, 72.

3. Joel Feinberg, *Harm to Others: The Moral Limits of the Criminal Law* (New York: Oxford University Press, 1984), 117.

4. The account of group harm that follows in the text is a short version of the account I offer in "A Feminist Definition of Sexual Harassment," forthcoming in the *Journal of Social Philosophy* 24, 2.

5. See Marilyn A. Friedman and Larry May, "Harming Women as a Group," *Social Theory and Practice* 11, 2 (Summer 1985): 207–34, and Ann E. Cudd, "Enforced Pregnancy, Rape, and the Image of Woman," *Philosophical Studies* 60 (1990): 47–59, for more detailed analyses of the group harm of women.

6. Laurie Shrage has argued that prostitutes reinforce and legitimate the oppression of women. But Shrage does not want to blame them for their behavior, but instead blames the system that creates them. Unfortunately, she does not elaborate on why we should not blame prostitutes. See Laurie Shrage, "Should Feminists Oppose Prostitution?," *Ethics* 99, 2 (January 1989): 347–61.

7. Cheshire Calhoun, "Responsibility and Reproach," *Ethics* 99, 2 (January 1989): 389-406, esp. pp. 393–96. In contrast, in abnormal moral contexts where individuals cannot be expected to know that their behavior is sexist (e.g., male bias in moral theory, the use of "he" neutrally) and where moral ignorance is the norm, they are not to blame for their sexist behavior.

8. Ibid., 393.

9. Ibid., 405.

10. See Catherine Itzin, "Margaret Thatcher Is My Sister: Counselling on Divisions Between Women," *Women's Studies International Forum* 8, 1 (1985): 73–83, esp. pp. 75-76.

11. Susan Faludi discusses the antifeminists who were responsible for what she calls "backlash," a term that refers to the political response by right-wing people to strides and gains made by the feminist movement. She is quick to point out that though many antifeminists took up their cause for personal reasons, including "private yearnings and animosities and vanities," there are some common threads running through all their stories that show why they have certain attitudes toward feminism. See Susan Faludi, *Backlash: The Undeclared War Against American Women* (New York: Crown Publishers, 1991): 282ff.

12. I do not mean to ignore the many other kinds of right-wing women, such as prostitutes and models for pornography. They are right-wing women because they "buy into" sexist stereotypes that men have defined for women. But it can hardly be said that they adopt a "traditional" lifestyle. I believe that, like other right-wing women, they adopt their lifestyle because it seems to be their best option. A lot of what I say about right-wing women applies to them, but I will focus mainly on those who adopt a "traditional" lifestyle.

13. Kristin Luker, *Abortion and the Politics of Motherhood* (Berkeley: University of California Press, 1984). The statistics in the following paragraphs are taken from pp. 194–97.

14. I use the term "religion" loosely, to refer to Catholicism and fundamentalist Christianity. I do not mean to suggest that *all* religions lead women to become right-wing.

Also, particularly in chapter 7 of Luker's book, many quotes from the women surveyed reveal that it is *religion*, not class issues as the statistics cited might suggest, that is at the root of the women's right-wing beliefs.

15. Ibid., 146.

16. Faludi, op. cit., 233. The passage is Ephesians 5:22–24.

17. Ibid., 233.

18. Luker, op. cit., 159–61.

19. Sandra Lee Bartky, "Foucault, Femininity, and the Modernization of Patriarchal Power," in *Femininity and Domination: Studies in the Phenomenology of Oppression* (New York: Routledge, Chapman and Hall, 1990): 63–82, esp. p. 77.

20. Luker, op. cit., 162.

21. Ibid., 205. The idea is that one would not "toss out" something sacred.

22. Faludi, op. cit., 240.

23. Ibid., 254.

24. Luker, op. cit., 207, 206. I do not think feminism does promote this view. A good feminist theory allows women to choose from a variety of "meaningful work" options, including motherhood.

25. Ibid., 146.

26. Faludi, op. cit., 364. Interestingly, Faludi reports that the media misconstrued this figure to 70 cents. This number was based on a faulty study that grossly exaggerated the salary of part-time workers, most of whom were women, but who did not work a full year. Faludi also reports that by 1988, women with college degrees earned only 59 cents to a man's dollar. The gap is even more severe in certain fields.

27. Andrea Dworkin, op. cit., 69–70.

28. The horrific story of Betty Riggs is recounted in detail by Susan Faludi, op. cit., 440. Apparently, the scientific studies conducted on the suspect chemicals were not conclusive for women, and were not even conducted on male subjects. Moreover, the men were not forced into sterilization: the solution in their case was to remove the suspicious chemicals. To top it all off, after Riggs and other women workers were sterilized, their positions were cut by the company.

29. Rosemarie Tong cites a study conducted by *Redbook* (1975) that showed that of 9,000 readers surveyed, 88 percent had experienced some form of harassment. See Tong, *Women, Sex, and the Law* (Savage, Md.: Rowman & Littlefield Publishers, 1984), 66.

30. It was because of this case that the Supreme Court ruled sexual harass-

ment to be a form of sex discrimination prohibited under Title VII of the Civil Rights Act of 1964. See *Meritor Savings Bank vs. Vinson*, 477 U.S. 57 (1986).

31. Dworkin, op. cit., 200.

32. Faludi, op. cit., 289, citing George Gilder, spokesperson for former Republican Senator Charles McC. Mathias.

33. Dworkin, op. cit., 103.

34. According to Dworkin, "... it is antifeminism that convinces right-wing women that the system of sex segregation and sex hierarchy is immovable, unbreachable, and inevitable . . . . it is the pervasiveness of antifeminism, its ubiquity, that establishes for women that they have no way out of the sex-class system." Ibid., 233.

35. Luker, op. cit., 139.

36. Ibid., 146.

37. Ibid., 201.

38. See the discussion in Dworkin, op. cit., 234ff.

39. Dworkin, ibid., 232. Between 22–35 percent of all emergency room visits by females are for injuries from domestic assaults. The March of Dimes reports that battering of women during pregnancy causes more birth defects than all diseases for which children are immunized combined. See Nancy Gibbs, "'Til Death Do Us Part," *Time* 141, 3 (January 18, 1993): 38–45, esp. p. 41.

40. Faludi, op. cit., 322.

41. This might seem to suggest that feminism is an elitist position, accessible only to those who benefit from higher education. I do not mean to suggest this. Though feminism is difficult to comprehend fully, it is not accessible only to those who have higher education—often, women who never attended college but who deal with the public in their jobs and who are exposed to sexism on a daily basis clearly grasp how feminism can free all women. Moreover, though I think women's lives would be better under feminism rather than patriarchy, the position I am advancing is that we ought not to blame women who opt for sexist lifestyles. Compare feminism versus patriarchy to atheism versus, say, Christianity. Also, it is not stupidity that prevents right-wing women from understanding feminism, but their deeply held beliefs and values.

42. Harriet Baber raised this objection in response to a short version of this paper that I presented to the Society for Analytical Feminism at the Pacific Division American Philosophical Association, March 27, 1993. Baber believes that *most* right-wing women are in this position.

43. Susan Faludi, op. cit., discusses such women in chapter 9. She describes them as follows: "They could indeed 'have it all'—by working to prevent all other women from having that same opportunity" (256).

44. The example comes from Harriet Baber.

45. Thomas Hill seems to argue that women have an obligation to themselves to change. See Thomas E. Hill, Jr., "Servility and Self-Respect," *The Monist*, 57, 1 (January 1973): 87-104. He argues that if the servile wife does not fully

understand what her rights are, then she is not to blame (94). But if she knows what she is doing and is too lazy or too timid to change, or obtains a minor advantage if she does not change, then she is to blame (96). If she respects the moral law, then she must respect her own rights. The servile person tolerates lightly abuses of morality and does not have the proper respect for morality to enable her to affirm it proudly (99).

I think this shows a lack of understanding of oppression. Women might, given their options, obtain minor advantages by buying into patriarchy. But because their choices are so limited, it would be wrong to blame them for the one they select. I do not think they fully understand the long-term benefits that feminism could bring them. Also, if women are too timid to change, that is hardly something for which they are to blame, given that it is the system of patriarchy that makes them so timid. This is part of the insidiousness of patriarchy—it has created a group of people who are so reticent and fearful that they will not complain, and in extreme cases it has made them believe they *like* their lifestyle.

46. My opponent might be Ann Cudd, who has offered me a similar argument.

47. In the case of the rape victim, the question is whether she is responsible for the harm done to her. In the case of right-wing women, the question is whether they are responsible for the harm they cause all women.

48. Marilyn Frye, "History and Responsibility," *Women's Studies International Forum* 8, 3 (1985): 215–17, esp. p. 216.

49. Susan Wendell worries about whether women are free to choose. If we say women cannot make free choices under patriarchy, this leads to the view, for example, that there is no distinction between rape and lovemaking. If we say women can make free choices, we must give some account of how they can do so given the effects of internalized oppression. See Susan Wendell, "Oppression and Victimization: Choice and Responsibility," in this volume.

50. The flip side of this is that feminists are at least in part responsible for *their* choices and actions. This would allow us to praise women who take the pains necessary in becoming feminists and rejecting patriarchy for the sake of all women. I thank Susan Hale for bringing this point to my attention.

51. Ann Cudd has suggested that it does not make them victims but frees them, since we benefit them by limiting their choices. I agree that ultimately it frees them, but I believe they paradoxically become victims by becoming free. While it may be unproblematic to limit the choices of those who cannot choose (e.g., children), it is problematic to do so for those who *can*.

52. The opponent is Ann Cudd. I have added a bit to her argument.

53. Some might argue that other kinds of right-wing behavior are also attempts to force this view on all women. For example, beauty magazines encourage women to adopt a certain look in order to be attractive to men and impose the view that this is the way all women should look.

54. Sommers, op. cit., esp. pp. 69–70.

55. Marilyn Friedman, "Does Sommers Like Women? More on Liberalism,

Gender Hierarchy, and Scarlett O'Hara,'' *Journal of Social Philosophy* 21, 2 (Fall 1990): 75–90, esp. p. 76.

Questions

1. According to Superson, what are right-wing women? What are the differences between right-wing women and feminists? What, if anything, are their similarities?
2. How might a person argue that as a whole, right-wing women cause more harm to feminists than right-wing men do? According to Superson, does this make right-wing women blameworthy for promoting sexist attitudes? What are Superson's reasons for *not blaming* right-wing women and *blaming* right-wing men?
3. What is the difference between right-wing women and right-wing men? Why would we make a distinction between these two groups? Could we say that men are as oppressed as women? Or that men are as blameless for sex discrimination as women? Why or why not?
4. Superson argues that right-wing women are restricted in their choices of lifestyles. How can it be argued that feminists are not also restricted in a similar way? If feminists and right-wing women are both as restricted, what causes the difference between them?
5. Discuss the reasons, other than religion, Superson cites as causes of women being or becoming right-wing.
6. Are right-wing women threatened by feminism? Is feminism threatened by right-wing women? Is it possible to want to live, in some ways, like a right-wing woman and simultaneously be a feminist?

Part II
Women at Work

5

Sexual Harassment, the Acquiescent Plaintiff, and the "Unwelcomeness" Requirement

Melinda A. Roberts

[W]hen the law fails to protect women from . . . harassment, it deprives them of one of the basic goods for which government was ordained, leaving them in an Hobbesian wilderness men do not share.

— *Cynthia Grant Bowman*[1]

Bowman draws the analogy to a Hobbesian wilderness to make a point about the political import of our failure to regulate, in any meaningful way, the sexual "street harassment" of women. *Workplace* sexual harassment is at least nominally regulated, by a broadly drawn federal law—a law, that is, that has the potential to control, if not to eradicate, the problem of sexual harassment in the workplace. Thus, as the courts struggle to formulate the practical rules for how this relatively recent law is to be interpreted and applied, the only impediment to achieving meaningful regulation of workplace sexual harassment may be judicial will.

The Law

Title VII of the Civil Rights Act of 1964, as amended, makes it illegal "to discriminate against any individual with respect to his compensation, terms, conditions, or privileges of employment, because of such individual's race, color, religion, sex, or national origin."[2] In 1980, the Equal Employment Opportunity Commission (EEOC) issued guidelines that interpreted Title VII to prohibit two distinct types of sexual harassment—"quid pro quo" sexual harassment and "hostile environ-

105

ment'' sexual harassment.[3] In 1986, the Supreme Court, in the pivotal case of *Meritor Savings Bank v Vinson*, agreed with the EEOC's interpretation.[4] The employee who can prove either type of harassment is considered to have been discriminated against, on the basis of sex, with respect to the "compensation, terms, conditions, or privileges" of her employment.[5]

Quid Pro Quo Sexual Harassment

The main element of the quid pro quo cause of action is the supervisor's express or implied conditioning of an employment benefit or detriment on the employee's response to a sexual advance.[6] Additionally, courts generally require the employee to show that she did not welcome the conduct at issue. Thus, for the purposes of Title VII a supervisor's conduct will be considered harassment only if "the employee . . . regarded the conduct as undesirable or offensive."[7]

Hostile Environment Sexual Harassment

The Supreme Court's decision in *Meritor*, recently reaffirmed in *Harris v Forklift Systems*,[8] recognized hostile environment sexual harassment as a form of discrimination for purposes of Title VII.

Hostile environment actions, which require no quid pro quo, are of two, nonexclusive types. We can think of the first type as involving "sweet" harassment, where the supervisor displays inappropriate and excessive affection toward the employee. While the supervisor might view himself as innocently "in love with" the employee, his attentions may in fact interfere with her ability to work and perhaps eventually force her to resign her position. The second type of case involves harassment "directed at women" and "motivated by animus against women."[9] Supervisors who display "animus" harassment reveal significant bias against and hostility toward women as a group and may make frequent deleterious comments about the ability, intelligence, or motivation of the women who work for them.

Under *Meritor*, the employee who claims hostile environment harassment of either type is required to show that the harassment is "sufficiently severe or pervasive 'as to alter the conditions of [the victim's] employment and create an abusive working environment.'"[10] In *Harris*, the Court adopts a "reasonable person" standard for determining when the harassment rises to an actionable level: "Conduct that is not severe or pervasive enough to create objectively hostile or abusive work environment—an environment that a reasonable person would find hostile or abusive—is beyond Title VII's purview."[11] The Court does not attempt to provide a "mathematically precise test." Rather, "whether an environment is 'hostile or abusive' can be determined only by looking at all the circumstances. These may include the frequency of the discriminatory conduct; its severity; whether it is physically threatening or humiliating, or a mere offensive utterance; and whether it unreasonably interferes with an employee's work performance."[12] Significantly, the Court states that the employee is not required to prove that she suffered any physical, economic, *or psychological* injury.[13] The Court reasons that "even without regard to these tangible effects, the very fact that the discriminatory conduct was so severe or pervasive that it created a work environment abusive to employees because of their . . . gender . . . offends Title VII's broad rule of workplace equality."[14]

It had generally been thought that the employee in a hostile environment case must demonstrate, as in the quid pro quo case, that the conduct complained of was unwelcome.[15] It is perhaps significant that the Court in *Harris* does not expressly refer to the unwelcomeness requirement, but rather states that the plaintiff, in addition to showing that the environment *would* reasonably be perceived as hostile, must also show that the work "environment . . . *is* perceived . . . as hostile or abusive."[16]

The unwelcomeness requirement has been the subject of controversy.[17] The "perception of abusiveness" requirement would seem to play the same role as the unwelcomeness requirement and to raise the same issues. The intent of both of these "state of mind" requirements is to ensure that Title VII does not apply where the supervisor and employee have a complete mutuality of interest. But one problem with imposing these requirements is that, in the case of the acquiescent employee, the record will often naturally be devoid of any suggestion that the employee was offended by the supervisor's conduct.[18] Consider the employee who needs her job, her raise and her promotion. To fulfill these needs, she acquiesces in her supervisor's wrongful conduct, hoping thereby to remain in his good graces. She now must explain to the judge or jury that the supervisor's conduct *was* in fact unwelcome to her, even though at the critical time she took care to behave as though it was *not*.[19]

Moreover, including either state of mind element in the Title VII cause of action means, of course, that the defendant will be entitled to present evidence of the *absence* of this element. And this evidence is likely to have the effect of shifting "the focus [of the inquiry] from the man to the woman.''[20] Consider, for example, the Supreme Court's evidentiary holding in *Meritor*, according to which the plaintiff's ''sexually provocative speech or dress'' is ''obviously relevant'' to the issue of unwelcomeness.[21] The Court does not explain why it thinks that dress, provocative or not, is relevant to the question of harassment. But this ruling will likely have two practical effects. First, deserving employees may be dissuaded from bringing claims under Title VII. They may well opt not to be embarrassed, or even humiliated, by evidence of speech, dress, or perhaps, prior sexual conduct. Second, employees willing to take these risks may still find their juries at least distracted from the critical work of determining whether the elements of Title VII are present and, very possibly, confused as to just what those elements are.

Finally, there are conceptual difficulties with the state of mind requirements. Designed to ensure that the employee who once enjoyed a romance with her supervisor does not, once the relationship ends, reap a windfall under Title VII, the state of mind requirements in fact act to bar relief in cases that are meritorious. Thus, the state of mind requirements lead us, I argue, to the wrong concept, defining not the concept that we should employ in interpreting Title VII, but a narrower concept—a concept that we might very roughly describe as ''sexual harassment recognized as the bad thing that it is.'' Pertinent examples will be discussed below.

My aim in this paper is to argue that the state of mind requirements should be eliminated. At the same time, I will argue, it would be a mistake to think that the elimination of these requirements will focus the spotlight of the harassment action exclusively on the conduct of the supervisor, leaving the matter of the employee's conduct entirely in the shadows. Rather, the employee's conduct will inevitably remain an issue under any sensible interpretation of Title VII.[22]

Sexual Harassment and the Acquiescent Employee

The Supreme Court expressly holds in *Meritor* that a Title VII action remains viable for the plaintiff who has acquiesced in her supervisor's request for a sexual favor or relationship and cannot prove economic injury.[23] *Meritor* is, however, a hostile environment case, and the question arises whether the Court's ruling extends to the quid pro quo case. Some commentators and courts since *Meritor* have suggested that the quid pro quo claimant must show that she has indeed been subject to a "tangible job detriment"—that is, to some economic loss.[24] But of course the acquiescent employee will presumably *not* have suffered economic loss, so on this view the acquiescent employee will not be entitled to claim quid pro quo harassment. However, the better view seems to be that the acquiescent employee does not lose her quid pro quo claim despite the fact that she suffers no economic injury. The supervisor's conduct in this case would seem to be just the kind of conduct that the "broad rule of workplace equality" embodied in Title VII is intended to prohibit. Supervisors should not require employees to perform sexual favors on pain of dismissal. Moreover, the bind in which the employee finds herself constitutes precisely the kind of harm Title VII should be construed to guard against. Employees are not harmed just when they lose a job as a result of refusing to grant a sexual favor, but also when they must grant a sexual favor to retain the job.

The Court of Appeals for the Second Circuit recently accepted this interpretation of Title VII on pragmatic grounds.[25] If the Court of Appeals is correct on this point—as it would seem to be—then the acquiescent victim of either quid pro quo harassment or, under *Meritor*, hostile environment harassment is entitled to relief under Title VII.

Quid Pro Quo and the "Unwelcomeness Requirement"

As noted above, the quid pro quo plaintiff claims that her supervisor has conditioned a job benefit or detriment on her response to his sexual demand. She must also argue that the controversial unwelcomeness requirement is satisfied. The first thing to note about the requirement in the quid pro quo context is how very limited in scope it would seem to be.

To see this, consider the various possible demonstrations plaintiffs could be required to make under the rubric of "unwelcomeness." One possibility is that the employee under Title VII is required to show that the *sexual relationship itself* is unwelcome. But since, as argued above, Title VII embraces the employee who agrees to provide the sexual favor as well as the employee who does not, in this view the employee must show that the very sexual acts that she *acquiesced* in—that she *consented* to—were acts that she did not *welcome*. But how is she to do this?

Certainly, we cannot require her to have voiced her protest *to the supervisor*. The employee in this case has already shown that she was subject to the quid pro quo and she has admitted, or it has been demonstrated by the defendant, that she acquiesced in the sexual demand. This is not an employee who is likely to have risked, or more to the point should be required to have risked, the substantial investment in job security that she is about to make by voicing her "unwelcomeness" in the hotel elevator or to her supervisor's superior. Thus, it is likely that the employee's best evidence of unwelcomeness will consist in her own testimony regarding her private thoughts and feelings during the critical period; and this testimony must, if her claim is to succeed, undo the passable record of welcomeness she has herself so carefully constructed. It is implausible to think that the law would require the acquiescent employee to walk this tightrope—that is, would provide the acquiescent employee a cause of action under Title VII but at the same time require her to prove an element that she is virtually certain to be unable to establish.

A more plausible interpretation of the unwelcomeness requirement would apply the requirement not to the sexual favor or relationship itself but rather to the *antecedent sexual advances.*[26] But even this statement of the requirement is ambiguous, and we must clarify what we mean by "sexual advances" in this context. There are two alternatives: (1) the sexual request *simpliciter* ("Will you have sex with me?") and (2) the conditioning of an employment benefit on the granting of this request ("If you say no, you lose your job").

The EEOC guidelines, quoted with approval by the Court in *Meritor*, seem to contemplate the first alternative. Further support for this alternative is found, of course, in *Meritor*'s evidentiary ruling on "provocative speech or dress." While we might disagree with the Court's ruling on this point, under the first alternative we can at least make sense of it. In contrast, if we adopt the second alternative, the Court's thinking becomes far more obscure. Provocative speech or dress, arguably, may suggest that an employee welcomed a sexual advance *simpliciter*; but it is hard to see under what circumstances provocative speech or dress will be probative on the issue of whether the employee welcomed a sex-for-employment-benefit deal.

But the evidence for alternative (1) is not completely determinate, particularly in view of the fact that it is unlikely that the EEOC or the courts have carefully considered the specific issue of interpretation. Moreover, on other grounds we can see that alternative (1) will not do. Suppose that an employee has fallen in love with her supervisor; she consequently heartily welcomes his initial inquiries regarding a sexual relationship; he then explains the quid pro quo arrangement he had in mind; she instantly loses her affection for him; she refuses to enter into the quid pro quo; and she is fired. In alternative (1), she had no case. But this result would seem to be incorrect. The employee's compelling claim of quid pro quo harassment surely cannot be undone by the finding that she welcomed the supervisor's initial indication of sexual interest.

We are left, then, with alternative (2).[28] Alternative (2) would seem to produce the correct results in the case of the once-in-love employee: a jury will readily understand that even an employee eager for her supervisor's sexual attention is very likely to find the *conditioning* of employment benefits on a sexual relationship unwelcome. After all, who *welcomes* any form of blackmail?

But the very unlikelihood of the claim that the employee welcomed the quid pro quo gives rise to the question of whether it is fair to retain the requirement in all quid pro quo cases. The fact that the claim itself is unlikely does not mean that its negation is trivially established. Defendants can be expected to argue, e.g., that the employee expressed anxiety about her chances for promotion during past employment reviews, that she expressed financial worries in the lunchroom, and, perhaps, that she was not the sort of person who would view casual sex with horror. In light of, particularly, the Court's evidentiary holding in *Meritor* regarding "provocative speech and dress," establishing the unwelcomeness of the quid pro quo thus may be enormously difficult. Since evidence of "provocative speech and dress" would seem to have no material relevance to the issue of whether the plaintiff welcomed a "sex-for-employee-benefit" deal, admitting it creates a substantial risk of confusing the jury about the very issue of interpretation we have been considering here: Are they to evaluate the "come hither" attitude the supervisor argues that the employee's clothes evince, or are they to restrict their inquiry to the employee's attitude toward "sexual blackmail?"[29]

There are other problems with the unwelcomeness requirement as well. A function of the fine line between the quid pro quo that is acquiesced in and is welcome and the quid pro quo that is acquiesced in and is unwelcome is that Title VII, so interpreted, will generate different results in cases that are factually extremely close. Consider, for example, the employee who, anxious to keep her job when other valuable employees are losing theirs and eager to achieve a sense of entrenchment within the company, greets the supervisor's quid pro quo with the proverbial sigh of relief. In a rather strained sense, she could be said to have "welcomed" the quid pro quo, even though she would never have proposed such an exchange herself; it relieves her mind, and sex outside of love is not a prospect that horrifies her. Is it so clear that this employee has any less of a claim under Title VII than the employee who is otherwise in the same position but who does not, in this sense, welcome the quid pro quo? Their difference in attitude may simply reflect the fact that one employee is more confident about her just deserts and therefore views the quid pro quo not as an insurance policy but as an unfair and outrageous demand. Or perhaps this employee is not more self-confident at all, but rather simply more worldly about supervisors and their quid pro quos, understanding that succumbing to sexual blackmail in the workplace will likely as not render her position as less, not more, secure.[30]

The distinction between these two cases does not seem to justify a difference in treatment. We have in both precisely the type of conduct on the part of the supervisor that Title VII is designed to combat; and in both cases the employee must grant the sexual demand or lose the job. In both cases the employee acquiesces. The only difference is a rather fuzzy variation in attitude that does not seem pertinent to the issue of what counts as a legitimate Title VII claim. It thus would seem that the two cases should be treated similarly under the law.

Hostile Environment and the "State of Mind" Requirement

As noted above, sweet harassment takes place when the supervisor is excessively affectionate toward the employee. In these cases, the smitten supervisor might write love letters to the employee, bombard the employee with invitations to lunch and dinner and pester her for a sexual relationship.

It seems clear that in certain circumstances such conduct should be considered harassment.[31] And it goes without saying that cases of sweet harassment are not always purely romantic; there is no fine line between sweet and animus harassment. In *Meritor*, for example, the employee testified not only that she had intercourse with her supervisor "some 40 or 50 times," but also that he raped her on several occasions, followed her into the restroom and exposed himself, and fondled her in front of other employees.[32]

The kind of conduct the employee complained of in *Harris* could be categorized as animus harassment. Here, the supervisor, in the presence of other employees, on several occasions said to the employee such things as, "You're a woman, what do you know," at least once called her a "dumb ass woman," and once suggested that the two of them "go to the Holiday Inn to negotiate [her] raise."[33] Perhaps because of the transparent implausibility of the proposition that the conduct was in any sense *welcome*, as noted above, the Court in *Harris* quietly substituted for the unwelcomeness requirement the requirement that the employee actually perceive the environment as hostile or abusive.

"Animus" Harassment and the Perception of Abusiveness

Let us consider two types of cases that will be excluded from Title VII if the perception of abusiveness requirement is retained. Imagine an environment that a reasonable person would find patently hostile and abusive toward women. But suppose that a "naive" employee has for years, even decades, found the same environment to be unexceptional.[34] The naive employee, in other words, is someone who does "not recognize harassment for what it is."[35] But she awakens one day to the fact that she has been badly mistreated in the workplace. She becomes aware that she has been inaccurately stereotyped as a person outside the arena of those to whom raises and promotions, influence, and privilege are due. Under *Harris*, she has no Title VII claim.

Consider the case of the "veteran" who has steeled herself to have no reaction at all in the face of abusive conduct within the workplace.[36] She needs the job and, cynically aware that men will be boys, she makes a point not to dwell even for a moment on the hostility or abusiveness of the environment. She too has no action under Title VII.

Perhaps the most obvious rationale for excluding these cases from Title VII derives from the view that harassment requires the *perception* of harassment. This would be to analyze harassment as we might analyze pain. The patient under general anesthesia, however intrusive the surgery, does not perceive pain and, we think, therefore is not in pain. But it is by no means clear that this analysis of the concept of harassment is correct. A competing analysis would treat harassment as we treat harm. Harm does not require the perception of harm. The unconscious patient due for a facelift is unequivocally harmed, even though completely unaware, when his left leg is amputated by accident; and the banking client may be blissfully unaware that her banker is at this moment looting her life's savings.

The conduct of the supervisor is hostile or abusive independently of whether the employee perceives this fact. I do not see any reason to recognize the claim of the employee who is sophisticated about the phenomenon of workplace sexual harassment and deny the claim of the naive employee, or deny the claim of the steel-minded employee but recognize the claim of her sensitive colleague.[37]

Moreover, the tightrope problem arises in the hostile environment case as well as the quid pro quo case. Here again we suppose an employee who meets the state of mind requirement—actual perception of abuse—but who, because she wants to keep her job, acquiesces in her supervisor's conduct. She has not scolded him for his biased jokes or scowled at him in response to his offensive comments. And so, at trial, she must prove false a record of conduct that she herself has already established.

One may worry that completely screening off the employee's conduct from consideration in a sexual harassment case will unfairly disadvantage the defendant; and one might believe that the perception of abusiveness requirement is the proper vehicle for bringing the employee's conduct into the equation. I agree that we ought not completely eliminate the employee's own conduct from consideration in a sexual harassment case. But I also believe that it is a misunderstanding to think that eliminating the perception of abusiveness requirement will have this effect.[38] For, even if this requirement is eliminated, to prevail the employee must still show that a "reasonable person" would view the environment as hostile or abusive. And the finder of fact (whether judge or jury) will not be able to satisfy itself on the issue of whether a reasonable person would perceive the environment as hostile by examining, in perfect isolation, the supervisor's conduct. To adapt a quite extreme example from *Harris*, suppose that an employee says to a supervisor, "I am a dumb ass woman." And he responds, quizzically, "You are a dumb ass woman?" In this context, his words do not represent an instance of "animus" harassment. Hearing only evidence of the supervisor's conduct, the jury might inaccurately conclude that the employer's comment was abusive, or might accurately, but without justification, conclude that the employer's comment was *not* abusive. Either result is unsatisfactory.

Here is another example. Supervisor and subordinate are partner and associate in a law firm and engage in an egalitarian shouting match on, say, whether a particular client is illegally selling short certain securities. The supervisor uses language that, while not so suggestive of bias as the language at issue in *Harris*, would offend a reasonable person and, given its sexual overtones, might well suggest, if taken in isolation, animus hostile environment harassment. In this case it is not at all obvious that the employee is suffering sex-based discrimination. But the most accurate statement of what is at issue here is whether the supervisor's conduct is in fact *abusive*, not whether the employee is *offended* by his conduct. She may, or may not, be offended by his language.

Critically, the Court in *Meritor* stated that a finding of a hostile environment harassment is to be made on "the record as a whole."[39] This requirement suggests that the employee's conduct, as well as the supervisor's, is to be examined. At the same time, the whole record requirement eliminates, I believe, all legitimate need for the perception of abusiveness requirement.

"Sweet" Harassment and the Unwelcomeness Requirement

A parallel debate arises in consideration of sweet hostile environment harassment. As in the case of animus harassment, the employee's need to keep her job may well prevent her from expressing how little she welcomes the attention she is receiving. Moreover, the naive employee case and the veteran case may arise just as readily in the context of sweet harassment as in the context of animus harassment. For these reasons, I believe it is appropriate to eliminate the state of mind requirement in the case of sweet as well as animus harassment.

As in the case of animus harassment, we need not worry that eliminating the state of mind requirement from the cause of action for sweet harassment will preclude consideration of the employee's conduct. It simply will not work to adopt a reasonable person test to determine whether the environment is hostile or abusive and then restrict the scrutiny of the finder of fact to the supervisor's conduct alone. A reasonable person can undoubtedly be counted on not to equate a dozen roses with a dozen obscene epithets and not to find abusive an environment where the supervisor invites the employee to dinner on one occasion. But invitations to dinner *every night* mean one thing if the employee is engaged to be married to the supervisor and quite another if the employee is otherwise engaged.

We still are left with the problem that, under *Meritor*, evidence of "provocative speech or dress" is "obviously relevant" to the question of unwelcomeness. For even if the unwelcomeness requirement is eliminated as an element of the cause of action, as argued above, the conduct of the employee is still pertinent in determining whether a reasonable person would find the environment hostile or abusive. Thus, there remains the risk that the employee's legitimate claim will be waylaid by the argument that she, if not by her words then by her pretty clothes, agreed, e.g., to become engaged to the supervisor. At least one commentator has argued for a per se rule of inadmissibility in the case of evidence based on clothing in rape and sexual harassment cases. Such a rule would quickly communicate the patently obvious truth to supervisors, potential rapists, and others that they ought not, and will not be permitted to, justify their behavior by reference to how a woman elects to dress.[40]

Conclusion

I have argued that the state of mind requirements should be eliminated from both the quid pro quo and the hostile environment causes of action under Title VII. Requiring the employee to establish unwelcomeness, or the perception of abusiveness, comes very close to nullifying the effect of the important recognition that employees who acquiesce in the face of their supervisor's wrongful conduct, as well as employees who resist, may suffer sexual harassment. Moreover, imposing a state of mind requirement both excludes meritorious Title VII claims of various categories of employees (e.g., claims like those of the hypothetical anxious employee, the naive employee, and the veteran) and creates a substantial risk of jury confusion. Finally, a state of mind requirement is not necessary to ensure the fair treatment of the defendant. As an initial matter, eliminating the state of mind requirements will appropriately focus the attention of the inquiry on the conduct of the supervisor rather than the conduct of the employee. While fairness requires that the pertinent aspects of the employee's conduct be subjected to scrutiny as well, this result will naturally be achieved as the employee seeks to establish and the defendant to rebut the remaining elements of the Title VII cause of action.

Research on the law valid through May 1, 1994 only.

Notes

The author is indebted to Timothy Bakken, Eva Bodanszky, Judith DeCew, Nancy Lasher, and Alan McMichael, as well as to the editors of this collection, for their insightful comments and criticisms of prior drafts of this paper. I also wish to thank Betty Dooley and the Women's Research and Education Institute for providing me with various materials relating to sexual harassment.

May 1, 1994

1. *Street Harassment and the Informal Ghettoization of Women*, 106 Harvard Law Review 517, 521 (Jan. 1993).
2. 42 U.S.C.A. § 2000e-2(a) (1) (1981 & Supp. 1994).
3. See *EEOC Guidelines on Discrimination Because of Sex: Sexual Harassment*, 29 C.F.R. § 1604.11(a) (1992).
4. 477 U.S. 57 (1986).
5. Catharine MacKinnon's pivotal work, *Sexual Harassment of Working Women: A Case of Sex Discrimination* (New Haven: Yale University Press, 1979), notably influenced the development of the law under Title VII. There, she argued that sexual harassment should be considered a form of sexual discrimination.

The case of the bisexual supervisor has been offered to refute this inference from harassment to Title VII discrimination. This example has been much discussed elsewhere. See, e.g., Rhode, *Justice and Gender* (Cambridge: Harvard University Press, 1989), 233. It is enough to say here that courts may if justice requires recognize a defense to the Title VII claim that would allow the supervisor to show that he equally harassed men and women. *Ibid.*

Justice Ginsburg suggests, more generally, that Title VII is triggered by *any* disadvantageous term or condition of employment—that is, by *any* term or condition making "it more difficult to do the job"—that applies to one sex but not the other. *Harris v Forklift Systems,* 114 Sup. Ct. 367, 372 (1993)(Ginsburg, J. concurring).

6. *Barnes v Costle* was one of the critical initial cases recognizing quid pro quo harassment as a form of discrimination under Title VII. In this case, the employee's job was eliminated in retaliation for her rejection of a supervisor's advances. The District Court held that Title VII did not apply, since the employee had been "discriminated against, not because she was a woman, but because she refused to engage in a sexual affair with her supervisor." The D.C. Court of Appeals reversed, on the grounds that the supervisor would not have exacted such a price from a male. "It is much too late in the day to contend that Title VII does not outlaw terms of employment for women which differ appreciably from those set for men and which are not genuinely and reasonably related to performance on the job." 561 F.2d 983, 990 (D.C. Cir. 1977).

7. *Henson v Dundee*, 682 F.2d 897, 903 (11th Cir. 1982). See also *Meritor*, 477 U.S. at 68 ("The gravamen of any sexual harassment claim is that the alleged sexual advances were 'unwelcome.' ").
8. 114 Sup. Ct. 367 (1993).
9. See *EEOC Notice of Proposed Rulemaking*, 58 Fed. Reg. 51266 (Oct. 1, 1993). The EEOC here proposes to categorize cases in which the supervisor displays excessive sexual interest in the employee as "sex-based discrimination" of a "sexual nature." The contrasting form of discrimination would be a form of harassment that is "gender-based but non-sexual in nature" and "motivated by animus."
10. 477 U.S. at 67.

11. 114 Sup. Ct. at 369.

12. 114 Sup. Ct. at 371.

13. 114 Sup. Ct. at 370. That it is not necessary for the employee to prove economic injury was established in *Meritor*. 477 U.S. at 64.

14. 114 Sup. Ct. at 370. Justice Scalia in his concurrence notes that the Court had no real alternative to ruling as it did on this issue. 114 Sup. Ct. at 372. There would be no sense to—and no justice in—denying Title VII relief to otherwise deserving women who through training, genes, will power, or plain good luck manage to retain both their positions and their mental health. Justice O'Connor, writing for the Court, puts the point this way: "Title VII comes into play before the harassing conduct leads to a nervous breakdown." 114 Sup. Ct. at 370.

15. 477 U.S. at 68.

16. 114 Sup. Ct. at 371 (emphasis added).

17. See, e.g., Susan Estrich, *Sex at Work*, 43 Stanford Law Review 813, 826ff. (April 1991). Estrich argues that the unwelcomeness element is superfluous in the causes of action for both quid pro quo harassment and hostile environment harassment.

18. Martha Chamallas notes that "[o]nly recently have the courts confronted the problem of the compliant sexual harassment victim." *Consent, Equality, and the Legal Control of Sexual Conduct,* 61 Southern California Law Review 777, 803 (May, 1988). Chamallas points out that one important reason for recognizing the compliant victim's claim is that, in many cases, "[w]omen tended to tolerate or acquiesce to the milder forms of sexual harassment. What passed for consent could be better described as a grudging accommodation to the fact of women's powerlessness to change the tone of the working environment or the social conventions of the workplace. When harassment became intolerable, the most common response by women employees was to quit their jobs." Chamallas, at 802. Thus, another way of analyzing the position of the acquiescent victim is to *deny* that she *genuinely* acquiesced in, or consented to, the supervisor's wrongful conduct.

19. Estrich points out that the employee "may be less powerful, and economically dependent, but she still must express unwelcomeness. Unless she does, no burden is placed on him to refrain from abusing his position of power." Estrich, at 828

20. See Estrich, at 830 and 833. Estrich argues that attempts to reform the law of rape foundered on just such a shift from the conduct of the defendant to the conduct of the plaintiff. "[R]eform failed not because feminists are not good at writing statutes, but because if there is one area of social behavior where sexism is entrenched in law—one realm where traditional male prerogatives are most protected, male power most jealously preserved, and female power most jealously limited—it is in the area of sex itself, even forced sex." Estrich, at 814–15

21. 106 Sup. Ct. at 2406. The D.C. Court of Appeals, in contrast, stated that

testimony as to the plaintiff's "dress and personal fantasies" had "no place in this litigation." See 753 F.2d at 146 n.36. Of course, a court may rule that the unfair prejudice associated with relevant evidence renders that evidence inadmissible. But courts are reluctant to exclude even highly prejudicial evidence, if they believe such evidence to be directly on point.

22. I consider here the prototypical workplace sexual harassment case, in which the supervisor is a man and the employee is a woman. I do not intend, however, to suggest that workplace sexual harassment does not arise in other cases as well.

My aim here is to examine a limited number of issues raised by the state of mind requirements, particularly in the context of claims made by acquiescent employees. For these purposes, I focus on the two Supreme Court opinions on sexual harassment and do not canvass the significant body of pertinent law at the appellate and district court levels.

23. 477 U.S. at 68.

24. See, e.g., Maureen E. McClain and Kevin G. Chapman, "Updates in Employment Discrimination," 491 *Practicing Law Institute* 7 (Jan. 1994) (hostile environment harassment, as distinct from quid pro quo harassment, "does not require tangible job detriment"); Ellen Frankel Paul, "Sexual Harassment as Sex Discrimination: A Defective Paradigm, *Yale Law & Policy Review* 8 (1990): 333, 341. ("Plaintiffs must show that they suffered a tangible economic detriment as a result of the harassment [e.g. discharge, constructive discharge, demotion, etc.]."); *Babcock v Frank*, 783 F.Supp. 800, 807 (S.D.N.Y. 1992) (mere threats of detriment insufficient to support Title VII claim when employee not actually harmed).

25. "We do not read Title VII to punish the victims of sexual harassment who surrender to unwelcome sexual encounters. Such a rule would only encourage harassers to increase their persistence." On the grounds that, "[i]n the nature of things, evidence of economic harm will not be available to support the claim of the employee who submits to the supervisor's demands," the Court of Appeals overturned the District Court's holding that quid pro quo victims must present evidence of actual economic loss. *Karibian v Columbia University* 14 F. 3d 773, 778 (1994). See also Chamallas, 61 Southern California Law Rev at 46ff. for an analysis of this issue.

26. The Supreme Court in *Meritor* suggests this approach: "The correct inquiry is whether respondent by her conduct indicated that the alleged sexual advances were unwelcome, not whether her actual participation in sexual intercourse was voluntary." 477 U.S. at 68.

27. "Unwelcome sexual advances, requests for sexual favors, and other verbal or physical conduct of a sexual nature constitute sexual harassment . . . when . . . submission to such conduct is made either explicitly or implicitly a term or condition of an individual's employment." 29 C.F.R. § 1604.11(a).

28. I take Estrich, at 831, to interpret the requirement in this way.

29. Of course, it is possible that the evidentiary holding in *Meritor* regarding

speech and dress is intended to be limited to the hostile environment action. Even so, the supervisor will obviously be permitted to produce some evidence to the effect that the employee herself welcomed the quid pro quo, that is, that she solicited or incited it, or that she did not find it "offensive." *Henson* 682 F.2d at 909.

30. The example of the nervous employee who welcomes the quid pro quo should be distinguished from Bayles' much-discussed mediocre graduate student example, wherein a chairman of a department offers an undeserving student a teaching assistantship is she will sleep with him. It is uncontroversial that a *deserving* student who is threatened with the loss of her teaching assistantship if she does not perform a sexual favor has been coerced. Hughes and May argue that the sexual offer, as well as the sexual threat, is coercive. See "Sexual Harassment," *Social Theory and Practice* 6 (1980): 255–56. As Tong puts the point, the chairman by making the sexual offer "has in fact boxed his graduate student into a corner from which she cannot emerge unscathed." "Sexual Harassment," *Women and Values*, ed. Marilyn Pearsall (Belmont, Calif.: Wadsworth, 1986).

But the issue of merit is not raised by my anxious employee example. Rather the pertinent exercise here is a comparison between employees who differ *only* in their *attitudes* toward the quid pro quo proposition, and we are free here either to assume that both deserve the job security *or* that both do not deserve the job security.

31. Carson McCullers sees this point clearly:

[T]he value and quality of any love is determined solely by the lover himself. It is for this reason that most of us would rather love than be loved. Almost everyone wants to be the lover. And the curt truth is that, in a deep secret way, the state of being be loved is intolerable to many. The beloved fears and hates the lover, and with the best of reasons.

The Ballad of the Sad Cafe (Bantam, 1971), p.27. Of course, in the workplace, at least, this "curt truth" is no longer a deep secret, if indeed it ever was one. McCullers may have broken up the word "beloved" toward the end of the quoted passage to emphasize the meaning and speculate regarding the possible etymology of the word.

32. 477 U.S. at 60.

33. 114 Sup. Ct. at 369.

34. One might argue that the case could not arise—that an environment a reasonable person would find hostile is one that the employee would find hostile as well. But of course if this were true there would be no need at all to impose the perception of hostility requirement in the first place.

35. Superson, at 55. This article examines the various possible scenarios in which a woman is clearly the target of sexual harassment but does not perceive this fact and thus presumably does not perceive the conduct as "hostile."

36. The example of the "veteran" is from Susan M. Dodds, Lucy Frost, Robert Pargetter, and Elizabeth Prior, "Sexual Harassment," *Social Theory*

and Practice 14 (Summer 1988): 111. It is used there to support the view that it is inappropriate to employ the mental state of the "harassee" or "harasser" to define sexual harassment. The authors favor a behavioral account of sexual harassment that would focus, not on the mental states themselves, but rather on the behaviors that are typically, but not always, associated with the mental states that the authors regard as pertinent. In contrast to the view suggested in this article, the authors of "Sexual Harassment" at least suggest that the victim of sexual harassment will be required to display "avoidance behavior." However, their aim is not, I take it, to provide a definitive list of elements of a cause of action for sexual harassment but rather to suggest a methodological approach.

37. Significantly, proposed EEOC supplemental guidelines on the issue of "animus" hostile environment harassment, issued prior to the announcement of the *Harris* decision, would not impose the additional requirement that the plaintiff actually perceive the environment to be hostile or abusive. See note 9 above.

38. As noted above, Estrich's objection to the unwelcomeness requirement is largely that it shifts the focus of the inquiry from "the man to the woman." For this reason and others, she argues for the elimination of the unwelcomeness requirement from the Title VII cause of action. But, as I argue here, it seems to me very clear that, even if the unwelcomeness requirement is eliminated, the inquiry will inevitably consider and, depending on the facts, may even focus on the employee's conduct. The issue, however, will not be the employee's state of mind or even the employee's outward behavior that might suggest one state of mind rather than another. The issue will be, rather, the hostility or abusiveness of the environment.

39. 477 U.S. at 69 (Citing EEOC guidelines).

40. T. L. Lennon, Sharon J. Lennon, and Kim K. P. Johnson, "Is Clothing Probative of Attitude or Intent: Implications for Rape and Sexual Harassment Cases," 11 *Law and Inequality* 11 (June 1993): 391, 413.

Questions

1. On *no* interpretation of the Title VII action for sexual harassment will all the deserving plaintiffs win and all the undeserving plaintiffs lose. So the mere fact that a single deserving plaintiff has a claim that will not be recognized under Title VII, interpreted in a particular way, does not count against that interpretation of Title VII. What, then, is the correct method for assessing the various competing interpretations of Title VII? What are some of the methods Roberts uses?

2. The "acquiescent" employee's claim is more difficult to establish under either a quid pro quo theory or a hostile environment theory of sexual harassment. Explain why this is so. Why does Roberts believe that imposing the requirement that the plaintiff find the supervisor's wrongful conduct

''unwelcome'' compounds the acquiescent employee's difficulty in establishing her claim?

3. Will the defendant in an action under Title VII always be the supervisor?
What other persons might find themselves named as defendants in Title VII
actions?

4. Do you believe that employees who consent to—that is, who acquiesce in—
the hostile and abusive conduct of their supervisors should be barred from
bringing a claim under Title VII? Do you believe that women who have
consented to sexual intercourse should, in all cases, be barred from subsequently complaining that they have been raped? Do you perceive any role
for the reasonable person test to play in the criminal law on rape?

5. Why does Roberts believe that no plausible interpretation of hostile environment sexual harassment will have the consequence that the employee's conduct is entirely irrelevant to the success or failure of her claim? Do you
agree with Roberts on this point? Explain.

6

Women, Equality, and the Military

Judith Wagner DeCew

Introduction

There is ample evidence that women in the military are granted neither equal treatment nor full equal opportunity. In recent years debates regarding inequality in the military have focused partly on sexual harassment and more centrally on the exclusion of women from combat duty. The combat exclusion was given implicit legal sanction by the Supreme Court in 1981 in *Rostker v Goldberg*,[1] a decision holding that there was no gender-based discrimination in requiring men but not women to register for the draft.

I shall begin by examining the arguments given by Justice William Rehnquist in his majority opinion in *Rostker* justifying this exclusion of women from combat. I then turn to dissenting arguments for the contrary view that the exclusion of women from the draft violated the Constitution's guarantee of equal protection of the laws. I argue that Rehnquist's opinion endorses, despite his disclaimers, unsubstantiated judgments about the ''proper role'' of women, relies on an overly narrow interpretation of Congress's stated purpose for registration for the draft, and accepts the combat exclusion based on a mistaken reading of the history of its adoption, thus undermining his arguments and perpetuating inequality for women in the military.

To make the last point I review and assess the history of the adoption of the combat exclusion, showing that the exclusion was never given adequate justification by Congress. Next I turn to further arguments that have been raised against the combat exclusion, many of which were not reflected in the earlier debates. I argue that there are strong replies to each and that most are based on sociopolitical considerations rather than military need. I then present additional reasons for lifting the combat exclusion.

We might well wonder why, given the wealth of arguments against the exclusion, it continues to be hotly debated and strongly supported by many. I argue that feminist analyses of equality help explain why the Supreme Court in *Rostker* and others in the current debate continue to defend the exclusion despite weak justifications and strong counterarguments.

Finally, I discuss recent proposals to ease bans on women's roles in combat in the armed services. I examine the extent to which these limited proposals genuinely enhance equal treatment and equal opportunity for women as proponents hope or ultimately hinder progress because they de-emphasize or even conceal persistent inequality for women. In conclusion, I point out why lifting the combat ban to gain equal opportunity for women has implications for equal or unequal treatment of women in the areas of sexual harassment and abuse.

For clarification, let me point out first that I am not assuming that there is a single feminist position on the exclusion of women from combat. For years feminists committed to equality have been divided over issues concerning the role of women in the military, and it is important to recognize this diversity of views.[2] Second, I am not arguing for the draft but use the *Rostker* case because it has major implications for the combat exclusion. Indeed, I have deep misgivings about a draft for both men and women. Third, by arguing against the combat exclusion I am not thereby endorsing current military activities. I believe we can and must discuss the egalitarian concerns raised by the exclusion, independently of assessments of general military practices, policies, and objectives.

The *Rostker* Legacy

The Military Selective Service Act required the registration of males but not females for possible military service. The purpose of such registration, as stipulated by Congress, was to facilitate conscription of military personnel. Rehnquist's majority opinion in *Rostker* sets forth a two-pronged argument justifying the registration of men but not women.

The majority's primary argument relies on deference to the legislature. Rehnquist claimed that the scope of congressional power is especially broad in the military context. In his view, courts in general should not substitute their own judgments concerning which policies will be desirable, and this customary deference is enhanced in military affairs and national defense contexts where courts are far less competent than Congress to pass judgment. Emphasizing that ''deference does not mean abdication''(70), Rehnquist argued that since Congress specifically considered the question of the registration of women for the draft and recommended against it, its decision was not an ''accidental by-product of a traditional way of thinking about females''(74) and hence it was inappropriate to overturn the legislative decision. He claimed, in fact, that the Constitution required this deference to the legislature. Rehnquist also explicitly chided the District Court for exceeding its authority and ignoring Congress's conclusions that the need for women in noncombat roles could be met by volunteers and that staffing non-combat positions with women during a mobilization would be ''positively detrimental'' to the important goal of military flexibility.

Rehnquist's second argument addressed the equal protection issue more specifically. He agreed that Congress's determination that any future draft would be characterized by a need for combat troops was sufficiently justified by testimony at the hearings. Since women were excluded from combat by statute in the navy and air force, and by military policy in the army and marines, he concluded that ''men and women are simply not similarly situated for purposes of a draft or registration for the draft''(78). Thus, he continued, excluding women from registration did not violate the due process clause of the Fifth Amendment.[3] Congress was entitled to base the decision on military need over equity.

Note that the District Court had rejected the defendant's deference to Congress argument as well as the plaintiff's request that the constitutional standard used be ''strict scrutiny,'' and instead relied on the mid-level ''heightened scrutiny'' or ''important government interest'' test articulated in previous sex discrimination cases.[4] In contrast, Rehnquist distinguished such cases as *Reed v Reed*[5] and *Frontiero v Richardson,*[6] which involved overly broad classifications, and cited other recent cases, such as *Schlesinger v Ballard,*[7] as supportive of his view. Schlesinger, which had challenged the navy's policy of allowing females a longer period than males to attain promotions needed for continued service, was cited as a case where the ''different treatment of men and women naval officers . . . reflects, not archaic and overbroad generalizations, but instead, the demonstrable fact that male and female line officers in the Navy are not similarly situated with respect to opportunities for professional service''(66).

Combat restrictions formed the clear basis for Congress's decision to exempt women from the draft registration. Given that women had been excluded from combat through statute and policy, Congress concluded that they would not be needed in the even of a draft and, therefore, decided not to register them. Thus, while we think of *Rostker* as the draft case, it is also crucially a combat exclusion case. According to Rehnquist, *Rostker*, like *Schlesinger*, relied appropriately on a Senate report that said in part, "In the Committee's view, the starting point for any discussion of the appropriateness of registering women for the draft is the question of the proper role of women in combat."[8] Rehnquist stressed in his own words that "Congress was fully aware not merely of the many facts and figures presented to it by witnesses who testified before its Committees, but of the current thinking as to the place of women in the Armed Services"(71). Clearly the idea was that women should be protected from combat situations. Furthermore, it is explicit in the opinion that the reason men and women were not "similarly situated" for a draft or registration for one was "because of the combat restrictions on women"(78). Rehnquist added gratuitously that women would not actually be excluded by the decision because they could always volunteer for military service.

Justice White's dissent in *Rostker* (joined by Brennan) is short and pointed. He argued that the majority accepted and merely assumed that excluding women from combat was not unconstitutional. And administrative convenience was not a sufficient reason for the gender-based discrimination of registering men but not women (84). Furthermore, even if the exclusion were constitutional, there were plenty of positions where women could serve that did not need to be filled by "combat-ready" men. Rather than relying on women volunteers, he continued, the services should register women because there were a substantial number of women who could be used in the military without sacrificing combat readiness.

Marshall's dissent (also joined by Brennan) is even stronger. He chastised Rehnquist's opinion as condoning the ancient view of the "proper role of women" and violating the constitutional guarantee of equal protection. *Rostker* was, in his view, a gender discrimination case requiring the "heightened scrutiny" advocated by the District Court. Although Marshall acknowledged the normal deference due to Congress, he argued that the gender classification of *Rostker* was part of federal law and hence raised a legitimate constitutional question the court had to decide. He declared, "In my judgment, there simply is no basis for concluding in this case that excluding women from registration is substantially related to the achievement of a concededly important governmental interest in maintaining an effective defense''(90).

Although the majority concluded that women could be excluded from draft registration because they would not be needed, Marshall rejected that argument as focusing on the wrong question. Rather, he maintained, the government had the burden of showing that excluding women furthered the goal of preparing for a draft of combat troops, or, in alternative words, it had to show that ''registering women would substantially impede its efforts to prepare for such a draft''(94). The government could not, however, meet this burden since registering women would in no way obstruct the governmental interest in preparing for a draft of combat troops. Governmental objectives could be as well served by a gender-neutral classification such as combat eligibility, which would exclude large subgroups of men as well as women. Marshall reminded the court that registration provides an inventory of available strength in a pool of qualified military personnel for some future conscription. Even if a restrictive conscription were later justified for a particular task, that would not imply that a law expressly discriminating between men and women for registration was justified (96).

Finally, Marshall charged that the majority argument rested on the false premise that registration prepares for a draft in which every single draftee must be available for combat assignment. Even the government, however, had admitted that only two-thirds of those drafted needed to have combat skills. While it was assumed there would be a primary need for combat troops, noncombat support troops would still be necessary for a future mobilization and women had served effectively in such positions before. He pointed out that many women were among the best qualified 18–26 year olds in the military and were thus needed for a national emergency. In sum, Marshall felt nothing supported the majority's view that women must be excluded from registration because combat eligibility was a prerequisite for all jobs. For some 60,000 out of 650,000 positions, women were eligible and hence were not situated differently from men. Yet the majority's gender classification precluded women from being drafted for positions where they would be useful. The crucial question was whether there was sufficient justification for not registering women. By any court test, this minority argued, the answer had to be no. Even if there were ''no need'' for women, that would not imply that the registration exclusion was equitable. Moreover, the court could not be sure there would be ''no need'' and that a volunteer force for women would be adequate.

It should be clear at this point that despite his disclaimers, Rehnquist repeatedly relied on and reasserted Congress's emphasis on the "proper role" of women in the military, as Marshall charged. This "proper role" was invoked as the justification for the combat exclusion, which in turn formed the basis for the exclusion of women for registration for the draft. In reply to the District Court he also cited further problems associated with registering women that had been raised in hearings: that "training would be needlessly burdened by women recruits who could not be used in combat," and "other administrative problems such as housing and different treatment with regard to dependency, hardship and physical standards''(81). Rehnquist's claims to the contrary, these arguments raise questions of convenience, not military need.

Second, while the case does not judge the combat restriction per se, the exclusion is accepted uncritically by Rehnquist and then given as the basis for the conclusion that men and women are not similarly situated in this instance and thus, as unlike cases, may be treated differently with no equal protection violation. The exclusion thus plays a pivotal role in the argument. Yet we can now see that Rehnquist's interpretation of the stated purpose of the registration, to facilitate preparation for a draft of combat troops, only justifies his conclusion when read far more narrowly than is reasonable. That is, even if the combat exclusion is accepted, preparing for a draft of combat troops does *not* imply that only combat positions will need to be filled. As Marshall emphasized, approximately one-third of the positions were acknowledged to be roles where women could serve effectively. Including women in a draft to gain their skills in communications, radar repair, navigation, jet engine mechanics, drafting, surveying, meteorology, transportation, administrative and medical specialties, etc., could save the time needed to train men in those fields and could release men from noncombat jobs to move to combat positions, thus facilitating rather than hindering a mobilization.

Third, Rehnquist's primary argument, relying on deference to Congress, is of course a common one. But, as White noted, it leaves the combat exclusion itself unchallenged from a constitutional point of view. It is thus staggering to discover that the combat exclusion for women was, when first enacted, merely an addition not originally part of the bill and not ever adequately justified in congressional testimony.[9]

History of the Adoption of the Combat Exclusion

The original Senate bills establishing a regular corps of women in each of the services were introduced in 1947 and did not contain any provisions that would have excluded women from combat roles. At the Senate Armed Services Committee hearings little attention was paid to the possibility of legislating a mandatory combat exclusion, although some discussion indicated the services' intentions not to use women in combat situations. General Eisenhower, for example, testified concerning the value of women in the military, but his compliments were laced with comments about the roles for which women were well suited.[10] In the House of Representatives, during the air force portion of the hearings there was no discussion of adding a combat exclusion for women. It was only during navy testimony that Representative Vinson proposed a legislative exclusion:

> I propose an amendment, if somebody will draft it. I am just throwing it out for what it is worth. Those are my views. I think it will strengthen the bill to have it positively understood by Congress that ships are not places to which these women are going to be detailed and nobody has authority to detail them to serve on ship.
>
> Of course, they are not going to be detailed to serve on ships, but you cannot tell what happens, you know, because somebody might say they need a few of them up there to do communications or other kinds of work and I do not think a ship is the proper place for them to serve. Let them serve on shore in the Continental United States and outside of the United States, but keep them off the ships. Of course, they ought to be on hospital ships.[11]

Despite testimony from Captain F. R. Stickney of navy personnel that "[w]e do not feel, though, that it was [sic] necessary to write that into law, Mr. Vinson,"[12] the proposed amendment appeared later in the hearing. There was further objection to the amendment, but the bill considered the following year included combat exclusions for the navy and air force. During the House debate, Representative Short commented, "[w]e have put in those safeguards which I think are wise. We do not want our women killed."[13] There was no other specific discussion on combat exclusions. There seemed merely to be a general understanding that women would fill noncombat roles. The bill passed the House with the exclusion amendment. When submitted to the Senate it was described as essentially the same bill that originally passed by the Senate, with no mention of the addition of the combat exclusion. Moreover, the conference report made no reference to the rationale behind the combat amendment.

Consider, however, related House testimony, which displays an attitude toward women in the military that was probably typical of the time:

> All these positions that will be filled by women at the present time are of a so-called housekeeping nature such as your excellent secretaries in many of your offices . . . . women that men would have to replace.
>
> *   *   *
>
> . . . for every job ashore filled by a Wave [sic] officer you deny a male officer, who, after several years at sea, [has] the right to come ashore and occupy such an assignment.
>
> *   *   *
>
> . . . enlisted men objected to the idea of having to take orders from a WAVE officer. Put yourself in the position of an enlisted man and I am sure you will agree with them.[14]

Clearly there was a prevailing view that if women were to serve in the military at all, it would be to do ''women's work,'' and this presumably influenced views on the combat exclusion. But in all the congressional discussions on the issue, no military purpose for the exclusion seems to have been articulated. It appears that the only reasons for the exclusion were paternalistic protectionism and stereotypical views about what work women were suited for.

We find corroboration for this conclusion in Judge John Sirica's 1978 opinion in *Owens v Brown*,[15] which held that the absolute ban on assignment of female personnel to sea duty, except in certain ships, violated the equal protection guarantee of the Fifth Amendment:

> The part of Section 6015 being challenged . . . was added casually, over the military's objection and without significant deliberation. . . . The provision was not directed at enhancing military preparedness . . . (n)or was it inserted to take account of the practical considerations associated with integrated shipbound personnel. . . . Instead, the sense of the discussion is that Section 6015's bar against assigning females to shipboard duty was premised on the notion that duty at sea is part of an essentially masculine tradition.[16]

It is worth remembering that despite all its restrictions,[17] the 1948 act ultimately provided permanent status to women in all the armed forces (both regular and reserve), and so provided for a group of trained women who could be mobilized in an emergency. This was a first step toward moving women from their second class status as citizens allowed only in auxiliaries.

Arguments For and Against the Combat Exclusion

Subsequently, there has been considerably more discussion of arguments both in favor and against the combat exclusion for women. We would do well to describe them in categories. One argument, exemplified in the quotation given above from Representative Short, mirrors the early paternalistic and protectionist justifications for the exclusion, namely that women should not be hurt or killed in combat. In General William Westmoreland's words, ". . . No man with gumption wants a woman to fight his Nation's battles. I do not believe the American public wants to see a woman . . . do a man's job and that is to fight."[18] The underlying premises are that only certain jobs are appropriate for women and that the public expects and demands that women will be kept out of harm's way so they do not become victims. One obvious reply is that women have often served at substantial risk of injury in noncombat and semicombat positions and have been prisoners of war (POWs) as well. They are surely exposed to combat when serving as nurses or administrative assistants at the front lines. These women are not out of harm's way and may be doubly vulnerable if they have received little training in self-protection.[19] Note, in addition, the ironic relation between service and risk for women:

> U.S. military history in fact demonstrates that when the nation's level of military activities is reduced, women are no longer needed in service and their military activity is commensurately reduced; however, when military emergencies arise a role for women in service is quickly rediscovered. This results in the irony that women have served in the military in greater numbers precisely when the risks were the greatest, but their military participation was less acceptable when the risks were lower.[20]

Furthermore, as the definition of "combat" changes over time or due to different guidelines in the four services, the protection afforded women by the combat exclusion is diminishing. Finally, battle versus homefront lines may be irretrievably blurred in nuclear warfare so that there is no choice about whether or not women "go to war." Some women receive training in nuclear/biological/chemical (NBC) defense, yet if women not "in combat" are subject to the threat of an NBC attack, the combat exclusions are obsolete to the extent they are based on the fear of risk to women.

A second common argument for the combat exclusion cites the physical disadvantages of women, such as strength, stamina, and muscle.

This diminished physical ability of women is often cited as the reason women cannot meet the physical demands of ground combat, including tasks such as carrying and lifting. Therefore, the argument continues, their presence impairs military efficiency.[21] Of course men who lack upper body strength are not for that reason prohibited from combat duty. Moreover, the statutes exclude women from combat ships and aircraft, not land activities. In reply, others point out that physical strength is only one of many attributes necessary to perform successfully as sailors and aviators, and physical conditioning may compensate for much lack of strength for ground troops. In addition, many have emphasized that the small physical stature of the Viet Cong and North Vietnamese did not lead to military success for larger American forces. The issue is not one of lowering standards for performance in order to allow women to participate. Rather, it seems that efficiency should dictate gender-neutral determinations of whether or not an individual (male or female) has the competence, skill, and strength to serve in any given position. Note also that with the growing complexity of modern weapons systems, technical ability and education are becoming far more important than physical strength in determining eligibility and qualifications for many military positions.

Another popular argument used to justify the exclusion of women stresses the purported psychological differences between men and women. It is often claimed that women are less able than men to withstand the stress of combat, that women are too emotional and volatile to perform under combat stress. There are two strong replies to this argument. First, critics note the overall performance record of women in World War II, Korea, and Vietnam, and more recently in Panama, Operation Desert Storm, and elsewhere, not only as nurses on the front lines but also as military police, pilots, and flight engineers. Second, they point to the record of women who serve as urban police officers and firefighters under analogous stress. There does not seem to be documented evidence to establish the claim that women will deal less well than men with combat pressure.

Fourth, pregnancy and childrearing are cited as reasons women cannot serve effectively in combat. It is claimed that pregnancy hinders military readiness, the ability to deploy rapidly, and the length of women's service careers.[22] These concerns may stem from a social perception of the "proper role" of women. But whatever their origin, they do not seem to acknowledge that women are pregnant only a short part of their lives, some women never become pregnant at all, and readiness procedures and policies could well accommodate the 5 percent to 10 percent of military women who are pregnant at any given time. Men have child care responsibilities as well as women, and all military personnel are expected to take responsibility for dependent care arrangements in case of a mobilization.

A fifth reason cited for excluding women from combat is the fear that some women will fail to develop a "team spirit" or "bond" with men in combat.[23] The assumption underlying this argument is that males will bond with males, and females with females, but bonding will not occur across the sexes. This argument mirrors similar claims about group cohesion used against allowing blacks in the military, indicating that fear and prejudice are at least partially at its base. Respondents argue that bonding is important, especially in military emergencies, but that it is more dependent on leadership, trust, organization for a common goal, the pressure of imminent danger, and a willingness to sacrifice than on any considerations relevant to sex differences. Respondents suggest the problem is not that women will not be active participants on the "team" but men's attitudes: men will not accept women with a "team" spirit unless encouraged to do so.

A sixth reason cited against allowing women in combat is that the presence of women will lead to sexual fraternization and disruption of discipline. But this argument relies on the dubious assumptions that existing rules against sexual fraternization will not be obeyed and that sexual fraternization will be more of a threat in combat situations than elsewhere in the military.

Finally, some have expressed worries that if women participate in combat, the image of the U.S. armed forces will suffer. The simple reply to this is that Canada and Great Britain have now made it a violation of law to bar women from combat or to place restrictions on their number, and Israel conscripts women into the military. These countries, and others that include women in the military, do not appear to have a tarnished image of military strength and preparedness. Preparations to commit women to combat might, in contrast, demonstrate especially strong resolve.

It is clear from this summary of justifications and replies that most of the arguments against allowing women in combat are based on sociopolitical considerations, some quite dubious, rather than military need. Not only are there readily available replies to these arguments favoring the combat exclusion, but also there are a variety of additional justifications for abolishing the exclusion. The most often cited is the impact on individual women in the military who face fewer job opportunities and choices (and therefore less access to medical, educational, retirement, and veterans' benefits), less opportunity for promotion and career advancement, and less opportunity to gain the experience needed to gain promotion. Sheila Tobias has argued that women's exclusion from combat has been a barrier to their political success as well.[24] Advocates for the exclusion argue that opening career opportunities for women is not a function of the armed forces,[25] but for years career opportunity has been an argument used to promote the military services for men.

More difficult to document is the morale problem for women who are capable of doing a job but who are nevertheless excluded, and who are thus not able to get recognition for the tasks they can perform or the risky service they endure. A flip side of the morale problem is the resentment felt by males who feel they must hold more than their share of some undesirable duties because women trained to do them are precluded from that service. Low morale surely can affect military capability and management. Excluding women from combat can also limit military flexibility. Shifting and disrupting a crew in wartime damages cohesiveness and military readiness, for example. And troop movement can be delayed while military officials try to determine whether or not female personnel can participate. As Sen. William Proxmire commented in 1986,

> Barring women from combat has resulted in complex and arbitrary restrictions that limit our military.[26]
>
> *   *   *
>
> The first consideration in any issue of military personnel must always be national security, and, indeed, that is my primary concern. The combat exclusion policies deprive our forward battle areas of available personnel resources and limit our flexibility. . . .
>
> I am not saying that every position should be open to every soldier. Of course no soldier should be assigned to a position for which he or she is not qualified. . . . Gender neutral physical requirements would address this concern without arbitrarily excluding qualified candidates. . . . We are wasting our personnel resources. . . .
>
> It is important that those women feel that they are a valued part of our armed services and that they be regarded with ample opportunities for advancement. We owe them that. The women in the military serve our country faithfully, and, despite the combat exclusion policy, many women risk their lives every day at dangerous posts like the Mx and Minuteman launch sites. They must not be treated like second-class soldiers.[27]

Finally, there is the serious problem of defining "combat duty." Military definitions differentiate combat missions, close combat, direct combat, combat support, and combat service support, to name a few. The definitions are not always consistent from one branch of the services to another, leading to confusion and inconsistency in determinations of which positions are open to women.[28] Redefinition of positions in which women can serve results in reassignment, retraining, and career uncertainty, which in turn can affect retention and morale.

Equality and Feminist Analysis

Bernard Williams has said, ''[e]quality is a popular but mysterious political ideal. People can become equal (or at least more equal) in one way with the consequence that they become unequal (or more unequal) in others. . . . It does not follow that equality is worthless as an ideal.''[29] Differentiating types of equality does not lessen its importance.

Equal opportunity and equal treatment are two of the most distinctive conceptions of equality, and both are at issue for women in the military. During the 1970s many gains in these areas were achieved through the federal courts. Women won the right to the same benefits for dependents as males, the right to remain in the military after bearing children, the right to attend military academies, and the right not to be discharged in the same time span as men, given that women had fewer promotional opportunities. Despite these successes the combat exclusion has remained in effect, and despite the numerous arguments and replies defending elimination of the exclusion, it is still widely supported both within and outside the military. Why is this? Why has the combat exclusion remained so entrenched? Why does the legacy of *Rostker* remain, leading many to deny the equality issues at stake?

I believe that feminist analysis applied to equal protection of the law can help us answer these questions. And understanding why the combat exclusion persists can help us determine strategies to gain further equality for women through its abolition. Martha Minow has recently discussed ways of applying feminist analysis to the legal doctrine of equal protection of the law. She calls attention in particular to three assumptions underlying that doctrine:

> feminist theorists stress and challenge three assumptions that usually remain unstated in analyses of equality and discrimination. The first is that the perspective of the excluded or subjugated person or group is irrelevant or untrustworthy in evaluating claims of discrimination: the perspective presumed relevant is that of those with the power to structure social institu-

tions and to rule on charges of discrimination. The second assumption is that the equality inquiry does and should use as the norm for whether likes are treated alike those who have been privileged in the past: generally, white, male, Christian, English speaking, able-bodied persons. The third assumption is that the status quo in social and economic institutions is sufficiently fair and uncoerced, and resists change.

In making these assumptions explicit, feminists suggest that the assumptions are themselves contestable and that alternative starting points should be used.[30]

Consider the first assumption that the only relevant perspective for evaluating equal opportunity claims is that of those in power, not that of the complainants. We see this clearly at play in *Rostker* as well as in later arguments. Rehnquist, for example, does not see *Rostker* as a legitimate equal protection case. But the history of the adoption of the combat exclusion shows that deference to the legislature is very suspect in that case. First, almost no women in the military were questioned during the original hearings on the 1948 bill and the exclusion amendment. One male representative suggested its addition and it was tacked on in a haphazard manner. Second, even in 1981, deference to the legislature basically meant deferring to the white males in power. It allowed virtually no input from women in general or women in the military. Even if not explicit or intended, women were treated from the early hearings to the *Rostker* decision as if they had no valuable or relevant input on the question. This is emphasized throughout later hearings when most testimony is from men who repeatedly refer to "them" or "those women." Clearly the perspective advanced is not that of women in the military.

Consider next the second assumption cited by Minow concerning who makes the determination when cases are "alike" or "similar" enough to require equal treatment. There is continued focus, from *Rostker* on, on the "proper role" for women, the need to protect women from harm, physical strength, psychological ability to handle stress, male bonding, and problems of pregnancy. That these are used repeatedly to differentiate men and women gives strong indication that the determination is being made by individuals who are reinforcing stereotypical views about women as fragile, emotional, and weak persons who should be home tending their children and who are not similar enough to men to be treated like them. The tendency to disregard the many counterarguments and contrary evidence on women's interest in serving in the military even under severe risks, on their effectiveness in military and civilian positions under combat-like stress, on their physical conditioning in the military, and on their qualifications for positions relying on education more than physical strength, points out that the norm being applied is one of a physically strong and unemotional male needed for ground combat. Given the contrast between the norm used and the stereotype of women appealed to, it is hardly surprising that women are judged not to be similarly situated to men and are thus automatically excluded.

The refusal of advocates of the combat exclusion to allow career advancement to be considered a relevant or important military goal for women, despite repeated emphasis on it as a legitimate goal for men in service, shows as well that the female perspective is being ignored and that the norm being used necessarily excludes women. But it also illustrates reliance on the third assumption, that the status quo in social and economic institutions is viewed as sufficiently fair by those making decisions about women's role in the military. According to those defending the exclusion, men need the jobs and there is no need to provide for or guarantee positions or promotions for women. The military is doing just fine as it is.

In sum, the arguments favoring the combat exclusion repeatedly ignore the perspective of women, rely on stereotypical views of their needs and abilities, and assume there is no difficulty with the status quo of the military, thereby ensuring that women can not and will not be deemed similar enough to men to be treated alike. Using Minow's analysis, therefore, we can see that the question of whether or not to allow women in combat generates a paradigm equal protection case.

If this is correct, then there may be hope for change as more women are able to speak up and be heard in positions of authority and power. With newly appointed Secretary of the Air Force Sheila Widnall, we can expect to have more military women called into hearings to voice their views on the qualifications and need for women in the services. Similarly, more military men and congressional leaders are taking views like that of Senator William Proxmire. For example, former President Bush's navy secretary, Sean O'Keefe, urged (before he left office) that the navy should permit women to fly combat aircraft and serve on all navy ships and amphibious vessels.[31] While his comments are not binding, they do signal a new attitude. We can also hope to look forward to more women joining Representative Pat Schroeder on the Senate Armed Forces Committee. And we now have the new voice of Ruth Bader Ginsberg on the Supreme Court articulately defending the strengths and abilities of women. These show, I believe, that we can

expect and should demand future testimony and arguments to expose
and reject the common assumptions made in the past.

The Current Debate: How Much Progress?

As time has passed, Congress and the president have removed the legislative combat ban for ships and aviation. For example, legislation
passed by Congress in 1991 repealed laws excluding women from flying air force and navy combat planes. Because that legislation did not
require changes in the services, women have been excluded since then
by Pentagon policies. Thus, although military policy has also changed,
restrictions still remain.

In terms of substantive argumentation, it is discouraging that recent
public debates on the combat exclusion have made little progress.
Bush's Presidential Commission on Women in the Military recommended that women continue to be barred from flying combat planes
and be prohibited from ground combat. But it said women should be
allowed on warships (though not submarines or amphibious vessels).
Unfortunately, the central arguments again focused largely on social
policy and the "proper role" for women rather than military considerations. For example, one panel member argued that "it was wrong to
allow women to kill," another feared danger to national security if
women pilots were captured, others cited the negative effects on cohesion of fighter pilot units including women, and the commission urged
that single parents of school age children not be allowed to deploy and
that spouses of parents not be allowed to enlist.[32] In addition, the justification given for the recommendation to allow women on warships was
that the commission had to recommend *some* change or else its credibil-
ity would be lost because people would not believe it considered the
issue seriously. The political makeup of the commission caused many
to question it legitimacy. Moreover, the commission's recommendations were not binding. Nevertheless, despite six months of work and
expenditures of four million dollars, the recommendations constituted
a reversal of the 1991 legislation repealing exclusion laws.

As another example, Ross Perot's recent critique of proposals to
allow women to fly combat planes or serve on combat ships echoes the
familiar paternalistic and "proper role" justifications. He has urged: (1)
that the military is not the place for social experimentation (that is, the
status quo is fine); (2) that combat is the "dirtiest" job (and thus too

dirty for women); and (3) that he is fearful of women being maimed or becoming POWs (presumably they should be protected instead).[33]

In contrast, the navy prepared a plan for ex-Defense Secretary Les Aspin, approved by retiring Admiral Frank Kelso, that would add women "in all its frontline combat jobs—as fighter pilots, submariners and warship crew members—within the next 4 years."[34] The navy is also allowing women to be trained for more advanced combat jobs. It is widely acknowledged, however, that the navy's initiatives were designed to repair that branch's image after the Tailhook scandal and other tales of sexual abuse in the navy and thus were not motivated primarily by considerations of equity and military need.

At the same time the navy has been recommending advances for women, the air force has been preparing to exclude women from flight missions needed to qualify for combat missions.[35] It is hoped that Air Force Secretary Sheila Widnall will reverse that trend. But it illustrates the services' uncoordinated approach. The newest arguments invoked by the air force for these restrictions refer to tight budgets and the claim that expensive training for women makes no sense if they will not actually fly. That is only a problem, of course, if the combat exclusion is maintained.

Before stepping down, Aspin requested a full review of all female combat roles. Thus many navy initiatives are being stalled until recommendations for an equal opportunity policy for female aviators and combatants can be consistent for all the branches of the military. It was claimed that Aspin planned to (1) order women be allowed in combat aircraft and helicopters; (2) ask Congress to repeal the laws banning women from warships; and (3) ask all four services to justify excluding women from ground combat units. He was apparently ambivalent to or opposed to women in ground combat.[36] Although the navy has now announced its first assignments of women to combat ships,[37] it is not yet clear what Defense Secretary William Perry will ultimately approve.

While we can applaud Aspin's efforts to gain consistency in the treatment of women in the armed services, maintaining the exclusion for ground troops continues to reinforce stereotypes and perpetuate inequality for women. A blanket ground combat exclusion is unacceptable. The relevant question must be who is qualified to do the job. What is required is full acknowledgment that the issue of women in the military *is* a question of equal opportunity and that assumptions and arguments supporting the exclusion from the past to the present are deeply flawed. Over the last twenty years arguments against women's combat service have changed to deemphasize arguments about the instability of women, but concerns about unit cohesion are still featured and considerations of strength keep reappearing, particularly for the army and marines. Future discussion must focus instead on the relevant considerations, equity and military need, both of which provide strong justifications for abolishing the combat exclusion.

One final point. I have focused until now on the combat exclusion, merely alluding to the sexual abuse and harassment now well-documented in the armed services. (Tailhook is only one case. There are also reports of rape and sexual assault in the Persian Gulf during Operation Desert Storm, and reports of women pressured for sex and being objects of sexual harassment and demeaning sexual jokes.) But the two are closely connected.

Harassment and abuse are made worse by the exclusion. Wherever women are barred, their absence leads to a culture that breeds sexism and domination. It is arguable that integrating women and giving them equal opportunity can lead to gains in equal treatment and can decrease sexism more effectively than a sexual harassment class. While harassment may initially increase with more inclusion of women, over the long term it will ease. Consider, for example, the experience in the air force where 97 percent of the jobs are open to women as opposed to only 59 percent of the jobs in the navy. The air force women who understand the technology are rarely harassed.[38] Until women can compete based on the same standards as men, they are likely to remain vulnerable to harassment and mistreatment. If they are not allowed to use their full abilities it will continue to be easy for them to be treated as if they do not have the skills and to be stereotyped as unable, unqualified, and unneeded, as "detriments" to military effectiveness rather than the assets they are. Thus, another major argument for the elimination of the combat exclusion is its effectiveness in minimizing sexual harassment and abuse in the military.[39]

Notes

1. *Rostker, Director of Selective Service v Goldberg et al.*, 453 U.S. 57 (1981). Quotations from this case are noted in the text by page numbers. Note that *Rostker* involved a male plaintiff and the executive branch at the time supported registering women for the draft but Congress disagreed.

2. The National Organization for Women, for example, submitted an amicus brief in *Rostker* supporting the draft of women as well as men. Other feminist groups disagreed. Similarly, with respect to the combat exclusion, women both within and outside the military hold different views. Many feminists have

committed themselves to pacifism and reject any female participation in current U.S. interventionist and militaristic endeavors, particularly under male orders. Therefore my argument provides just one liberal feminist approach but, I believe, it is a compelling one.

3. The guarantee of equal protection is found in two amendments to the U.S. Constitution. The Fourteenth Amendment applies to actions of state governments, whereas the prohibitions of the Fifth Amendment apply to actions of the federal government and so are at stake here. Although the text of the Fifth Amendment does not expressly guarantee equal protection of the law, the U.S. Supreme Court has held that this guarantee is included within the due process clause of the Fifth Amendment in *Bolling v Sharpe*, 347 U.S. 497 (1954).

4. See *Craig v Boren*, 429 U.S. 190 (1976).

5. 404 U.S. 71 (1971).

6. 411 U.S. 677 (1973).

7. 419 U.S. 498 (1968).

8. S. Rep. No. 96–826, cited by Rehnquist at 67.

9. See Marilyn A. Gordon and Mary Jo Ludvigson, "A Constitutional Analysis of the Combat Exclusion for Air Force Women," *Minerva: Quarterly Report on Women and the Military* 9, no. 2 (1991): 1–34, published in different form in the U.S. Air Force *Journal of Legal Studies* 1 (1990) and *The Naval Law Review* 1 (1990): 4.

10. Ibid., 4.

11. Ibid., 8.

12. Ibid., 8.

13. Ibid., 11.

14. Ibid., 12, comments from Representative Andrews followed by two comments from Representative van Zandt. Cong. Rec. 2 June 1948: 6969 and 6869–70. Beginning in 1943, women serving in the naval reserve had been known as Women Accepted for Voluntary Emergency Services (WAVES).

15. 455 F. Supp. 291 (D.D.C. 1978).

16. Cited in "The Combat Exclusion Laws: An Idea Whose Time Has Gone," The Association of the Bar of the City of New York Committee on Military Affairs and Justice, *Minerva: Quarterly Report on Women and the Military* 9, no. 4 (1991): 1–55, at 4.

17. Other restrictions included a separate rank and promotion structure for women and men, different minimum age restrictions on enlistment for women and men, a limitation on total female enlisted strength of 2 percent of personnel on duty in each service, a 10 percent ceiling on female officers who could serve as permanent regular lieutenant colonels and navy commanders, and a 20 percent ceiling in the navy for the number of lieutenant commanders. Many of these restrictions on rank and percentage limits were reversed in 1967. Ibid., 3–5.

18. Hearings on Women in the Military, 1979 at 75. Ibid., 9.

19. Susan Brison has pointed out to me that combat training provides impor-

tant self-defense skills useful in nonmilitary contexts and is arguably of equal or even greater value for women than for men.

20. Ibid., 22. See also Cynthia Enloe, *Does Khaki Become You? The Militarization of Women's Lives* (Boston: South End Press, 1983): 181, 189, for a description of how the government campaigned hard during the war to recruit women for military service and factory jobs (to replace the men who went off to war), and then after the war engaged in a full-scale propaganda blitz to send women back to their homes so men could have their civilian jobs back.

21. Jeff M. Tuten, "The Argument Against Female Combatants," in *Female Soldiers—Combatants or Noncombatants: Historical and Contemporary Perspectives*, ed. Nancy Loring Goldman (Westport, Conn.: Greenwood, 1982), 247.

22. See B. Mitchell, *Weak Link: Feminization of the American Military* (Washington, D.C.: Regnery Gateway, 1989), and J. Yarborough, "Sex and the Military: The Feminist Mistake," *Current* (November 1985): 27–32, at 31, cited in "The Combat Exclusion Laws . . . ," op. cit., 25.

23. See Francine D'Amico, "Women at Arms: The Combat Controversy," *Minerva: Quarterly Report on Women in the Military* 8, no. 2 (1990): 7.

24. Jean Bethke Elshtain and Sheila Tobias, eds., *Women, Militarism, and War: Essays in History, Politics, and Social History* (Lanhan, Md.: Rowman & Littlefield, 1990): 163–188.

25. For example , see opposing statements by J. Philip Anderegg and Nicholas Kamillatos in "The Combat Exclusion Laws . . . ," op. cit., 49 and 51.

26. Congressional Record, March 21, 1986: S3182–83. Cited in Gordon and Ludvigson, op. cit., 16.

27. Gordon and Ludvigson, op. cit., 16–17.

28. "The Combat Exclusion Laws," op. cit., 11–14.

29. Bernard Williams, "What Is Equality? Part 1: Equality of Welfare," *Philosophy and Public Affairs* 10, no. 3 (1981): 185.

30. Martha Minow, "Equalities," *The Journal of Philosophy* 88, no. 11 (1991): 639.

31. "Women pilots in combat urged," *Boston Globe*, January 7, 1993. Note as well that Vice Admiral Richard Dunleavy, the navy's aviation commander, has said he has "no problem" with putting women in combat jets and has a year-old plan to do so should Congress allow it. Dunleavy is now under censure for being in a position of responsibility during the Tailhook episode. Interestingly, in 1992 he had said he should be fired for the Tailhook events because he was a top navy man in charge at the time. "Sex abuse incident my fault—officer," *Boston Globe*, May 6, 1992.

32. "Panel is Against Letting Women Fly in Combat," *New York Times*, November 3, 1992.

33. "Perot assaults wide range of Clinton policy," *Boston Globe*, April 29, 1993.

34. "Navy has plan to put women in combat jobs," *Boston Globe*, April 5,

1993. Mary Rowe of MIT, author of the navy's most recent sexual harassment guidelines, has reported that despite Kelso's position during Tailhook, many navy women have found him to be their most supportive advocate. Defense Secretary William Perry has noted Kelso's failure of leadership at Tailhook, but has also cited him for "developing policies against sexual harassment and promoting the place of women in command positions in the navy. . . . Perry says Kelso shouldn't be demoted for Tailhook," *Boston Globe*, April 13, 1994.

35. "Air Force plans to cut women's pilot training," *Boston Globe*, April 7, 1993. Defense officials and air force documents are cited as sources. The plan is said to include changing training for supersonic jets and air combat tactics (now open to all) to exclude women, to limit women to training in slower, subsonic planes, regardless of skill or aptitude, and to stop allowing women to serve as supersonic jet flight instructors by using only experienced combat pilots, all of whom are men.

36. "Pentagon expected to ease curbs on women in combat," *Boston Globe*, April 28, 1993.

37. "Navy to assign women to warship," *Boston Globe*, March 7, 1994.

38. "An Officer, Not a Gentleman," *Time*, July 13, 1992: 36.

39. Parts of this paper are drawn from an earlier version presented at a conference on Feminist Ethics and Social Policy at the University of Pittsburgh Graduate School of Public and International Affairs, November 6, 1993, which appears in *Hypatia* as "The Combat Exclusion and the Role of Women in the Military." I am grateful to participants at the conference as well as Cynthia Enloe, Virginia Held, Susan Brison, and James Sterba for helpful material and comments, though they may not all agree with my conclusions.

Questions

1. Describe what you believe are the two main arguments of the majority opinion and the two main arguments from the minority opinions in the *Rostker v Goldberg* case.
2. Why is the *Rostker* case, concerning the draft, relevant for a discussion of equality in the military and relevant for a discussion of the combat exclusion for women?
3. What can be learned from the history of the adoption of the combat exclusion?
4. Explain four major arguments in favor of the military combat exclusion and think of possible replies to each.
5. What are three unstated assumptions in analyses of equality and discrimination as described by Martha Minow? How do they apply to the role of women in the military?
6. Describe how recent arguments in the public debate over the role of women in the military have changed or have reflected arguments of the past.

7. According to DeCew, how are sexual harassment and abuse related to the exclusion of women from combat in the military?
8. In sum, which do you believe are more persuasive: arguments favoring the combat exclusion or arguments against it? Why?

Part III
Reproductive Technology and Liberty

7

New Reproductive Technologies

Susan Sherwin

New technologies in human reproduction have provoked wide-ranging
arguments about their desirability and moral justifiability. Authors in
the fields of both bioethics and feminist ethics have been active participants in public policy debates on the implementation of these technologies and related practices. Once again, there are striking differences in
the focus of the arguments as they are presented by feminist ethicists
and by their counterparts among nonfeminist medical ethicists: feminist
writers see reproductive practices as having very broad social implications, but most nonfeminist commentators have adopted a comparatively narrow perspective on the topic. I shall show why I believe it
is necessary to incorporate an explicitly feminist analysis into ethical
evaluations of the various reproductive technologies.

Although public attention focuses on a few sophisticated and dramatic innovations in the area of reproductive control, the category of
reproductive technologies is broad and has a long and interesting history. It includes the full range of means that have been employed or
pursued to gain control over human reproduction from conception
through to birth. We can consider this label to include the various measures and devices that are used to monitor and sometimes intervene in
pregnancy and birth, such as ultrasound, electronic fetal monitors, and
surgical deliveries. It also encompasses the means that are pursued to
prevent or terminate unwanted pregnancies (contraception and abortion).

Most commonly, the label of "new reproductive technologies" is
applied to a variety of techniques that are employed to facilitate conception or to control the quality of fetuses that are produced, including
such increasingly common practices as artificial insemination, ova and
embryo donation, in vitro fertilization (IVF), gamete intrafallopian

147

transfer (GIFT), embryo freezing, prenatal screening, and sex preselec-
tion. Included among the technologies now emerging or still on the
horizon are embryo flushing for genetic inspection or transfer to another
woman's womb, genetic surgery, cloning, and ectogenesis (fetal development wholly in an artificial womb). Other practices, such as racial
eugenic planning or contractual pregnancy (so-called surrogate mothering), are sometimes also raised in this context; although they need not
involve any specific use of new technology, they pose some of the same
social and political issues that arise in conjunction with some of the
techniques of reproductive technology. Almost all of the reproductive
technologies are carried out on women or on the fetuses they carry.

Private versus Public Interests

Complex cultural attitudes toward both technology and reproduction
shape the meanings and values that the various reproductive technologies carry in our society. In evaluating a particular technology in this
area, it is important to consider its place within the vast network of
measures that have been designed to control human reproduction. The
degree and extent of possible human manipulation of reproduction is
rapidly expanding, but it is useful to remember that the desire to control
reproduction is a long-standing one in human history. Therefore, it is
especially significant that the new forms of reproductive technology
promise a much greater scope for the direction and management of
reproduction than has ever been possible before.

Although both technological and reproductive choices are usually
placed in the sphere of private decision making, feminist methodology
directs us to evaluate practices within the broader scheme of oppressive
social structures. Therefore, the ethical evaluation of reproductive technologies requires us to ask questions about their social, political, and
economic effects, in addition to questions about their place in the lives
of those individuals who seek to use them. After all, reproductive practices carry profound social as well as private implications.

The pursuit of technological intervention in reproduction is part of a
larger general pattern in our society in which a search for technological
solutions is often the first response to the recognition of human problems—a commitment that Barbara Wright has dubbed "technophilia."[1]
Kathryn Ratcliff observed that medicine is a discipline particularly oriented toward the use of technology (what she calls "technological fa-
voritism"),[2] because medical education, public policy, and the profit

motive combine to ensure that technological innovation is seen as the measure of medical progress. In a technophilic society such as ours, specific problems generate technological solutions, which are then marketed wherever they may be put to use. Decisions about implementation are usually left in the hands of those individuals who are directly involved, even though the use of a new technology often involves consequences that extend far beyond its immediate intended effects.

Elisabeth Beck-Gernsheim argues that a common pattern of evolution seems to govern the use of new forms of medical technology.[3] They usually begin as innocent contributions to specific health problems, but they often end up with a nearly universal, coercive application to the population (for example, electronic fetal monitors and ultrasound). There is already evidence that some clinicians envisage such an extension for some of the more sophisticated forms of reproductive technologies, such as prenatal screening and IVF.[4] Thus many (perhaps even most) women—not just those who choose to make use of the new reproductive technologies—eventually may find themselves directly affected by the development and implementation of some of these technologies. Private decision making cannot be sufficient for evaluating a new reproductive technology if its introduction is likely to produce political, social, and economic changes beyond its effects on specific users.

Within the sphere of technologies involving human reproduction, it is particularly important to explore the possibility that they will bring about profound cultural change. Because effective forms of reproductive technology increase the possibilities for human intervention in reproduction, they create opportunities for greater power in the hands of whoever controls that technology. Throughout history, those who have been in positions of power and authority have sought to exercise their power over the sexual and reproductive lives of the less powerful: for example, among the powers that Plato reserved for the philosopher-kings of the republic was the authority to arrange the reproductive pairings for all classes, and in the American South slaveholders bred their slaves as they did their livestock. Through this century, legislators and religious leaders have tried to restrict sexual activity to married partners by such means as declaring sex outside of marriage to be illicit, labeling as "whores" the women who participated in extramarital sex (and making such labels sting by devaluing the humanity of prostitutes), and classifying any offspring produced through such unauthorized unions as illegitimate. Until quite recently, the male-dominated medical, religious, and legal communities conspired to keep contraceptive knowledge from women.[5] Even in this century, when contraceptive information is more widely available than ever before, economic factors serve to restrict the poor from access to the means of personal control over conception.[6] In much of the developing world, contraception is governed by policies of population control where control and choice belong to the state, not to the women concerned.[7]

Although the new reproductive technologies can provide individuals with greater power to determine their own procreative choices,[8] actual control may belong to others. It is, therefore, extremely important that in evaluating each practice we be clear about where that control will actually reside. Each reproductive technology presents its own risks and benefits and demands its own evaluation with regard to its place within the general scheme of technologically controlled reproduction; some technologies will prove to be socially desirable, whereas other will not.

In the struggle to decide on public policy regarding the various innovations in reproductive technology, authors in the medical ethics and feminist traditions have differed dramatically in their conceptions of how the discussion should be constituted. I shall take a detailed look at the debate surrounding one form of reproductive technology, in vitro fertilization, to show the contrast between feminist and nonfeminist approaches to bioethics and to give some indication of the importance of evaluating these technologies from the perspective of feminist ethics. Because it is the most widely discussed of the new reproductive technologies, in vitro fertilization offers a particularly clear example of the difference in emphasis found in the approaches of feminist and nonfeminist bioethicists.

IVF in Bioethics Literature

In vitro fertilization (IVF) is the technology responsible for what the media like to call "test-tube babies." It attempts to circumvent, rather than cure, a variety of barriers to conception, primarily those of blocked fallopian tubes and low sperm counts. Several stages make up the complex technology of IVF: artificial hormones are administered to stimulate the ovaries to release eggs; the released ova are removed from the woman's body (usually by a surgical procedure known as laparoscopy, although newer, less dangerous techniques of vaginal access are being pursued); semen is collected from the woman's partner (or, more rarely, from an anonymous donor) through masturbation, and the sperm is "washed"; the ova and sperm are then combined to promote fertilization. If all has gone according to plan, then some number of the newly fertilized eggs are transferred directly into the woman's womb, with the hope that one will implant itself in the uterus and pregnancy will continue normally from this point on.[9] This procedure requires that a variety of hormones be administered to the woman (often leading to dramatic emotional and physical changes), that her blood and urine be monitored daily at three-hour intervals, and that the extremely uncomfortable procedure of ultrasound be used to determine when ovulation occurs. In some programs the woman is required to remain immobile for forty-eight hours after the fertilized eggs are introduced to her womb (including up to twenty-four hours in the head-down position). The procedure may fail at any point and, in the majority of cases, it does. Most women undergo multiple attempts and may be dropped from the program at any time. Although many practitioners of IVF have tried to obscure the information, IVF is, at best, successful in 10 to 15 percent of the cases selected as suitable.[10]

The issues that bioethicists have judged important in evaluating IVF and other methods of laboratory controlled conception (such as artificial insemination) vary with the philosophic traditions of the authors. Those who adopt a theological perspective tend to object to all forms of reproductive technology, on the grounds that they are not "natural" and undermine God's plan for the family. Paul Ramsey, for instance, is concerned about the artificiality of IVF and other sorts of reproductive technology with which it is potentially associated:

> There is as yet no discernable evidence that we are recovering a sense for man [*sic*] as a natural object . . . toward whom a . . . form of "natural piety" is appropriate. . . . Parenthood is certainly one of those "courses of action" natural to man, which cannot without violation be disassembled and put together again."[11]

Leon Kass argues a similar line in " 'Making Babies' revisited."[12] He worries that our conception of humanness will not survive the technological permutations before us and that we will treat these artificially conceived embryos more as objects than as subjects; he also fears that we will be unable to track traditional human categories of parenthood and lineage and that this loss will cause us to lose track of important aspects of our identity.

Philosophers in the secular tradition prefer a more scientific approach; they treat these sorts of concerns as sheer superstition. They carefully explain to their theological colleagues that there is no clear sense of what is "natural," and no sense that demands special moral status. All medical activity, and perhaps all human activity, can be seen in some sense as being "interference with nature," but that is hardly grounds for avoiding such action. "Humanness," too, they point out, is a concept that admits many interpretations; generally, it does not provide satisfactory grounds for moral distinctions of the sorts that Ramsey and Kass propose.

Where some theologians object that "fertilization achieved outside the bodies of the couple remains by this very fact deprived of the meanings of the values which are expressed in the language of the body and in the union of human persons,"[13] secular philosophers quickly dismiss objections against reproduction that occurs without sexuality in a properly sanctified marriage. For instance, Michael Bayles argues that "even if reproduction should occur only within a context of marital love, the point of that requirement is the nurturance of offspring. Such nurturance does not depend on the sexual act itself. The argument confuses the biological act with the familial context."[14]

IVF is a complex technology involving research on superovulation, "harvesting" of ova, fertilization, and embryo implants. It is readily adaptable to technology that requires the transfer of ova and embryos, and hence their donation or sale, as well as to programs for the "rental of womb space"; it also contributes to an increasing ability to foster fetal growth outside of the womb and, potentially, to the development of artificial wombs covering the whole period of gestation. IVF is sometimes combined with artificial insemination and is frequently used to produce "surplus" fertilized eggs, whose moral status is in doubt. Theological ethicists worry that these activities and further reproductive developments that we can now anticipate (for example, human cloning) violate God's plan for human reproduction. They worry about the cultural shift that occurs when we view reproduction as a scientific enterprise, rather than as the "miracle of love" that religious proponents prefer: "[a child] cannot be desired or conceived as the product of an intervention of medical or biological techniques; that would be equivalent to reducing him [sic] to an object of scientific technology."[15] Moreover, they are concerned that we cannot anticipate the ultimate outcome of this rapidly expanding technology; they fear that it leaves us balancing precariously on a slippery slope, in danger of sliding down into yet more troubling practices.

The where-will-it-all-end hand-wringing that comes with this sort of religious futurology is rejected by most secular philosophers; they urge us to realize that few slopes are as slippery as the pessimists would have us believe. In their experience, scientists are moral people and quite capable of evaluating each new form of technology on its own merits. Hence, they argue, IVF must be judged by its own consequences and not the possible result of some future technology with which it may be linked. Samuel Gorovitz is typical of the secular philosophers: "It is not enough to show that disaster awaits if the process is not controlled. A man walking East in Omaha will drown in the Atlantic—if he does not stop. The argument must also rest on the evidence about the likelihood that judgement and control will be exercised responsibly. . . . Collectively we have significant capacity to exercise judgment and control. . . . Our record has been rather good in regard to medical treatment and research."[16]

The question of the moral status of the fertilized eggs is another area of controversy for some critics. Superovulation is chemically induced to produce multiple eggs for collection, because the process of collecting eggs is so difficult and the odds against conception on any given attempt are very slim. Therefore, several eggs are usually fertilized at once. A number of these fertilized eggs will be introduced to the womb with the hope that at least one will implant and gestation will begin, but there are frequently some "extras" produced. Moral problems arise as to what should be done with these surplus eggs. They can be frozen for future use; alternatively, they can be donated to other women who cannot produce viable or genetically acceptable eggs, used as research material, or simply discarded. Many clinics are ambivalent about the moral status of these developing embryos, and some choose to deal with the problem by putting them all into the woman's womb or by limiting the numbers of available eggs that are collected. The former option poses the devastating threat of four or more eggs "successfully" implanting and a woman being put into the position of carrying a litter—something her body is not constructed to do.[17] The latter option risks not collecting sufficient eggs to guarantee successful fertilization of some.

Those who take a hard line against abortion and argue that the embryo is a person from the moment of conception object to all these procedures, because each places the fertilized egg at risk and treats it merely as an object; hence, they argue, there is no morally acceptable means of conducting IVF. Nonreligious theorists offer the standard responses to this argument: personhood involves moral, not biological, categories, so a being neither sentient nor conscious is not a person in any meaningful sense. For example, Gorovitz argues: "Surely the concept of person involves in some fundamental way the capacity for sentience, or an awareness of sensations at the very least." Bayles says: "For fetuses to have moral status they must be capable of good or bad in their lives. . . .What happens to them must make a difference to them. Consequently some form of awareness is necessary for moral status.''[18] Fertilized eggs (which are now called "pre-embryos" by clinicians who are eager to establish their ontological status as distinct from that of embryos and fetuses) do not meet such criteria of consciousness.

Many bioethicists have agreed here, as they have in the abortion debate, that the principal moral question of IVF concerns the moral status and rights of the (pre-)embryo. Once they resolve that question, they can, like H. Tristram Englehardt, Jr., conclude that because fetuses and their precursors are not persons and because reproductive processes occurring outside a human body pose no special moral problems, ''there will be no sustainable moral arguments in principle . . . against in vitro fertilization.''[19] He argues that

> in vitro fertilization and techniques that will allow us to study and control human reproduction are morally neutral instruments for the realization of profoundly important human goals, which are bound up with the realization of the good of others: children for infertile parents and greater health for the children that will be born.[20]

Nonfeminist moral theorists do express worries about the safety of the process, by which they tend to mean the safety to fetuses with regard to this technique; although there is evidence of a higher incidence of birth complications and defects among IVF-produced fetuses, most bioethicists conclude that the practice is safe enough.[21] There is no mention in their discussions of the dangerous side effects that IVF poses for women. The bioethics literature has not considered the chemical similarities between clomid, an artificial hormone that is commonly used to increase women's rate of ovulation, and DES, a drug that has belatedly been implicated as carcinogenic for the offspring of women who were prescribed it decades before.[22] The uncertainties surrounding superovulation and use of ultrasound and the dangers associated with administering a general anesthetic for egg collection and embryo transfer have not been deemed worthy of attention in the nonfeminist bioethics literature. Women who do succeed in achieving and sustaining pregnancies through this method experience a very high rate of surgical births, but those risks also are generally ignored.[23] Furthermore, most ethical discussions do not explore the significant emotional costs for women that are associated with this therapy. To date, only feminists have raised these issues.

Having disposed of the religious objections, most bioethicists in the secular tradition conclude that the focus of discussion should be on the values of patient autonomy and individual rights. Most judge IVF to be simply a private matter, to be decided upon by the couple concerned in consultation with a medical specialist. The desire to have and raise children is a common one; it is generally thought of as a paradigm case of a purely private subject. Because, for most people, conception is automatically a matter of private choice (or accident), bioethicists generally argue that "it would be unfair to make infertile couples pass up the joys of rearing infants or suffer the burdens of rearing handicapped children."[24] Concern for the desires or needs of individuals is the most widely accepted argument in favor of the use of this technology.

What is left, then, in most of the nonfeminist discussions of IVF, is usually some hand-waving about costs. For instance, Gorovitz says: "There is the question of the distribution of costs, a question that has heightened impact if we consider the use of public funds to pay for medical treatment."[25] IVF is an extremely expensive (and profitable) procedure, costing several thousand dollars per attempt. Because it is often not covered by public or private health plans, it is financially inaccessible for most infertile couples.[26] Discussion in the nonfeminist forum generally ends here, in the mystery of how to balance soaring medical costs, with the added comment that IVF poses no new ethical problems.

The Feminist Perspective

A widening of perspective to include all the effects of IVF and other reproductive technologies on the women involved is called for in bioethical evaluations. In theory, mainstream approaches to bioethics could accommodate such concerns, should the philosophers involved think to look for them, and it is significant that, for the most part, they do not appear to have perceived them.

Like their nonfeminist counterparts in bioethics, most feminists are concerned to promote personal freedom. Feminists have a long history of supporting the protection of personal reproductive control in the areas of abortion and contraception. As I argued in chapter 5, women's ability to avoid unwanted pregnancies is both personally and politically important.[27] There is a distinction to be drawn between voluntary and involuntary childlessness, however, for where the former is desired, involuntary childlessness can be devastating in specific lives. From the point of view of those whose infertility is involuntary, IVF is likely to be positively valued, because it holds the promise of increasing their own reproductive freedom. Any public policy that restricts access to this technology will be experienced by those in search of relief for their childless condition as a serious interference with their personal reproductive freedom.

Indeed, most arguments in support of IVF are based on appeals to the rights of the individual to choose such technology. Feminists urge us to look carefully at these autonomy-based arguments, however, because as IVF is usually practiced, it does not altogether satisfy the motivation of fostering personal freedom. Like many other forms of reproductive technology, IVF is controlled by medical specialists and not by the women who seek it. It is not made available to every woman who is medically suitable but only to those who have been judged worthy by the designated medical practitioners. In almost every clinic a woman is considered eligible for this procedure only if she is involved in a stable (preferably married) relationship with a male partner. A couple must satisfy the specialists in charge that they have appropriate resources to support any children produced by this arrangement (in addition to the funds required to purchase the treatment in the first place), and they must demonstrate that they genuinely ''deserve'' this support. In other words, IVF is usually unavailable to single women, lesbian women, or women who are not securely placed in the middle class or beyond. Furthermore, women who are themselves affected by genetic handicaps are likely to be turned down by medical authorities who feel responsible for protecting future generations against the passing on of genetic defects (even if the condition at issue is one that the woman herself has come to terms with). IVF is also refused to those who have been judged as deficient according to the professionals' norms of good mothering.

The supposed freedom of choice, then, is provided only to selected women who have been screened according to the personal values of the experts administering the technology. Because most clinics deny service to single women, IVF may be accurately described as a technique that is available to men who are judged worthy, even though it is carried out on the bodies of their wives. Not only is this a far cry from individually controlled reproductive freedom, the selection criteria serve as one more instrument to establish the superior power and privilege of favored groups in society.

Feminist ethics directs us to examine the practice of IVF within the broader context of medical involvement in women's reproductive lives. There is a clear pattern of ever-increasing medical control over the various aspects of women's reproductive lives. Menstruation, pregnancy, delivery, lactation, childbearing, abortion, and menopause have already been subjected to medical control. In both Canada and the United States medical societies have removed midwives from their traditional place of influence and thereby have eliminated woman-centered control of reproduction. Medically supervised pregnancies and hospital births are demanded of everyone; women who fail to comply may be subject to criminal prosecution for endangering the health of the fetus. In most hospital settings it is doctors, not the women in labor, who determine the level of technology to be invoked in monitoring a woman's labor: doctors decide when to use cesarean sections and are even prepared to get court orders to perform them if the pregnant woman does not "consent."

Among its other effects, this increasingly interventionist, medicalized approach to reproduction alienates women from their own reproductive experiences. In seizing control of the various aspects of reproduction, physicians have tended to treat women as passive bodies to be subjected to medical manipulations. They focus their professional attention on the technology, rather than on the woman present, being more concerned with the product than the process of reproduction. The fetus-child is often viewed as the dominant subject of obstetric care; women may be assigned a merely passive role. With IVF, women's role is to permit their bodies to be subjected to forms of medical manipulation that they hope will "give" them the baby they desire. Here especially, women are portrayed as the passive containers for a medical miracle; their responsibility is to be compliant and accepting of the physician's active intervention. Doctors are represented as the real producers of the children created.

Viewed in the context of medicine's historical pursuit of control over women's reproductive lives and the role of the medical community in the general oppression of women, the issue of professional gatekeeping and monitoring in IVF is a matter of deep concern. IVF and most other new forms of reproductive technology constitute further areas for medical intervention in women's reproductive lives. They allow still greater decision-making power to be concentrated in the hands of medical specialists.

Some formal indication of "informed consent" is generally sought from clients, but many of the forms of reproductive technology have a poor track record in meeting the ethical demands of consent. Some of these technologies are offered to women as if they were established therapies, although they are still in a highly experimental stage; often the techniques are transferred directly from agricultural experience in animal husbandry, without the benefit of careful clinical trials performed on primates.[28] Other technologies, such as the use of ultrasound and electronic fetal monitors, represent new applications of military research, which have also been used extensively on women's bodies without adequate safety studies.[29] Women's experiences with thalidomide, DES, the Dalkon Shield, as well as the widespread use of fetal X rays until the mid-1970s and the belated warnings of the hazards of chemical contraceptives, provide ample reason for women to distrust reproductive technologies that have not yet been thoroughly tested for safety, but most bioethicists have been willing to rely on medical assurances about risks.

In many clinics relevant information is deliberately withheld from clients, which calls into question the informed nature of patients' choices and the degree of control that women actually exercise when receiving this technology. Many of the clinics that offer IVF are notoriously poor at keeping records and seldom offer full information on their low success rates to potential clients.[30] They encourage the media to present pictures of smiling parents with babies, which distract from the fact that the technology requires disruptive and dangerous hormone therapy, intrusive monitoring of the woman's blood and urine, surgery, a period of immobility, and a high likelihood of failure. Women are persuaded that only the application of complex technology can meet their needs, and therefore they feel compelled to rely on medical authority for their well-being. Doctors have been willing to take extraordinary risks with women's health in the hope of helping them to become mothers. Clearly, there is cause for concern about forms of technology that involve increased medical control over women's reproduction.

Putting IVF in Context

Feminist ethics expands the scope of ethical discussions of IVF and the other forms of new reproductive technologies in other respects. Although feminists share with their nonfeminist counterparts in bioethics an interest in matters of personal freedom, safety, fairness, and the overall contributions to human happiness and suffering that such technology may produce, they also identify many other important moral issues, which must be investigated. In evaluating the new reproductive technologies, a principal concern of feminist ethics is to see how each innovation fits into existing patterns of oppression. Technology is not neutral, so it is important to consider who controls it, who benefits from it, and how each activity is likely to affect women's subordinate status in society.

There are infertile couples with a strong desire to produce a child, and IVF does benefit many of them while it holds out hope to the rest. It is worth keeping in mind, however, that patients are not the only ones who benefit from this technology; IVF also serves the interests (commercial, professional, scholarly, and patriarchal) of the medical specialists who create and manipulate it. As the birth rates drop in the West and the traditional market for obstetric services shrinks, new reproductive technologies fill a potential void in the demand for specialist services. There is the prospect of significant prestige and profit at stake in the development of successful technologies. Michelle Stanworth observes: "Reproductive technologies often enhance the status of medical professionals and increase the funds they can command, by underpinning claims to specialized knowledge and by providing the basis for an extension of service. Such technologies may, in addition, help a profession in its attempts to dominate other competitors for control in an area of work. . . . Perhaps, most significantly, new technologies help to establish that gynecologists and obstetricians 'know more' about pregnancy and about women's bodies than women do themselves."[31] Renate Klein is blunter; she claims that "it is *not* the concerns of people with fertility problems that matter most. Much higher priority is given to the concerns of those who invent, practice and promote the new technologies."[32]

Moreover, it is important to investigate why so many couples feel compelled to seek technological solutions to involuntary childlessness. Why do people place such emphasis on the desire to produce their "own" child? With respect to this question, theorists in the mainstream tradition of bioethics seem to shift to previously rejected ground and suggest that this is a natural or, at least, a proper desire. Englehardt, for example, says, "The use of technology in the fashioning of children is integral to the goal of rendering the world congenial to persons." Bayles more cautiously observes that "a desire to beget for its own sake . . . is probably irrational"; nonetheless, he immediately concludes: "These techniques for fulfilling that desire have been found ethically permissible." Robert Edwards and David Sharpe confidently state that "the desire to have children must be among the most basic of human instincts, and denying it can lead to considerable psychological and social difficulties."[33] They do not seem interested in probing the desire to procreate or the expectations placed on people to develop such desires.

Generally, practitioners and critics alike accept without question the assumption that involuntary childlessness leads to "desperation," but as Naomi Pfeffer argues, this perspective is a caricature of the complex feelings that are actually experienced by infertile people.[34] Infertility is not simply a biological state; it is a socially defined and interpreted category that is addressed through many distinct strategies, including not only the pursuit of medical solutions but also such nonmedical options as acceptance, denial, changing partners, and adoption. Attention to the specific concerns voiced by childless people reveals a complex range of responses that does not readily fit into a single social category of "desperation," but the characterization of need implied by that label rationalizes radical medical intervention as a supportive response.[35] This way of conceptualizing the problem promotes a sense of urgency that denies scope for the investigation of other options. Infertile clients are regarded as desperate by the professionals they consult, and they learn to comply with the stereotyped expectations applied to them, so that they may ensure their place in oversubscribed infertility programs. They seek to establish their "normalcy" and worthiness of treatment by being eager and compliant thereby verifying the professionals' stereotypical expectations.

These observations are not meant to deny that involuntary childlessness is a cause of great unhappiness for many people. Many individuals and couples suffer from their inability to procreate when they choose to do so; many are indeed eager to pursue whatever techniques might be offered to relieve this condition. Their motivations cannot be dismissed as irrational or misguided or judged unethical. As long as the technology that offers relief from their condition is available, it is appropriate for individuals to seek access to it.

Feminist ethics asks us to look at the social arrangements and cultural values that underlie people's drive to assume the risks that are posed by IVF and its variants. In our culture involuntary childlessness is made all the more painful by the fact that many adults have no opportunity for emotional attachment to children outside their own home. Children are valued as privatized commodities that reflect the virility and heredity of their parents. Because adults are often inhibited from having warm, stable interactions with the children of others, those who wish to know children well may find that they must have their own.

Moreover, many women are persuaded that their most important purpose in life is to bear and raise children; they are told repeatedly that their lives are incomplete, that they are lacking in fulfillment if they do not have children. Furthermore, many women do face a hollow existence without children. Far too often children remain their one hope for real intimacy and for the sense of accomplishment that comes from doing work one judges to be valuable. Children are sometimes the only means women have to secure their ties to their husbands, in a culture that makes a husband a financial and social necessity for many women.

Children also serve important symbolic functions. They are, for instance, part of the glue that holds together the institution of heterosexuality. It is significant to feminists that many of the new reproductive technologies unquestioningly accept the pronatalist and heterosexist values of our society and the sexual division of labor on which they rest. Rather than challenge the assumptions that women's destiny is best expressed in the time-honored roles of wife and mother, these technologies legitimize those assumptions and help to entrench them even more deeply by demonstrating the lengths to which women will go to achieve this status.

Furthermore, IVF is entangled within the racist and classist value system that underlies the powerful eugenic forces in our culture. For many people, one significant attraction of IVF is that it is a means of allowing for specifically biological parenthood. Although some couples who pursue IVF would be willing to accept adoption if waiting lists were shorter, many others are not interested in raising children who are not genetically related to them. As Christine Overall argues, such decisions can rest on a variety of considerations, such as the sense of continuity with previous generations of the family, the desire to experience pregnancy and childbirth, or the prospective father's unwillingness to contribute to the support of a child produced by another man's sperm; some motives, although not all, raise serious obstacles to feminist ideals of greater social equality and the elimination of oppression.[36] Whatever the actual motivation, the practice of IVF itself serves to accept and support the sorts of individualistic values that say it is fine to invest vast resources into reproducing a child of one's own genes, despite the unmet needs of millions of existing children.

Feminist analysis requires us to examine how the various forms of reproductive technology reinforce the social prejudices that constitute the oppressive structures of our society. Doctors use their own values, which reflect their privileged position in society, to determine who qualifies for artificial insemination and IVF on the one hand and sterilization on the other hand. Different criteria are invoked to foster reproduction among the preferred groups and to repress reproduction among the disadvantaged. Laurie Nsiah-Jefferson and Elaine J. Hall observe: ''Population control groups have historically tended to define the prob-

162   *Susan Sherwin*

lem of infertility as the absence of white babies for married couples who are able to pay for them.''[37] They note that although the black community in the United States suffers significantly higher rates of infertility than the white community, infertility treatment programs are overwhelmingly directed at the latter group. The technologies of ova and embryo donation and genetic screening allow the medical specialists in charge to decide which genes are worth perpetuating. Embryo transfer, for example, allows the possibility of ''pure surrogate mothering,'' where a couple from the dominant class can engage an economically disadvantaged member of a subordinate class to gestate their fetus for them, sparing the genetic parents the dangers and inconvenience of pregnancy but assuring them of a child of the ''right'' genetic makeup at the end. Sex-selection technology allows the social preference for males to be translated into coming generations of increased numbers of males and, potentially, increased influence of male values.

Feminist ethics invokes a concept of reproductive freedom under which women should be free to say no or yes to reproduction. This concept cannot be understood in terms of traditional conceptions of individual autonomy, however, for the latter tends to leave out analysis of the factors of oppression. Freedom cannot always be determined in isolated cases but requires attention to a person's whole life situation. The reproductive freedom that feminists appeal to in abortion arguments is the freedom for women to choose their status as childbearers, which is especially important in the face of the social, economic, and political significance that are associated with reproduction for women.

Reproductive freedom for women requires that they have control over their sexuality, protection against coerced sterilization (or iatrogenic sterilization caused by prescribed contraceptives), and access to the social and economic support necessary to care for any children each may choose to bear. It requires that women be free to define their roles in society according to their concerns and needs as women. Feminism helps us understand that reproductive freedom involves being free from the economic, racist, and sexist oppression that prevents choices in other aspects of life. This freedom cannot be captured by focusing on single choices, in isolation from other factors.

In contrast, most nonfeminist bioethicists (outside of the theological tradition) treat reproductive freedom as if it were the consumer freedom to purchase technology. Often such choices are, by their very nature, available only to relatively few couples of the privileged classes (who are situated in traditionally approved relationships). Rather than increasing women's general freedom from oppression, this narrow concept of freedom of choice may help entrench more deeply the patriarchal notion of woman's role as childbearer. Under current social conditions, not all such choices can be seen to foster autonomy for women collectively.

From the point of view of feminist ethics, the central question is whether IVF and other forms of reproductive technology threaten to reinforce the lack of autonomy that most women now experience in our culture—even though these technologies appear to increase particular aspects of freedom for some women. Although the new reproductive technologies are advertised as increasing women's autonomy, feminists mistrust them as long as they remain intertwined with key social forces that are oppressive to women in general and, especially, to women who are multiply oppressed. By accepting the presupposition that (particular) women ought to bear children, even if they must risk their lives to do so, IVF implicitly reinforces many of the sexist, classist, and often racist assumptions of our culture. It helps to support the existing power structures, because it provides reproductive assistance to the affluent and accepts the view that it is more important for the privileged to produce children of their own genetic type than to adopt a child of a different background. On our revised understanding of freedom, the contribution of this technology to the general autonomy of women collectively seems largely negative.

Therefore, it seems appropriate to resurrect the old slippery-slope arguments against IVF. Women's existing lack of control in reproductive matters begins the debate on a pretty steep incline. Technology with the potential to remove further control of reproduction from women makes the slope very slippery indeed. IVF is a technology that will always include the active involvement of designated specialists; it will never be simply a private matter for the couple or women concerned. Although offered under the guise of increasing some individuals' reproductive freedom, IVF threatens to result in a significant decrease in freedom for women as a class.

Feminist analysis guides us in rethinking the values that drive the search for new forms of reproductive technologies. It urges us to question the appropriateness of encouraging people to spend huge sums on creating certain sorts of children through IVF and other forms of reproductive technology, while so many other children starve to death each year. IVF, like other forms of new reproductive technology, seems to strengthen, rather than weaken, the social attitudes that underlie the politics of dominance and supremacy in our world.

More positively, feminist ethics looks elsewhere for solutions to the problems of infertility. It seeks to make changes in the prevailing social arrangements that can lead to a reduction of the sense of need for this sort of solution. On the medical front, research and treatment should be stepped up to reduce the rates of sexually transmitted disease and other causes of pelvic inflammatory disease, which often result in tubal blockage; a significant percentage of female infertility is preventable, and feminist concern with reproductive freedom entails the view that involuntary sterilization should be prevented. Feminists can also support the need to direct more attention to the causes of and possible cures for male infertility. Research into eliminating the environmental and social factors (for example, malnutrition) that contribute to infertility is clearly vital. In addition, we should pursue techniques that will permit safe, reversible sterilization in both women and men, providing better fertility control options than are now available.

On the social front, we must continue the pressure to change the statuses of women and children in our society from those of breeder and possession respectively: hence we must develop a vision of society as a community where women and children are valued members. We must challenge the notion that having one's wife produce a child with one's own genes is sufficient cause for the wives of men with low sperm counts to undergo the physical and emotional assault that IVF and genetic technology involves.

In contrast to their nonfeminist bioethicist colleagues, feminists attend closely to the often devastating consequences of various reproductive technologies on the particular women who undergo them. Nonfeminist bioethicists have chosen to skip over the significance of the hazards to which women are exposed by this technology; they assume that the generic informed consent requirements that they have spelled out for all medical procedures will provide adequate protection against excessive threats to individual patients. Feminists, however, painstakingly monitor the cumulative effects of these new technologies.[38] Such effects are not mere details, unconnected with the theoretical moral question of the acceptability of reproductive technologies (as most traditional ethicists would have it). The data demonstrate the willingness of the medical profession to risk the lives and well-being of women to try to ensure that all women can fulfill their biological role in reproduction. Such information leads feminists to look more deeply for explanations for the phenomenon of fertility treatments as the new growth industry in medicine.

Traditional ethics and nonfeminist bioethics would have us evaluate individual cases without also looking at the implications of the practices as reviewed from a wide perspective. Examination of IVF as one form of new reproductive technology demonstrates the inadequacy of that approach for the moral evaluation of some medical practices. Feminist ethics provides the necessary wide perspective, because its different methodology is sensitive to both the personal and the social dimensions of issues.

Notes

1. Barbara Drygulski Wright, "Introduction," in *Healing Technology: Feminist Perspectives*, ed. Kathryn Strother Ratcliff (Ann Arbor, Mich: University of Michigan, 1989), 13.
2. Kathryn Strother Ratcliff, ed. *Healing Technology* (Ann Arbor, Mich.: University of Michigan, 1989.)
3. Elisabeth Beck-Gernsheim, "From the Pill to Test-Tube Babies: New Options, New Pressures in Reproductive Behavior," in *Healing Technology: Feminist Perspectives*, ed. Kathryn Strother Ratcliff (Ann Arbor: University of Michigan, 1989).
4. Renate D. Klein, *Infertility: Women Speak Out about Their Experiences of Reproductive Medicine* (London: Pandora Press, 1989).
5. It was not until 1965 that the United States overturned state laws that prohibited the sale of contraceptives to married couples and not until 1973 that single persons could claim similar rights. In Canada regulations restricting the provision of contraceptive information and devices were removed in 1969.
6. Robin Morgan, ed., *Sisterhood Is Global: The International Women's Movement Anthology* (Middlesex: Penguin Books, 1984), reports that only one-third of the women in the world have access to the information and means necessary for contraception.
7. Lyn Duggan, "From Birth Control to Population Control: Depo-Provera in Southeast Asia," in *Adverse Effects: Women in the Pharmaceutical Industry*, ed. Kathleen McDonnell (Toronto: Women's Press, 1986). See Vimal Balasubrahmanyan, "Finger in the Dike: The Fight to Keep Injectables Out of India," in *Adverse Effects*, and Cary LaCheen, "Pharmaceuticals and Family Planning: Women are the Target," in *Adverse Effects*. And also see Kim Yanoshik and Judy Norsigan, "Contraception, Control, and Choice: International Perspectives" in *Healing Technology*.
8. We should keep in mind that much of the promise of the new forms of reproductive technology remains unfulfilled at this time; most cannot achieve the control they are meant to accomplish.
9. A very useful description of the process involved in this technique and its variations can be found in Lynda Birke, Susan Himmelweit and Gail Vines, *Tomorrow's Child: Reproductive Technologies in the 90's* (London: Virago, 1990).

10. Therefore, Renate D. Klein, *Infertility: Women Speak Out about Their Experiences of Reproductive Medicine* (London: Pandora Press, 1989) concludes, "In reality, it is a *failed* technology."

11. Paul Ramsey, "Shall We Reproduce?" *Journal of the American Medical Association* 220: 1484, (1972).

12. Leon Kass, " 'Making Babies' revisited," *Public Interest* 54:32–60, 1979.

13. Joseph Card Ratzinger and Alberto Bovone, "Instruction on Respect for Human Life in its Origin and on the Dignity of Procreation: Replies to Certain Questions of the Day" (Vatican City: Vatican Polyglot Press, 1987), 28.

14. Michael Bayles, *Reproductive Ethics* (Englewood Cliffs, N.J.: Prentice Hall, 1984), 15.

15. Joseph Card Ratzinger and Alberto Bovone, "Instruction on Respect for Human Life in its Origin and on the Dignity of Procreation: Replies to Certain Questions of the Day" (Vatican City: Vatican Polyglot Press, 1987), 28.

16. Samuel Gorovitz, *Doctors' Dilemmas: Moral Conflict and Medical Care* (New York: Oxford University Press, 1982), 168.

17. Multiple births are a relatively frequent occurrence in IVF and other technological responses to infertility; the preferred technological solution to this iatrogenic problem is the new technique of selective abortion, wherein some fetuses in the womb are given a lethal injection and the other(s) are allowed to continue their development.

18. Samuel Gorovitz, *Doctors' Dilemmas: Moral Conflict and Medical Care* (New York: Oxford University Press, 1982), 173; Michael Bayles, *Reproductive Ethics* (Englewood Cliffs, N.J.: Prentice Hall, 1984), 66.

19. Tristram H. Englehardt, Jr., *The Foundations of Bioethics* (Oxford: Oxford University Press, 1986), 237.

20. Englehardt, 241.

21. Having a healthy baby with an uncomplicated birth is an extremely rare achievement for IVF technology. A survey conducted by the Australian government reported that fewer than 5 percent of cases resulted in an unproblematic, live birth cited in Renate D. Klein, *Infertility: Women Speak Out about Their Experiences of Reproductive Medicine* (London: Pandora Press, 1989).

22. For a discussion of some of the already apparent dangers of clomid use in the treatment of infertility, including deaths attributed to irresponsible prescriptions, see Renate D. Klein, *Infertility: Women Speak Out about Their Experiences of Reproductive Medicine* (London: Pandora Press, 1989).

23. Elizabeth Beck-Gernsheim, "From the Pill to Test-Tube Babies: New Options, New Pressures in Reproductive Behavior." In *Healing Technologies: Feminist Perspectives*, ed. Kathryn Strother Ratcliff (Ann Arbor: University of Michigan Press, 1989) reports that over half of the women who give birth to IVF babies do so by cesarian section (36).

24. Michael Bayles, *Reproductive Ethics* (Englewood Cliffs, N.J.: Prentice-Hall, 1984), 32.

25. Samuel Gorovitz, *Doctors' Dilemmas: Moral Conflict and Medical Care* (New York: Oxford University Press, 1982), 177.

26. The province of Ontario is a remarkable exception; it does include IVF under the rubric of provincially funded medical services. In Britain only one clinic is fully funded under the National Health Service, and waiting lists are extremely long. See Lesley Doyal, "Infertility-A Life Sentence? Women and the National Health Service." In *Reproductive Technologies: Gender, Motherhood and Medicine* ed. Michelle Stanworth (Minneapolis: University of Minnesota Press, 1987); Lynda Birke, Susan Himmelweit, and Gail Vines, *Tomorrow's Child: Reproductive Technologies in the 90's* (London: Virago, 1990).

27. Susan Sherwin, *No Longer Patient: Feminist Ethics and Health Care* (Philadelphia: Temple University Press, 1992), 99.

28. When I raised this point in a panel discussion on the ethics of reproductive technologies at the University of Alberta, the gynecologist on the panel patiently explained the reason for this omission: primates are expensive research animals. Although I do not mean to imply that there are no ethical problems in the experimental use of animals, animal experimentation and careful documentation are usually demanded before any new medical technology can be implemented; but here, where the technology is directed exclusively at women, no such research was performed. Further, the women on whom this technology is practiced are not advised of this omission; many assume that they are undergoing an established treatment, rather than participating in a broad, uncontrolled clinical trial.

29. Ann Oakley, "From Walking Wombs to Test-Tube Babies," in *Reproductive Technologies*; see Doyal 1987; Rosalind Pollack Petchesky, "Reproductive Freedom: Beyond 'a Woman's Right to Choose,' " in *Women—Sex and Sexuality*; see Person 1980; and Judith R. Kunisch, "Electronic Fetal Monitors: Marketing Forces and the Resulting Controversy," in *Healing Technologies*; see Beck-Gernsheim 1989.

30. Michael Soules, "The In Vitro Fertilization Pregnancy Rate: Let's Be Honest with One Another," *Fertility and Sterility* 43(4) (1985): 511–13. Much of the difficulty has to do with the unwillingness of practitioners to establish meaningful guidelines on what constitutes success. For women contemplating such therapy, "success" naturally is interpreted as meaning that the process produces a healthy baby, but for practitioners, success can mean success at any of the stages of the program. Even with the most generous interpretation, however, there is evidence that some clinics have been less than honest.

31. Michelle Stanworth, ed., *Reproductive Technologies: Gender, Motherhood and Medicine* (Minneapolis: University of Minnesota Press, 1987), 13.

32. Renate D. Klein, *Infertility: Women Speak Out about Their Experiences of Reproductive Medicine* (London: Pandora, 1989), 247.

33. Tristram H. Englehardt, Jr., *The Foundations of Bioethics* (Oxford: Oxford University Press, 1986), 239; Michael Bayles, *Reproductive Ethics* (Englewood Cliffs, N.J.: Prentice Hall, 1984), 31; and Robert G. Edwards and David

168   *Susan Sherwin*

J. Shapre, "Social Values and Research in Human Embryology," *Nature* 231: 87.

34. Naomi Pfeffer, "Artificial Insemination, In-vitro Fertilization, and the Stigma of Infertility," in *Reproductive Technologies;* see Doyal 1987.

35. See Naomi Pfeffer, "Artificial Insemination," 1987.

36. Christine Overall, *Ethics and Human Reproduction: A Feminist Analysis* (Boston: Allen and Unwin, 1987); e.g., a man may be interested in producing a genetically linked child because genetic inheritance is likely to be his only real connection with the child, if he does not assume any child-rearing responsibilities, or a racist may choose this technology to ensure that only "racially pure" genes go into the creation of the child.

37. Laurie Nsiah-Jefferson and Elaine J. Hall, "Reproductive Technology: Perspectives and Implications for Low-Income Women and Women of Color," in *Healing Technologies.* See Beck-Gernsheim 1989.

38. See, e.g., Helen B. Holmes, Betty B. Hoskins, and Michael Gross, eds., *The Custom-Made Child? Women-centered Perspectives* (Clifton, NJ: Humana Press, 1981); Gena Corea, *The Mother Machine: Reproductive Technologies from Artificial Insemination to Artificial Wombs* (New York: Harper and Row, 1985b); Renate D. Klein, *Infertility: Women Speak Out about Their Experiences of Reproductive Medicine* (London: Pandora Press, 1989); and Linda S. Williams, "No Relief until the End: The Physical and Emotional Costs of In Vitro Fertilization," in *Future of Human Reproduction.* See Colodny 1989.

Questions

1. Explain why Sherwin believes it is important to have a distinctly feminist investigation and evaluation of the different reproductive technologies. What specific problems does she see in not having a feminist ethics evaluation of these new technologies?

2. How is it possible that a technology like ultrasound could adversely affect the population? What different aspects of women's reproductive systems have been relegated to the medical community? What is beneficial about this? What is not beneficial?

3. What might some theologians object to in the technology of in vitro fertilization? How do secular philosophers dismiss these objections? What is Sherwin's position? What do you think about the objections?

4. In what ways does feminist ethics approach aspects of women's reproductive lives? What do some feminists see as the physician's role in our society today? How does the physician's role affect women's oppression?

5. What does Sherwin suggest feminists do regarding infertility problems? Do you agree?

8

Markets in Women's Reproductive Labor

Debra Satz

Much of the evolution of social policy in the twentieth century has occurred around conflicts over the scope of markets. To what extent, under what conditions, and for what reasons should we limit the use of markets?[1] Recently, American society has begun to experiment with markets in women's reproductive labor. Many people believe that markets in women's reproductive labor, as exemplified by contract pregnancy,[2] are more problematic than other currently accepted labor markets. I will call this the asymmetry thesis because its proponents believe that there ought to be an asymmetry between our treatment of reproductive labor and our treatment of other forms of labor. Advocates of the asymmetry thesis hold that treating reproductive labor as a commodity, as something subject to the supply-and-demand principles that govern economic markets, is worse than treating other types of human labor as commodities. Is the asymmetry thesis true? And, if so, what are the reasons for thinking that it is true?

My aims in this article are to criticize several popular ways of defending the asymmetry thesis[3] and to offer an alternative defense. Other foundations for an argument against contract pregnancy are, of course, possible. For example, several of the arguments that I examine in this article have sometimes been raised in the context of more general anti-commodification arguments. I do not examine such general arguments here. Instead, I focus my discussion on those arguments against contract pregnancy that *depend* on the asymmetry thesis. I believe that the asymmetry thesis both captures strong intuitions that exist in our society and provides a plausible argument against contract pregnancy.

Many feminists hold that the asymmetry thesis is true because women's reproductive labor is a special kind of labor that should not be treated according to market norms. They draw a sharp dividing line between women's reproductive labor and human labor in general: while human labor may be bought and sold, women's reproductive labor is intrinsically not a commodity. According to these views, contract pregnancy allows for the extension of the market into the "private" sphere of sexuality and reproduction. This intrusion of the economic into the personal is seen as improper: it fails to respect the intrinsic, special nature of reproductive labor. As one writer has put it, "When women's labor is treated as a commodity, the women who perform it are degraded."[4]

Below, I argue that this is the wrong way to defend the asymmetry thesis. While I agree with the intuition that markets in women's reproductive labor are more troubling than other labor markets, in this article I develop an alternative account of why this should be so. My analysis has four parts. In the first part, I criticize the arguments against the commodification of women's reproductive labor that turn on the assumption that reproductive labor is a special form of labor, part of a separate realm of sexuality. I argue that there is no distinction between women's reproductive labor and human labor generally, which is relevant to the debate about contract pregnancy. Moreover, I argue that the sale of women's reproductive labor is not ipso facto degrading. Rather, it becomes "degrading" only in a particular political and social context.[5]

In the second part, I criticize arguments in support of the asymmetry thesis that appeal to norms of parental love. Here, the asymmetry between reproductive labor and labor in general is taken to derive from a special bond between mothers and children: the bond between a mother and her child is different from the bond between a worker and his product. In response, I argue that the bond between mothers and children is more complicated than critics of contract pregnancy have assumed and that, moreover, contract pregnancy does not cause parents to view children as commodities.

The third part of the article examines an argument that stresses the potential negative consequences of contract pregnancy for children. While this argument has some merit, I argue that it is unpersuasive.

The first three parts of the article argue that the various reasons given in the literature for banning contract pregnancy on the basis of its asymmetry with other forms of labor are inadequate. Nonetheless, most people think that there should be some limits to commodification, and there does seem to be something more problematic about pregnancy contracts than other types of labor contract. The question is, what is the basis for and the significance of these intuitions? And what, apart from its agreement with these particular intuitions, can be said in favor of the asymmetry thesis?

In the fourth part of my article, I argue that the asymmetry thesis is true, but that the reason it is true has not been properly understood. The asymmetry thesis should be defended on external and not intrinsic or essentialist grounds. The conditions of pervasive gender inequality in our society are primary to the explanation of what is wrong with contract pregnancy. I claim that the most compelling objection to contract pregnancy concerns the background conditions of gender inequality that characterize our society. Markets in women's reproductive labor are especially troubling because they reinforce gender hierarchies in a way that other accepted labor markets do not. My defense of the asymmetry thesis thus rests on the way that contract pregnancy reinforces asymmetrical social relations of gender domination in American society. However, not all of the features of contract pregnancy that make it troubling concern gender inequality. Contract pregnancy may also heighten racial inequalities[6] and have harmful effects on the other children of the gestational mother.[7] In addition, the background conditions of economic inequality that characterize our society raise questions about the equal status of the contracting parties. I do not address these points in detail here. However, these latter considerations would have to be addressed in order to generate a complete argument against contract pregnancy.

The Special Nature of Reproductive Labor

A wide range of attacks on contract pregnancy turn out to share a single premise, viz., that the intrinsic nature of reproductive labor is different from that of other kinds of labor. Critics claim that reproductive labor is not just another kind of work; they argue that unlike other forms of labor, reproductive labor is not properly regarded as a commodity. I will refer to this thesis as the essentialist thesis, since it holds that reproductive labor is *essentially* something that should not be bought and sold.

In contrast to the essentialist thesis, modern economic theories tend to treat the market as "theoretically all encompassing."[8] Such theories tend to treat all goods and capacities as exchangeable commodities, at least in principle.[9] Economists generally base their defense of markets as distributive mechanisms on three distinct ideas.

First, there is the idea that markets are good for social welfare. Indeed, the fundamental theorem of welfare economics states that every competitive (market) equilibrium is Pareto optimal.[10] A Pareto optimum is a distribution point at which, given the initial distribution of resources, no individual can become better off (in view of her preferences) without at least one other individual becoming worse off. The so-called converse theorem of welfare economics states that every Pareto optimum is a competitive equilibrium.

Second, there is the idea that markets promote freedom. The agent of economic theory is a free, autonomous chooser.[11] Markets enhance her capacities for choosing by decentralizing decision making, decentralizing information, and providing opportunities for experimentation. Markets also place limits on the viability of unjust social relationships by providing avenues for individual exit, thereby making the threat of defection a credible bargaining device.

Third, there is the idea that excluding a free exchange of some good, as a matter of principle, is incompatible with liberal neutrality. Liberalism requires state neutrality among conceptions of value. This neutrality constrains liberals from banning free exchanges: liberals cannot mandate that individuals accept certain values as having "intrinsic" or ultimate worth.[12] Liberals can, of course, seek to regulate exchanges so that they fall within the bounds of justice. But any argument prohibiting rather than regulating market activity is claimed to violate liberal neutrality.[13]

If we accept the logic of the economic approach to human behavior, we seem led to endorse a world in which everything is potentially for sale: body parts, reproductive labor, children, even persons.[14] Many people are repulsed by such a world. But what exactly is the problem with it? Defenders of the essentialist thesis provide the starting point for a counterattack: not all human goods are commodities. In particular, human reproductive labor is improperly treated as a commodity. When reproductive labor is purchased on the market, it is inappropriately valued.

The essentialist thesis provides support for the asymmetry thesis. The nature of reproductive labor is taken to be fundamentally different from that of labor in general. In particular, proponents of the essentialist thesis hold that women's reproductive labor should be respected and not used.[15] What is it about women's reproductive labor that singles it out for a type of respect that precludes market use?

Some versions of the essentialist thesis focus on the biological or naturalistic features of women's reproductive labor. (1) Women's reproductive labor has both a genetic and a gestational component.[16] Other forms of labor do not involve a genetic relationship between the worker and her product. (2) While much human labor is voluntary at virtually every step, many of the phases of the reproductive process are involuntary. Ovulation, conception, gestation, and birth occur without the conscious direction of the mother. (3) Reproductive labor extends over a period of approximately nine months; other types of labor do not typically necessitate a long-term commitment. (4) Reproductive labor involves significant restrictions of a woman's behavior during pregnancy; other forms of labor are less invasive with respect to the worker's body.

These characteristics of reproductive labor do not, however, establish the asymmetry thesis. (1) With respect to the genetic relationship between the reproductive worker and her product, most critics object to contract pregnancy even where the "surrogate" is not the genetic mother. In fact, many critics consider "gestational surrogacy"—in which a woman is implanted with a preembryo formed in vitro from donated gametes—more pernicious than those cases in which the "surrogate" is also the genetic mother.[17] In addition, men also have a genetic tie to their offspring, yet many proponents of the asymmetry thesis would not oppose the selling of sperm. (2) With respect to the degree to which reproductive labor is involuntary, there are many forms of work in which workers do not have control over the work process; for example, mass-production workers cannot generally control the speed of the assembly line, and they have no involvement in the overall purpose of their activity. (3) With regard to the length of the contract's duration, some forms of labor involve contracts of even longer duration, for example, book contracts. Like pregnancy contracts, these are not contracts in which one can quit at the end of the day. Yet, presumably, most proponents of the essentialist thesis would not find commercial publishing contracts objectionable. (4) With regard to invasions into the woman's body, nonreproductive labor can also involve incursions into the body of the worker. To take an obvious example, athletes sign contracts that give team owners considerable control over their diet and behavior, allowing owners to conduct periodic tests for drug use. Yet there is little controversy over the sale of athletic capacities.[18] Sales of blood also run afoul of a noninvasiveness condition. In fact, leaving aside the genetic component of reproductive labor, voluntary military service involves features 2 through 4; do we really want to object to such military service on *essentialist* grounds?

Carole Pateman suggests a different way of defending the asymmetry thesis as the basis for an argument against contract pregnancy. Rather than focusing on the naturalistic, biological properties of reproductive labor, she argues that a woman's reproductive labor is more "integral" to her identity than her other productive capacities. Pateman first sketches this argument with respect to prostitution:

> Womanhood, too, is confirmed in sexual activity, and when a prostitute contracts out use of her body she is thus selling herself in a very real sense. Women's selves are involved in prostitution in a different manner from the involvement of the self in other occupations. Workers of all kinds may be more or less "bound up in their work," but the integral connection between sexuality and sense of the self means that, for self-protection, a prostitute must distance herself from her sexual use.[19]

Pateman's objection to prostitution rests on a claim about the intimate relation between a woman's sexuality and her identity. It is by virtue of this tie, Pateman believes, that sex should not be treated as an alienable commodity. Is her claim true? How do we decide which of a woman's attributes or capacities are essential to her identity and which are not? In particular, why should we consider sexuality more integral to self than friendship, family, religion, nationality, and work?[20] Yet we allow commodification in each of these spheres. For example, rabbis or priests may view their religion as central to their identity, but they often accept payment for performing religious services, and hardly anyone objects to their doing so. Does Pateman think that *all* activities that fall within these spheres and that bear an intimate relationship to a person's identity should be inalienable?

Pateman's argument in the above passage appears to support the asymmetry thesis, by suggesting that a woman's sexuality is *more* intimately related to her identity than her other capacities. Yet she provides no explicit argument for this suggestion. Indeed, at times, her argument seems intended not so much to support the asymmetry thesis as to support a more general thesis against alienating those activities that are closely tied to the identity of persons. But this more general argument is implausible. It would not allow individuals to sell their homes or their paintings or their book manuscripts or their copyrights.

A similar argument about the close connection between sexuality and identity underlies the objection to contract pregnancy raised by the British government-commissioned Warnock Report on Human Fertilization and Embryology. The Warnock Report links reproductive labor to a person's dignity, claiming that "it is inconsistent with human dignity that a woman should use her uterus for financial profit."[21] But why is selling the use of a woman's uterus "undignified" while selling the use of images of her body in a television commercial is not?

The Warnock Report's argument implicitly rests on the assumption that women's sexuality and reproduction belong to a sacred, special realm. In the words of another author, it is a realm "worthy of respect."[22] Even if this is so, however, the idea of respect alone cannot guarantee the conclusion that reproductive labor should not be treated as a commodity. We sometimes sell things that we also respect. As Margaret Radin puts it, "we can both know the price of something and know that it is priceless."[23] For example, I think that my teaching talents should be respected, but I don't object to being paid for teaching on such grounds. Giving my teaching a price does not diminish the other ways in which my teaching has value.

This point undermines Pateman's argument as well. For although Pateman would not endorse the idea that sexuality is part of a private realm, she does believe that it bears a special relationship to our identities and that by virtue of that relationship it should be inalienable. But we sometimes sell things intimately tied to our identities, without ceasing to be the people that we are. For example, as I suggested above, a person's home may be intimately tied to her identity, but she can also sell it without losing her sense of self.[24]

Finally, I believe that it is a mistake to focus, as does the Warnock Report, on maintaining certain cultural values without examining critically the specific social circumstances from which those values emerge. Thus, the view that selling sexual or reproductive capacities is "degrading" may reflect society's attempts to control women and their sexuality. At the very least, the relations between particular views of sexuality and the maintenance of gender inequality must be taken into account. This is especially important insofar as one powerful defense of contract pregnancy rests on its alleged consequence of empowering poor women.[25] Indeed, there is something hypocritical in the objection to contract pregnancy as "degrading," when the fundamental background conditions of social inequality—many of which are at least equally "degrading"—are ignored.

The Special Bonds of Motherhood

Sometimes what critics of pregnancy contracts have in mind is not the effect of such contracts on the relationship between reproductive labor and a woman's sense of self or her dignity, but its effect on her views (and ours) of the mother-fetus and mother-child bond. On this view, what is wrong with commodifying reproductive labor is that by relying on a mistaken picture of the nature of these relationships, it degrades them. Further, it leads to a view of children as fungible objects. In part 1 of this section I examine arguments against contract pregnancy based on its portrayal of the mother-fetus bond; in part 2 I examine arguments based on contract pregnancy's portrayal of the mother-child bond.

1. Mothers and Fetuses

Some critics of contract pregnancy contend that the relationship between a mother and a fetus is not simply a biochemical relationship or a matter of contingent physical connection. They claim that the relationship between a mother and a fetus is essentially different from that between a worker and her material product. The long months of pregnancy and the experience of childbirth are part of forming a relationship with the child-to-be. Elizabeth Anderson makes an argument along these lines. She suggests that the commodification of reproductive labor makes pregnancy an alienated form of labor for the women who perform it: selling her reproductive labor alienates a woman from her "normal" and justified emotions.[26] Rather than viewing pregnancy as an evolving relationship with a child-to-be, contract pregnancy reinforces a vision of the pregnant woman as a mere "home" or an "environment."[27] The commodification of reproductive labor thus distorts the nature of the bond between the mother and the fetus by misrepresenting the nature of a woman's reproductive labor. What should we make of this argument?

Surely there is truth in the claim that pregnancy contracts may reinforce a vision of women as baby machines or mere "wombs." Recent court rulings with respect to contract pregnancy have tended to acknowledge women's contribution to reproduction only insofar as it is identical to men's: the donation of genetic material. The gestational labor involved in reproduction is explicitly ignored in such rulings. Thus, Mary Beth Whitehead won back her parental rights in the "Baby M" case because the New Jersey Supreme Court acknowledged her genetic contribution.[28]

However, as I will argue in section 4 below, the concern about the discounting of women's reproductive labor is best posed in terms of the principle of equal treatment. By treating women's reproductive labor as identical to men's when it is not, women are not in fact being treated equally. But those who conceptualize the problem with pregnancy contracts in terms of the degradation of the mother-fetus relationship rather than in terms of the equality of men and women tend to interpret the social practice of pregnancy in terms of a maternal "instinct," a sacrosanct bonding that takes place between a mother and her child-to-be. However, not all women "bond" with their fetuses. Some women abort them.

Indeed, there is a dilemma for those who wish to use the mother-fetus bond to condemn pregnancy contracts while endorsing a woman's right to choose abortion. They must hold that it is acceptable to abort a fetus, but not to sell it. While the Warnock Report takes no stand on the issue of abortion, it uses present abortion law as a term of reference in considering contract pregnancy. Since abortion is currently legal in England, the report's position has this paradoxical consequence: one can kill a fetus, but one cannot contract to sell it.[29] One possible response to this objection would be to claim that women do not bond with their fetuses in the first trimester. But the fact remains that some women never bond with their fetuses; some women even fail to bond with their babies after they deliver them.

Additionally, are we really sure that we know which emotions pregnancy "normally" involves? While married women are portrayed as nurturing and altruistic, society has historically stigmatized the unwed mother as selfish, neurotic, and unconcerned with the welfare of her child. Until quite recently, social pressure was directed at unwed mothers to surrender their children after birth. Thus, married women who gave up their children were seen as "abnormal" and unfeeling, while unwed mothers who failed to surrender their children were seen as selfish.[30] Such views of the mother-fetus bonding relationship reinforce this traditional view of the family and a woman's proper role within it.

2. Mothers and Children

A somewhat different argument against contract pregnancy contends that the commodification of women's reproductive labor entails the commodification of children. Once again, the special nature of reproduction is used to support the asymmetry thesis: the special nature of maternal love is held to be incompatible with market relations. Children should be loved by their mothers, yet commercial surrogacy responds to and promotes other motivations. Critics argue that markets in reproductive labor give people the opportunity to "shop" for children. Prospective womb-infertile couples will seek out arrangements that "maximize" the value of their babies: sex, eye color, and race will be assessed in terms of market considerations.[31] Having children on the basis of such preferences reflects an inferior conception of persons. It brings commercial attitudes into a sphere that is thought to be properly governed by love.

What are the reasons that people seek to enter into contract pregnancy arrangements? Most couples or single people who make use of "surrogates" want simply to have a child that is "theirs," that is, genetically related to them. In fact, given the clogged adoption system, some of them may simply want to have a child. Furthermore, the adoption system itself is responsive to people's individual preferences: it is much easier, for example, to adopt an older black child than a white infant. Such preferences may be objectionable, but no one seriously argues that parents should have no choice in the child they adopt or that adoption should be prohibited because it gives rein to such preferences. Instead, we regulate adoption to forbid the differential payment of fees to agencies on the basis of a child's ascribed characteristics. Why couldn't contract pregnancy be regulated in the same way?

Critics who wish to make an argument for the asymmetry thesis based on the nature of maternal love must defend a strong claim about the relationship between markets and love. In particular, they must claim that even regulated markets in reproductive services will lead parents to love their children for the wrong reasons: love will be conditional on the child's having the "right" set of physical characteristics. While I share the view that there is something wrong with the "shopping" attitude in the sphere of personal relations, I wonder if it has the adverse effects that the critics imagine. Individuals in our society seek partners with attributes ranging from a specified race and height to a musical taste for Chopin. Should such singles' advertisements in magazines be illegal? Should we ban dating services that cater to such preferences? Isn't it true that people who meet on such problematic grounds may grow to love each other? I suspect that most parents who receive their child through a contract pregnancy arrangement will love their child as well.

Even if contract pregnancy does not distort our conception of personhood per se, critics can still associate contract pregnancy with baby-selling. One popular argument runs: In contract pregnancy women not only sell their reproductive services, but also their babies. Because baby-selling is taken to be intrinsically wrong, this type of argument attempts to use an analogy to support the following syllogism: If baby-selling is wrong, and contract pregnancy is a form of baby-selling, then contract pregnancy is wrong. The Warnock Report, for example, makes this charge.[32] Suppose that we grant, as seems plausible, that baby-selling is wrong (perhaps on essentialist grounds). Is this argument successful?

It is important to keep in mind that pregnancy contracts do not enable fathers (or prospective ''mothers,'' women who are infertile or otherwise unable to conceive) to acquire children as property. Even where there has been a financial motivation for conceiving a child, and whatever the status of the labor that produced it, the *child* cannot be treated as a commodity. The father cannot, for example, destroy, transfer, or abandon the child. He is bound by the same norms and laws that govern the behavior of a child's biological or adoptive parents. Allowing women to contract for their reproductive services does not entail baby-selling, if we mean by that a proxy for slavery.

Anderson has argued that what makes contract pregnancy a form of baby-selling is the way such contracts treat the ''mother's rights over her child.''[33] Such contracts mandate that the mother relinquish her parental rights to the child. Furthermore, such contracts can be enforced against the mother's wishes. Anderson argues that forcing a woman to part with her child and to cede her parental rights by sale entails treating the child as a mere commodity, as something that can be sold. Even if this is true, it does not necessarily lead to the conclusion that pregnancy contracts should be banned. There are many similarities between contract pregnancy and adoption. Like adoption, pregnancy contracts could be regulated to respect a change of mind of the ''surrogate'' within some specified time period; to accord more with an ''open'' model in which all the parties to the contract retain contact with the child; or by making pregnancy contracts analogous to contracts that require informed consent, as in the case of medical experiments. Pregnancy contracts could be required to provide detailed information about the emotional risks and costs associated with giving up a child.[34]

Finally, some writers have objected to pregnancy contracts on the ground that they must, by their nature, exploit women. They point to the fact that the compensation is very low, and that many of the women who agree to sell their reproductive labor have altruistic motivations. Anderson writes, ''A kind of exploitation occurs when one party to a transaction is oriented toward the exchange of 'gift' values, while the other party operates in accordance with the norms of the market exchange of commodities.''[35]

Two responses are possible to this line of argument. First, even if it is the case that all or most of the women who sell their reproductive labor are altruistically motivated,[36] it is unfair to argue that the other parties to the contract are motivated solely in accord with market values. The couples who use contract pregnancy are not seeking to make a profit, but to have a child. Some of them might even be willing to maintain an "extended family" relationship with the "surrogate" after the child's birth. Second, even if an asymmetry in motivation is established, it is also present in many types of service work: teaching, health care, and social work are all liable to result in "exploitation" of this sort. In all of these areas, the problem is at least partially addressed by regulating compensation. Why is contract pregnancy different?

The Consequences of Contract Pregnancy for Children

Susan Okin makes an argument against contract pregnancy that is based on its direct consequences for children, and not on the intrinsic features of reproductive labor or the bonds of motherhood. She argues that the problem with pregnancy contracts is that they do not consider the interests of the child.[37] Okin thus focuses on a different aspect of the concern that contract pregnancy leads us to adopt an inferior understanding of children. She points not to the conception itself, but to its consequences for children. The asymmetry, then, between reproductive labor and other forms of labor is based on the fact that only in the former are the child's interests directly at stake.

Putting aside the difficult question of what actually constitutes the child's best interests,[38] it is not certain that such interests will always be served by the child's remaining with its biological parents. Some children may be better off separated from their biological parents when such parents are abusive. No one would claim that children should always remain with their biological parents. Nevertheless, I agree with Okin that one problem with pregnancy contracts lies in their potential for weakening the biological ties that give children a secure place in the world.[39] If it can be shown that pregnancy contracts make children more vulnerable, for example, by encouraging parental exit, then such a consideration might contribute to calls for restricting or prohibiting such contracts.[40] Such an argument will have nothing to do with the special nature of reproductive labor, nor will it have to do with the special biological relationship between a parent and a child. It will remain valid even where the child bears no genetic relation to its parents. Children are vulnerable and dependent, and this vulnerability justifies the moral obligations parents have toward them. While this objection can be used to support the asymmetry thesis, it is important to note that asymmetrical vulnerabilities are found throughout the social world; they are not unique to the spheres of the family, sex, and reproduction. The same principles that will mandate against pregnancy contracts will also mandate against the use of child labor and argue for helping the disabled and the aged.

Nonetheless, this objection does point out an asymmetry between reproductive labor and other forms of labor. Can it be used to justify prohibiting contract pregnancy? One of the difficulties with evaluating pregnancy contracts in terms of their effects on children is that we have very little empirical evidence of these effects. The first reported case of pregnancy contract in the United States occurred in 1976.[41] Even with the more established practice of artificial insemination, no research is available on the effects of donor anonymity on the child. Nor do we know how different family structures, including single-parent and alternative families and adoption, affect children. We should be wary of prematurely making abstract arguments based on the child's best interests without any empirical evidence. Moreover, in the case of families whose life situation may be disapproved of by their community, we may have moral reasons for overriding the best interests of an individual child.[42] For example, if the child of a single or lesbian mother were to suffer discrimination, I do not think that this would justify removal of the child from the mother. Thus, while pregnancy contracts may threaten the interests of children, this is not yet established; nor is this consideration by itself a sufficient reason for forbidding such contracts.

Reproductive Labor and Equality

In the preceding three sections I have argued that the asymmetry thesis cannot be defended by claiming that there is something "essential" about reproductive labor that singles it out for different treatment from other forms of labor; nor by arguing that contract pregnancy distorts the nature of the bonds of motherhood; nor by the appeal to the best interests of the child. The arguments I have examined ignore the existing background conditions that underlie pregnancy contracts, many of which are objectionable. In addition, some of the arguments tend to accept uncritically the traditional picture of the family. Such arguments take current views of the maternal bond and the institution of motherhood as the baseline for judging pregnancy contracts—as if such views were not contested.

If we reject these arguments for the asymmetry thesis, are we forced back to the view that the market is indeed theoretically all-encompassing? Can we reject contract pregnancy, and defend the asymmetry thesis, without claiming either that reproductive labor is essentially not a commodity, or that it necessarily degrades the bonds between mothers and children, or that it is harmful to children?

I think that the strongest argument against contract pregnancy that depends upon the asymmetry thesis is derived from considerations of gender equality. It is this consideration that I believe is tacitly driving many of the arguments; for example, it is the background gender inequality that makes the commodification of women's and children's attributes especially objectionable. My criticism of contract pregnancy centers on the hypothesis that in our society such contracts will turn women's labor into something that is used and controlled by others[43] and will reinforce gender stereotypes that have been used to justify the unequal treatment of women.

Contrary to the democratic ideal, gender inequality is pervasive in our society. This inequality includes the unequal distribution of housework and child care that considerably restricts married women's opportunities in the workforce; the fact that the ratio between an average full-time working woman's earnings and those of her average male counterpart is 59.3:100,[44] and the fact that divorce is an economically devastating experience for women (during the 1970s, the standard of living of young divorced mothers fell 73 percent, while men's standard of living following divorce rose 42 percent).[45] These circumstances constitute the baseline from which women form their preferences and make their "choices." Thus, even a woman's choice to engage in commercial surrogacy must be viewed against a background of unequal opportunity. Most work done by women in our society remains in a "female ghetto": service and clerical work, secretarial work, cleaning, domestic labor, nursing, elementary school teaching, and waitressing.

I assume that there is something deeply objectionable about gender inequality. My argument is that contract pregnancy's reinforcing of this inequality lies at the heart of what is wrong with it. In particular, reproduction is a sphere that historically has been marked by inequality: women and men have not had equal influence over the institutions and practices involved in human reproduction. In its current form and context, contract pregnancy contributes to gender inequality in three ways:

1. Contract pregnancy gives others increased access to and control over women's bodies and sexuality. In a provocative book, Carmel Shalev argues that it is wrong to forbid a woman to sell her reproductive capacities when we already allow men to sell their sperm.[46] But Shalev ignores a crucial difference between artificial insemination by donor (AID) and a pregnancy contract. AID does not give anyone control over

men's bodies and sexuality. A man who elects AID simply sells a product of his body or his sexuality; he does not sell control over his body itself. The current practices of AID and pregnancy contracts are remarkably different in the scope of intervention and control they allow the "buyer." Pregnancy contracts involve substantial control over women's bodies.[47]

What makes this control objectionable, however, is not the intrinsic features of women's reproductive labor, but rather the ways in which such control reinforces a long history of unequal treatment. Consider an analogous case that has no such consequence: voluntary (paid) military service, where men sell their fighting capacities. Military service, like contract pregnancy, involves significant invasions into the body of the seller; soldiers' bodies are controlled to a large extent by their commanding officers under conditions in which the stakes are often life and death. But military service does not *directly* serve to perpetuate traditional gender inequalities.[48] The fact that pregnancy contracts, like military contracts, give someone control over someone else's body is not the issue. Rather, the issue is that in contract pregnancy the body that is controlled belongs to a woman, in a society that historically has subordinated women's interests to those of men, primarily through its control over her sexuality and reproduction.

Market theorists might retort that contract pregnancy could be regulated to protect women's autonomy, in the same way that we regulate other labor contracts. However, it will be difficult, given the nature of the interests involved, for such contracts not to be very intrusive with respect to women's bodies in spite of formal agreements. The purpose of such contracts is, after all, to produce a healthy child. In order to help guarantee a healthy baby, a woman's behavior must be highly controlled.[49]

Moreover, if the pregnancy contract is a contract for reproductive labor, then, as in other types of labor contracts, compliance—what the law terms "specific performance"—cannot be enforced. For example, if I contract to paint your house, and I default on my agreement, you can sue me for breaking the contract, but even if you win, the courts will not require me to paint your house. Indeed, this is the salient difference between even poorly paid wage labor and indentured servitude. Thus, by analogy, if the woman in a pregnancy contract defaults on her agreement and decides to keep the child, the other parties should not be able to demand performance (that is, surrender of the child); rather, they can demand monetary compensation.[50]

This inability to enforce performance in pregnancy contracts may have consequences for the *content* of such contracts that will make them especially objectionable. Recall that such contracts occur over a long period of time, during which a woman may undergo fundamental changes in her willingness to give up the child. The other parties will need some mechanism to ensure her compliance. There are two mechanisms that are likely to produce compliance, but both are objectionable: (a) The contract could be set up so that payment is delivered to the woman only after the child is born. But this structure of compensation closely resembles baby-selling; it now looks as if what is being bought is not the woman's services, but the child itself. Thus, if baby-selling is wrong, then we should be very troubled by the fact that, in order to be self-enforcing, contract pregnancy must use incentives that make it resemble baby-selling. (b) The contract could mandate legal and psychological counseling for a woman who is tempted to change her mind. Given that it is hard to imagine in advance what it means to surrender a child, such counseling could involve a great deal of manipulation and coercion of the woman's emotions.[51]

2. Contract pregnancy reinforces stereotypes about the proper role of women in the reproductive division of labor. At a time when women have made strides in labor force participation, moving out of the family into other social spheres, pregnancy contracts provide a monetary incentive for women to remain in the home.[52] And, while some women may "prefer" to stay at home, we need to pay attention to the limited range of economic opportunities available to these women, and to the ways in which these opportunities have shaped their preferences. Under present conditions, pregnancy contracts entrench a traditional division of labor—men at work, women in the home—based on gender.

Additionally, pregnancy contracts will affect the way society views women: they will tend to reinforce the view of women as "baby machines."[53] It is also likely that they will affect the way women see themselves. Insofar as the sale of women's reproductive capacities contributes to the social subordination of women, and only of women, there are antidiscrimination grounds for banning it.

3. Contract pregnancy raises the danger, manifested in several recent court rulings, that "motherhood" will be defined in terms of genetic material, in the same way as "fatherhood." Mary Beth Whitehead won back parental rights to Baby M on the basis of her being the genetic "mother." On the other hand, Anna Johnson, a "gestational" surrogate, lost such rights because she bore no genetic relationship to the child.[54] These court rulings establish the principle of parenthood on the basis of genetic contribution. In such cases, women's contribution to

reproduction is recognized only insofar as it is identical to that of men. Genes alone are taken to define natural and biological motherhood. By not taking women's actual gestational contributions into account, the courts reinforce an old stereotype of women as merely the incubators of men's seeds.[55] In fact, the court's inattention to women's unique labor contribution is itself a form of unequal treatment. By defining women's rights and contributions in terms of those of men, when they are different, the courts fail to recognize an adequate basis for women's rights and needs. These rulings place an additional burden on women.[56]

Given its consequences for gender inequality, I think that the asymmetry thesis is true, and that pregnancy contracts are especially troubling. Current gender inequality lies at the heart of what is wrong with pregnancy contracts. The problem with commodifying women's reproductive labor is not that it "degrades" the special nature of reproductive labor, or "alienates" women from a core part of their identities, but that it reinforces a traditional gender-hierarchical division of labor. A consequence of my argument is that under very different background conditions, in which men and women had equal power and had an equal range of choices, such contracts would be less objectionable.[57] For example, in a society in which women's work was valued as much as men's and in which child care was shared equally, pregnancy contracts might serve primarily as a way for single persons, disabled persons, and same-sex families to have children. Indeed, pregnancy contracts and similar practices have the potential to transform the nuclear family. We know too little about possible new forms of family life to restrict such experiments on a priori grounds; but in our society, I have argued that there are consequentialist reasons for making this restriction.

At the same time, there are potential caveats to the acceptability of a regulated form of pregnancy contract even under conditions of gender equality: (1) the importance of background economic inequality;[58] (2) the effect of the practice on race equality; (3) the need to ensure the woman's participation in the overall purpose of the activity; and (4) the need to ensure that the vulnerable—children—are protected. We know very little about the prerequisites for psychologically healthy children. We know very little about the effects of pregnancy contracts on parental exit or on the other children of the birth mother.[59] For this reason, even under more ideal circumstances, there is reason to be cautious about the potential use of such contracts. For the time being, I believe that pregnancy contracts should be discouraged. This can be done by making such contracts unenforceable in the courts. Furthermore, in contested cases, the courts should recognize no distinction between genetic and gestational "surrogates" with respect to parental rights. Finally, brokerage of pregnancy contracts should be illegal. These proposals aim to discourage contract pregnancy and to strengthen the position of the "surrogate," who is the most economically and emotionally vulnerable party in any such arrangement.

Conclusion: Wage Labor, Reproductive Labor, and Equality

In this article, I have analyzed various grounds for forbidding markets in women's reproductive labor. While I rejected most of these grounds, including the essentialist thesis, the opposing approach of market theorists misses the point that there are noneconomic values that should constrain social policy. Market theorists, in representing all of human behavior as if it were a product of voluntary choice, ignore the fact of unequal power in the family and in the wider society.

While market theorists often defend their approach in terms of the values of liberty, welfare, and neutrality, they abstract away from the inegalitarian social context in which an individual's preferences are formed. But how preferences are formed, and in the light of what range of choices,[60] has a great deal to do with whether or not acting on those preferences is liberty- and welfare-enhancing.[61] Under some circumstances, for example, it could be welfare-enhancing to sell oneself into slavery.[62]

What about liberal neutrality? Market theorists may claim that the asymmetry thesis is a violation of liberal neutrality: it imposes a standard of gender equality on free exchanges. Furthermore, it may seem biased—distinguishing activities that harm women from those that harm everyone. The issue of neutrality is a difficult matter to assess, for there are many interpretations of neutrality. At the very least, however, two considerations seem relevant. First, why should existing distributions serve as the standard against which neutrality is measured? I have argued that it is a mistake to assume that the realm of reproduction and sexuality is "neutral"; it is a product (at least in part) of the unequal social, political, and economic power of men and women. Second, most liberals draw the line at social practices such as slavery, indentured servitude, labor at slave wages, and the selling of votes or political liberties. Each of these practices undermines a framework of free deliberation among equals. If such restrictions violate viewpoint "neutrality," then the mere violation of neutrality does not seem objectionable.

Contract pregnancy places women's bodies under the control of others and serves to perpetuate gender inequality. The asymmetries of gender—the fact of social relations of gender domination—provide the best foundation for the asymmetry thesis. However, not all of the negative consequences of contract pregnancy involve its effects on gender inequality. I have also referred to its possible effects on children, and to the problematic form that such contracts will have to take to be self-enforcing. In addition, a full assessment of the practice would have to consider both its potential for deepening racial inequality and the unequal bargaining power of the parties to the contract. Some of these features of pregnancy contracts are shared with other labor contracts. Indeed, there is an important tradition in social philosophy that argues that it is precisely these shared features that make wage labor itself unacceptable. This tradition emphasizes that wage labor, like contract pregnancy, places the productive capacities of one group of citizens at the service and under the control of another. Unfortunately, there has been little attention in political philosophy to the effects of gender and class inequality on the development of women's and workers' deliberative capacities or on the formation of their preferences. We have to ask: What kinds of work and family relations and environments best promote the development of the deliberative capacities needed to support democratic institutions?

Notes

1. See Karl Polanyi, *The Great Transformation* (Boston: Beacon Press, 1970); Gosta Esping-Anderson, *Politics Against Markets: The Social Democratic Road to Power* (Princeton: Princeton University Press, 1985); Michael Walzer, *Spheres of Justice: A Defense of Pluralism and Equality* (New York: Basic Books, 1983); Richard M. Titmuss, *The Gift Relationship: From Human Blood to Social Policy* (New York: Pantheon Books, 1971); Margaret Jane Radin, "Market-Inalienability," *Harvard Law Review* 100 (1987): 1849–1937; Viviana A. Zelizer, "Human Values and the Market: The Case of Life Insurance and Death in Nineteenth Century America," *American Journal of Sociology* 84 (1978): 591–610.

2. I will use the terms *contract pregnancy* and *pregnancy contract* in place of the misleading term *surrogacy.* The so-called surrogate mother is not a surrogate; she is the biological and/or gestational mother. In this article, I do not make any assumptions about who is and who is not a "real" mother.

3. See Elizabeth S. Anderson, "Is Women's Labor a Commodity?" *Philosophy and Public Affairs* 19, no. 1 (Winter 1990): 71–92; Christine Overall,

188   *Debra Satz*

Ethics and Human Reproduction: A Feminist Analysis (Boston: Allen and Unwin, 1987); Mary Warnock, *A Question of Life: The Warnock Report on Human Fertilization and Embryology* (Oxford: Basil Blackwell, 1985); Martha Field, *Surrogate Motherhood: The Legal and Human Issues* (Cambridge, Mass.: Harvard University Press, 1988); Gena Corea, *The Mother Machine* (New York: Harper and Row, 1985); Carole Pateman, *The Sexual Contract* (Stanford: Stanford University Press, 1988). Not all of the arguments against contract pregnancy in these texts depend on the asymmetry thesis.

4. Anderson, "Women's Labor," 75.

5. I believe that my argument can also be applied to the case of prostitution, but I do not pursue that point in this article.

6. See Anita Allen, "Surrogacy, Slavery and the Ownership of Life," *Harvard Journal of Law and Public Policy* 13 (1990): 139–49.

7. See Amy Z. Overvold, *Surrogate Parenting* (New York: Pharos Books, 1988); Elizabeth Kane, *The Birth Mother* (San Diego: Harcourt Brace Jovanovich, 1988).

8. Radin, "Market-Inalienability," 1859. Radin refers to this view as "universal commodification."

9. The theoretical assumption that everything is commodifiable characterizes a range of modern economic theories. It is found in both liberal welfare economics and in the conservative economics of the Chicago School. In welfare economics, there are technical reasons for this assumption: Walrasian equilibrium theory, as generalized by Arrow and Debreu, depends on there being markets in everything, including futures, uncertainty, and public goods. In order to demonstrate the existence of a general equilibrium, all goods must be included in the equations.

The economists of the Chicago School argue that most things should be treated as commodities. They start with the assumption that rational human beings make their choices according to economic principles. Gary Becker, for example, has claimed that all human behavior can be understood in terms of maximizing efficiency, market equilibrium, and stable preferences. Becker's work uses these assumptions to explain criminal punishment, marriage, childbearing, education, and racial discrimination. See Becker, *The Economic Approach to Human Behavior* (Chicago: University of Chicago Press, 1976). (For criticisms of the application of Walrasian equilibrium theory to certain domains, see Joseph Stiglitz, "The Causes and Consequences of the Dependence of Quality on Price," *Journal of Economic Literature* 25 [1987]: 1–48; Louis Putterman, "On Some Recent Explanations of Why Capital Hires Wage Labor," in *The Economic Nature of the Firm*, ed. Putterman [Cambridge: Cambridge University Press, 1986]; Samuel Bowles and Herbert Gintis, "Contested Exchange: New Microfoundations for the Political Economy of Capitalism," *Politics and Society* 18 [1990]: 165–222.)

10. The first welfare theorem holds only under specific conditions, for example, where external economies and diseconomies are absent.

11. See Milton Friedman, *Capitalism and Freedom* (Chicago: University of Chicago Press, 1962).

12. See Will Kymlicka, "Rethinking the Family," *Philosophy and Public Affairs* 20, no. 1 (Winter 1991): 95–96.

13. In *Birthpower* (New Haven, Conn.: Yale University Press, 1989) Carmel Shalev develops a powerful defense of contract pregnancy that draws on considerations of liberty, welfare, and liberal neutrality. She argues that it is a matter of the "constitutional privacy" of individuals to define legal parenthood in terms of their prior-to-conception intentions; that contract pregnancy will empower women and improve their welfare by unleashing a new source of economic wealth; and that the market is neutral between competing conceptions of human relationships.

14. See Robert Nozick, *Anarchy, State and Utopia* (New York: Basic Books, 1974), 331.

15. See Anderson, "Women's Labor," 72.

16. In cases of in vitro fertilization, reproductive labor is divided between two women.

17. See Katha Pollitt, "When Is a Mother Not a Mother?" *The Nation* (31 December 1990): 843.

18. See Orlando Paterson, *Slavery and Social Death* (Cambridge, Mass.: Harvard University Press, 1982) for comparisons between slaves and athletes.

19. Pateman, *The Sexual Contract*, 207.

20. Freudian theory, with its emphasis on "natural" drives, might give us such reasons, but Pateman does not explicitly endorse such a theory.

21. Warnock, *A Question of Life*, 45.

22. See Anderson, "Women's Labor," 72.

23. Margaret Jane Radin, "Justice and the Market Domain," in *Markets and Justice*, ed. John W. Chapman and J. R. Pennock (New York: New York University Press, 1989), 175.

24. However, I believe that there should be limits on the sale of housing: poor people should not be displaced from their homes for someone else's profit. But in this case, as in contract pregnancy, I think that markets should be limited by considerations of equality. For an interesting alternative approach, see Margaret Jane Radin. "Residential Rent Control," *Philosophy and Public Affairs* 15, no. 4 (Fall 1986): 350–380.

25. Radin calls our attention to the problem of the "double bind": under current conditions of inequality, there are negative external effects of both banning and allowing pregnancy contracts. See Radin, "Market-Inalienability," 1917.

26. Anderson, "Women's Labor," 81.

27. See Orange County Superior Court Judge Richard Parslow's ruling in which he referred to birth mother Anna Johnson as a "home" for an embryo and not a "mother" (*New York Times,* 23 October 1990).

28. *In the Matter of Baby M,* 537 A. 2d 1227 (N.J. 1988).

29. Michael Bratman has suggested that the analogy between abortion and contract pregnancy breaks down in the following way. In contract pregnancy, a woman gets pregnant with the intention of giving up the child. There is presumably no analogous intention in the case of abortion: few women, if any, intentionally get pregnant in order to have an abortion. Critics of contract pregnancy might claim that intentionally conceiving a child either to give it up for money or to abort it is immoral. I am not persuaded by such arguments. If abortion is murder, then it is so regardless of the intentions involved. My own view is that the best argument in favor of the right to abortion makes no reference to intentions, but concerns the consequences of abortion restrictions for women, restrictions that, moreover, directly burden only women.

30. See Adrienne Rich, *Of Women Born: Motherhood as Experience and Institution* (New York: Norton, 1976).

31. See Radin, "Market-Inalienability," 1927.

32. Warnock, *A Question of Life,* 45.

33. Anderson, "Women's Labor," 78.

34. I owe this suggestion to Rachel Cohon.

35. Anderson, "Women's Labor," 84.

36. Philip Parker, "Motivation of Surrogate Mothers: Initial Findings," *American Journal of Psychiatry* 140 (1983): 117–18. I am grateful to Elizabeth Anderson for bringing this article to my attention.

37. Susan Okin, "A Critique of Pregnancy Contracts: Comments on Articles by Hill, Merrick, Shevory, and Woliver," *Politics and the Life Sciences* 8 (1990): 205–10.

38. See Jon Elster, *Solomonic Judgements* (Cambridge: Cambridge University Press, 1989) for a discussion of the difficulties of ascertaining the best interests of the child. Elster is also skeptical of the idea that the best interests of the child should necessarily prevail in custody disputes.

39. Anderson raises this point as well. See "Women's Labor," 80.

40. We must be careful in considering the scope of this argument. Divorce and adoption, for example, may weaken the ties between children and parents, but very few people would be willing to give the state the right to forbid divorce or adoption on such grounds.

41. D. Gelman and E. Shapiro, "Infertility: Babies by Contract," *Newsweek* (4 November 1985).

42. See Elster, *Solomonic Judgements,* 148ff.

43. Of course, pregnancy contracts also give another woman, the adoptive mother, control over the body of the surrogate mother. The important point here is that in a society characterized by gender inequalities, such contracts put women's bodies at the disposal of others.

44. This figure compares the earnings of white women and white men. In 1980, black and Hispanic women earned, respectively, 55.3 percent and 40.1 percent of white men's earnings. See Sara M. Evans and Barbara Nelson, *Wage Justice: Comparable Worth and the Paradox of Technocratic Reform* (Chicago: University of Chicago Press, 1989).

45. Leonore J. Weitzman, *The Divorce Revolution: The Unexpected Social and Economic Consequences for Women and Children in America* (New York: The Free Press, 1985), 323.

46. Shalev, *Birthpower.*

47. A man who buys women's reproductive labor can choose his "surrogate"; he does not legally require his wife's permission; pregnancy contracts include substantial provisions regulating the surrogate's behavior. Such provisions include agreements concerning medical treatment, the conditions under which the surrogate agrees to undergo an abortion, and regulation of the surrogate's emotions. Thus, in the case of Baby M, Mary Beth Whitehead consented to refrain from forming or attempting to form any relationship with the child she would conceive. She agreed not to smoke cigarettes, drink alcoholic beverages, or take medications without written consent from her physician. She also agreed to undergo amniocentesis and to abort the fetus "upon demand of William Stern, natural father" if tests found genetic or congenital defects. See "Appendix: Baby M Contract," *Beyond Baby M,* ed. Dianne Bartels (Clifton, N.J.: Humana Press, 1990).

48. This is not to imply that voluntary military service is not objectionable on other grounds, a question that I cannot discuss here.

49. There is already legal precedent for regulating women's behavior in the "best interests" of the fetus. A Massachusetts (sic) woman was charged with vehicular homicide when her fetus was delivered stillborn following a car accident. See Eileen McNamara, "Fetal Endangerment Cases on the Rise," *Boston Globe,* 3 October 1989; cited in Lawrence Tribe, *Abortion: The Clash of Absolutes* (New York: Norton, 1990).

50. This analogy may be complicated by the fact that the other parties to the contract may have at least some biological relationship to the child.

51. Anderson also makes this point. See "Women's Labor," 84ff.

52. This is not to imply that the current sexual division of labor, in which women are disproportionately involved in unpaid domestic work, is just.

53. See Corea, *The Mother Machine.*

54. Anita Allen, in "Ownership of Life," has pointed to the disturbing possibilities contract pregnancy poses for racial equality. In cases like *Johnson v. Calvert,* where the gestator (surrogate), Johnson, was a black woman and the Calverts were white and Filipina, it is difficult to imagine a judge awarding the baby to Johnson. For example, there are almost no adoption cases in which a healthy white infant is placed with black parents. In his ruling in *Johnson v. Calvert,* Judge Parslow referred to Johnson as the baby's "wet nurse." Any full assessment of contract pregnancy must consider the implications of the practice for women of color.

55. The medieval church held that the male implanted into the female body a fully formed homunculus (complete with a soul). See Barbara Ehrenreich and Deidre English, *Witches, Midwives and Nurses: A History of Women Healers* (Old Westbury, N.Y.: Feminist Press, 1973).

56. For a perceptive discussion of the ways in which the social treatment of difference has been used to perpetuate inequalities, see Martha Minow, *Making All the Difference* (Ithaca, N.Y.: Cornell University Press, 1990).

57. Of course, under different conditions, the importance of genetically based ties between parents and children might decline.

58. According to a 1987 study by the U.S. Office of Technology Assessment, the typical clients of surrogate parenting agencies are white; 64 percent have annual incomes of over $50,000. By contrast, 66 percent of the "surrogates" reported annual incomes of less than $30,000.

59. See n. 7 above.

60. I am indebted to Elisabeth Wood for many discussions about the importance of the "range of choice" in evaluating social practices.

61. Cass Sunstein has criticized the tendency of a wide range of political views to take preferences as given, without attention to the background conditions that shaped them. See his "Preferences and Politics," *Philosophy and Public Affairs* 20, no. 1 (Winter 1991): 3–34.

62. See Patterson, *Slavery and Social Death,* for a discussion of such circumstances.

Questions

1. How does reproductive labor differ from other forms of labor? If essentialists use these characteristics as an argument to support asymmetry, according to Satz, what problems arise?

2. Satz's argument against contract pregnancies is based on gender inequality. Explain her argument. Do you agree with her position? If an apparently autonomous woman wants to make her living as a contracted mother, should feminists criticize her?

3. How might someone who defends the asymmetry thesis argue that a contract pregnancy causes parents to view children as mere commodities? How does Satz respond?

4. Discuss Satz's beliefs about the asymmetry thesis. How does she apply the asymmetry thesis to contract pregnancies? Do you agree? Explain your reasons.

5. How is the work of a woman who has joined the military for one year and is on call twenty-four hours a day similar to the work of a woman with a contracted pregnancy? What differences are there between the two? Can you think of other occupations that might be compared with contracted pregnancy?

6. How might Satz's argument about reproductive labor be applied to the case of prostitution?

9

Privacy and Reproductive Liberty

Anita L. Allen

Privacy is commonly pointed to as part of what is at stake in the choice between competing reproductive rights policies. Yet it is not always clear what is meant by "privacy" and hence what forms of privacy are at stake. This essay will identify the most important forms of privacy at stake in the quest for basic reproductive liberties and explain why respect for these forms of privacy should be deemed a major impetus toward policies that maximize women's choices.

Motherhood and Intrafamilial Privacy

Seclusion, Solitude, and Anonymity

Complete privacy is as undesirable as its opposite. Nevertheless, a degree of privacy is of value to individuals and the communities to which they potentially contribute. Personal privacy can be characterized as a degree of inaccessibility of persons, their mental states, or information about them to the senses and surveillance devices of others. Seclusion, the inaccessibility of the physical person, is a basic, indeed, paradigmatic form of personal privacy in this sense. Solitude, or being alone, is a particular kind of seclusion, namely, solitary as opposed to shared seclusion. People who live alone normally achieve solitude simply by entering their homes. The story is quite different for cohabitants of a shared residence. Without space or rooms of their own in which to further seclude themselves, they may seldom possess either solitude or the form of privacy known as anonymity.

In a familiar sense of the term, "anonymity" denotes not having one's name or identity known to others. In the broader sense favored by privacy theorists and intended here, "anonymity" denotes not having attention paid to one.[1]

In this broader sense, anonymity can be a reasonable expectation of privacy even in the context of nuclear family life where, it goes without saying, one's name, identity, and background are known. When attention is being paid a person, it is accompanied by implied pressure to limit conduct to publicly acceptable standards. One seeks to fit in and to avoid opprobrium, shame, embarrassment, and negative sanctions.[2] While conformity to public norms is relaxed considerably within the typical family, there are often further, family norms that govern conduct. Family members reasonably seek periodic relief from such norms. Intrafamilial privacy provides opportunities to be free of the social requirements imposed by both the public and the family.

The family home has come to symbolize what it does not in fact always represent—both the shared seclusion of good times spent with others and the solitudinous, anonymous seclusion of good times spent alone. Sharing a home can make seclusion within it anything but satisfying. The burdens and responsibilities that arise out of commitments, dependencies, crowding, incompatible lifestyles, clashing personalities, and emotional conflicts can make a shared residence oppressive. Crowding, for example, diminishes opportunities for solitude and anonymity and can diminish the pleasure of intimate contact. In some cases the most meaningful opportunities for solitude and anonymity in a person's life may be time spent at work in a private office or in a public park, where the obligation to interact with others is circumscribed. Life outside the home may be the truer haven.

Is Motherhood Consistent with Privacy?

The foregoing points are obvious, but have the greatest importance for a woman's decision whether to have a child. Motherhood and family life typically entail that women sacrifice a good deal of their privacy. In many circumstances the birth of a child will entail that too much privacy be sacrificed. Feminist Charlotte Perkins Gilman only slightly overstated the conflict between family life and privacy when she wrote in 1898:

> Such privacy as we have at home is family privacy, an aggregate privacy; and this does not insure—indeed, it prevents—individual privacy. . . . The home is the one place on earth where no one of the component individuals can have any privacy. . . . At present any tendency to withdraw and live

one's own life on any plane of separate interest or industry is naturally resented, or at least regretted, by the other members of the family. This affects women more than men, because men live very little in the family and very much in the world.[3]

Contrary to Gilman, there *can* be privacy in a family home. Indeed, where family size is limited, space is sufficient, and there are mutual respect, discipline, and cooperation, a household can offer quite a lot of intrafamilial privacy. Family life, however, plainly presents the potential for conflict between adequate privacy, especially solitude and anonymity, and adequate participation in and responsibility toward the family. Gilman was correct in her recognition that women's roles as guardians of the private sphere have been a special obstacle to their attainment of adequate privacy.

If I am right that intrafamilial privacy is possible, then it follows that advocacy of meaningful opportunities for privacy and the conditions of life that make them practicable is not a rejection of motherhood and the family. Should motherhood and the family be rejected for other reasons? The family is not beyond reproach as a social institution. The family has been celebrated in Western society in sentimental, moral, and pragmatic terms as both a valuable educational vehicle for the transmission of culture and as an efficient economic unit, satisfying the need for food, clothing, shelter, and productive work. The philosopher who may have been the first to examine carefully the question of the justice of the family was ambivalent about the institution. While he rejected the family as a form of life for the ruling elite of his ideal republic, Plato not only embraced it for the artisans or "working classes," but also prescribed that elites live together in communes and be encouraged to think of themselves as family kin, for the sake of social harmony.[4]

Sharing Plato's ambivalence, some modern political theorists have viewed the moral justice of the family for individuals and that aggregate of society as an open question. In *Theory of Justice,* John Rawls suggested that the result of grouping persons into families with unequal social, educational, and economic resources is the imperfect carrying out of what he called the "principle of fair opportunity."[5] This principle requires that social institutions be constituted so as to ensure that each person has a fair chance to enjoy society's benefits. Children from happier and wealthier families tend to have better opportunities than equally deserving children from troubled and poorer families. Rawls maintained that because of the inequalities it perpetuates, the family is consistent with justice only to the extent that it contributes goods that redound even to the benefit of those most disadvantaged by family life.[6]

Ambivalence about the family has also stemmed from recognition of its implications for moral justice toward women. In recent decades feminist theorists have advocated the rejection or reform of the family. With analyses reminiscent of Frederick Engels's *The Origin of the Family, Private Property and the State,*[7] radical feminists have concluded that the male-dominated modern monogamous family has been inimical to social justice for its subjugation of women (and children) and should be rejected. Others have rejected the male-dominated family, but urged that the family is a redeemable institution. In this vein, Jean Bethke Elshtain has argued for family reconstruction. Elshtain perceives the family as a moral imperative for the human nurturance of children. But she rightly calls for the articulation of a "particular idea of family life that does not repeat the terms of female oppression and exploitation."[8]

While the problem of privacy at home for mothers can be especially severe in the male-dominated family, it exists as well in female-headed families and in egalitarian families where women share decision-making authority with partners. Women welcome some of the obstacles to privacy posed by motherhood. Maternal and familial love, like romantic love, make solitude and anonymity less attractive. Mothers often want nothing more than to be in the company of their families and to have their attention. Familial love is an obstacle to privacy. Nevertheless, many women doubtless undertake family life precisely to have and give love. They are anxious to assume the characteristic commitment of responsiveness to the emotional, social, and economic needs of children and partners. These women "no longer want to exist as persons for themselves as they do in the area of abstract right characterized by property, contract, and punishment for injustice, or as mere isolated subjects with their own private resolutions, intentions, conscience . . . but as real social members, living with each other."[9] Still, some obstacles to solitude and anonymity are not welcomed and could not be welcomed, even by women who have voluntarily undertaken family life.

A child can be such an obstacle.[10] While older children are capable of intentionally invading the privacy of those with whom they live, it is not chiefly for this reason that children in general constitute an obstacle to privacy for their mothers. The main reason they are a privacy obstacle is that children must be closely cared for and must have ready access to those who care for them.

Planning for Privacy

Simply put, contraception and abortion can be utilized to assure that children are not born who would constitute an obstacle to the attainment of privacy. Safe contraception is an inexpensive tool for assuring privacy. Abortion, the emotional costs of which are often substantially greater than the emotional costs of contraception, is also a birth prevention tool. It reduces the number of persons with whom a sexually active younger woman is likely to have to share a home and for whom she would be responsible. Absent contraception and abortion, there would be more unwanted pregnancies, more births, and more children to be cared for by women. It is impossible to know precisely how many births are prevented through the use of contraceptives, but we do have a good idea of how many births are prevented as a result of medical abortions.

Approximately 1.5 million abortions are performed in the U.S. each year. Viewed as a social phenomenon, abortion rights may have the effect of indirectly preventing more births than the number of annual abortions procedures suggests. In *Abortion and the Politics of Motherhood* (1984), Kristin Luker cited empirical evidence that outlawing abortion could turn public opinion against the pill, the IUD, and treatment after rape. Public disapproval of birth control could reduce reliance on contraception and raise the birthrate.

Mothers, rather than fathers or couples, still typically assume primary responsibility for the direct care of children. Mothers closely share their lives with each of their children for eighteen years or more. Spouses, fathers, and extended families can relieve women of responsibilities that compete with privacy. Increasingly, due to mobility, divorce, and women working outside the home, such assistance is not readily available. Few birth-mothers, even teen-aged and unmarried birth-mothers, exercise the adoption option afforded by law. Instead, typical mothers choose to retain responsibility for their offspring.

Creating adequate privacy for herself (and any other members of her household) may require financial resources that women with children do not have. Affluent women can purchase professional childcare, babysitters, additional living space, and vacations, all of which allow family members to escape from one another from time to time. However, not all women of means view giving over childcare responsibilities to others as a viable option. Consideration of the child's best interest and of doing what is morally best may preclude apparent options. For example, many thoughtful women reasonably conclude—with expert concurrence—that the well-being and safety of their children should not be entrusted to preschool day-care centers.[11] As another example, conscientious women may feel morally compelled by traditional secular and religious values to reject day care and similar options, even at great cost to their freedom and privacy. Moral and religious considerations, as well as financial limitations and considerations for the safety and well-being of the child, help to determine the extent to which having a child obstructs a woman's attainment of privacy.

Sharing a life with a child has a psychological dimension that may undermine a woman's effort to create privacy and freedom by delegating childcare responsibilities. Few women today have fallen prey to the late-nineteenth-century middle-class myth that failure to lavish every moment upon one's children could jeopardize the whole of civilization. Nonetheless, a mother's active concern and sense of responsibility do not end when her infant is placed under the charge of a sitter or her child heads off to school or to play. Carol Gilligan and others have pointed out that women with children strongly identify with them and their needs. A mother may cease to define herself as an individual and view herself as the composite of her child and herself. Mothers have been known to feel without purpose and identity when children to whom they have devoted themselves leave home for good.

Sexually active younger women who do not want children, who want no more children, or who want to postpone children must rely on contraception and abortion to preserve and achieve desired levels of solitude and anonymity in their lives. Most deeply, privacy must be valued for promoting individuating traits and well-being called for by personhood, social participation, and contribution. And while individuality is not as important among family members, who inevitably share a common history and many of the same values and aspirations, it goes without saying that respect for personhood, participation, and contribution have value inside the family as well as out.

While solitude and anonymity can represent vacant, nongoal-directed time of one's own, these forms of privacy are often prerequisites for fulfilling educational, artistic, and professional aspirations. Privacy in private life provides the best opportunity in our society for relaxation, rejuvenation, reflection, and nurturing traits that can potentially distinguish one in the larger, public world. Contributions within the private sphere are not to be demeaned, but contributions to the public must not be foreclosed. It is plain why privacy, as opportunity for self-development, is essential for women if they are to continue progress toward social equality.

Contraception

The use of contraception is lawful in the United States. Respect for privacy and privacy-related liberties demands that it remain so. Where the law prohibits contraception, sexually active fertile women are exposed to the possibility of recurrent pregnancies. Each pregnancy represents potential privacy losses for women and others in their households. Laws prohibiting contraception also expose women to privacy intrusions by persons outside the family. Enforcement of laws banning contraception invite law enforcement officials into the seclusion of the bedroom. Beyond that, laws banning contraception would invite the courts to inspect the intimacies and privacies of home life to ascertain whether contraceptive practices measure up to the legal standard.

Supreme Court Justice William O. Douglas raised these privacy concerns in *Griswold v. Connecticut* when he posed the now-famous question "Would we allow the police to search the sacred precincts of marital bedrooms for telltale signs of the use of contraceptives?"[12] Douglas answered the question as he knew his readers would: "The very idea is repulsive to . . . notions of privacy."

With the *Griswold* case, the Supreme Court struck down unconstitutional Connecticut anticontraception statutes. The statutes provided, first, that persons using any "drug, medicine or instrument for the purpose of preventing contraception" be fined, imprisoned, or both; and second, that any person "who assists, abets, or counsels, causes, hires, or commands another to commit an offense," including use of contraception, be prosecuted as if he were the principle offender. The executive and medical directors of the Planned Parenthood League of Connecticut, Estelle T. Griswold and Dr. Charles Lee Buxton, had been arrested and convicted after giving contraception information, instruction, and medical advice to a married couple. Ms. Griswold was determined to test the legality of the state laws criminalizing contraception and virtually sought out arrest after she opened a birth control clinic in New Haven.[13] In the ensuing Supreme Court proceedings, the two directors were found to have the legal standing to raise in their own defense the constitutional rights of the married people with whom they had a professional relationship. On the basis of rights of privacy and repose emanating from the penumbra of the Bill of Rights, the Court held that states may not prohibit use of contraceptives by married couples.

In a later case, *Eisenstadt v. Baird,* the Court went further, holding a Massachusetts statute prohibiting distribution of contraceptives to unmarried persons unconstitutional.[14] Defendant William Baird had been convicted of violating provisions of the Massachusetts General Laws after he exhibited contraceptive articles in the course of a lecture at Boston University and gave an unmarried woman a package of Emko vaginal foam. As a result of *Griswold* and *Baird,* the decisional privacy of adult women to safeguard their privacy at home through contraceptive use is now legally protected. The Court has not always taken care to distinguish decisional privacy from paradigmatic forms of privacy, such as solitude and anonymity. It is now evident that they can and should be distinguished, and that decisional privacy is a key to women's attainment of paradigmatic forms of privacy.

Aborting for Privacy

It is conceivable that attempts to enforce laws regulating abortion could lead to intrusions upon the seclusion of women in their homes and in the offices of health-care providers. Seclusion interests number among those privacy interests women have that oppose abortion prohibitions and some abortion control laws. Even so, women's interests in decisional privacy rather than privacy in the sense of seclusion were the focus of pathbreaking abortion rights cases.

In *Roe v. Wade* and *Doe v. Bolton,* the Supreme Court invalidated statutes criminalizing procurement or administration of abortion.[15] *Roe* plaintiff "Jane Roe" was actually Norma McCorvey, a poor, uneducated Dallas woman. Unable to obtain a legal abortion in Texas, she felt compelled to have the child and put it up for adoption. Her suit alleged that the Texas abortion statutes were unconstitutionally vague and abridged her right of personal privacy protected by the First, Fourth, Fifth, Ninth, and Fourteenth Amendments. Additional *Roe* plaintiffs were a childless couple, "John and Mary Doe," and a licensed physician, Dr. James Hallford. The Texas abortion statutes before the Court in Roe provided for prison sentences of up to ten years. Statutes in various states criminalizing attempted abortion were also at issue in *Roe.* For example, under Massachusetts law, attempted abortion was a crime that carried fines up to $1,000.

Writing for the majority in *Roe,* Justice Harry Blackmun explained that while states may assert a legitimate interest in safeguarding health, maintaining medical standards, and protecting prenatal life, women have a fundamental constitutional right of privacy to decide for themselves in the early stages of pregnancy whether or not to give birth to a child. Their right of privacy—choice free of governmental interference—is implicit in the concept of liberty.[16] As a result of the *Roe* decision and later cases clarifying its meaning, pre-viability abortions are available to adult women "on demand" and to some minors without parental consent. *Roe,* its progeny, and the moral and jurisprudential problems they raise have been extensively analyzed and debated.[17]

Decisional privacy was the focus of *Roe,* but the concepts of seclusion and solitude arose subtly in the Court's opinion in the context of explicating the nature of the pregnant woman's claims against her unborn and the right of the state to interfere on behalf of viable fetal life. Justice Blackmun suggested that the pregnant woman shares whatever condition of physical privacy she enjoys with a developing entity, and that therein lies the problem: "The pregnant woman cannot be isolated in her privacy. She carries an embryo and, later, a fetus. . . . [A]t some point in time . . . [t]he woman's privacy is no longer sole and any right of privacy she possesses must be measured accordingly."[18] This confused passage has doubtless helped to convince opponents of *Roe* that the Supreme Court's privacy analysis is incoherent. Justice Blackmun's words suggest that he subscribes to a non sequitur: as an embryo approaches maturity it becomes progressively less true that the pregnant woman possesses actual physical privacy and therefore less true that she possesses a right to decisional privacy.

Why suppose with Blackmun that a woman's decisional privacy rights diminish as her physical privacy correspondingly diminishes? It is not clear what sense it makes to suppose that her physical privacy is significantly diminished by pregnancy. Here the definition of privacy-as-inaccessibility becomes useful. Privacy means a degree of inaccessibility to the senses and surveillance devices others can employ to learn what we are, do, think, and feel. At no stage in their development do the unborn have the combination of sensory experiences and understanding that could make their presence in the womb a significant privacy diminution for others. A pregnant woman's privacy never ceases to be virtually sole, despite her pregnancy. Thus pregnancy itself cannot have the impact on a woman's privacy that Justice Blackmun suggested it must. Moreover, even if pregnancy did lessen physical privacy, it would not follow as a matter of logic alone that decisional privacy rights have to be compromised.

The point Justice Blackmun sought to make on behalf of the Court was simply that the right of decisional privacy respecting childbirth cannot be deemed absolute. At the point at which the fetus becomes a "viable" entity, it is reasonable for the state to assert an interest in its well-being and put an end to a woman's right lawfully to choose abortion. The decisional privacy rights to decide whether to enjoy heterosexual adult sex or read pornography in the home are less subject to lawful state interference. They are, in Blackmun's words, "inherently different," because they do not normally have the life-and-death implications of abortion. The problem with Blackmun's *Roe* analysis is that viability strikes many conservatives and liberals as an arbitrary, vague dividing line.

In addition to seclusion and solitude, other paradigmatic privacy concepts, namely information nondisclosure and anonymity, have joined decisional privacy in playing a role in abortion rights cases. In *Thornburgh v. American College of Obstetricians and Gynecologists,* the Supreme Court found provisions of Pennsylvania's Abortion Control Act unconstitutional.[19] The act was enacted to discourage abortion by making it expensive, time-consuming, and psychologically burdensome to offer or obtain abortion services. Concern for secrecy, confidentiality, and anonymity motivated invalidating provisions of the act that required modes of record keeping and reporting by abortion facilities, which threatened to subject abortion recipients to public exposure and harassment. The Court recognized that protecting these paradigmatic privacy interests was an important means of protecting free choice. Women who fear they cannot obtain an abortion in a context of secrecy, confidentiality, and anonymity are constrained in their decision making. The Court upheld the principle that women are entitled to make the abortion decision, and to make it without undue risk of public scrutiny and its inhibiting consequences: "Few decisions are more personal and intimate, more properly private, or more basic to individual dignity and autonomy, than a woman's decision . . . whether to end her pregnancy."[20]

Four tiers of privacy and privacy-related concerns are implicated by *Thornburgh* and earlier abortion cases. They are (1) privacy at home, (2) bodily integrity and self-determination, (3) decisional privacy, and (4) informational privacy. The first tier, not expressly addressed by the court cases but emphasized here, is privacy at home. Abortion, like contraception, helps women create seclusion, solitude, and conditions of limited attention-paying at home. The second tier, bodily integrity and self-determination, are privacy-related concerns for managing one's own body, a prerequisite of managing one's self. A third tier of privacy and privacy-related concerns is decisional privacy. An aspect of liberty, it protects bodily integrity and self-determination (tier two) and allows women to assure adequate privacy for themselves and their households (tier one). A fourth tier, informational privacy, protects decisional privacy (tier three) and through it bodily integrity and self-determination (tier two), as well as privacy at home (tier one). Secrecy and confidentiality assure that women can elect abortions without fearing that family members or others in possession of the knowledge will cause them harm.

Arguments for permissive abortion policies generally relate to the second, third, and fourth tiers. Can an argument for permissive, woman-centered abortion policies be based on the importance of the first tier of privacy concerns? Yes, but such an argument will not always be persuasive to women who oppose abortion on certain religious, cultural, or moral grounds.

Religion, Character, and Ethnicity

An argument based directly on the value of seclusion, solitude, and anonymity in home life is likely to be unpersuasive to those who oppose contraception and abortion on religious grounds. A woman may believe seclusion, solitude, and anonymity in the family have legitimate significance (as opportunities for meditation and prayer, for example) but view preserving privacy in these senses as less important than the child-bearing and child-rearing duties ascribed by religion. Christian doctrines provide that releasing new souls into the world to do God's work or be put to God's test is a central aspect of women's duties. Likewise, some Christians regard the moral education of the young in a family context to be an aspect of women's religious duty. Religious beliefs such as these cause some women to oppose abortion for themselves and for others, and to oppose contraception as well.

In addition, some secular opponents of abortion would not be persuaded by an argument for abortion based on the importance to women of privacy at home. Secular moral opposition to abortion is commonplace on such grounds as (1) bearing and rearing children are required by virtue, women's natural duty, or social obligation; (2) human life, even in embryonic and fetal stages, has inherent value; and (3) the unborn have a right to life. The cogency of these grounds has been exhaustively debated, and those debates will not be duplicated here.

The dialectic of one abortion debate is worth noting. The expression "person" is commonly used to mean *human being*.[21] A number of philosophers have argued that only persons in the moral sense have inherent moral value or rights, and that fetuses are not persons.[22] To be a person in the moral sense is to possess consciousness of oneself as a subject of experiences and a minimal rational capacity to view oneself as having a past and a future, qualities that embryos, fetuses, and even neonates do not have. Critics of such arguments have contended that only arbitrary reasons can be given for withholding the protected moral status that pertains to persons from the unborn since they have unquestioned potential to develop traits of moral personhood. One reply to this potential-persons-count-too rejoinder is to concede personhood to the unborn, but to deny that abortion is therefore without justification. Even if the unborn have the highest moral status, the reply goes, women have the same high status. Their moral status countermands that they be required either to sacrifice their bodies, happiness, and potential, or to yield to others decisional authority concerning matters so deeply tied to their individual identities.

While both pro-life and pro-choice activists rely heavily on the language of children's and women's rights, some ethicists have urged that discussion of rights has no place in family and reproductive ethics.[23] The notion of those ethicists—that there are special, onerous, sui generis family obligations—is a potentially self-serving one, too easily used to mandate sacrifices for women. Theories claiming that individualistic rights analysis is appropriate in connection with the public sphere (male world) but has no place at all in the private sphere of family and reproductive concerns (female world) are cause for suspicion. If pregnancy and motherhood impose particular sui generis abstract obligations upon women, it is notoriously unclear what they are. This is not to say that family and reproductive ethics is naught but a battleground of rights in which the arsenal of other ethical concepts guiding human conduct are necessarily unwelcome.

For example, the evaluation of character in the framework of abortion decision making might be appropriate. Having an abortion after deliberately becoming pregnant could indicate a frivolous character. Suppose, for example, a woman sought to obtain an abortion after discovering she would have a girl, because she really wanted a boy. Refusal to bear a child would also show a lack of integrity if one unilaterally decided to remain childless after carefully planning a pregnancy with a devoted spouse. I must add, however, that it is doubtful that the abortion decision is often a product of lapses of character. There is evidence that adult women make the abortion choice carefully. Carol Gilligan's studies of abortion decision making indicates that women agonize over the abortion choice, because they perceive themselves as having serious obligations of caretaking, sacrifice, and benevolence.[24]

Abortion is not always the less sacrificial of the choice between giving birth and abortion. For women who know they are unable adequately to provide for a new child, but who still desire to see their pregnancy through, abortion may be the greater act of self-sacrifice. Character can be presumed to cut inevitably against abortion only where one assumes that electing abortion is inherently of greatest appeal to women without good characters. It is easy to fall prey to this assumption because, traditionally, having a good female character has meant being a woman of saintly sacrifice, rather than a person of temperate and just disposition. In any case, permissive abortion laws may be precisely what is required if reproduction is to be fully within the realm of character. Meaningful exercises of character can occur only where individuals have realistic choices.

Opposition to birth control can arise out of a woman's identification with the traditions of her cultural group. These traditions may expressly oppose abortion, contraception, and laws that permit them. But even if they do not, a woman may nonetheless view herself as having an obligation to sacrifice privacy at home and perpetuate her group by bearing children whom she will rear in its traditions. Thus, some Jewish women view themselves as having special obligations to rear children and to rear them as Jews. To do otherwise would be virtually to continue what Hitler began with the Holocaust. Some black women recognize special obligations to bear children, obligations that arise out of a tradition of large families. Large families serve as a source of pride and as a network of economic and moral support in a hostile world. During the 1960s and 1970s, genocidal concerns not unlike those raised among Jewish women were raised among black women in intellectual circles, who feared emphasis on birth control was less women's liberation than a conspiracy to thin the African American population. More recently, capable black women have come to believe themselves under an obligation to sustain black progress and promote further social and economic improvement by rearing children with racial identity but with the special resources needed for self-help and success in a multiracial society.

The role of felt moral obligations of culture are typically overlooked in scholarly discussions of the morality of birth control. This may be because prevailing political moralities in the United States are, broadly speaking, liberal. Liberalism cannot straightforwardly accommodate the recognition of nonuniversal obligations. Liberals typically recognize universal obligations that are the correlatives of universally ascribed individual rights. The liberal perspective recognizes morally binding laws, but does not recognize publicly cognizable genuine moral obligations binding women as members of particular cultural groups to have children (or to do anything). In the liberal view, the individual is "incapable of membership in any community bound by moral ties antecedent to choice."[25] At most, the liberal would allow that an individual woman could undertake an obligation to have a child through a voluntary promise or commitment made to a spouse, parent, or community.

If real and not simply felt moral obligations can flow from cultural identity, then the argument that abortion is morally acceptable and ought not be prohibited because the unborn have no independent moral status faces a particularly strong challenge. Yet, the difficulty of knowing what membership in a particular cultural group truly requires is a weak link in arguments from culture against birth prevention. The tendency of such arguments to preserve the status quo, however unjust, is another difficulty that cuts against reliance on culture-based arguments. The acceptance of ancillary child-bearing and child-rearing roles has been a historic feature of what culture after culture has defined as the moral obligation of women. It may be necessary for a woman recognizing strong bonds to a cultural heritage to reject its traditional opposition to birth prevention as a step toward reshaping that heritage in a more equitable direction. Doing so may serve to strengthen the heritage's chances of survival in a world of improved opportunity for women.

Privacy arguments based directly on the value to women of privacy at home can seem to condone selfishness in the same way that economic arguments for abortion can seem to condone materialism. An economic realism argument for permissive abortion and contraception laws is sometimes made by pro-choice activists. They argue that it is morally wrong to allow an unwanted child to be born who will be economically underprivileged and an economic burden to its family. The economic argument is countered by pro-lifers with the claim that human life is more important than economic comfort. It is better to be born poor and unloved, conditions that can be overcome, than to be killed before birth; it is better to suffer the malnourishment and miseducation that poverty entails than to have one's life snuffed out in its inception. This rebuttal pits life against mere money. It suggests that to embrace the economic argument is to condone materialism and demean human life.

Arguments from privacy may not appear persuasive when interpreted to pit the value of privacy at home from women against the value of life itself for the unborn. Mere privacy, after all, cannot be more important than a chance at life itself. Is not the right to privacy surely outweighed by the right to life?

A basic level of privacy is more need than luxury. For this reason the value of privacy is not always outweighed, so to speak, by the value of life. The right to privacy is not always outweighed by the right to life. The strongest possible privacy-at-home argument is one that highlights the importance of privacy by showing its connection to those attributes that give individual lives moral significance. As a practical matter, such an argument is powerless against someone wedded to the premise that mere life is the ultimate, preeminent value, and that public policies ought to be shaped accordingly. Nonetheless, the present generation, more than any other in history, has had its faith in the absolute value of creating and extending life tested. We have seen that death can be better than life spent in a coma or in slow agony aided by technological life supports.[26] That is not something we want for ourselves or for our families and friends. It is not merely life but the quality of the life that merits protection.

Lives ended through abortion, or never begun because of contraception, would not, for the most part, have been valueless lives. This means women's privacy is typically pitted not against altogether dreadful lives, but against crowded, impoverished, stressful, and perhaps unhappy lives. Nonetheless, there is a strong privacy-at-home argument against restrictive abortion and contraception laws. It starts with the premise that lack of abortion choice is detrimental to women's full development, and that the personal development of women is every bit as important as the personal development of the unborn. What gives human life its special value is that it can be an experience in which persons find happiness and satisfaction through self-directed participation and contribution. Lives spent bearing and rearing children and without adequate solitude and seclusion from others are stunted lives. These lives can lack the levels of fulfillment and satisfaction that are the hallmark of happiness; such lives may be lives of sacrificial contribution, but they are lives that fall far short of those that might otherwise have been. Women are justified in refusing to bear children to the extent that the privacy they need to be happy, to participate, and to make their most meaningful and best contributions would be obstructed by motherhood. The argument from privacy at home asserts that it is better to have a population of adult women who are satisfied, fulfilled participants and contributors than simply to have more people. It further asserts that it is worse to perpetuate a social order in which some persons are unhappy, stunted, and inferior because of their sex, than to permit termination of human life prior to birth.

Decisional Privacy

Thus far I have emphasized seclusion, especially anonymous and solitudinous seclusion, as the form of privacy threatened by laws placing constraints on the availability of abortion and contraception. But free choice regarding whether or not to bear a child, choice free from governmentally imposed constraints, is the "privacy" more often emphasized in connection with reproductive rights. Strictly speaking, free choice is not a form of privacy. Solitude, anonymity, and information nondisclosure are aptly described as forms of privacy, because they designate respects in which persons, their mental states, and information about them are to some extent inaccessible to others. Free choice is not a form of privacy, even though it relates to one's capacity to control one's privacy, one's private life, and one's own body. Free choice designates the absence of governmental (in that sense, "public") interference with decisions made by individuals and families about aspects of life deemed unsuited to such interference. Decisional privacy, that is, nongovernmental decision making, is an important part of what autonomous choice is all about.

The Supreme Court has relied mainly on decisional privacy rights in stating the rationales for leading reproductive rights cases. Thus, in *Eisenstadt* Justice Brennan wrote, upholding the right of single women to birth control, that "If the right of privacy means anything it is the right of the *individual,* married or single, to be free from unwarranted governmental intrusion into matters so fundamentally affecting a person as the decision whether to bear or beget a child."[27]

Decisional privacy has distinct implications for women's ability to secure important forms of privacy. The free choice implied by decisional privacy can be exploited to promote privacy interests. Whether or not the right to free choice—the right to be free from unwarranted governmental intrusion into the decision whether to bear a child—is aptly construed as a right to privacy, it is a right whose recognition and protection have profound implications for women's ability to achieve privacy. Seclusion, solitude, anonymity, and information nondisclosure are forms of privacy implicated by free choice and the right to free choice. Thus we must strenuously reject the conclusion of George Sher that "despite what the Supreme Court has said about [the right to privacy], its connection with abortion seems too tenuous and indirect to be credible."[28]

Liberty versus Privacy

A number of legal scholars and philosophers have sought to drive a wedge between the privacy concept and reproductive rights.[29] They have sought to recast questions about whether abortion or contraception choices ought to be preempted by government as questions about liberty rather than about privacy. Their basic argument has a philosophical and a jurisprudential variant. The philosophical variant takes as its focus the requirements of conceptual clarity; the jurisprudential version relies on the requirements and constraints of constitutional adjudication in American law.

The philosophical variant contends that the government is limiting liberty when it takes away free choice respecting reproduction and with it women's control of their bodies and lives. Liberty, it is often observed, has a positive and a negative interpretation.[30] Negative liberty is noninterference; freedom from direct restraints, constraints, or coercion. Demonstrators in a rally protesting world hunger exercise negative liberty to the extent they are left alone by officials and members of the general public. And women possess an aspect of negative liberty to the extent that they are left alone by government and others in the procurement of abortion and contraception.

Positive liberty, on the other hand, is freedom from indirect constraints. It is freedom from want, relative to basic needs whose satisfaction is presupposed by egalitarian conceptions of liberty. The argument that the liberty of women on welfare is impaired by the exclusion of abortion and contraception from the package of medical and health benefits made available by state and federal government relies upon the positive interpretation of liberty.[31] Lack of access to abortion and contraception means that the cycle of poverty will be perpetuated as the size and number of dependent families mount. It also means that poor women do not have the same opportunity for self-determination through family planning as do middle-class and affluent women, since their private choices are ineffective.[32] This is particularly troubling since children represent the greatest burden for poor women, who lack the economic bases of privacy in private life.

Liberty is conceptually distinct from privacy. This is the central message of the philosophical wedge-drivers. They are correct, I believe, on the basic point that privacy and liberty are distinct concepts. The concepts are distinct in the sense that certain conditions to which the expression "privacy" and its synonyms apply could not be aptly described by the term "liberty" or its synonyms and vice versa. "Privacy" and expressions referring to paradigmatic forms of privacy, such as "seclusion," "solitude," "anonymity," and "confidentiality," are best defined in terms of inaccessibility to others. I do not offer a full-fledged philosophical definitional analysis of "liberty" here. Yet liberty, whether positive or negative, is invariably defined in terms of the absence of restraint, constraint, or coercion. While conditions of inaccessibility (privacy) are often marked by the absence of restraint, constraint, or coercion (liberty), this is not always the case. Thus, assuming the plausibility of the definitional understandings indicated, one must conclude that liberty is conceptually distinct from privacy.

The concept of decisional privacy has closer conceptual affinities to liberty than to paradigmatic senses of privacy. So too does the conception of family privacy elaborated later in this chapter. Both are best construed as aspects of liberty, understood as the absence of coercive interference. To refer to aspects of liberty that relate to reproduction and parenting as privacy simply because they relate to private life is to blur some of the conceptual boundaries suggested by everyday discourse and by careful attempts at philosophical definition. The occurrence of "privacy" in the phrases "decisional privacy" and "family privacy" reflects a usage of "privacy" that is probably derivative of the public/private distinction, rather than of the concept of privacy as restricted access. Under this usage "privacy" refers to a particular aspect of liberty—namely, freedom from governmental interference with what is properly left to nongovernmental control. By extension, we have come to use the expressions "decisional privacy" and "family privacy" even when the outside interference in the private sphere is not strictly governmental.

The jurisprudential version of the attempt to drive a wedge between privacy and reproductive concerns is motivated by criticism of the Supreme Court's "right to privacy" analyses of contraception and abortion rights. It characterizes the analysis under which government is said, metaphorically, to enter the zone of constitutionally protected privacy when it preempts abortion and contraception choices as inaccurate and confusing. It depicts the Court as second-guessing legislative balances and reading vague substantive due process rights into the Constitution.[33] It construes laws preempting the choices of citizens as coercive and, consequently, as involving a denial of liberty. The proper test for deciding the constitutionality of coercive state abortion and contraception laws, it declares, is whether such laws abridge the Fourteenth Amendment proscription against deprivation of liberty without due process. The question becomes one of whether abortion laws are rationally related to legitimate state interests, which have been held by the Court to include promoting family life, regulating health care, and collecting statistical data on reproduction. The federal courts go too far, the legal wedge-drivers argue, when they grasp for a penumbral or fundamental due process right of privacy and rely on it as a strict, substantive test of the constitutionality of prohibitive abortion laws.

I propose an obvious response to both the philosophical and jurisprudential versions of the argument that the concept of privacy does not belong in discussions of reproductive concerns. Laws preempting decision making admittedly constrain choice. They compel sexually active fertile women to give birth to unwanted children. They involve a denial of women's liberty. But they also involve a denial of privacy, for women lose privacy when they undertake motherhood. Assuming the most plausible account of what privacy centrally denotes (that is, degrees of inaccessibility), there is good reason for concluding that free choice (decisional privacy) and the right to it cannot be equated with paradigmatic privacy and the right to it. But, since coercive laws preempting free choice also result in significant deprivations of paradigmatic forms of privacy, discussion of privacy and whether the state may constitutionally impose privacy sacrifices on women has a place in legal discussion of reproductive rights. Since a loss of privacy is invariably implicated in reproductive rights cases, a federal court would be justified in appealing both to the concept of privacy and to the concept of liberty in explaining the rationale for outcomes that favor free choice for women. (This is not to say the federal courts have always made good use of the privacy concept in handing down opinions in reproductive rights cases.) The unresolved jurisprudential questions are questions of interpretation and judicial review. Does the Constitution in fact protect the reproductive liberties known popularly as decisional privacy? Does it embody substantive safeguards against the deprivations of seclusion, solitude, anonymity, or information that result from legislative constraints on the free choice of pregnant women? Are such safeguards fundamental in the constitutional sense?

While much is made of these philosophical and jurisprudential controversies in the scholarly literature, they are not of central import for understanding what is at stake for women. For these controversies concern not so much what is at stake, but how what is at stake is to be labeled. What is of central import is clear recognition that decisional privacy, whether or not properly labeled "privacy," is important and promotes the existence of conditions that properly bear the privacy label. Seclusion, in particular solitudinous and anonymous forms of seclusion, is the clearest form of privacy afforded by free choice to sexually active fertile women.

Equal Protection versus Privacy and Liberty

Many scholars now believe that sex equality and equal citizenship countermand restrictive reproductive laws, and that the Equal Protection Clause should be marshalled against state and federal abortion restrictions. In *Planned Parenthood v. Casey*, the Supreme Court reaffirmed much of *Roe*'s traditional privacy jurisprudence. However, Justice O'Connor's opinion for the Court expressly linked abortion rights to equality as well as privacy. Without their "unique" reproductive liberty, women are unable to "participate equally in the economic and social life of the Nation," she wrote. A year after the *Casey* decision Justice Ruth Bader Ginsburg joined the Court. Ginsburg has gone on record as a strong advocate of the equality perspective on abortion rights.[34] Her view is that sex inequality is perpetuated by abortion restrictions and that, because it is, the equal protection clause of the Fourteenth Amendment is, in principle, a strong basis for claiming abortion rights under the Constitution. It is so strong that *Roe* was weakened by "concentration on a medically approved autonomy idea, to the exclusion of a constitutionally-based sex-equality idea."[35]

The growing affinity among justices of the Supreme Court for an equality jurisprudence of reproductive rights is consistent with an increasingly popular view in the scholarly community that equality arguments are, not only available, but better that privacy or liberty arguments with respect to abortion. A number of feminist legal theorists who advocate strong abortion rights, favor constitutional alternatives to the doctrine of privacy-related liberty. They view privacy law as distorting the truths of women's lives and impeding women's lives and impeding women's equal citizenship. Catherine MacKinnon has broadly assaulted privacy jurisprudence in abortion law,[36] arguing that "the doctrine of privacy-related liberty has become the triumph of the state's abdication of women in the name of freedom and delf-determination."[37] Privacy doctrine works only if women are equals within the private sphere. MacKinnon argues that privacy law and other "legal attempts to advance women," wrongly treat women, "as if women were citizens—as if the doctrine was not gendered to women's disadvantage, as if the legal system had no sex, as if women were gender-neutral persons temporarily trapped by law in female bodies."[38] Joan Williams complex ambivalence about arguments premised on "choice," "liberty," and "privacy" stems from the observation that women seeking abortion do not feel especially free.[39] The language of privacy implies that women are choosers against a background of a number of realistic alternatives. Pregnant women who consider abortion are not so situated. The concepts of privacy, liberty and choice are at odds with the sense of choicelessness women seeking abortion actually feel. In general, "choice rhetoric is not appropriate where patterns of individual behavior follow largely unacknowledged gender norms that operate to disempower women."[40]

Ruth Colker's rejection of the privacy doctrine is partly ontological. She insists that the privacy-related liberty doctrine relies on the false assumption of the existence of an autonomous sphere—women and fetuses—beyond public life. Colker sees a connection between reproductive rights and compassionate social participation that she believes equality perspectives capture better that privacy perspectives: "equality doctrine doesn't demand that women be allowed to choose to have abortions because women are entitled to be treated with autonomy," but "insists that women be allowed to choose to have abortions because of women's position in society—the roles and responsibilities of women in society."[41]

For feminist theorists who believe the privacy doctrine should be abandoned, equal protection doctrine promises to replace, not just supplement, the constitutional case against abortion restrictions. They believe it is a superior constitutional framework. Some jurists and lawyers suggest that such an equal protection rationale for abortion rights is superior to rationales that rely either on the concept of privacy or the concept of liberty.[42] Again many leading legal feminists argue that privacy jurisprudence fails to fully promote, and may actually harm, women's interests. Catherine MacKinnon's *Feminism Unmodified* (1987), which rejects the privacy rationale, may be viewed in this vein. While her argument reveals some of *Roe*'s shortcomings, MacKinnon understates the positive influence *Roe* has had in the quest for women's equality, and obscures the ways in which women can use abortion as a means for establishing significant privacy rights. The real problem is not with the right to privacy as such, but that women have had too much of the wrong kinds of privacy. The "wrong" kind—that which MacKinnon emphasizes in her attack on *Roe*—is the "privacy" of the domestic sphere, where a dominant man controls sex and home life. The "right" kind of privacy, which MacKinnon disregards, gives women real choices. Privacy can enable some women to escape unhappy and oppressive lives, and others to experience the peace of mind conducive to their making contributions both inside and outside the domestic sphere.

Feminists sometimes blame privacy jurisprudence for the Supreme Court's refusal to grant poor women the right to state and federal assistance for elective of "non-therapeutic" abortions.[43] The usual argument is that conceptually privatizing abortion as in *Roe* rules out public assistance.[44] Critics say the right to privacy means limited government involvement; it would be reasoning against the grain of privacy jurisprudence to find in the idea of a governmental duty to leave people alone, the idea of a governmental duty to assist the poor in seeking abortion.

This criticism of *Roe* implies that liberal values in principle rule out all public programs. Although extreme libertarians have taken this view, more modern and nuanced liberal political theories that value limited government do not proscibe all forms of public assistance. Relevantly, the "liberal" Western nations have sought in practice to balance independence from government interference with reliance on government aid needed to make meaningful independence possible. A number of feminists have suggested that American constitutionalism could accomodate affirmative understandings of privacy-related liberty that are broad enough to support abortion funding. For example, responding critically to the abortion funding cases, Rachael Pine and Sylvia Law countered with a "feminist concept of reproductive freedom" based on "affirmative liberty" and the idea that "government has the obligation to insure that people can make reproductive decisions freely."[45] Reacting to *Rust v. Sullivan*,[46] Dorothy Roberts describes a "liberation theory" version of constitutional liberty that would "recognize the importance of information for self-determination and therefore "place an affirmative obligation on the government to provide [abortion] information to people who are dependent on government funds."[47] Those who say privatizing abortion access conceptually rules out public subsidies needlessly abdicate privacy theory to its least progressive interpreters.

It may be possible to make a moral argument for abortion rights that does not expressly refer to privacy. However, I conjecture that most contemporary American women would be unable to articulate fully their concerns about antiabortion laws without appealing to notions of privacy. In talking about abortion, women commonly say that government should mind its own business. By using the term "privacy" in connection with abortion, women are able to draw on a wealth of shared meanings, including connotations of autonomy, independence, and respect for others. One wisely refuses to jettison privacy's rich semantic heritage when one embraces an equal protection analysis to support a woman's right to choose.

Bodily Integrity and Self-determination

Bodily integrity and self-determination are both sometimes equated with privacy. By "self-determination" I mean autonomous determination of the course of one's life, especially one's private or family life. Like free choice, bodily integrity and self-determination cannot be straightforwardly identified with privacy. In the context of contraception and abortion, bodily integrity is not privacy. It is a possible consequence of private reproductive choices with implications for privacy. Bodily integrity for a woman means, inter alia, that if she elects otherwise, her physical person will not undergo a pregnancy and its characteristic physical strains and mortal risks.

The idea of bodily integrity is sometimes articulated in terms of self-ownership, owning one's own body and doing with it as one pleases. But this is a misleading way to put it, since human beings surely do not own their bodies but *are* their bodies. Our claims to exclusive access to our bodies can be based directly on our being persons in the moral sense whose bodies should not be reduced to involuntary instruments of service for others' needs.[48] Hence, the concept of self-ownership is as superfluous as it is misleading. Moreover, arguments based on bodily ownership have no particular logical clout in abortion arguments. Conservatives on the abortion issue are free to assert that fetal rights include a right of the fetus to bodily integrity of its own. Pro-lifers can assert that fetuses have rights of self-ownership, too, if that is what the liberal is claiming for women in virtue of their humanity. Even pro-choice liberals may want to say that a pregnant woman's putative right of bodily integrity or self-ownership is not absolute in the later stages of pregnancy, because the viable fetus also has rights of bodily integrity and self-ownership.

This was, I think, what the Court in *Roe v. Wade* was getting at when it expressly rejected the notion argued by *amici* that the constitutional privacy right implies "one has an unlimited right to do with one's body as one pleases."[49] In response, the Court argued that the state has a legitimate (paternalistic) interest in safeguarding health and medical standards affecting maternal well-being. Moreover, the Court argued that the state's interest in protecting viable fetal life is legitimate and provides a reason to interfere with bodily integrity by prohibiting later-term abortions: "it is reasonable and appropriate for a state to decide that at some point in time another interest, that of potential human life, becomes significantly involved."[50]

Self-determination respecting childbearing is a condition enabling women to protect their health directly, and their privacy indirectly. By the final stages of pregnancy some of the risks to health have passed. For some women abortion at any stage of pregnancy is less likely to end in mortality than is childbirth. But risks to the privacy of the pregnant woman are as strong on the day of delivery as at the moment of conception.

Both bodily integrity and self-determination are forms of access control; they are privacy control mechanisms. Free choice makes these privacy control mechanisms operative and makes it more possible for women to achieve desired levels of privacy. Free choice signals sexual equality, too. It is likely that many women with powers of self-determination will choose lives that make the most of their educational, artistic, and professional potentials.

I now want to turn to a consideration of what decisional privacy or free choice-based arguments, over and above paradigmatic privacy-based arguments, add to the case for permissive birth prevention policies.

Liberal Democracy

The prevailing ideal of government in the United States is the liberal democracy. It is democratic in its commitment to consensual government of citizens who meaningfully participate in their own governance. It is liberal in virtue of its commitment to individualism and neutral protection of individual rights. Democratic liberalism so described is capable of multiple interpretations. "Conservative," "liberal," and "libertarian" are names commonly used to designate adherents of influential interpretations of American democratic liberalism.

Many self-described conservatives are "pro-life." They reject abortion as a personal choice, and they reject permissive abortion laws. In addition, some conservatives are "pro-choice" rather than "pro-life." The pro-choice conservatives who rely on decisional privacy arguments rely essentially on libertarian argument. The libertarian holds dear the principle that, to the extent the prevention of injury and the protection of property allow, government ought to refrain from limiting individuals' liberty. Reproductive liberty being no special case, the government should grant individual women the freedom to choose what they do to avoid and terminate pregnancies. On the libertarian view, abortion should be legally permissible up to the point at which it makes sense to ascribe individual rights to the unborn.

The argument for permissive birth prevention based on the importance of paradigmatic privacy asserts that seclusion and other paradigmatic forms of privacy are something all women need and ought not be deprived of. In contrast, the libertarian/conservative decisional privacy argument asserts that women should be free as individuals to choose to possess privacy (because, for example, they want it or think it best) or to choose to give privacy up (because, for example, they enjoy the idea of having and raising children). For the libertarian/conservative the importance of negative liberty rather than the importance of privacy is more fundamental to understanding why governmental interference with free abortion choice is wrong.

The liberal proponent of American democratic liberalism holds dear the ideal of liberty, but treats principles of equality and government neutrality as limiting individual and collective liberty. Ronald Dworkin has argued that a conception of equality requiring that government treat citizens with "equal respect and concern" is constitutive of liberal thinking. He has maintained that this conception is what distinguishes liberal thought from conservatism, libertarianism, collectivism, and other less similar political moralities.[51] Dworkin rejected a second liberal version of liberalism that takes equality to be an important but derivative value. On the rejected version, the principle of neutrality that the government ought not favor particular conceptions of the good life by which citizens live is regarded as constitutive.[52] For the "neutral principle" liberal, the concept of equal respect and concern is merely a device by means of which government can assure its own neutrality. This rejected form of liberalism, Dworkin contended, is "vulnerable to the charge that liberalism is a negative theory for an uncommitted people"—a theory for the wishy-washy.[53] Dworkin rejected "neutral principle" liberalism because it offers no effective argument against utilitarianism and other contemporary justifications for economic inequality.[54] It undervalues equality by treating it as just another preference.

The form of liberalism Dworkin embraced is grounded on a constitutive principle of equality requiring "equal respect and concern." It regards a principle of neutrality as a derivative principle, adopted to promote equality. Critics have typically gone after the "neutral principle" liberal, holding that neutrality is impossible and self-contradictory. Critics argue that a liberal conception of the good life is embodied in liberal policies as much as a nonliberal's conception of the good life is embodied in policies preferred by the nonliberal, who makes no pretense of neutrality. By arguing that equality is the fundamental substantive liberal principle and neutrality a derivative rule of thumb, Dworkin aimed to escape the criticisms leveled at the wishy-washy liberal. Dworkin has argued that neutrality as a derivative position is not self-contradictory. Nor is it a pointless impossible ideal. Approximating neutrality among citizens with competing interests and values is a way government can strive to treat citizens as equality requires, with equal respect and concern, even if strict neutrality is impossible.

Dworkin has described the roots of the conception of equality as "equal respect and concern" as Kantian.[55] In his essay "Why Liberals

Should Care About Equality,'' Dworkin gave an account of the liberal principle of equality and the nature of the constraint it imposes on interference by government. The account was both deontological and contractarian: government "must impose no sacrifice or constraint on any citizen in virtue of an argument that the citizen could not accept without abandoning his sense of equal worth."[56] This principle limiting citizen "sacrifice or constraint" is contractarian in its requirement that government be morally constrained by what a citizen could *accept* or *agree to.* It is deontological in its implication that a rational self-respecting person, one whose dignity is intact, is an end in itself. According to Dworkin, adherence to this principle of equality limiting state action entails (1) a principle of social justice that precludes enforcement of private morality, and (2) a principle of economic justice that precludes citizens having less than their equitable share of the resources available to all.[57]

The former entailment is the one that concerns us here. It would follow from the liberal principle of equality as articulated by Dworkin that government is precluded from impermissive restriction of reproductive liberties if these are matters of "private morality." For some liberals it has gone without saying that abortion and contraception fall within the realm of private morality. If private morality consists of rules of conduct governing what our culture has traditionally treated as falling within the private sphere and zone of privacy, this assumption is a reasonable one. Contraception and abortion do fall within the traditional "zone of privacy." They relate to the body, sexuality, marriage, family, and the home. All of these are closely tied to a person's sense of identity and individuality. Based on this analysis of private morality, many liberals readily conclude that restrictive birth prevention policies must be rejected, because government may not reach into the zone of privacy for purposes of interfering with private morality. As long as a person is acting within that zone, he or she ought to be off-limits to government and other unwanted third parties.

Opponents of permissive birth prevention policies would insist that even though matters of contraception and abortion fall within the private sphere of sex and family life, they are not matters of private morality. Abortion is a matter of public morality and legitimate governmental intervention because of the harm it represents for fetuses, they argue. In response, liberals have made two moves. They have claimed that "harm" to fetal life is of no moral consequence (because fetuses are not persons, or have no right to life, or have no rights that are not overcome by women's rights). They have also claimed that the lack of moral and philosophical certainty about the moral status of the fetus means government is not justified in constraining abortion choice.

Roger Wertheimer's liberal pro-choice argument fits into this second mold.[58] He maintained that the moral status of the fetus has so far proven to be an irresoluble metaphysical question. Since the ideal of political freedom places the burden on government rationally to justify its coercive powers, as long as the state cannot establish that a fetus is a person or human being that counts, it must refrain from enacting a coercive law. For Wertheimer, metaphysical indeterminacy is what keeps abortion within the confines of private morality. But Wertheimer's argument is too timid. The point is not that the status of the fetus is an unresolved metaphysical question and government must keep its hands off until the philosophical truth be known. The point is that the truth pertains to a choice that is of a type individuals ought to decide for themselves even though fetal life may be extinguished as a consequence. Government must leave us alone in the making of the basic reproductive choice if it is to respect each of us as a person and an individual.

Even if reproductive liberties do not fall within private morality in the above sense, Dworkin's Kantian/contractarian account of governmental constraint provides a reason to accord women free choice. Imposing motherhood on women by denying them the right to decide whether to bear and rear children imposes a heavy burden of sacrifices and constraints in virtue of an argument a woman cannot accept without abandoning her sense of equal worth. Without abandoning their sense of equal worth, women cannot accept the pro-lifers' argument that the existence of an anonymous embryo or fetus is of greater value than full personhood, participation, and contribution by women.

While decisional privacy arguments are the preferred arguments for libertarians and liberals, paradigmatic privacy arguments are highly congenial to these interpretations of liberal democracy. Women may or may not make privacy-promoting reproductive choices where government is permissive. But if they do, they partake more fully of the bounties of individual liberty and public participation. Liberals and libertarians have a reason to encourage women to make paradigmatic privacy-enhancing choices and a reason to demand that government permit free choice by affording decisional privacy.

Indirect Constraints

It should go without saying that if in a liberal democracy privacy interests counsel against direct, blanket governmental constraints on birth prevention measures, such interests counsel as well against indirect, piecemeal constraints. Just as blanket prohibitions on abortion and contraception have implications for women's privacy, so too do regulatory schemes that impair freedom of choice. State regulations that make it unduly onerous for a woman to obtain an abortion and contraception impair decisional privacy and thereby affect her ultimate ability to obtain and exploit solitude and anonymity.

Since *Roe v. Wade*, government officials have sought to restrict abortion through:

1. restrictions on the advertisement of abortion services;

2. zoning restrictions on abortion facilities;

3. record-keeping and reporting requirements;

4. spousal and parental notification or consent requirements;

5. the requirement of pre-abortion ''informed consent'' counseling by a physician;

6. the requirement of mandatory pre-abortion waiting periods;

7. the requirement of the presence of a second physician during the abortion procedure;

8. the requirement that a method calculated to spare fetal life be employed in post-viability abortions, if possible without substantial risk to the mother;

9. the requirement that all tissue removed during an abortion be sent to a laboratory for analysis by a certified pathologist;

10. a requirement that insurance companies offer at a lower cost a health insurance policy without coverage for elective abortion, other than for elective abortion precipitated by incest or rape;

11. legislating a state-wide information campaign to communicate an official state policy against abortion;

12. legislating criminal sanctions against physicians knowingly aborting viable fetuses;

13. a requirement that all nonemergency abortions after the first trimester of pregnancy be performed in a hospital;

14. banning Medicaid funding or other public abortion subsidies;

15. "gag" rules prohibiting abortions or abortion couseling by physicians at publicly funded facilities.

Aspects of devices 3, 5, 6, 7, 8, and 12 have been found unconstitutional by the Supreme Court. Yet certain restrictions, including "gag rules" and waiting periods once deemed constitutionally problematic, have been recently upheld by the court.

Given the infrequency of second- and third-trimester abortions,[59] actual ethical conflicts involving the fate of viable fetuses are rare. Nonetheless, the most difficult abortion restrictions to assess are those that aim at protecting *viable* fetal life, even against the wishes of pregnant women.[60] These statutory provisions shift the focus from women's decisional privacy to fetal survival. The Pennsylvania statue challenged before the Supreme Court in *Thornburgh v. American College of Obstetricians and Gynecologists* (1986) required that physicians employ the method of aborting viable fetuses that results in greater likelihood the fetus will be aborted alive unless, in the physician's good-faith judgment, that technique "would present a significantly greater medical risk to the life or health of the pregnant woman."[61] One objection to this requirement denies that there is a procedure that would not add risk to the woman that would decrease risk to a viable fetus. This is more or less the ground on the basis of which the Supreme Court invalidated the Pennsylvania provision.

Suppose there were a method to save fetuses without additional risk. If a child "born" as a result of this method were to be deemed the responsibility of its mother, as it presumably would be in the absence of a statute to the contrary, her purposes for seeking abortion would have been thwarted. Is part of the abortion right a right not to give birth to a living child? A right not only not to bear a child, but not to have a child conceived of one's body alive in the world? The privacy arguments relating to seclusion, solitude, and anonymity are not obviously arguments that justify killing a fetus or letting a fetus die, if the state will assume complete care of the child. While it may cause the noncustodial mother a loss of solace and unhappiness to know a child she begat has survived an abortion, its survival does not diminish paradigmatic forms of her privacy. Fetal survival does, arguably, render her decisional privacy ineffective.

Decisional privacy arguments can be used to defend the idea that women are entitled to have abortions that are fatal for the fetus. Steven Ross has argued that women's desire for fatal abortion can be an understandable concomitant of a conception of parenting that obliges us to bear and rear children, if at all, in a responsible, personal, attentive, loving way.[62] A woman who cannot do that might prefer that there be no child of hers in existence at all. A fetal death wish can be nobly motivated.

State laws prohibiting abortion techniques calculated to destroy fetal life create special dilemmas for women. So too do state laws that automatically deny a woman custody of a child "born" in the course of an abortion. Consider this statute enacted in Missouri:

> In every case where a live born infant results from an attempted abortion which was not performed to save the life or health of the mother, such infant shall be an abandoned ward of the state under the jurisdiction of the juvenile court wherein the abortion occurred, and the mother and father, if he consented to the abortion, of such infant shall have no parental rights or obligations whatsoever relating to such infant, as if the parental rights had been terminated.[63]

The guiding idea behind this statute is that once a woman seeks abortion, expressing thereby a fetal death wish, custody of a child surviving abortion passes from her. It goes to the state or the natural father if he did not share in the death wish by consenting to the abortion. This statute creates an ethical dilemma for women that negatively affects their freedom of choice. Fewer women will choose to abort if they know that the fetus might survive and that if it did, it would either be given up for adoption or left to the state. Thus, "There is clearly an inverse relationship between advancements in fetal sciences and the degree to which the right of privacy [i.e., decisional privacy] as it pertains to abortion may be exercised."[64]

Were techniques developed whereby even the youngest pre-embryos could be brought to term outside the women who conceived them, women might come to view pregnancy as a trap. In many instances a woman would wish not to be pregnant, but would be unwilling to have her pre-embryo, embryo, or fetus "rescued" and be permitted to develop into a child who would be an unwanted ward of the state, or given away to unknown adoptive parents. In the words of Janet Benschof:

"The increasing tendency to view the fetus as an independent patient or person occurs at the cost of reducing the woman to the status of little more than a maternal environment."[65]

Information Nondisclosure

Lack of informational privacy can eviscerate decisional privacy altogether. Secrecy and confidentiality about procurement of birth control information, contraception, or abortion effect free choice in any number of respects, in a variety of circumstances.

It has been proposed that married women should be required to disclose abortion plans to their husbands, or more strongly, obtain their consent. This is because husbands are presumed to be prospective fathers when their wives are pregnant. Laws requiring spousal notification or consent would compel disclosure of what could otherwise have been a secret a woman kept to herself, or shared in confidence with her health care provider or others. The Supreme Court has found spousal notification and consent requirements unconstitutional.[66] There are many legitimate reasons a woman might desire not to notify her spouse of a pregnancy and of her plans to terminate it. She might desire to choose not to communicate plans to abort:

> 1) where the husband is not the father of the fetus; for instance, where the fetus is the product of an extramarital affair; 2) where the wife has been a rape victim, has not disclosed the incident to her husband, and has subsequently become pregnant; 3) where the husband, because of strong religious beliefs or moral precepts, would strenuously object; 4) where the husband is seriously ill or emotionally unstable and is unable to participate in the abortion decision; and 5) where the woman is a "battered wife" and fears that discussion concerning an abortion may precipitate physical violence.[67]

Spousal notification and consent requirements can discourage abortion by women who fear the consequences of information disclosure. So too can requirements that abortion facilities keep records and file reports subject to public disclosure. In the *Thornburgh* case the special relationship between record-keeping and reporting requirements and "free choice" was recognized by the Court. Fear of disclosure and harassment may work to discourage women from having abortions. While medical records are generally subject to disclosure to researchers, government statisticians, and insurance companies, it is important that information collection and disclosure practices mandated in the abortion context be designed to reflect the social reality that abortion patients need anonymity, secrecy, and confidentiality. Without them, free choice is seriously constrained.

The relationship between a woman and the facility from which she obtains an abortion is in some respects a consensual transaction between players in an economic setting.[68] Indeed, it may be inappropriate to characterize it as a "private relationship." It is not a "private relationship" in the sense in which, for example, marriage is. But this is not dispositive of the need to recognize rights of confidentiality in the abortion setting.

Minors have a constitutional right protecting access to contraceptives and contraception information.[69] Moreover, every minor has a constitutional right to go directly to court, without parental notification, to attempt to establish that she is a mature minor who must be permitted to obtain an abortion without parental consent.[70] Many argue that the state ought to protect family privacy values and teen welfare by requiring parental approval or notification of sex counseling, prescription of contraceptives, and abortion.

There is a certain cogency to the argument that younger teens have a right to paternalistic protection, and that that protection is best got from their families. If teens are permitted by law on decisional privacy grounds to obtain contraception and abortion without the knowledge or consent of their parents, parents may feel the state is interfering with family privacy. In this context, family privacy signifies the freedom of parents to exercise their authority and judgment in accordance with their own values to promote the interests and well-being of themselves and their children. This is no trivial matter, since birth control devices such as the intrauterine device (IUD) have proven to involve risks to health and fertility that a teenager, even in consultation with a physician, cannot be expected always to assess fully.

The ability of parents to be genuinely helpful to teenagers desiring information and advice is open to question. Parental consent and notification requirements can discriminate against and burden mature minors:

> Abortions are sought by minor women because of the weighty and often adverse consequences of having a child. These range from interruption of the woman's education to early and unstable marriages. Economic effects of childbirth can be particularly severe when a minor drops out of high school and attempts to support herself and a child. Health consequences

for minor women can also be harsh. Maternal mortality and non-fatal complications from premature births are higher with women under twenty than with adult women. Access to an abortion is therefore a vital option for pregnant minor women faced with such consequences. Access to an abortion free from parental interference can be just as vital. For some minor women parental notification will prevent them from obtaining an abortion. . . . One study on the probable impact of parental notification estimates that 19,000 minor women would resort to self-induced or illegal abortions and that 18,000 more minor women would bear unwanted children, were parental notification required. In addition, another 5,000 minors would run away from home either to have the unwanted child or to obtain an illegal abortion. [The] infant death rate is higher for children born to women under twenty, and minor women are far more likely to have premature or low-birth weight babies.[71]

Paradigmatic privacy arguments are not irrelevant to the case for unconstrained birth control choice for teens. Young women have many of the same underlying interests in solitude, seclusion, and anonymity that mature women have. There is more controversy, however, over whether they are entitled to use occasions of private seclusion as opportunities for sexual intercourse. If we start with the realistic assumption that even very young girls will have sex and become pregnant in the absence of accessible contraception and sex education, the decisional privacy arguments against state-imposed obstacles are clear. Abortion must be realistically accessible, too. Since teens are sometimes slower to discover and act on their pregnancies, access to abortion in the second and third trimesters has special importance. To be saddled with a child at a young age is to be saddled with responsibilities that limit opportunities for education and privacy called for by personhood, participation, and contribution in the adult world.

Decisional Privacy Revisited

Giving Birth

Free to choose, some women will choose childbirth. And some of these will prefer giving birth in an intimate setting to giving birth in an institution in which strangers take charge and to which strangers have wide access.[72] At least 1 percent of all births occurring in the United States occur at home. Being free to choose conditions of birth without governmental or other third-party interference can be styled as yet another aspect of decisional privacy. Although state and federal courts have not faced the issue squarely, home birth and midwifery raise "two basic constitutional claims—that home birth is encompassed within the . . . right of privacy, and that the right of privacy includes one's choice of an unlicensed birth attendant."[73] Here, too, the privacy implications of constraints on reproductive free choice are clear, even if the appropriateness of the "privacy" label is not. As in the abortion context, the possibility of a legitimate state interest in protecting the health of pregnant women and their offspring presents itself. Some studies indicate that home birth is between two and five times as likely to result in newborn mortality than hospital birth. Home birth advocates argue that planned, midwife-assisted home birth is not significantly more risky than hospital birth.

Women typically have been more directly concerned with achieving intimacy and privacy in hospital births through the elimination of superfluous supervision and technology than with doing away with physician and government interference. The private birthing issue has not been prominent in philosophical and legal discussions of reproductive liberties. It nevertheless merits brief mention here to clarify the senses in which privacy is at stake in the choice of childbirth settings.

One of the earliest reported American cases in which the plaintiff expressly alleged an invasion of privacy involved privacy of birth. *DeMay v. Roberts*, an 1881 Michigan case, was brought by a Mrs. Roberts against a Dr. DeMay and a Mr. Scattergood. Dr. DeMay took Mr. Scattergood to the Robert's tiny home when he went to deliver a child on what the court described as a "dark and stormy" night.[74] At the time, Roberts and her husband assumed Scattergood was a trained medical assistant. In fact he was an "unprofessional young unmarried man," brought along to carry Dr. DeMay's lantern. Scattergood remained at Roberts's house for the many hours of Mrs. Roberts's protracted labor and delivery. At one point during the night he helped Dr. DeMay and the attending midwife by taking Mrs. Roberts's hand to restrain her from "rocking herself and throwing her arms."

Mrs. Roberts won her lawsuit alleging deceit, assault, and invasion of privacy. In his opinion the judge declared:

> To the plaintiff the occasion was a most sacred one and no one had a right to intrude unless invited because of some real and pressing necessity which it is not pretended existed in this case. The plaintiff had a legal right to the privacy of her apartment at such a time, and the law secures to her this right by requiring others to observe it, and to abstain from its violation.[75]

In addition to the conception of childbirth as a ''sacred'' occasion, the DeMay case reflects its era's norms about women's privacy in general. These norms are apparent in another case of the same period unrelated to childbirth but also involving medical procedures. In *Gulf v. Butcher,* a case brought before the Supreme Court of Texas in 1892, the argument was noted that a court order compelling a woman who claimed to have been injured in a rail accident to be examined by a physician was ''an intrusion upon her privacy and modesty and should never have been permitted or been availed of.''[76] The *DeMay* court's choice of terms to describe Scattergood—''unprofessional young unmarried man''—says a great deal about the requirements of female modesty in the nineteenth century.

Contemporary arguments for the right to private childbirth rest on the ideals of freedom and control over privacy and intimacy rather than on the need for modesty or respect for the sacred character of birth. The familiar principle implicit in commonly heard arguments is that individuals should be free to achieve desired self-regarding and family ends. Free choice is constrained only by the obligation that one commit no harms or cognizable offenses against others. Applied to childbirth, this principle seems to entail that if a woman wants a private birth for any reason—including but not limited to modesty or a sense that child-birth is sacred—then the power should lie with her, prima facie, to have precisely that. Maternal health, public health, and the well-being of the newborn justify some unwanted third-party regulatory interference with the choice of procedures and setting of childbirth. But women's free-dom mandates that any such interference be strictly limited to what is demonstrably necessary for health and safety.

Consider the account one woman gave of her reasons for desiring to give birth at home rather than in a hospital:

> What were the other reasons? It had something very basic to do with con-trol, power, and authority. At home, I would have them, in the hospital they would be handed over to the institution. I heard arguments for home rather than hospital birth that spoke about privacy. For me it was less a question of privacy and more a question of authority. At home nobody was coming in the door whom I did not choose to come in.[77]

Physical privacy was *one* of this woman's concerns. Being inaccessible to unwanted others was one of her reasons for preferring home birth. In her own mind, however, physical privacy was not the deepest reason to reject hospital delivery. She was concerned about physical privacy but also the de jure authority and power to have her choice of privacy re-spected. To put it differently, she wanted privacy in two senses: both seclusion from unwanted others *and* decisional privacy, the right to freely decide birth conditions without unwarranted interference.

Heading Families

With the birth of a child a multitude of parental obligations begin. Notable among them are obligations of maintenance, education, and health care. Freedom to decide for oneself how such obligations will be discharged is a key aspect of what is sometimes referred to as "family privacy." Another conception of family privacy is enjoyment of a se-cluded home life with spouse, children, or kin. This is the aggregate family privacy feminist Charlotte Perkins Gilman condemned as anti-thetical to individual forms of personal privacy. I want to focus on the former conception of family privacy: decisional family privacy.

The claim of moral entitlement to be free from third-party, and espe-cially governmental, interference in the discharge of familial obliga-tions is commonly advanced as a claim of a right to family privacy. A moral right of family privacy is deemed to be a right of family members to be free from uninvited, unwarranted interference with the rearing, education, discipline, health, and custody decisions made by family members (usually adults) on behalf of members of the same family (usually infants, children, teenagers, the elderly, or the infirm). Increas-ingly, women are becoming family heads as a consequence of conscious design, divorce, separation, and desertion. The number of female heads of household increased 25 percent from 8.7 million in 1980, to 10.9 million in 1990. Thirteen million children lived in primarily female-headed families in 1990, compared to 3.4 million in 1970. Since women are more and more likely to be heads of households, concern for the right to family privacy in many cases boils down to concern for wom-en's right to decisional privacy.

The decisional brand of family privacy is appealing, but it is also troubling. It is appealing because the idea of the family itself has sub-stantial appeal. Like individual privacy, family privacy can function to promote the development of meaningful, intimate familial relationships. In general, it can allow individual family members the opportunity to make autonomous choices regarding how their personal lives will be ordered, and assure opportunities for unfettered, unobserved enjoyment of those lives. It can function to provide a context in which young per-sons develop responsibility and judgment requisite for meaningful social participation. Parental autonomy afforded by family privacy gives parents their due liberty and at the same time benefits children by maximizing their chances for normal development. As argued by Goldstein, Freud, and Solnit in *Before the Best Interests of the Child,* to ensure timely development of children's capacities for physical closeness, emotional attachment, identification, and self-reliance, the state must recognize a trio of interlocking family integrity rights: a right to family privacy; a parental right to be presumed to have the "capacity, authority, and responsibility to do what is 'good' for one's children and what is 'best' for the entire family"[78]; and a right of children to autonomous parents.

It has been widely argued that the state has a considerable interest in protecting the family. Alan F. Westin argued in *Privacy and Freedom* that family autonomy to permit preferred modes of education, religion, and home life is a basic commitment of liberal democratic societies.[79] It is one of the respects in which liberal democracy acknowledges the interests persons have in a life apart from the state. The axiom of American life that families achieve ends in virtue of which the government has an interest in protecting families has a corollary. Neither the state nor its agents, nor any other institution adequately achieves the same ends. Thus, although the interest the state is presumed to have in protecting the family might be thought to justify broad regulatory intervention, there is widespread contrary belief that the state's own ends are best served by a "hands-off" family policy.[80]

Yet, the notion of family privacy is a problematic, potentially dangerous one. It is problematic whether it practically vests in men alone, women alone, or is shared among family members. If a moral right of family privacy is ascribed a family unit, who is entitled to exercise that right? Who is the spokesperson for the family's interest? What if family members disagree about the desirability of governmental intervention? Of private third-party involvement? Family privacy is a troubling concept because:

1. in traditional families, family privacy can amount to male domination of the women and children;

2. in child abuse or neglect cases and in child custody contexts where parents are at odds, family privacy policies can and may stand in the way of efficient, essential state intervention on behalf of a child;

3. for teenagers mature enough to make up their own minds about, for example, religion, education, contraception, and abortion, family privacy can amount to parental tyranny;

4. family privacy can be a tool of discrimination when judicially interpreted so as to protect only the interests of traditional families to the exclusion, for example, of families headed by homosexual and unmarried persons; and

5. emphasis on family privacy, if at the expense of individual decisional privacy, "obfuscates privacy's deeper meaning."[81]

All of these concerns arise out of concern for the implications of family privacy for individual rights and freedoms.

Family violence is one of the contexts in which the risks attendant to application of the family privacy concept become apparent.[82] Family privacy cloaks even physical brutality in a protective mantle. Interfamilial violence has been treated as a "personal" and "private" affair, with the result, critics claim, that the law enforcement response to battered women's pleas for help has been to discount them. The "hands-off" notion of family privacy has played a role in denying spouses the rights enjoyed by other crime victims.

The risks attendant to application of the concept of family privacy come into sharper focus in cases involving the allocation of authority between teenagers and their parents. The right to family privacy can be interpreted as giving parents the authority to make choices about their teenaged children's education. But mature teenagers living at home are arguably justified in the desire to enlist state protection for some of their own preferences regarding their education. For example, they should be able to exercise the choice of a public over a private parochial school.

Teenage sex and pregnancy raise problems for both the conceptualization and application of the right to family privacy. Teenage pregnancy and parenthood is sometimes described as a national crisis. According to a recently completed two-year study of the National Research Council, a congressionally chartered research arm of the National Academy of Sciences, a 15-year-old American girl is at least five times more likely to give birth than girls her own age in other countries. Teen mothers and their babies are at high risk for medical complications; teen parents have severely limited career opportunities and are more likely to become dependent upon public assistance. In 1985 the economic burden for maintaining teen families was an estimated $16.6

billion in outlays for aid to dependent children, Medicaid, and food stamps. The burden has grown.

Everyone agrees teen pregnancy is potentially a problem. Opinions will vary about how much parental involvement is warranted in the resolution of an unemancipated minor's pregnancy. The age of the teenager, the circumstances of conception, disagreement among grandparents-to-be, economic resources, and drug problems can affect our views as to the best resolution of particular teenage pregnancies. But it is clear that the idea of the right to family privacy cannot have a central role in shaping policy in this area. Where society's prescriptive norms respecting the timing of procreation have been violated, the individuation of families for purposes of ascribing family privacy rights is complicated by the processes by which families are naturally perpetuated. The pregnant teen may believe that she and her unborn child, or she, the child, and its father are a family apart. The grandparents-to-be may believe their minor children are inside the proper sphere of their family authority, despite sexual activity and pregnancy. The problem with family privacy in the teen pregnancy context is that as youth approach adulthood and, biologically speaking, begin families of their own, the justification of parental authority becomes progressively less clear.

Conclusion

Typical discussions of privacy in connection with contraception and abortion focus exclusively on questions of decisional privacy. Decisional privacy is centrally at stake in the choice among competing contraception and abortion policies. However, my discussion of reproductive liberties shifted the focus from decisional privacy to physical and informational privacy.

The argument for reproductive liberties is not only that the exercise of free choice belongs to women as a requirement of moral justice. It is also that the decisional, physical, and informational privacy called for by moral concern for the quality of individual and group life depends upon the ability of women to determine when and if they have children. Women need privacy and ought to exploit opportunities for meaningful individual privacy in the private sphere. These opportunities depend, inter alia, upon the abrogation of patterns of dependence, marriage, and childcare in virtue of which a woman's time and fate belong to others. To have a private life that is her own, a woman must have powers of

effective decision making respecting contraception, abortion, childbirth, and child care.

Notes

1. For example, Ruth Gavison ("Privacy and the Limits of Law," *Yale Law
Journal* 89 [1980]: 421, 432) uses "anonymity" in the broader sense identified.
2. See, in general, Arnold H. Buss, *Self-Consciousness and Social Anxiety*
(San Francisco, Calif.:W. H. Freeman, 1980); C. Schneider, *Shame, Exposure
and Privacy* (Boston, Mass.:Beacon Press, 1977).
3. Charlotte Perkins Gilman, *Women and Economics,* ed. Carl N. Degler
(New York: Harper & Row, 1966; first published in 1898 by Small, Maynard
and Company, Boston), 258.
4. See Paul Shorey, trans., *The Republic,* in *Plato: Collected Dialogues,* ed.
Edith Hamilton and Huntington Cairns (Princeton, N.J.: Princeton University
Press, 1961), Book V.
5. John Rawls, *The Theory of Justice* (Cambridge, Mass.: Belknap Press of
Harvard University Press, 1971), 511–12. The problems of social justice created
by the family and the "hands-off" approach to the family associated with liberalism are admirably addressed in James S. Fishkin, *Justice, Equal Opportunity,
and the Family* (New Haven, Conn.: Yale University Press, 1983.)
6. Rawls asks (p. 511), "Is the family to be abolished then?" He answers:
"Taken by itself and given certain primacy, the idea of equality inclines in this
direction. But within the context of the theory of justice as a whole, there is
much less urgency to take this course. The acknowledgment of the difference
principle redefines the grounds for social inequalities as conceived in a system
of liberal equality."
7. Frederick Engels, *The Origin of the Family, Private Property and the
State,* ed. Eleanor Burke Leacock (N.p.: International Publishers, 1972).
8. See Jean Bethke Elshtain, "Family Reconstruction," *Commonwealth*
(August 1, 1980): 430–36. See also her *Public Man, Private Woman* (Princeton,
N.J.: Princeton University Press, 1981), 323.
9. See Rudolf J. Seibert, "Hegel's Concept of Marriage and Family: The
Origin of Subjective Freedom," in Hegel's *Social and Political Thought,* ed.
Donald P. Verene (Atlantic Heights, New Jersey: Humanities Press, 1980), pp.
177–210, 178. The quoted passage is a description of Hegel's conception of the
consequences of familial love for individuality.
10. For Arabs, an understanding of the privacy implications of child rearing
are reflected in the language. In *Bargaining for Reality: The Construction of
Social Relations in a Muslim Community* (1984), anthropologist Lawrence
Rosen points out that the literary Arabic word for "child" shares etymological
roots with Arabic words that mean to "intrude," "disturb," "impose upon,"

"sponge," "live at other's expence," and "arrive uninvited or at inconvenient time," 23.

11. See Deborah Fallows, *A Mother's Work* (Boston: Houghton Mifflin, 1986). Fallows argues that the quality of day care in the United States is so low that we should "create the circumstances that allow more parents to care for their children themselves."

12. *Grisold v. Connecticut*, 381 U.S. 479, 486–87 (1965).

13. *See* F. Friendly and M. Elliot, *The Constitution, That Delicate Balance* (New York: Random House, 1984), 188–202; Marian Faux, *Roe v. Wade* (New York: Mentor, Penguin Books, 1993); Sarah Weddington, *A Question of Choice* (New York: Putnam, 1992); David Garrow, *Liberty and Sexuality* (New York: Macmillan, 1994).

14. *Eisenstadt v. Baird*, 405 U.S. 438, 453 (1972).

15. *Roe v. Wade*, 410 U.S. 113 (1973) (Texas statute restricting abortion access invalidated); *Doe v. Bolton*, 410 U.S. 179 (1973) (Georgia statute restricting abortion access invalidated).

16. *Roe,* 410 U.S. at 153.

17. For a discussion and analysis of abortion cases and the normative and policy issues raised by them, see Nanette J. Davis, *From Crime to Choice* (Westport, Conn.: Greenwood Press, 1985); Jay L. Garfield and Patricia Hennessey, *Abortion: Moral and Legal Perspectives* (Amherst, Mass.: University of Massachusetts Press, 1984); Rosalind Petchesky, *Abortion and Women's Choice* (Boston: Northeastern University Press, 1985); Kristin Luker, *Abortion and the Politics of Motherhood* (Berkeley: University of California Press, 1984); Eva R. Rubin, *Abortion, Politics and the Courts* (Westport, Conn.: Greenwood Press, 1982); Carl E. Schneider and Maris A. Vinovskis, *The Law and Politics of Abortion* (Lexington, Mass.: Lexington Books, 1980).

18. *Roe,* 410 U.S. at 159.

19. *Thornburgh v. American College of Obstetricians and Gynecologists,* 737 F.2d 283 (3rd Cir. 1984), 106 S. Ct. 2169 (1986).

20. Ibid. at 2185.

21. Jenny Teichman, "The Definition of Person," *Philosophy* 60 (1985): 175–86.

22. See, for example, Michael Tooley, "Abortion and Infanticide," *Philosophy and Public Affairs* 2 (1972): 37–65.

23. See, for example, Stanley Hauerwas, "The Moral Meaning of the Family," *Commonwealth* 1 (August 1980): 432–33.

24. Carol Gilligan, *In a Different Voice: Psychological Theory and Women's Development* (Cambridge: Harvard University Press, 1982).

25. Michael Sandel, *Liberalism and the Limits of Law* (New York: Cambridge University Press, 1982), 135.

26. Cf. *Matter of Quinlan*, 355 A.2d 647 (1976) (comatose woman without apparent hope for improvement may be removed from artificial life-support systems); *Cruzan v. Director* 497 U.S. 261 (1990).

27. Emphasis in the original. *Eisenstadt,* 405 U.S. at 253.

28. George Sher, "Subsidized Abortion: Moral Rights and Moral Compromise," *Philosophy and Public Affairs* 10 (1981): 361, 363.

29. See, for example, W. A. Parent, "Privacy, Morality and the Law," *Philosophy and Public Affairs* 12 (1983): 269; idem, "Recent Work on the Conception of Privacy," *American Philosophical Quarterly* 20 (1983): 341, 346; Gavison, "Privacy and the Limits of Law," 421; Sher, "Subsidized Abortion"; John Hart Ely, "The Wages of Crying Wolf: A Comment on *Roe v. Wade,*" Yale 82 (1973): 920, 932. But see David A. J. Richards, *Toleration and the Constitution* (Oxford, 1986).

30. See S. I. Benn and R. S. Peters, *The Principles of Political Thought: Social Foundations of the Democratic State* (New York: Collier Macmillan, 1959), 248–49; L. Tribe, *The Constitutional Protection of Individual Rights* (Mineola, N.Y.: Foundation Press, 1978), § 15–2, 889. Cf. James Childress, "Negative and Positive Rights," *Hastings Center Report* 10 (1980): 19. The negative conception of liberty was defended as the sole liberty properly guaranteed by government by conservative F. A. Hayek in *The Constitution of Liberty* (Chicago: University of Chicago Press, 1960).

31. Related issues arose in *Harris v. McRae,* 488 U.S. 297 (1980) and *Maher v. Roe,* 432 U.S. 464 (1977) (state may withhold funds for nontherapeutic abortion even though childbirth would be funded). More recent cases relating to restrictions on public abortion funding include *Webster v. Reproductive Health services.,* 492 U.S. 490, 507 (1989) and *Rust v. Sullivan,* 500 U.S. 173 (1991). See also Sher, "Subsidized Abortion."

32. See, in general, Leslie Goldstein, "A Critique of the Abortion Funding Decision: On Private Rights in the Public Sector," *Hastings Constitutional Law Quarterly* 8 (1981): 313; David T. Hardy, "*Harris v. McRae*: Clash of a Nonenumerated Right with Legislative Control of the Purse," *Case Western Reserve Law Review* 31 (1981): 465; Note, "Abortion Funding Restriction: State Constitutional Protections Exceed Federal Safeguards," *Washington and Lee Law Review* 39 (1982): 1469, 1473–74, n.14; Note, "The Hyde Amendment: New Implications for Equal Protection Clause," *Baylor Law Review* 33 (1981): 295.

33. Richards, in *Toleration and the Constitution,* argued that the jurisprudential basis of the Court's constitutional "right to privacy" analysis is sound. He maintained that the right to privacy would support further judicial intervention to invalidate state laws, in particular, laws criminalizing consensual adult homosexuality. For sympathetic discussion of the Supreme Court's "substantive due process" approach in the reproductive rights cases, see Laurence Tribe, "Forward: Toward a Model of Roles in the Due Process of Life and Law," *Harvard Law Review* 87 (1973): 1, where he defended *Roe* on ground the Court was "choosing among alternative allocations of decision-making"; idem, "Structural Due Process," *Harvard Civil Rights-Civil Liberties Law Review* 10 (1975): 269 (court may facilitate evolution of a new moral consensus). Cf.

Laurence Tribe, *Constitutional Choices* (Cambridge: Harvard University Press, 1985). For an unsympathetic discussion, see Ely, "Crying Wolf"; and cf. John Hart Ely, *Democracy and Distrust: A Theory of Judicial Review* (Cambridge: Harvard University Press, 1980).

34. See Ruth Bader Ginsburg, "Some Thoughts on Autonomy and Equality in Relation to *Roe v. Wade,*" *North Carolina Law Review* 63 (1985): 375.

35. Ibid., 386.

36. See Catharine A. MacKinnon, "Privacy v. Equality Beyond *Roe v. Wade,*" in *Feminism Unmodified* (Cambridge, Mass.: Harvard University Press, 1987), 93–102.

37. Catharine A. MacKinnon, "Reflections on Sex Equality under Law," *Yale Law Journal* 100 (1991): 1281–1311.

38. Ibid., 1286.

39. Joan Williams, "Gender Wars: Selfless Women in the Republic of Choice," *New York University Law Review* 66 (1991): 1559–84. She writes, "[t]he choice rhetoric is not the simple unadulterated truth of women's lives: many aborting women feel they have no choice but to abort." Williams refers to "choice" as a libertarian rhetoric and an autonomy/self development rhetoric.

40. Ibid., 1633.

41. Ruth Colker, *Abortion and Dialogue: Pro-Choice, Pro-Life, and American Law* (Bloomington: Indiana University Press, 1992), 86. In another work, Ruth Colker explains that, "[M]y defense of women's ability to choose to have a baby is not absolute . . . it is not embedded in the argument that a woman has the right to control her body under any circumstances. . . . A woman in my view has the right to seek an abortion to protect the value of her life in a society that disproportionately imposes the burdens of pregnancy and child care on women and does not sufficiently sponsor the development and use of safe, effective contraceptives." ("Feminism, Theology, and Abortion: Toward Love, Compassion, and Wisdom," *California Law Review* 77 (1989): 1011–1050.

42. I discuss this suggestion more fully in "The Proposed Equal Protection Fix for Abortion Law: Reflections on Citizenship, Sex, and the Constitution," forthcoming in the *Harvard Journal of Law and Public Policy.*

43. See *Harris v. McCrae*, 448 U.S. 297 (1980) and *Maher v. Roe*, 432 U.S. 464 (1977), holding that neither state nor federal government must pay for a poor woman's abortion. See also *Rust v. Sullivan* (1991), holding, under Title X of the Public Health Act, that "[t]he Government has no affirmative duty to commit any resources to facilitating abortions"; *Webster v. Reproductive Health Services*, 492 U.S. 490 (1989), holding a state may restrict the use of public funds and facilities "for the performance or assistance of nontherapeutic abortions"; *Beal v. Doe*, 432 U.S. 438 (1977), holding "Title XIX of the Social Security Act does not require" a state to fund "nontherapeutic abortions as a condition of participation in the Medicaid program established by that Act."

44. See Ruth Colker, "Feminism, Theology, and Abortion: Toward Love,

Compassion, and Wisdom," *California Law Review* 77 (1989): 1011. But see Laurence H. Tribe, "The Abortion Funding Conundrum: Inalienable Rights, Affirmative Duties, and the Dilemma of Dependence," *Harvard Law Review* 99 (1985): 330, concluding "it becomes difficult indeed to justify the government's decision not to fund an impecunious woman's choice of abortion," on p. 338.

45. Rachel Pine and Sylvia Law, "Envisioning a Future for Reproductive Liberty: Strategies for Making the Rights Real," *Harvard Civil Rights-Civil Liberties Law Review* 27 (1992): 407–18.

46. 111 S. Ct. 1759 (1991).

47. Roberts, "*Rust v. Sullivan* and the Control of Knowledge," *George Washington Law Review* 61 (1994): 587–640.

48. See Sara Ann Ketchum, "The Moral Status of the Bodies of Persons," *Social Theory and Social Practice* 10 (1984): 25, 26.

49. *Roe*, 410 U.S. at 154.

50. Ibid., at 159.

51. Ronald Dworkin, *A Matter of Principle* (Cambridge: Harvard University Press, 1985), 181–213. Cf. Immanuel Kant, *Groundwork of the Metaphysic of Morals*, trans. H. J. Paton (New York: Harper & Row, 1964). According to Kant, "Man is not a thing—not merely something to be used merely as a means: he must always in all his actions be regarded as an end in himself" (97).

52. Dworkin, *A Matter of Principle*, 206–13.

53. Ibid., 205.

54. Ibid., 209–10.

55. Ronald Dworkin, *Taking Rights Seriously* (Cambridge: Harvard University Press, 1977), 198.

56. Dworkin, *A Matter of Principle*, 205–6.

57. Ibid., 206.

58. Roger Wertheimer, "Understanding the Abortion Argument," *Philosophy and Public Affairs* 1 (1971): 67–95.

59. David A. Grimes, "Second-Trimester Abortion in the United States," *Family Planning Perspectives* 16 (1984): 260–66.

60. "Viability" is an inexact term. It refers, roughly to the date after which a fetus could survive after removal from a woman's uterus. On some measures, this date has shifted back four weeks since 1973, from 28 weeks to 24 weeks, due to advances in fetal life-support technology. Toward contrary ends, feminists and conservatives alike have argued that the "viability" limitation on women's right to abortion is untenable in light of the impact of technology. See "Late Abortion and Technological Advances in Fetal Viability," *Family Planning Perspectives* 17 (1985): 160-64. Cf. David A. Grimes, "Second-Trimester Abortion."

61. *Thornburgh*, 476 U.S. 747, 763 (1986).

62. Stephen Ross, "The Death of the Fetus," *Philosophy and Public Affairs* 11 (1982): 234. It is not clear how far Ross would push his thesis. He defends it only with respect to embryos and fetuses in the earliest stages.

63. Missouri: Annotated Statutes, Section 188.040 (Vernon 1982).
64. Note, "Current Technology Affecting Supreme Court Abortion Jurisprudence," *New York Law School Law Review* 27 (1982): 1221, 1257. Cf. Comment, "Fetal Viability and Individual Autonomy: Resolving Medical and Legal Standards for Abortion," *UCLA Law Review* (1980): 1340, 1361.
65. Benschof is cited in Daniel Callahan, "How Technology Is Reframing the Abortion Debate," *Hasting Center Report* (February 1986), 33, 40.
66. *Planned Parenthood v. Danforth*, 428 U.S. 52, 68 (1976) (a state cannot delegate power to veto abortion to a spouse). *Planned Parenthood of Southeastern Pennsylvania v. Casey*, 112 Sup. Ct. 2791 (1992) (invalidating spousal notification statute).
67. *Scheinbert v. Smith*, 482 F. Supp. 529, 538 (S.D. Fla. 1979).
68. *Roe*, 410 U.S. at 172 (Justice Rehnquist, dissenting).
69. *Carey v. Population Services Int'l*, 431 U.S. 678, 681 (1976); *Planned Parenthood v. Danforth*, 428 U.S. 52, 74 (1976).
70. See *Belloti v. Baird*, 443 U.S. 622 (1968); *Planned Parenthood v. Danforth*, 428 U.S. 52, 68 (1976); cf. *Planned Parenthood Association of Kansas City v. Ashcroft*, 462 U.S. 476 (1983); and *Akron v. Akron Center for Reproductive Health, Inc.*, 462 (1983). But see *H. L. v. Matheson*, 450 U.S. 398 (1980) (Court upheld Utah statute requiring physician to give notice to parents prior to performing abortions on unemancipated daughters living at home who make no claim or showing as to independence); *Hodgson v. Minnesota*, 110 Sup. Ct. 2926 (1990), *Ohio v. Akron Center for Reproductive Health*, 110 Sup. Ct. 2972 (1990) (upholding notification, restrictions on teen abortions).
71. Note, "Parental Notification: A State-Created Obstacle to a Minor Woman's Right of Privacy," *Golden Gate Law Review* 12 (1982): 579, 584–85, 587.
72. See Barbara Rothman, *In Labor: Women and Power in the Birthplace* (New York: W. W. Norton, 1991). Cf. *Fitzgerald v. Porter Memorial Hospital*, 523 F2d 716 (7th Cr. 1975) (husband not entitled to be present at childbirth if medical authorities do not permit it).
73. Charles Wolfson, "Midwives and Home Birth: Social, Medical, and Legal Perspectives," *Hastings Law Journal* 37 (1986): 909, 929 n.117; see also Note, "Respecting Liberty and Preventing Harm: Limits of State Intervention in Parental Choice," *Harvard Journal of Law and Public Policy* 8 (Winter 1985): 19; Note, "Childbearing and Nurse Midwives: A Woman's Right to Choose," *New York University Law Review* 58 (June 1983): 661; Walker, "A Matter of the Quality of Birth: Mothers and Midwives Shackled by the Medical Establishment and Pennsylvania Law," *Duquesne Law Review* 23 (1984): 171.
74. *De May v. Roberts*, 46 Mich. 160, 9 N.W. 146 (1881).
75. Ibid. at 147.
76. *Gulf, C. & S. F. Ry. Co. v. Butcher et ux.*, 18 S.W. 583, 585, 83 Texas 309 (1892).
77. B. Rothman, *In Labor*, 15. The desire for private childbirth can be a desire to exclude not only nonfamily members but also unsupportive members of one's own family:

Nothing's private in a one-room house . . . . I had nine children in that room, back there, and I suppose I'll die there the same way—with all the men in the family sitting around the fire muttering. "Why doesn't she hurry up about it." My father, my brothers, my husband's brothers, they all sat there by the fire and drank wine and waited. If you make a sound, if a pain catches you by surprise, or the baby won't come out and you can't stand it and you moan, you've disgraced yourself. You keep a towel shoved in your mouth, and every time it hurts so bad, you bite down on it and pray to God no noise comes out. I always tied a knot in one end so I could bite real hard, and my sister had a way of crooning and stroking me that made it better . . . . So many times it was all for nothing too. Six of nine died. I could have wailed then—that's all right—but there are some hurts that stay inside . . . . Nothing's private here, not birth, not death, not anything. No matter what any one says, though, you never get used to it."

See Lisa Leghorn and Katherine Parker, *Women's Worth: Sexual Economics and the World of Women* (London: Routledge & Kegan Paul, 1981).

78. J. Goldstein, A. Freud, J. Solnit, *Before the Best Interests of the Child* (New York: Macmillan, 1979); cf. idem. *In the Best Interest of the Child* (New York: Free Press, 1985).

79. Alan F. Westin, *Privacy and Freedom* (New York: Atheneum, 1967), 27.

80. See, for example, *Meyer v. Nebraska,* 262 U.S. 390 (1923); *Pierce v. Society of Sisters,* 268 U.S. 510; *Prince v. Massachusetts,* 321 U.S. 510 (1925); and *Wisconsin v. Yoder,* 406 U.S. 205 (1972).

81. June A. Eichbaum, "Towards an Autonomy-Based Theory of Constitutional Privacy: Beyond the Ideology of Familial Privacy," *Harvard Civil Rights-Civil Liberties Law Review* 14 (1979): 361.

82. See David Finkelhor and Richard J. Gelles, eds., *The Dark Side of Families: Current Family Violence Research* (Beverly Hills, Calif.: Sage Publications, 1983); M. Boulard, *Violence in the Family* (Atlantic Heights, N.J.:Humanities Press, 1976); Karen MacKinnie, "Battered Wives," *University of California Law Review* 52 (1981): 587. See also, Elizabeth M. Schneider, "The Violence of Privacy," *Connecticut Law Review* 23 (1991): 861–954.

Questions

1. According to Allen, what does privacy have to do with the birth of a child? Can there be privacy inside a family's home? Is a desire for privacy necessarily a rejection of motherhood and family? Do you think that everyone has a right to privacy?
2. What is decisional privacy? What relationship, if any, is there between decisional privacy and physical privacy? In what ways does pregnancy affect a woman's decisional privacy and physical privacy?
3. Allen notes that some ethnic women see themselves as obligated to bear

children. Why might holding this view weaken the survival of the heritage, especially regarding women?

4. What is the difference between positive and negative liberty? How does liberty relate to privacy?

5. How do laws restricting abortion place a burden on women's ability to be socially and economically equal to men?

6. Explain Allen's argument regarding reproductive liberties. What role do the concepts of physical and informational privacy play in her argument?

10

Coerced Birth Control and Sexual Discrimination

Lenore Kuo

[Judge Howard Broadman] gave [Darlene Johnson] prison time for whipping two of her four children with a belt and a cord. Then, having just heard of Norplant®, the new long-lasting contraceptive, he casually decreed that she have it implanted in her arm or else serve more time. When critics protested that Ms. Johnson had medical conditions that might make Norplant® harmful to her, the judge left it up to some doctors to decide whether the device would be safe.[1]

In the past year, a Kansas State legislator has introduced two bills aimed at using Norplant® to control pregnancies. . . . The first measure . . . proposed giving women on welfare $500 to have Norplant® inserted and $50 for each year it remained in place . . . The second proposal . . . would make insertion of Norplant® an acceptable condition of probation for women convicted of certain drug offenses.''[2]

In January of 1991, the Norplant® system was introduced into the United States. Norplant is an implant of six flexible tubes containing a hormone used in many birth control pills. These tubes are implanted below the skin on the inside of the upper arm of a woman (through a 2 mm incision). Once implanted, the tubes provide a steady level of the hormone levonorgestel for as much as five years. Current studies indicate that it has a cumulative success rate of 99.4 percent in preventing pregnancy, making it "the most effective reversible method of contraception available."[3]

The manner in which Norplant functions as well as its success rate in preventing pregnancy makes it the first birth control device that can effectively be used coercively "because it's so long lasting and doesn't require any cooperation after it's implanted, and can be monitored by a parole officer [or other governmental official] just by looking at the woman's arm."[4] It may, at first, appear peculiar to consider specifics of the technology of Norplant in answering the apparently theoretical question of the justification of coerced birth control. I will argue, however, that issues specific to the development and functioning of birth control technology are central to understanding an adequate answer to the more general theoretical question of the ethical justifiability of coerced birth control.

The scope of this discussion will be limited to the issue of whether or not coercing birth control, a *temporary* prevention of the capacity to reproduce, may ever be justified. I shall not here be directly concerned with the question of whether or not coercing sterilization, the *permanent* destruction of a capacity to reproduce, is ever justified. Many of the issues relevant to coerced sterilization are different from those relevant to coerced birth control and historically, both ethical doctrine and legal precedent have tended to judge coerced sterilization as unjustifiable.[5]

It is in part because of this perceived difference between sterilization and birth control that the issue of coerced birth control is only now becoming a source of significant controversy. Prior to January 1991, the question of forced birth control was pretty much a purely academic concern.[6] Although some methods of birth control that existed prior to that time could, in theory, have been coerced, any policing of such a practice would have constituted an unacceptable invasion of privacy. The development of Norplant has made the coercion of birth control practically possible.

Limiting Basic Rights

Part of the reason coercion to use birth control is such a highly controversial and emotionally charged issue is because such a policy involves limiting four distinct and basic human rights, that of (1) one's procreative or reproductive right (and/or potentiality); (2) one's right to bodily autonomy; (3) one's right to privacy; and (4) one's right to practice one's religion of choice. Although no rights are ever absolute, these rights are viewed as fundamental, not only by ethical tradition but also by legal precedent.[7]

The U.S. government explicitly acknowledges the right to reproduce, describing it as a "liberty" right—a right to noninterference so that one "is at liberty to take any action that is not coercing or restraining or designed to injure other persons."[8] Furthermore, this right is acknowledged to be fundamental to freedom and autonomy. "The right to reproduce appears to be linked to freedom and autonomy in the most basic way: the desire to have children and create a family is a natural expression of generative urges and commitments to religious, ethnic, and familial values that have characterized the human race from its beginning."[9]

The right to bodily autonomy, the right of competent adults to determine what will happen in and to their own body, is basic to virtually all ethical systems as well as to all democratic political systems. This right is considered so fundamental that it is regularly used as the basis for deriving other rights[10] and is treated as virtually absolute by the medical profession. For example, competent adults have regularly been permitted to refuse medical procedures (e.g., blood transfusions), even when death is likely to result without such treatment. A policy of coerced birth control not only limits one's right to bodily autonomy by forcing the individual not to reproduce but also limits this right by coercing the *form* of birth control an individual can use. That is, policies of coerced birth control, as evidenced above, are only possible (can only be monitored and policed) if the individual agrees to utilize specific *methods* of birth control. Therefore such a policy not only coerces an individual's capacity to reproduce, but also coerces the manner in which this end is to be achieved.

In addition, based on precedent, such a policy would be legally viewed as limiting a basic right to privacy. In *Roe v. Wade*, for example, the court argued that a woman's right to have an abortion (in the first two trimesters of pregnancy) was guaranteed by her right to privacy.[11] A similar view is held in traditional ethical theory. That is, an individual's right to privacy (including the right to decide the private issue of reproduction) is generally viewed as decisive in the absence of unusual or extenuating circumstances.

Finally, a policy coercing the use of birth control would have to be made conditional upon the religious convictions of the individual. Many religious sects severely and explicitly condemn the use of any methods (or of any "unnatural methods") of birth control. As such, any blanket coercion of birth control would potentially deny religious freedom. Policies can and have been made conditional upon the individual's religious convictions. Quakers, for example, have been permitted to do "alternative service" rather than fight during war times. So at least in theory, a policy of coerced birth control could avoid violating one's right to religious freedom if the policy was made appropriately conditional.

Despite how fundamental the rights of reproduction, bodily autonomy, and privacy are, they, like all rights, are never absolute. All rights may be restricted at times. A right is not absolute when one's exercising it violates the rights of another. (For example, my right to free bodily movement does not include a right to enter your home since this violates your right to privacy and private property.)

Traditionally, ethicists have argued about what grounds justify limiting individual's rights and liberties. J. S. Mill held that "the only purpose for which power can be rightfully exercised over any member of a civilized community, against his will, is to prevent harm to others"[12] where "harm to others" includes both harm to other individuals or harm to society and/or its institutions.

Although many other grounds for limiting individual rights have been considered by traditional ethicists,[13] no other grounds have historically been viewed, either by most ethicists or by U.S. legal or medical policies, as sufficient to limit the right of a competent adult to bodily autonomy.[14]

In addition, policies restricting basic rights have been held to be justifiable only where the harm is "highly probable or in the case of a very serious harm, reasonably probable."[15] Thus, for example, we have permitted officials to quarantine areas where bubonic plague was discovered because it is a serious disease with a high probability of transmission through casual contact with infected individuals.[16] We have not permitted officials to quarantine areas where AIDS was discovered because, although AIDS is a serious disease, the probability of transmission through casual contact with infected individuals is extremely low.[17] Thus we cannot limit rights in order to prevent all possible harm. Common sense alone makes it clear that we would have virtually no rights whatsoever if our rights could be limited whenever there was a possibility (or low probability) of causing harm. (We could not, for example, drive cars since there is always a possibility or low probability of injuring a pedestrian.)

Thus, to summarize what has been said so far, we can maintain that limitation of basic human rights, particularly of the right to bodily autonomy, can be justified only if the following condition is met:

1. Such a limitation is required to prevent harm to others that is either highly probable or very serious and reasonably probable (The Harm Principle).

There are two additional conditions generally acknowledged to be required in order to justify limiting basic rights.

First, the manner or method used to limit a right must be rationally related to the harm it is intended to prevent. I cannot limit your right to sing in order to prevent you from using drugs (even if it turned out that many people who sing take drugs). This condition is explicitly recognized by ethicists[18] and by U.S. law.[19] Thus, for example in *Jew Ho v. Williamson*, the courts held: "If . . . a statute purporting to have been enacted to protect the public health, the public morals, or the public safety, has no real or substantial relation to those objects . . . it is the duty of the courts to so adjudge, and thereby give effect to the constitution."[20]

Thus in order to justify limiting individual rights, the following condition must be met:

2. Such a limitation must be directly relevant to the prevention of the anticipated harm (The Test of "Rational Relationship").

The third condition, which is also recognized by precedents in ethics and the law, requires that the manner or method used to limit individual freedoms be the least restrictive and least intrusive possible to prevent the anticipated harm. It is, for example, part of the reason for rejecting a policy of quarantining those infected with AIDS since preventing the spread of AIDS can be achieved through far less intrusive means.[21] It is also part of the basis for the court's decision regarding the forcible administration of drugs in *Rennie v. Klein* where it was held that "a patient's constitutional right to be free from treatment may be limited only by the least intrusive infringement required by needed care or legitimate administrative concerns."[22] Thus we may limit basic rights only if the following condition is met:

3. Such a limitation is justified only if no less-restrictive or intrusive remedy is available (Least Restrictive or Intrusive Remedy Principle).

Finally, one clarification should be made explicit here. Neither ethicists nor legal theorists presume that in order to justify limiting basic rights, the individual whose rights are to be limited need be in any way culpable or morally responsible for any possible harm they may cause. We allow officials to quarantine populations of people to prevent the spread of highly contagious diseases even though those to be quarantined are in no respect morally or legally responsible for their exposure to the disease. As such, the harm principle justifies limiting basic rights of those who are, in every respect, innocent of any wrong doing.

So far, we have considered requirements for the limitation of individual rights that are part of the canon of traditional ethics. Now I will consider two additional requirements, which are presumed, if not explicitly stated, by both ethical and legal theorists. They are: (1) that any justifiable policy may not discriminate against individuals on irrelevant grounds (including race, sex, class, etc.)[23]; and (2) that no policy can be instituted without adequate evidence of possible harm.

We have come to recognize the moral unacceptability of behavior that is the result of discriminating between individuals on the basis of class membership when such membership is irrelevant to the issue at hand. It is also apparent that one cannot offer a coherent judgment of a policy unless one is adequately informed of the probable consequences of such a policy. Although these requirements seem straightforward and uncontroversial, they are the basis for holding that *no* policy of coerced birth control can, at this time in history, be justified.

Birth Control and Sexual Discrimination

The history of the development of birth control technology has demonstrated an extraordinary degree of discrimination against women. Both in research and testing of possible birth control devices, scientists have exhibited a willingness to experiment upon and intervene in the reproductive processes of women *rather than* men as well as a willingness to knowingly place women at tremendous health risks while demonstrating no such inclination towards men.

Funding of birth control research has traditionally been notoriously unbalanced. As recently as 1985, 75 percent of birth control research funded by the National Institutes of Health was directed towards methods of controlling female fertility.[24] In response to political pressure, NIH moved towards more equitable distribution of birth control research funding. According to a recent study[25] the proportional funding of birth control research in 1991 was 57 percent directed towards female fertility while 43 percent of the $18 million budget was directed toward male fertility. Lest we take too much comfort in these improved statistics, it should be noted that, with regard to infertility research, which is certainly likely to yield information helpful to the development of birth control technology, the proportional spending of funds is abysmal. Indeed, "the government still does not include men in its national fertility survey."[26]

Discrimination is also evident in the manner in which the medical establishment has pursued possible birth control technologies. Methods of birth control directed against female fertility have been marketed despite knowledge of significant possible side effects and/or lack of knowledge of side effects altogether.[27] Conversely, birth control methods directed towards controlling male fertility have been abandoned on the basis of mild side effects[28] or simple lack of interest.[29]

Time constraints prevent me from presenting a full summary of the history of birth control research[30]; I will instead focus the discussion that follows on comparative attempts to develop a female birth control pill versus efforts to develop a male birth control pill.

In 1960, female birth control pills were marketed based on extremely limited studies. Since that time, the pill has been associated with more than fifty side effects including blood clotting disorders that require hospitalization in one of every two thousand women. Pill-takers have a three to nine times greater risk of stroke, are twice as likely to have arteries burst in their brains, and have a 2.7 to 5.7 times greater risk of coronary thrombosis than nonusers. Of women using the pills, 10–15 percent suffer a loss of sexual drive (libido). At the time the FDA approved the pill as safe for marketing, it was also suspected of increasing the likelihood of breast cancer. In addition, pill usage is known to cause "harmless" side effects such as nausea, rashes, weight gain, bloating, etc.[31] Yet, in 1969, despite detailed evidence of "endless adverse side effects," the relevant FDA advisory committee declared the pill "safe." In 1970, during congressional hearings, the chair of the FDA's Advisory Committee on Obstetrics and Gynecology explained that it had been determined that female birth control pills were safe for distribution by comparing the benefits of the pill "*in curtailing population growth* against the risks of the Pill to individual women."[32] Thus the decision was made to place individual women at significant health risks for the benefit of *society* and despite the fact that other safe and effective though "less convenient" birth control methods were already available and on the market. At those same hearings, it was discovered that two-thirds of women on the pill who had been questioned had not been told that the pill had any serious long-term effects. Despite this fact, "the A.M.A. and the American College of Obstetrics and Gynecology subsequently opposed package inserts explaining side effects and risks of the Pill directly to Pill users."[33]

Evidence from these hearings and other sources indicate that governmental and scientific decisions regarding the pill were significantly affected by a desire for population control—especially of "the indigent and non-white." Dr. Herbert Ratner, then public health director, testified at the 1970 Senate hearings that the pill became immune to criticism "because it was promoted as the solution to the population problem in the undeveloped countries, and to the growing welfare problem in the U.S."[34] When we combine such testimony with the fact that the original testing of the pill was done on 132 Puerto Rican women, and that, as Dr. Philip Ball testified, the pill was considered particularly advantageous because "It could be used on the poor, ignorant, illiterate woman who scarcely knew what birth control was all about," we uncover not only sexual discrimination but intentional class and racial discrimination as well.

Compare this history to attempts to develop male birth control pills. In 1971, Dr. Robert Kistner, a staunch defender of the female birth control pill explained that a male birth control pill had not been attempted prior to the development of a female birth control pill because "the male is more sensitive to the psychological factors of the sex act than the female."[35]

Indeed, although it has been known for some time that sufficient amounts of testosterone will effectively suppress spermatogenesis, no extensive research into its utilization has occurred because (1) "There would have to be regular checks of sperm"; and (2) "There would be risks involved. Testosterone is a powerful hormone. You can't get sex hormones with impunity. We don't know what the long-term effects would be but they might be considerable."[36] Such a justification is noteworthy given that the female birth control pill is composed of sex hormones. And we actually do have some knowledge of the potential side effects of testosterone, namely, that "it is likely to increase the chance of blood clotting as well as other side effects similar to those suffered daily by women who are taking the pill."[37]

In September 1981, the *New York Times* reported the testing of LHRH, a substance secreted by the brain that activates the testes. Testers reported that they had "achieved cessation of spermatogenesis which is totally reversible." However, treatment of subjects was discontinued due to reports of impotence and decreased libido in some of the test subjects. Despite stated intentions to continue the study, no product utilizing these results is expected on the market as of this writing.

There are a variety of reasons for the discrimination evident in the researching and testing of birth control technology. As Dr. Philip Corfman, former director of the Center for Population Research at NIH, admitted, "Most physicians are male and some males are afraid of tampering with themselves."[38] This natural bias against using one's own sex as a guinea pig for reproductive technology then becomes rationalized in a variety of ways including claims that because women's repro- ductive physiology is more complex, it is a more promising locus of intervention. Not only is this claim illogical, it is also indefensible on biological grounds.[39] As Rita Arditti eloquently argues:

> it is easy to construct a case for males being the ideal target for contracep- tion if one cared to do so. . . . The fact is that their reproductive system is less complex and a concentrated research effort aimed at understanding one or two areas could conceivably bring more results. Males do not have a cycle, and complications arising from changing levels of hormones would be avoided. Their sex glands, placed outside the body are more accessible and easier to work on than women's organs. In statistical terms, male birth control is an ideal method because males can produce as many children as the number of women they have intercourse with, while women are restricted to about 1.4 pregnancies per year.[40]

I would add that the more complex a biological system, the more difficult it is to predict or detect long-term side effects. This constitutes an additional reason for holding that male contraception should, in the- ory, be easier to develop than female methods.

In response to accusations of sexual discrimination in the develop- ment of reproductive technologies, it has been alleged that:

> Among the . . . reasons for concentration on techniques for women is that women must assume the serious physical dangers and discomforts associated with pregnancy.[41] Since women have the most at stake when it comes to matters of reproductive control, it is not surprising that women have been far more anxious to effectively control their fertility than men have been. And since they have the most at stake, it is crucial to the well- being of women that safe and effective means of fertility control be readily available to them.[42]

Clearly, pregnancy does place women at physical risks that men do not have to face. It is therefore likely that women will be more moti- vated to insure birth control than men. This fact, however, is not suffi- cient to justify the extraordinary imbalance of birth control availability.

Although men are not at any physical risk in cases of pregnancy, they, in theory, should be at financial and personal risk with regard to the support and rearing of any child that they father. But because of societal discrimination, which fails to hold men responsible for their offspring, such risks need not be balanced by men against the potential risks to their female partners. In addition, although men are not as sig-

nificantly impacted by pregnancies as women, many men feel sufficiently morally responsible for their sexual behavior to sincerely desire
to be able to control their procreative capacities. Therefore, although
one might expect some greater focus on female fertility control over
male fertility control, one could not expect or justify the degree to
which the focus of research has been almost exclusively directed
towards women. Finally, although women are at greater risk than men
with regard to pregnancy, the standard of "who is at greater risk" is
not reflected in other medical technology and research policies. One
need only consider instances in which diseases are carried and transmitted by individuals who do not actively contract the disease to locate a
long tradition in which medical research has been directed towards
those who, though not at risk themselves, pose a risk to others.

An additional reason for bias in the development of birth control
technology appears to be the assumption that women should be the
responsible and self-controlled participants in sexual acts, while men,
whose sexual drives are held to be much stronger, are viewed as incapable of controlling and being responsible for their sexual behavior. On
this basis it is held that men cannot be expected to participate in birth
control. Feminist literature has dealt with this assumption in a number
of contexts and has clearly demonstrated that such a view is indefensible.[43] But the mythology appears to persist. In 1994 the only dependable
temporary form of birth control available for men is still the condom.
Due to renewed interest in the condom because of its ability to significantly lessen the transmission of the HIV virus, it has been redesigned
and is now being marketed as a barrier device *for women*.[44] This device,
the so called "female condom," has been approved for marketing despite the fact that when an FDA panel approved it, they admitted that
"the . . . data did not support claims that the female condom prevents
the spread of sexually transmitted diseases and did not provide enough
statistical basis for calculating effectiveness in preventing pregnancy."[45] Clearly, a sexist bias for birth control devices to be utilized
by, applied to, and the responsibility of women persists.

Ultimately, one suspects that Rosalind Pollack Petchesky is correct
when she maintains that: "One senses that where sex (as opposed to
reproduction) is at issue, the male of the species is still regarded by a
patriarchal culture and medicine as the delicate and vulnerable one."[46]

It is therefore not surprising that the *only* individuals currently capable of being coerced to use birth control are women. The only temporary birth control device that has been developed to interfere with the
male's role in reproduction, the condom, could not be coerced without

an extraordinary violation of privacy. Indeed, no technology that could be used in a policy of coerced birth control for men is expected within the next decade. But as the evidence clearly indicates, this is not the result of some accident of nature or fate but, rather, of a long-standing practice of discrimination in the development of birth control technology.

As such, any policy of coercing birth control is defacto discriminatory at this time because birth control technology is de facto discriminatory at this time. One cannot avoid the charge of discrimination in such instances by maintaining that such policies would neither be innately nor intentionally discriminatory. Even if a policy neither explicitly nor intentionally discriminates against any particular group, it would still be discriminatory if discrimination would, in fact, occur as a result of factors independent of the policy itself. In this instance, we are dealing with secondary discrimination, i.e., discrimination that occurs when a practice or policy depends upon some other practice that *is* innately and/or intentionally discriminatory. Although the law is not always consistent in recognizing and rejecting secondary discrimination,[47] both ethical tradition and common sense acknowledge the unacceptability of secondary discrimination.[48] Whenever a practice or policy A utilizes or depends upon a discriminatory practice or policy B, policy A can still be appropriately charged with discrimination. As such, no policy of coerced birth control can be considered justifiable until such a policy can be equally enforced against *both* men and women.

Adequate Assessment of Consequences

A second factor in the history of the development of birth control devices must be explicitly considered when discussing the justifiability of any such policy. Specifically, the history of birth control technology has involved an abysmal failure on the part of the medical profession and the FDA to protect women against the marketing of devices that have ultimately proven to be dangerous and, in some instances, fatal. Even cursory familiarity with the history of birth control pills,[49] IUDs,[50] and Depo-Provera[51] indicate an alarming lack of concern and responsibility in the development and marketing of birth control devices. As such, any policy that would coerce the use of birth control devices, either for women or men, must minimally require higher standards than currently employed to assure the safety of such devices. Without long-term, careful analysis of data to ensure adequate evidence of the safety of such devices, our knowledge of the true consequences of a policy coercing usage would be insufficient to support any claim that such a policy was justifiable.

The discussion above thus indicates two additional conditions required if a policy of coerced birth control is to be justified. They are:

4. A policy of coerced birth control must be nondiscriminatory in nature.

5. A policy of coerced birth control must be restricted to birth control technologies that are established to be safe for the user.

Coerced Birth Control and the Three Suggested Policies

Having identified five conditions necessary to justify the limitation of the individual rights of privacy, reproduction and bodily autonomy, we are now in a position to consider the three policies suggested at the outset of this chapter. Specifically, we will consider whether coercion of birth control could be justified in order to:

1. prevent child abuse (physical assault);
2. prevent increasing the number of children receiving welfare; and
3. prevent those convicted of certain drug offenses from reproducing.

Clearly, given the discussion in the preceding section, no policy of coerced birth control whatsoever is currently justifiable due to the discriminatory nature of birth control technology. Therefore, in this section we will consider the following question: if, in the future, birth control devices were available for use by both men and women that posed no significant health risk to the user, would it be justifiable to coerce their use in any of these instances?

The Prevention of Child Abuse

On the basis of the test of "rational relationship," a policy coercing the use of birth control to prevent child abuse is always unjustifiable. The individual who abuses a child does so in his/her capacity and role as *custodial* parent and not in his/her role as *biological* parent. But there are a variety of reasons why an individual might choose to biologically parent a child even though he or she may not be able to obtain parental custody of that child. Because biological and custodial parenting are separate and separable functions, such a policy would fail to meet the criterion of "rational relationship." Thus, although one can certainly justify limiting an individual's right to act as custodial parent in order to prevent child abuse,[52] one cannot justify coercing birth control in order to do so.

In addition, the coercion of birth control is a far more intrusive and restrictive measure with regard to privacy, bodily autonomy, and reproductive rights than is the removal of (all) custodial parenting right. Certainly one might hope that an individual who was denied custodial parenting rights on the basis of child abuse would elect to prevent future births.[53] But it is far more intrusive and restrictive to coerce birth control (including choosing the method of birth control) than to deny an individual custodial rights to any future children. As such, such a policy also fails the criterion of The Least Restrictive or Intrusive Remedy Principle.

Prevention of Increasing the Number of Children on Welfare

A policy offering $500 to a woman on welfare for agreeing to have Norplant inserted may be touted as "an inducement," but to a woman with children living on welfare, such an "inducement" must be viewed as coercive. Although technically women on welfare could "choose" not to have the implant, our understanding of "coercion" traditionally allows for other "choices" than the one being coerced. Ms. Johnson (cited in the California case at the beginning of the paper) could "choose" to go to prison for an additional three years rather than have a Norplant implant. Similarly I could "choose" to let you pull the trigger of the gun you are holding to my head rather than agree to rob the poor box. In all three cases however, the "inducement" to perform the desired action is so heavily weighted on that side, that no true free choice is possible. For a woman on welfare who is raising children, a $500 "inducement" fee could make the difference in her ability to provide adequate nutrition for her children, to obtain the child care necessary for her to receive training that could provide her with employment, or to provide medical treatment for her children that would not be available through public assistance. This is why Julie Mertus, a lawyer with the ACLU, has stated:

> We would be delighted if this were part of a package to improve reproductive health care for women, and there were no monetary incentives, but it's a bribe that pushes women into one choice instead of creating more choices. When a woman receiving Aid to Families with Dependent Children is offered $500, it crosses the line into unconstitutional coercion.[54]

But even if such policies are acknowledged as being coercive, we still must determine whether or not they constitute justified coercion. I will argue that such policies are not justifiable because they violate three criteria necessary for limiting rights.

First, even if the policy were considered only after birth control devices are made available for coercion of both sexes, without a major change of societal structures and practices the policy would still be discriminatory, both sexually and racially. Since welfare mothers are not *solely* responsible for the reproduction of their children, they should not be the sole targets of such a policy. But because society and the court discriminate against men being given (sole) custody of their children and because the welfare system strongly discriminates against giving welfare to two-parent families, women become the sole target of such policies. In addition, because racial discrimination keeps minority women disproportionately unemployed or underemployed, such a policy would impact disproportionately on minority populations. For this reason, when a similar policy was suggested in an editorial in the *Philadelphia Inquirer*, "The editorial was so widely denounced by both the newspaper's staff and readers as racist that the newspaper later printed an apology."[55]

Even if such a policy were not racially and sexually discriminatory, it is not clear that it would satisfy the harm principle. The harm to be avoided would presumably be the harm to society of producing another child to be supported on welfare. But is this harm adequate to limit fundamental rights of welfare recipients? So long as government is capable of funding projects that are not absolutely necessary (and few governments are not) it is doubtful that the harm done to society is sufficient to deny welfare recipients their rights to bodily autonomy, privacy, and reproductive freedom. Such a policy also presumes a good number of questionable probabilities. Since the harm principle requires that the harm is highly probable (or, if very serious, reasonably probable), it would have to be demonstrated that someone currently on welfare is likely to remain on welfare in order to justify the policy. In addition, in order to be nonarbitrary and nondiscriminatory, it would be necessary to demonstrate that individuals currently on welfare are (far) more likely to remain on welfare than those not currently on welfare, e.g., those near the poverty level who are likely to require welfare in the future. Otherwise, the latter group, posing equal or near equal potential "harm" to the society should also, in theory, be liable to similar coercion.

Finally, such a policy appears to fail the criterion of "least restrictive remedy." Funds to coerce birth control under such a policy could be utilized to provide (even coerce) skill or job training that could enable welfare recipients to get themselves (and their existing children) off welfare. Such a measure would surely be both less restrictive and less intrusive than a policy of coerced birth control.

Coerced Birth Control and Drug Offenders

Can we justify a policy of coerced birth control as a condition of probation for individuals convicted of certain drug offenses? Notice that two separate issues are being conflated into this one question. On the one hand, we must contend with the question of what punishment is reasonable and appropriate for those convicted of specific drug offenses. On the other hand, we are concerned with preventing birth defects that may be caused by using drugs during pregnancy. But one can be convicted of a drug offense without personally abusing drugs. Conversely, many people are guilty of drug (or other chemical) abuse that is potentially harmful to future offspring even though they have not been convicted of any drug offense. As such, there is no "rational relationship" between conviction for drug offenses and birth control. Therefore, on the whole, most policies coercing birth control as a condition of probation for drug offenses would fail the test of "rational relationship." It would be far more rational and effective to establish a policy of coerced drug testing rather than a policy of coerced birth control in these instances. We can require that convicted drug offenders undergo mandatory drug testing and drug abuse rehabilitation and counseling rather than mandatory birth control as a condition of their probation. If these mandatory test results are positive for usage, the offender could and should be returned to jail. As such, the suggested policy of coerced birth control for drug offenders would violate our understanding of the justifiable limitation of the fundamental rights to privacy, bodily autonomy, and reproduction.

What shall we say of instances in which drug offenses are connected with birth defects, instances in which drug offenses involve abusing drugs that are prone to lead to birth defects? Although the abuse of some illegal drugs is known to cause serious birth defects (particularly when used prior to conception or during pregnancy), abuse of alcohol and abuse of many legal drugs are also known to cause serious birth defects.[56] Therefore, on the basis of consistency, we must hold that if we decide to coerce birth control to prevent birth defects in instances involving illegal drug usage, we must adopt a policy that will apply equally to instances in which birth defects are caused by alcohol abuse or legal drug abuse. If concern about birth defects is at the heart of the suggestion that we coerce drug offenders to use birth control, then it is their chemical abuse and not their criminal offense that is the basis of this policy. As such, we need to consider a policy that would coerce birth control in order to prevent the birth of severely defective infants rather than consider a policy directed solely (and irrelevantly) at convicted drug offenders. I shall consider such a policy in the final section of this essay.

Is the Coercive Use of Birth Control Ever Justified?

Given the discussion above, I believe that there is a rather narrow range of situations that could, in theory, justify the coercive use of birth control. Such situations would be ones in which an individual would be likely to cause serious harm to others in his/her role as biological parent and when no less intrusive or restrictive means is available for preventing the harm. Such instances would justify a policy of coerced birth control if the policy were used in a nondiscriminatory fashion (racially, sexually, etc.) and involved only those birth control devices that, based on adequate research trials, could be demonstrated to be safe for its users.

What sorts of instances would these criteria include? I will now discuss what I take to be the most obvious instances in which birth control would appear to be justified—instances in which birth control is coerced in order to prevent the birth of severely defective children.[57]

Preventing the Birth of Severely Defective Children

Coerced birth control might be justified in the event that an individual or couple were *very* likely to produce a child with serious abnormalities or diseases, ones likely to produce a very poor quality of life for the child and its family (as well as creating a serious drain on community resources). This could occur as the result of genetic weaknesses, diseases, or chemical abuse.

Thus, if our knowledge of genetics ever reaches the point where we can predict that a particular couple has a very high probability of producing a child that is profoundly mentally or physically handicapped, we might be justified in coercing birth control. If an individual has a serious disease that significantly affects quality of life and if there is a high probability of the disease being transmitted to an unborn child, this might also justify coercing birth control.[58] If an individual is abusing alcohol and/or drugs and we can establish a high probability of his or her producing a child with serious abnormalities as a result of the abuse, we might also be justified in coercing birth control.

But even these instances are not straightforward. Our knowledge of genetics and physiology would have to be far more advanced than is currently the case. We would need a consistent set of standards for determining how probable the harmful outcome would have to be in order to justify coerced birth control. As the Harm Principle indicates, the less serious the possible harm, the more probable it must be in order to justify limiting individual rights. Thus we would have to determine, *with regard to each particular disease or abnormality*, how probable the harm must be in order to justify limiting individual rights. If, for example, a couple had a 30 percent chance of producing a hydrocephalic child, would this be a sufficiently high probability to justify coercing the use of birth control? Would 80 percent? 95 percent? It is far from clear that we could establish such standards on any nonarbitrary basis.

We would also have to be sufficiently knowledgeable regarding genetics and diseases to determine that what appears to be a harmful anomaly or disorder is not tied to a significant beneficial quality. For example, although the sickle cell anemia trait appears to be a highly undesirable genetic quality potentially leading to the development of sickle cell anemia disease, carriers of the sickle cell anemia trait have greater protection against falciparum malaria.[59] As such, it is not clear that the sickle cell anemia trait would be a satisfactory candidate for elimination from the gene pool.

In addition, adequate genetic information may ultimately suggest that virtually all humans carry genetic propensities for highly undesirable traits. Is the likelihood of producing daughters prone to develop breast cancer less harmful than the likelihood of producing a Down's Syndrome child? If we determine that it is acceptable to coerce birth control in order to avoid producing children with genetic weaknesses, abnormalities, or specific diseases, we may discover that none of us would be a suitable biological parent.

What should we say in instances in which children are born with profound disabilities due to a parent abusing alcohol or drugs? Can we, for example, justify coercing birth control for a woman who has already produced children with fetal alcohol syndrome or birth defects resulting from cocaine usage? Assume in such instances that this woman has already been provided with adequate counseling for her addiction but continues to abuse her chemical of choice. Is she a legitimate candidate for coerced birth control? Unfortunately, even in this instance, a remedy of coerced birth control is not unproblematic. We do not, for example, know enough about drug and alcohol abuse to know to what extent environmental factors precipitate the abuse. There is good evidence that poverty contributes significantly to drug usage (a disproportionate percentage of drug users appear to be poor).

In addition, it is far more likely that an individual using publicly funded agencies will be detected as fitting this criterion than one receiving services through private agencies and health professionals. Thus a disproportionately high percentage of those recognized to constitute a danger to the health of their fetuses due to chemical abuse will be poor. As such, this suggested policy is liable to be unjustly discriminatory on the basis of class and (as a result of racial discrimination) race.

Finally, with regard to all of the instances above, it is not clear that the harm to be prevented is adequate to justify the potential harm to society that such a policy may precipitate. Do we want to live in a society in which government determines who may and may not reproduce, one in which the government's decision is based on the likelihood of producing "defective" children? Or is the potential harm of producing such children not as serious as the potential harm of establishing a government with the legitimate capacity to intervene in what is traditionally recognized as a very private decision? The answer to this question largely rests on our evaluation of the number of defective children likely to be produced through genetic abnormalities, diseases passed through reproduction and drug and alcohol abuse. There may come a time when these numbers are perceived to be sufficiently high to justify governmental intervention. But at this time, both our knowledge of these issues as well as the number of defective children born annually do not appear adequate to justify a policy of coerced birth control.

In addition, given that in at least two of the above instances[60] no culpability rests with the potential parent, it would seem that less restrictive, less intrusive means *might* be equally satisfactory. Thus, rather than coercing the use of birth control, the state would be more justified in offering or even coercing individuals to attend courses that would educate prospective parents on the problems connected with their biological parenting and then allow them to choose alternative methods of birth control or abortion. If such a policy were equally or nearly equally efficacious in preventing the birth of profoundly handicapped children, then on the basis of the criterion of Least Restrictive Remedy, coerced birth control would still not be justifiable.

Conclusion

What should we conclude, given the discussion above? Perhaps, most obviously, that simply because technological developments make certain policies possible, this in no way makes them desirable. The fact that individuals within both legislative and judicial branches of government have attempted casually, simplistically, and precipitously to coerce the usage of Norplant (within months of its initial marketing) should be a significant source of alarm to the American public. Little, if any, weight appears to have been given to consideration of the extent to which such policies would limit individual rights, affect the health of those forced to use the technology, or further sexual and racial discrimination.

In addition, we must recognize that although there may be instances in which coerced birth control could be justified, the impact of such policies on personal autonomy, the potential health risks innate to almost all methods of birth control, and the danger of such policies being the basis for de facto discrimination support the view that such policies should be among the last considered to remedy any anticipated harm.

Notes

Part of this paper was published as ''Coerced Birth Control, Individual Rights, and Discrimination,'' *Biomedical Ethics Review: 1992,* ed. James M. Humber and Robert F. Almeder (Totowa, N.J.: Humana Press, 1993) and from ''Norplant© and Coercion: Secondary Discrimination as a Standard for Applied Feminist Ethics,'' presented to the Society for Analytical Feminism at the American Philosophical Association Central Division Meetings, April 1993.

1. *New York Times*, Jan. 5, 1991.
2. *New York Times*, Oct. 19, 1991.
3. *American Family Physician*, July 1991, 103–8.
4. *New York Times*, Jan. 10, 1991.
5. This was established in 1942 in *Skinner v. Oklahoma*, a sterilization case in which the court maintained "this legislation involves one of the basic civil rights of man. Marriage and procreation are fundamental to the very existence and survival of the race. . . . There is no redemption for the individual whom the law touches. He is forever deprived of a basic liberty." Congress of the United States, Office of Technology Assessment, *Infertility: Medical and Social Choices* (U.S. Government Printing Office, May 1988), 220.
6. Ibid., 103–4.
7. Although the courts have traditionally considered the right to bodily autonomy to be fundamental, there are two different types of instances in which the courts have recently ruled against the individual's right to decide what will happen in and to his or her body. In *Webster v. Missouri* and in *Bowers v. Hardwick*, the courts ruled against an individual's right to use his or her body in specific practices (i.e., with regard to abortion and homosexual acts). In addition, there have been a number of instances of late in which the court has forced a woman to undergo medical treatments and/or procedures to protect the health of her unborn child. (See "Here Come the Pregnancy Police," *Glamour Magazine*, August 1990, 203–5, 263–66.) Neither of these instances, however, is relevant to the issue of coerced birth control.
8. *Infertility: Medical and Social Choices*, 204.
9. Ibid., 205.
10. See, e.g., Joel Feinberg, *Harm to Self*, vol. 3. (Oxford: Oxford University Press, 1986), 52–53 where he uses bodily autonomy as the basis for explaining personal autonomy and sovereignty. See Carolyn M. Shafer and Marilyn Frey, "Rape and Respect," in *Women and Values: Readings in Recent Feminist Philosophy*, by Marilyn Pearsall (Belmont, Calif: Wadsworth Publishing Company, 1986), 188–96, where bodily autonomy is the basis for explaining domain and rightful power of consent and, thus, why one has a right not to be raped. See Janet Jarvis Thomson, "A Defense of Abortion," in *Women and Values*, 268–79, where bodily autonomy is part of her justification for the right to an abortion.
11. In *Roe v. Wade*, the court held:

going back perhaps as far as *Union Pacific R. Co. v. Botsford* (1891), the Court has recognized that a right of personal privacy, or a guarantee of certain areas of zones of privacy, does exist under the Constitution. . . . These decisions make it clear that only personal rights that can be deemed "fundamental" or "implicit in the concept of ordered liberty," . . . are included in this guarantee of personal privacy. They also make it clear the right has some extension to activities relating to marriage . . . procreation . . . contraception . . . family relationships . . . and child rearing and education. . . . The Court's decisions recognizing a right of privacy also acknowledge that some state regulation in areas protected by that right is appropriate. . . . a state may properly assert important interests in safe-guarding health, in maintaining medical standards, and in protecting potential life. From Thomas A. Mappes and Jane S. Zembaty, *Social Ethics: Morality and Social Policy*, 4th ed. (New York: McGraw-Hill, 1992), 41–42.

12. John Stuart Mill, *On Liberty* (New York: Bobbs-Merrill, 1956), chapter 1, paragraph 9.

13. For example, Feinberg considers five other grounds for limiting individual liberties (offense to others, harm to self, punishment of sin, benefit to self, and benefit to others) in "Grounds for Coercion," *Social Philosophy* (Englewood Cliffs, N.Y.: Prentice Hall, 1973), 20–45.

14. A similar view is maintained by the *European Convention on Human Rights*. (See *European Law Review*, vol. 8, 1983, Dudgeon Case, 205.)

15. Carol A. Tauer "AIDS: Towards an Ethical Public Policy," in *AIDS and Ethics (Biomedical Ethics Reviews*: 1988), eds. Robert F. Almeder and James Humber (Totowa, N. J.: Humana Press, 1989), 79–102.

16. See, e.g., "*Jew Ho v. Williamson*," *Federal Reporter*, 1900:103, 10–27 (Northern District of California Circuit Court).

17. See, e.g., Michael Mills, Constance Wofsy, and John Mills, "The Acquired Immunodeficiency Syndrome: Infection Control and Public Health Law," *New England Journal of Medicine* 314 (April 3, 1986): 931–36 and Bonnie Steinbock, "Harming, Wronging, and AIDS" in *AIDS and Ethics (Biomedical Ethics Reviews: 1988)*, 27–43.

18. Tauer, op. cit.; Mills, Wofsy, and Mills, op. cit.

19. See *Jew Ho v. Williamson* and *Camara v. Municipal Court, United States Reports*, 1967; 387:523–40.

20. See *Jew Ho v. Williamson*, 18.

21. See, e.g. Mills, Wofsy, and Mills, "The Acquired Immunodeficiency Syndrome" and Bonnie Steinbock, "Harming, Wronging, and AIDS."

22. *Federal Reporter* 653, 2nd Series, "*Rennie v. Klein*," 836. See also, Mills, Wofsy, and Mills, "The Acquired Immunodeficiency Syndrome"; *Rock v. Carney, Michigan Reports* 1921; 216:280–91 (Supreme Court); *Barmore v. Robertson, Northeastern Reporter* 1922; 134:815–21 (Illinois Supreme Court).

23. See, e.g., *Jew Ho v. Williamson*, 11.

24. Gena Corea, *The Hidden Malpractice* (New York: Harper Colophon Books, 1985), 150.

25. The study was an in-house study made at my request by the Program Analysis Branch of the National Institute of Child Health and Human Development of NIH.

26. Susan Faludi, *Backlash: The Undeclared War Against Women* (New York: Crown Publishers, 1991), 31–32. This is true despite the fact that men's sperm counts have dropped by more than half in thirty years, an important consideration given that low sperm count is a significant cause of infertility. As

a result, a common treatment for "infertile couples" whose infertility is caused by a low sperm count in the male partner is to subject the female partner to in vitro fertilization, a process that involves "pumping a woman full of hormones so she will release more than the usual number of eggs . . . placing her under general anesthesia, . . . sucking her eggs out; fertilizing the eggs in a dish and . . . inserting the embryo through her vagina and into her uterus. . . . it is a complicated procedure that rarely works." Gena Corea, "The New Reproductive Technologies," in *The Sexual Liberals and the Attack on Feminism*, ed. Dorchen Leidholdt and Janice G. Raymond (New York: Pergamon Press, 1990), 87–88.

27. See Corea, *The Hidden Malpractice*, 149–76. See also Vimal Balasubrahmanyan, "Women as Targets in India's Family Planning Policy," and Scarlet Pollock, "Refusing to Take Women Seriously: 'Side Effects' and the Politics of Contraception," in *Test-Tube Women: What Future for Motherhood?*, ed. Rita Arditti, Renate Duelli Klein, and Shelley Minden (Boston: Pandora Press, 1984), 153–64, 138–52.

28. Corea, *The Hidden Malpractice*, 178–88; Rita Arditti, "Have You Ever Wondered About the Male Pill?" in *Seizing Our Bodies: The Politics of Women's Health*, ed. Claudia Dreifus (New York: Random House, 1977), 126–27.

29. Corea, *The Hidden Malpractice*, 150, 177, 179–188; Arditti, 121–28.

30. I strongly recommend Gena Corea's *The Hidden Malpractice* for an in-depth discussion of the issue.

31. Linda Gordon, *Woman's Body, Woman's Right: Birth Control in America* (New York: Penguin Books, 1990), 422.

32. Corea, *The Hidden Malpractice*, 157–58.

33. Corea, *The Hidden Malpractice*, 155. In 1983, two government agencies encouraged use of the pill by "issuing a report claiming that its use benefitted arthritis victims, a claim that has since had to be retracted." Linda Gordon, *Woman's Body, Woman's Right: Birth Control in America* (New York: Penguin Books, 1990) 422.

34. Corea, *The Hidden Malpractice*, 159.

35. Corea, *The Hidden Malpractice*, 178.

36. Corea, *The Hidden Malpractice*, 179.

37. Rita Arditti. "Have You Ever Wondered About the Male Pill?" 127.

38. Corea, *The Hidden Malpractice*, 178.

39. See Corea, *The Hidden Malpractice*, 177–78; Rita Arditti, *Seizing Our Bodies*, 121–22.

40. Arditti, *Seizing Our Bodies*, 122.

41. Knight also argues that "high child mortality rates can be devastating to women, and in the past have led some women to seek a means of avoiding pregnancy. . . . Moreover, the burden of primary responsibility for child rearing has traditionally (fairly or not) fallen on women." But given that the reasons cited are considerations only because of past and existing cultural discrimination against women, they themselves constitute secondary discrimination.

42. James W. Knight and Joan C. Callahan, *Preventing Birth: Contemporary Methods and Related Moral Controversies* (Salt Lake City: University of Utah Press, 1989), 12.

43. See, e.g., Shafer and Frye, "Rape and Respect." See also Pamela Foa, "What's Wrong with Rape," in *Feminism and Philosophy*, ed. Mary Vetterling-Braggin et al. (New Jersey: Littlefield, Adams & Co., 1977), 313–332 and Susan Rae Peterson, "Coercion and Rape: The State as a Male Protection Racket," 360–71.

44. The "female condom" is designed to be inserted into a woman as opposed to being put on a man.

45. *New York Times National*, Feb. 1, 1992, 7.

46. Rosalind Pollack Petchesky, *Abortion and Woman's Choice: The State, Sexuality, and Reproductive Freedom* (Boston: Northeastern University Press, 1990), 173.

47. For a discussion of the treatment of secondary discrimination in the law, see Catherine A. MacKinnon, *Feminism Unmodified: Discourses on Life and Law* (Cambridge: Harvard University Press, 1987), 64–65.

48. If I own a contracting company and only employ carpenters belonging to union X, a union that I know discriminates against minority workers, I cannot avoid the charge of discrimination by insisting that *I* personally am not discriminating. Nor can I claim that I have no moral responsibility for discrimination when I knowingly join a restricted country club. Even if I join the club simply because I wish to use its facilities (and not because I want or intend to discriminate), I am still morally culpable for supporting unjustifiable discrimination.

49. Corea, *The Hidden Malpractice*, 151–59, 170–75. Barbara Seaman, "The Dangers of Oral Contraception," in *Seizing Our Bodies*, 75–85.

50. Corea, *The Hidden Malpractice*, 150, 159–65. Mark Dowie and Tracy Johnston, "The Case of Corporate Malpractice and the Dalkon Shield," in *Seizing Our Bodies*, 86–104.

51. Corea, *The Hidden Malpractice*, 165–69, 175–76. Phillida Bunkle, "Calling the Shots? The International Politics of Depo-Provera," in *Seizing Our Bodies*, 165–87.

52. Indeed, I would argue that one should do so. Sadly, the courts often neglect to do so and as a result, far too many children remain under custodial control of abusive parents.

53. I do not here intend to suggest that this alternative is one which does not have serious drawbacks. The plight of children who are in the custodial care of the state would be difficult in the best of circumstances; and unfortunately, given the state of foster care in the United States currently, the plight of such children is very difficult indeed. I am simply maintaining that the harm caused to children who would be born under these circumstances (and placed in foster care) would not be as great as the harm done to those whose basic rights would be abrogated under a policy of coerced birth control as well as the harm done to the society as a result of adopting such a policy.

54. *New York Times*, February 9, 1991.

55. *New York Times*, February 9, 1991.

56. Indeed, according to Beth Conover, R.N., M.S. (in genetic counseling) of the Nebraska Terategon Project, University of Nebraska Medical Center, studies linking birth defects with chemical use have only established a *significant* risk of birth defects in the instance of alcohol abuse and the use of accutane, a prescription drug used to treat acne. (In fact women are coerced to use birth control as a condition of receiving a prescription for accutane.) Preliminary studies on illegal drugs indicate a moderate risk of birth defects linked to cocaine usage, but it has not yet been established to what degree this risk is connected to the concurrent abuse of alcohol. Finally, it should be noted that this is the only policy that is discussed in this paper for which men may not be targets. Based on current studies, there is no clear evidence that male chemical abuse is linked to any birth defects.

57. There are certainly other instances that might justify coerced birth control that I have not considered here. For example, a policy of coerced birth control might be justified in situations of serious overpopulation. Thus, in countries where population significantly outreaches available food supply, the state might be justified in coercing birth control to prevent large-scale harm to the society of further overpopulation. But not only would it be necessary to construct such policies so they would be nondiscriminatory in nature, it would also be necessary to determine that no less restrictive policy (e.g., education, readily available selection of birth control devices, etc.) would be equally efficacious.

58. Note that this description does not appear to apply in the instance of AIDS. This is because "most infants who become infected acquire the virus [AIDS] during the birthing process" (*New York Times*, January 7, 1992, C-3). Studies are currently underway that are testing methods to prevent the spread of the disease during the birth process. If successful, having AIDS will not affect one's role as biological parent. In addition, "All children with HIV-infected mothers test positive at birth. In the first few years of life, however, many "seroconvert" as their own immune systems develop, and they grow up free of the disease" (*Parade Magazine*, February 23, 1992). We are not currently able to determine the probabilities of an HIV-infected parent producing a child with AIDS.

59. See Jean D. Wison et al., eds., *Harrison's Principles of Internal Medicine*, 12th edition (New York: McGraw-Hill, 1991).

60. I would argue that in the third scenario, alcohol or drug abuse is a disease and, as such, no culpability should attach to the individual.

Questions

1. According to Kuo, what is the relationship between religion and forced birth control? Do you agree with Kuo?

2. In your opinion, are there any rational reasons to coerce a person to undergo minor surgery? Is having the physical ability to bear children sufficient to claim also the moral right to bear children? Do you think that having children is necessarily good? If not, in what ways might it be bad?
3. What does it mean to have a right to bodily autonomy? Is this an absolute right? How does such a right relate to the harm principle?
4. According to Kuo, in what way does sex discrimination enter into the medical community's pursuit of birth control technology? What does Kuo mean when she speaks of "methods of birth control directed against female fertility?"
5. What sorts of birth control devices are now available to men? Do you believe that men's sexual drives are stronger than women's? How would we know? What does this have to do with Kuo's paper?
6. If a woman is offered only two possibilities—go to jail or use Norplant—can she make an autonomous choice? Do you believe coercion of birth control with Norplant—will solve the problem of child abuse? Explain.

11

Is IVF Research a Threat to Women's Autonomy?

Mary Anne Warren

Many of the moral objections to in vitro fertilization (IVF) and to research on human pre-embryos are based upon beliefs about the moral status of the pre-embryo itself. I shall consider a different moral objection to the experimental production and use of IVF pre-embryos, an objection based not on the supposed rights of pre-embryos, but on those of the persons from whom they originate. This objection is central to a number of feminist critiques of the new reproductive technologies. It is that women, in particular, do not freely choose to be subjects or donors in IVF and other reproductive research. Women's "choices" about the new reproductive technologies, it is argued, are controlled by coercive social pressures, and thus are neither free nor autonomous.[1] If women cannot autonomously choose or refuse to be experimental subjects or donors to reproductive research, then their participation in such research cannot be viewed as an exercise of their medical/reproductive rights. Nor can it easily be defended as in their own best interests, since most women who serve as subjects or donors are not greatly benefited, and some are subjected to significant medical risks.

Medical professionals respond to this objection by pointing to the practice of obtaining patients' "informed consent" for medical treatment or research. Today, at least in much of the world, physicians and researchers are required by law and/or institutional policy to obtain the consent of any person whose gametes or pre-embryos are used in medical or reproductive research. But is informed consent an adequate protection for women's autonomy in the context of IVF research? That is the question this chapter addresses.

In the first section I examine some of the reasons for requiring autonomous consent, from male as well as female donors, for research on human gametes or pre-embryos. In the second section I consider some sexual asymmetries that make the presumption of autonomous consent more problematic in the case of women. In the third section I consider the concept of informed consent and argue that adherence to ordinary standards of informed consent is not enough to enable all competent patients to make autonomous decisions. Women's practical options with respect to reproductive therapy and research might be such that it would be inappropriate to speak of choice, even when informed consent is given.

But there is no reason to conclude that this must be the case. In the fourth section I argue that most women who consider IVF therapy are capable of making substantially autonomous decisions about donating oocytes or spare pre-embryos to reproductive research. Nevertheless, respect for the autonomy of these women requires more than adherence to the usual requirements for informed consent. In the last section, I suggest some ways to counter the danger that reproductive research will compromise women's medical and reproductive autonomy.

Why Should Donor Consent Be Required?

To most people, it seems obvious that research on human gametes or pre-embryos should not be done without the consent of the individuals from whom these gametes or pre-embryos originated. The Warnock Report recommended that donor consent be required as "a matter of good practice."[2] Those who believe that IVF research violates the rights of pre-embryos will deny that donors' consent can justify such research. In their view, that would be morally analogous to allowing parents to volunteer their children for dangerous medical experiments that are of no possible benefit to the children themselves.[3] But few would argue that IVF or pre-embryo research should proceed *without* the donors' consent, except perhaps in exceptional cases. (The donor consent requirement might reasonably be waived, for instance, to enable a spouse or family member to donate a deceased person's stored sperm, oocytes, or spare pre-embryos.)

What is the basis of the claimed right of individuals to authorize or veto any experimental uses of their in vitro gametes or pre-embryos? Is there, in fact, any such right? It is relatively easy to explain why competent persons should not be subjected to medical interventions without their consent: the infliction of medical treatment upon unwilling persons constitutes a physical assault. But in vitro gametes or pre-embryos are no longer part of the persons from whom they originated, and experiments on them pose no direct physical threat to the latter. Why, then should their consent be required?

There are obvious pragmatic arguments for obtaining consent. Evidence that researchers were surreptitiously appropriating patients' gametes or pre-embryos for unauthorized purposes could do much to turn opinion against IVF research. But such practical considerations cannot be central to the right in question. If there is such a right, then the covert appropriation of gametes or pre-embryos would be wrong even if it caused researchers no detrimental publicity or other misfortune.

This right is sometimes treated as a property right, arising from explicit contractual agreements. Couples undergoing IVF treatment are usually given this right by law and/or by the terms of the agreement between themselves and those providing IVF services. The couple's reproductive cells are treated as their legal property, which is temporarily held in trust by the IVF program, and which may be used only in ways the couple have authorized. But such legal or contractual arrangements cannot be the primary basis of this right either. If there is a general right to control the uses others make of one's gametes or pre-embryos, it must be a moral right and not entirely derivative from specific laws or contracts. Otherwise, in the absence of legal or contractual prohibitions, researchers would do nothing seriously wrong in using human reproductive cells in ways the "donors" would find unacceptable.

The physical origin of human reproductive cells may provide another basis for the right in question. Perhaps the right to control one's own body has, as an implication or corollary, the right to control the uses made of any tissues or cells derived from one's body. True, so-called "discarded tissue" is not usually regarded as the patients's property, and should it be needed for some research project the patient's consent is not usually sought. But this may be appropriate only because most people do not care what is done with such material. Perhaps, when individuals do have strong preferences about what is done with cells or tissues derived from their bodies, those preferences ought to be respected.

This is a plausible claim, at least in many instances. A person's discarded tissues are related to that person in potentially important ways. For instance, hair like blood and other body fluids, can be analyzed to detect the use of certain proscribed drugs—though often not very reliably. Tissue analyses may also detect disease or predisease conditions, the knowledge of which, in certain hands, could result in the loss of employment or health insurance. For these and other reasons, individuals have a legitimate interest in controlling what others do with their discarded tissues. That interest will become even more important as additional procedures for extracting information from human cells, tissues, and body fluids are developed and marketed.

But gametes and pre-embryos are unlike (other) discarded tissues in one crucial respect. Not only are they a possible source of information about the individual from whom they came; they also have the potential to contribute to the development of a new human being, the genetic child of that individual. If it were possible to clone human beings from the genetic material contained in any living human cell, then any such cell would have that potential. But that kind of cloning is currently impossible, and likely to remain so for a long time. In this respect, then, reproductive cells are unique.

I strongly doubt that the possible developmental future of gametes or pre-embryos is enough to establish moral rights *for them*.[4] But it is enough to give both women and men a legitimate interest in controlling the uses made of their reproductive cells. This developmental potential means that the unauthorized use of gametes and pre-embryos is objectionable, in part, because it may violate reproductive rights.

Like other moral rights, reproductive rights are social creations, attempts to create zones of protection for certain interests that are vital to individual or societal well-being. The right to reproductive autonomy protects the powerful interest that most people have in controlling their own reproductive lives—or at least in not being unjustly prevented from doing so. Reproductive autonomy is a special case of the right to self-determination, which many regard as the most basic moral right.

The right to reproductive autonomy precludes a large range of coercive interventions into the reproductive lives of individuals, particularly (but not exclusively) interventions that prevent them from having children when they wish to or that force them to have children when they wish not to. It is, to that extent, a "negative" right, a right that others refrain from certain actions. But, like other moral rights, it also sometimes requires that positive steps be taken to enable individuals to enjoy the benefits that the right is intended to protect.

In most analyses of the right to reproductive autonomy, some coercive limitations of individuals' medical/reproductive options may be permissible. It might, for instance, be appropriate to ban the sale of some medically dangerous contraceptive—provided that safer and equally affordable substitutes are available. But reproductive autonomy requires that such exceptions be made only on the basis of a clear necessity. Those who wish coercively to limit the medical/reproductive choices of others must show, not only that there are some probable net benefits from these limitations, but also that these limitations are likely to be less objectionable and costly to each of the affected individuals than the alternative policy of letting them make their own decisions, on the basis of the best information available.

Should the right to reproductive autonomy include the right to control the uses made of one's in vitro gametes or pre-embryos? It might seem odd that reproductive autonomy should extend to a veto over procedures that (so far as can be predicted) will neither cause the birth of unwanted children, nor prevent the birth of wanted ones. Why, for instance, should a couple undergoing IVF treatment retain the right to control the disposition of their spare pre-embryos once they have decided not to use them to try to start a pregnancy?

One answer is that the in vitro fertilization of a human ovum by a human sperm is a part of the reproductive lives of at least two persons. Even if this event will probably never lead to the birth of an infant, it is at least theoretically possible that it might, e.g., with the aid of a "surrogate" mother. The fact gives those persons a legitimate interest in this event and its eventual outcome. They may also have moral, religious, or other reasons for attaching importance to the conception and pre-embryonic development of their own potential children. Some of these reasons may be debatable, but that is not the point. In the absence of clearly compelling reasons to the contrary, they are entitled to conduct their reproductive lives as they think best. Neither scientific curiosity nor the possibility of therapeutic benefits to other persons could justify the use of coercive or deceitful means to obtain human gametes or pre-embryos for research purposes.

Some Sexual Asymmetries

These arguments for requiring consent for IVF research are applicable to both female and male donors. But donating gametes or pre-embryos is a different proposition for women than for men. One difference is that it is not sperm, but oocytes, that are a scarce and limiting resource in such research. Whereas most fertile men regularly produce millions of spermatozoa, women normally produce only one mature oocyte each month. Furthermore, while sperm donation usually requires no medical intervention, "oocyte recovery" involves the physical invasion of the woman's body and, typically, the administration of drugs or hormones to alter the functioning of her reproductive system.

In contemporary IVF programs, oocytes are collected from the surface of the ovary either through incisions in the woman's abdominal wall—the laparoscopic method[5]—or through the use of ultrasound to guide an aspiration needle.[6] While the latter method usually does not require surgery or general anaesthesia, it is still invasive and carries some risk of infection or damage to internal organs. In addition, the woman is usually given antioestrogenic drugs or gonadotrophic hormones to cause her to produce multiple mature oocytes in a single monthly cycle. The long-term effects of these drugs are not yet known. Oocytes may also be obtained from women who undergo surgery for other reasons, e.g., hysterectomy or tubal ligation for sterilization.[7] In such cases oocyte recovery may create additional risks to women.

These women are potentially vulnerable to medical exploitation. The researchers' need for oocytes and pre-embryos may create a conflict of interest that adversely affects the medical care some women receive. In the worst case, women might be coerced or deceived into undergoing unnecessary surgery, drug exposure, or other potentially harmful procedures in order to provide reproductive researchers with additional opportunities for the collection of oocytes. There have already been allegations of this sort of abuse. Gena Corea reports that, according to physician and author Michelle Harrison, the decision to remove the healthy ovaries of premenopausal hysterectomy patients has sometimes been made in apparent response to requests for these organs from infertility researchers.[8]

The danger that women will be victimized by what Corea calls "egg snatchers"[9] has little or no practical parallel in the case of men. Researchers are unlikely to engage in "sperm-snatching," since sperm can generally be obtained without much difficulty from willing donors. If sperm donated for one purpose (e.g., contraceptive research) were used from some other purpose (e.g., artificial insemination) without the donor's consent, then his right to reproductive autonomy may well have been violated. But he would not, in addition, have been unwillingly or unwittingly subjected to potentially harmful medical interventions.

Women are also particularly vulnerable because of the predominantly male membership and hierarchy of the biomedical professions. Medicine has historically excluded women and is still not free of patronizing and misogynist attitudes towards female patients. Thus, it is difficult for some medical professionals to respect women as autonomous decision makers.

It is also difficult for many men to understand women's interests in the area of medical/reproductive care. Much of what women experience in that context is foreign to their experience. For not only do they lack a female reproductive system, but their perceptions are inevitably influenced by the different cultural world that they inhabit as members of the dominant gender. Consequently, male physicians and researchers are prone to certain sorts of error. They may underestimate the severity of the side effects that women experience from particular treatments, and they may disbelieve women's reports of their own symptoms. They may also fail to understand the effects upon women of the *absence* of certain medical/reproductive options; e.g., advice from a doctor who is also a woman; or home birth with a physician or midwife in attendance. Consequently, the forms of care offered by the predominantly male medical profession often limit women's options in ways that cannot be justified.

Realities outside the medical context can also limit women's reproductive autonomy. One feminist concern has been the influence of pronatalism. Pronatalism has been defined as "any attitude or policy that . . . encourages reproduction, that exalts the role of parenthood."[10] As Judith Blake has argued, most women and men everywhere are "channelled" towards parenthood, e.g., by the influence of religion, education, public opinion, art, and scientific theory.[11] The impact of pronatalist ideology upon women is especially severe, because cultural norms of femininity are more insistently linked to parenthood than are the equivalent standards of masculinity. It is women who are persistently exposed to the message that they cannot be worthy, happy, or fulfilled unless they have children.

In Blake's view, the power of pronatalism is such that women cannot (be correctly said to) *choose* to have children.[12] Others have drawn a similar conclusion about women's participation as patients or donors in reproductive research. For instance, Corea argues that women's consent to undergo IVF treatment is so strongly conditioned by the pronatalist culture that it must be seen as a product of social coercion rather than autonomous individual choice.[13] In her view, women's socially reinforced desire for motherhood is so powerful that it inevitably interferes with their capacity critically to evaluate therapies that purport to offer a means of fulfilling that desire. Worse, it can make them vulnerable to a form of implicit blackmail, whereby they are expected to lend their bodies and cells to reproductive research in return for receiving the benefits of the new reproductive therapies.

If it is true that women cannot make autonomous decisions about their involvement as subjects or donors in reproductive research, then such research probably should not be done at all—or not until the unjust conditions that may control women's reproductive choices are over-come. But is it true? I will argue that, despite the unjust conditions that limit reproductive freedom, women are not incapable of making autonomous choices with respect to reproductive therapy or research. The argument requires more than an appeal to informed consent; how-ever, it will be useful to begin with an examination of that concept.

Autonomy and Informed Consent

The view that mentally competent adults have the right to make autono-mous decisions about their own medical treatment is relatively new to the medical profession. Before this century, the dominant model of the doctor-patient relationship was markedly paternalistic. Patients were generally expected to follow doctors' orders, not make decisions about their own therapy. What they were told about their medical condition, the nature of the proposed therapy, its risks and possible benefits, and any possible therapeutic alternatives was largely left to the discretion of the physician.[14]

In contrast, the contemporary ideal of patient autonomy treats the doctor more as an expert advisor to the patient than as one empowered to issue orders. Since the 1950s, legal and other regulatory protections of patients' autonomy in some countries have often included the re-quirement that informed consent be obtained for any treatment or ex-perimental research undertaken. In *A History and Theory of Informed Consent,* Ruth Faden and Tom Beauchamp present an analysis of the concept of informed consent that captures its essential features.

Faden and Beauchamp define informed consent as *autonomous* con-sent. Autonomous actions are those that are performed intentionally, with understanding, and in the absence of improper controlling influ-ences.[15] Autonomy, they note, is a practical concept. When we ask whether some action is autonomous, we are not asking whether it is fully autonomous, i.e., performed with total understanding and in total freedom from any inappropriate outside influence, for that is an impos-sible ideal. In practical contexts such as medicine, what is required is not full autonomy but rather substantial autonomy.

Substantial autonomy requires not total understanding, but a reason-able grasp of the clearly relevant information; and not total freedom from all improper influences, but the absence of coercion or morally objectionable forms of manipulation. Substantially autonomous deci-sion making by patients requires that they be provided with adequate, accurate, and comprehensible information and that their consent not be obtained through deliberate coercion or improper manipulation. Patient autonomy is the moral goal that ought to motivate the implementation of informed consent regulations. It is, they conclude, "a reasonable and achievable goal," in medicine as in other practical contexts.[16]

One reason Faden and Beauchamp find it relatively easy to equate informed consent with autonomous decision making is that they employ definitions of coercion and wrongful manipulation that are suspiciously narrow. Coercion is defined as "an extreme form of influence by another person that completely controls a person's decision."[17] This influence must be intentional; typically, it involves a threat that the threatened person cannot resist. Manipulation is also defined as an intentional influence by another person, but one that could be resisted, although it is not.[18] Unlike coercion, manipulation is not necessarily inconsistent with substantial autonomous decision making. However, autonomy can be defeated through the manipulation of information, e.g., by lying, withholding pertinent facts, or presenting facts in a deliberately misleading way. Autonomy can also be defeated by deliberate psychological manipulations, such as playing upon fear, anxiety, or guilt in order to interfere with the person's ability to understand or deliberate effectively. Offers (e.g., of financial compensation) are often manipulative, but never coercive. They are inconsistent with autonomous decision making only if they are unwelcome—i.e., repugnant to those to whom they are made, yet very difficult for them to refuse.[19]

This account of coercion and wrongful manipulation rules out some of the most important feminist concerns about women's reproductive autonomy. In this account, coercion and wrongful manipulation can only occur through the intentional actions of individuals. But many of the social, economic, and other influences that feminists hold to be coercive are not readily reducible to the intentional actions of specific individuals. Pronatalism would certainly resist any such reduction. Thus, in the account that Faden and Beauchamp give, it is not even a logically possible obstacle to autonomous choice.

On this conceptual issue, the feminist critics are surely right. Informed consent, as Faden and Beauchamp define it, is not a guarantee of autonomy. An individual's decision may not be deliberately coerced or wrongly manipulated by any other individual, yet can be controlled by social or economic factors that preclude autonomous choice. Even welcome offers may be coercive—or part of a coercive situation—if they are welcome only because other options have been unjustly foreclosed.

Sex-selective abortion may (sometimes) be a case in point. Where this service is in great demand—e.g., parts of India and Southeast Asia—women are under powerful social and economic pressure to have sons. Daughters have little earning power and will in any case leave the family once they marry; moreover, they may need large dowries. Consequently, the birth of a daughter is often regarded as a great misfortune. Unwanted daughters, and women who do not produce sons, may be abused, neglected, or abandoned. In these circumstances, a woman might find it impossible to refuse to abort a female fetus, even though the prospect offends her strongest moral convictions. If social and economic conditions have effectively blocked all her other options, then her informed consent provides only the appearance of autonomy.

Reproductive autonomy may be defeated without intentional coercion or manipulation. Sometimes coercion is inherent in a particular culture or economic system. When unjust circumstances preclude autonomous choice, it is appropriate to speak of a violation of the right to reproductive autonomy—even though it may be difficult to fix the blame on any individual.

Informed consent is not necessarily autonomous consent. It is, however, a necessary condition for it. The implementation of informed consent requirements is a landmark in the evolution of the enforceable rights of patients and research subjects. The right to make informed and uncoerced decisions about one's own medical treatment is as yet incompletely won. In too much of the world, safe means of contraception and abortion remain unavailable, or available only to the affluent. At the same time, middle-class women are often sold unproven or unnecessary medical procedures—a trend illustrated by the massive overuse of cesarean section in the United States. It is essential to extend women's autonomy with respect to both the older reproductive technologies and the newer ones such as IVF. Although the formal requirement of informed consent cannot guarantee reproductive autonomy, it is a protection we could ill afford to lose.

Autonomous Choice in an Unjust World

All women are influenced by pronatalism. Meredith Michaels has described motherhood as a "narrative" into which women are born, even if they never become mothers. Relatively few women deliberately avoid motherhood altogether, and those who do often find that resisting the call of this cultural narrative requires "a continual act of will."[20] Yet for many women, the range of reproductive options is wider than in the past.

Throughout recorded history, most women have had little choice about becoming mothers. Married young, with no effective means of contraception or abortion, they had babies whether they wished to or not. Such knowledge about the control of human fertility that did exist was often systematically suppressed. There have always been women who have defied pronatalist pressures, through marriage resistance, voluntary celibacy, or the clandestine practice of contraception, abortion, or infanticide. But the greater availability of contraception and abortion, in this century has made childbearing more often a matter for deliberate choice by women. For women who are poor, underage, or subject to legal or religious prohibitions, preventing unwanted births can still be difficult and dangerous. But now there are also countless women who take for granted their ability to limit their fertility.

This expansion of (some) women's freedom not to have children is, in Mary O'Brien's words, a "world historic event."[21] The further growth of reproductive freedom is possible, but by no means inevitable. Women need more universal access to contraception and abortion, as well as to prenatal, obstetric, and pediatric care. The prevention and treatment of involuntary infertility needs to be taken as seriously as the prevention of unwanted pregnancies and births, but not more so. Reproductive freedom requires that economic security not be contingent upon the production of children. Conversely, economic security must be consistent with parenthood; in both socialist and capitalist societies, the structure of paid work needs to better accommodate the needs of childbearers.

The medical profession can claim only modest credit for past expansions of reproductive freedom, which have often been opposed by much of that profession. (For instance, nineteenth-century physicians and medical associations led successful movements to criminalize abortion in the United States and elsewhere.) In much of the world, better access to the old reproductive technologies is probably a more urgent need than the development of new ones. Nevertheless, if IVF research yields improvements in contraception or the treatment of involuntary infertility, then it may eventually contribute much to the growth of reproductive freedom.

Inevitably, the new reproductive technologies also have the potential for harmful or coercive uses. Rather than expanding reproductive freedom, they might give rise to new forms of tyranny. Even without overt coercion, the influence of social expectation, medical authority, and media oversell could make it all but impossible for infertile women *not* to undergo IVF or whatever reproductive therapy is in vogue. Just as it is now very difficult for many women to avoid unnecessary obstetric interventions, so it may become difficult to avoid dangerous and unnecessary interventions into the processes of conception and gestation. Women will need to make decisions about the use of the new reproductive technologies that are not only autonomous but also wise and clear-sighted. Otherwise, these technologies may some day be used against women, rather than by and for women.

But for now the question is whether the situation of women who undergo innovative reproductive therapies such as IVF makes autonomous choice impossible. Two facts suggest that it does not. First, pronatalist influences have by no means eliminated these women's capacity for intelligent deliberation about reproductive technologies. Many have already used reproductive technologies to postpone childbearing. Given what they have already been through in the pursuit of motherhood, they often are somewhat more reflective about their reasons for wanting children than the average prospective parent.

Second, most of these women have been subject not only to *pro*natalist social influences, but also to powerful *anti*natalist influences. The high cost of IVF treatment ensures that it will be marketed primarily to middle-class women. As Germaine Greer has argued, there are aspects of the Western middle-class lifestyle that strongly discourage childbearing.[22] Rearing children has become very expensive and difficult for most women to combine with paid work—which is increasingly essential for economic survival. These facts help to explain the transition to lower birth rates that generally coincide with industrialization and economic development. When raising children becomes more difficult, people tend to raise fewer children, in spite of pronatalist institutions and ideologies.

It is unlikely, therefore, that the choice to undergo IVF treatment will be made unreflectively. Women are not under economic pressure to undergo IVF therapy; on the contrary. If they conclude that for them the possible benefits are worth the costs and risks, then it is reasonable to presume that their decision is substantially autonomous. They cannot prove that their autonomy has not been in some way impaired, but it is not up to them to prove this. In the absence of decisive evidence to the contrary, the presumption must be that a competent adult is capable of making autonomous decisions about her own medical treatment.

This presumption of patient autonomy is essential. Health care providers must be reluctant to disregard a patient's expressed will without compelling evidence that this particular person is not acting autonomously in this particular instance. Any choice an individual makes about her own medical treatment may have been controlled by some subtle form of social coercion. But this possibility cannot be used to discredit that choice or to deny her the right to make it. If it could, then medical paternalism would replace patient autonomy altogether. Unless the burden of proof is firmly placed upon those who would deny a patient's capacity to make autonomous choices, there will be unlimited scope for coercive paternalistic intervention.

Complete reproductive freedom is a utopian ideal; but partial reproductive freedom is better than none. The long-term value to women of IVF and other new reproductive technologies remains to be seen. For that very reason, it is vital that individual women's decisions about the use of IVF be respected. Neither physicians nor legislators have the wisdom to override women's own informed judgments about matters so central to their reproductive lives.

If these reflections are correct, then IVF and pre-embryo research need not violate patients' or donors' rights to medical and reproductive autonomy. Yet obtaining patients' informed consent does not exhaust the obligation of therapists and researchers to respect patients' autonomy. They also need to be alert to the possibility that some patients are subject to covert forms of coercion or manipulation. And, as I shall argue below, they need to avoid inadvertently exploiting the unjust circumstances to which patients may be subject.

Beyond Informed Consent

There are circumstances in which proceeding on the basis of informed consent may not be the best way to show respect for autonomy. Sometimes there is a fine line between helping individuals whose reproductive options have already been unjustly limited to carry out the best choice that is now possible and complicity with the forces that have created those unjust limitations. There are, however, some dangers that reproductive researchers need to recognize.

First, they should be extremely reluctant to purchase the cooperation of subjects and donors. Modest financial compensation for minor inconveniences may sometimes be appropriate, as in the case of sperm donation. But it is morally problematic for medical researchers to use financial incentives to induce individuals to undergo significant and largely unpredictable risks. Oocyte collection or embryo donation can subject women to substantial risks to health, fertility, and sometimes life itself. To recruit paid volunteers is to risk exploiting vulnerable individuals whose consent is based upon desperation.

But why should poor or financially pressed individuals not be free to sell their services as subjects or cell donors? Would it not be unfair to deprive them of what might be much-needed income? Some women might be quite willing to sell their own oocytes or pre-embryos and might benefit from the transaction. But others might agree because of extreme financial need and despite powerful misgivings. For them, the offer might be unwelcome but difficult to refuse. In these instances, the transaction would be exploitative and possibly a violation of reproductive autonomy. It is the exploitation, not the sale itself, that is wrong. But the pervasiveness of what has been called "the feminization of poverty" suggests that exploitation will be difficult to avoid if women are offered substantial sums for serving as subjects or donors to IVF research.

A second problem arises from the relative powerlessness of those who may be asked to donate reproductive cells for research purposes. Asking individuals to participate in research that involves substantial risk to themselves is morally problematic when those individuals are in a powerless and dependent situation: if, for instance, they are prisoners. Even if no reward or penalty is announced in connection with the request, powerless individuals may rationally believe that they must avoid the displeasure of those who control their fate. They may, therefore, agree because of the fear of reprisals if they do not.

While the circumstances of IVF patients are not usually comparable to those of prisoners, nevertheless they often perceive their situation as one of dependence and powerlessness. They may fear that, should they decline to cooperate with any research projects associated with the IVF program, they may be dropped from the program or otherwise penalized. Thus, it should consistently (and truthfully) be stressed that they will under no circumstances be penalized, either directly or indirectly, should they decide not to donate gametes or pre-embryos for research purposes. Unless this is mutually understood, their consent may be obtained through the unintentional exploitation of their fear of the consequences of refusal.

A third danger is the creation, encouragement, or exploitation of unrealistic hope. There are, by many accounts, women who seek IVF therapy or have it recommended to them, but whose chances of success are clearly remote. IVF applicants have sometimes objected to the use of selection criteria, such as age, to exclude from IVF programs women whose chances of a successful pregnancy are thought to be unacceptably low.[23] But while any particular criterion may be subject to debate, there must be some point beyond which the odds of success are so slight that it would be wrong to provide IVF treatments on the basis of so small a hope. If women in this situation are offered IVF therapy, and also asked to donate reproductive cells for research, then both therapists and researchers may be exploiting this unreasonable hope.

These are some of the dangers that reproductive researchers need to avoid if they are to respect the autonomy of women as subjects and donors. I do not suggest that these dangers are more severe in reproductive research than in other medical research. The point is, rather, that respect for autonomy cannot be construed strictly in terms of informed consent. Equally essential is an awareness of the economic, social, and psychological pressures faced by potential subjects or donors and of the ways that reproductive research might wrongly exploit those pressures.

Is it realistic to expect such an awareness from medical professionals who, after all, are not usually social theorists or psychologists? It will certainly call for better communication than has often occurred between patients and health care providers. It will require not just the communication of information from the professional to the patient, but attentive, responsive dialogue aimed at bringing to light any coercive or exploitative situation that might exist. Mandatory counselling is resented by some IVF patients as paternalistic and an invasion of privacy. However, given the potential for conflicts between the interests of patients and those of physicians and researchers, it is important that independent professional counselling be available on a voluntary basis.

Efforts should also be made to extend the protection offered by standard procedures for obtaining informed consent, by incorporating more explicit safeguards against some of the forms of covert coercion or exploitation that are of concern to feminists. If such efforts are successful, then informed consent requirements may come to provide a more nearly adequate protection for medical and reproductive autonomy.

The goal of reproductive research must be not only to respect the autonomy of individual patients and donors, but also to expand reproductive freedom in the long run. To this end, there must be more equal participation in the medical and research professions by women and members of racial and other minority groups. Researchers must understand the effects of what they do, not just on cells and organisms but also on human lives. To do that, they will need the insights of those who are personally affected by the new reproductive technologies.

Summary and Conclusion

Research on IVF pre-embryos, if carried out without the autonomous consent of the donors, would violate their right to reproductive autonomy. In the case of female donors, it might also subject them to substantial medical dangers. Informed consent cannot guarantee that autonomous choice will be possible, because coercive circumstances can render women's choices about reproductive research less than substantially autonomous.

But it does not follow that such research should not be done. Autonomous decision making does not presuppose an improbable freedom from all unjust or inappropriate social influences. On the contrary, respect for autonomy requires the presumption that most people can make substantially autonomous decisions about their own reproductive lives and research participation—provided that they are given an opportunity to do so. Women who seek IVF therapy are probably at least as capable of making autonomous choices about their reproductive lives as are most persons of their time and culture. Informed consent requirements cannot ensure autonomous choice, but they can reduce the risk that women (or men) will be coerced, deceived, or underinformed by reproductive therapists or researchers.

Reproductive therapists and researchers are not obliged to ascertain that patients' decisions are entirely wise or ultimately free before accepting them as autonomous. Yet they need to be alert to the possibility that certain patients' or donors' consent is controlled by unjust circumstances. In such cases, they must ask whether to take that consent at face value is to respect the autonomy of those individuals or might instead constitute a form of complicity with those injustices. They must also be sensitive to the inadvertent exploitation of economic need, individual powerlessness, or unreasonable hope. These moral pitfalls take on a special urgency in the context of IVF and pre-embryo research, where both women's reproductive autonomy and their physical integrity may be at stake.

Notes

1. See Gena Corea, *The Mother Machine: Reproductive Technologies from Artificial Insemination to Artificial Wombs* (New York: Harper & Row 1985), 166; and Jalna Hammer, ''A Womb of One's Own,'' *Test-Tube Women: What*

Future for Motherhood?, ed. Rita Arditti, Renate Duelli Klein, and Shelly Minden (London Press, 1984), 438–48.

2. Mary Warnock, *A Question of Life: The Warnock Report on Human Fertilisation and Embryology* (New York: Basil Blackwell, 1984), 81.

3. See Paul Ramsey, *The Ethics of Fetal Research* (New Haven, Conn.: Yale University Press, 1975), 28.

4. See M. Warren, "Do Potential People Have Moral Rights?," *Canadian Journal of Philosophy* 7, no. 2 (1977).

5. J. Webster "Laparoscopic Oocyte Recovery," *In Vitro Fertilization: Past, Present, Future,* ed. S. Fishel and E. M. Symonds (Oxford: IRL Press, 1986), 69–76.

6. Matts Wikland, Lars Hamberger, and Lennart Enk, "Ultrasound for Oocyte Recovery," in Fishel and Symonds, op. cit., 59–67.

7. A. McLaren, "Discussion," in *Human Embryo Research: Yes or No?*, CIBA Foundation (London: Tavistock, 1986), 203.

8. Gena Corea, "Egg Snatchers," in Arditte, Klein, and Minden, op. cit., 39.

9. Ibid.

10. Ellen Peck and Judith Senderowitz, eds., *Pronatalism: The Myth of Mom and Apple Pie* (New York: Thomas J. Crowell, 1974), 1.

11. Judith Blake "Coercive Pronatalism and the American Population Policy," in Peck and Senderowitz, op. cit., 26–97.

12. Ibid., 66.

13. Corea, *The Mother Machine,* 169.

14. See, for instance, Jay Katz, *The Silent World of Doctor and Patient* (New York: The Free Press, 1984).

15. Ruth Faden, and Tom Beauchamp, *A History and Theory of Informed Consent* (Oxford: Oxford University Press, 1986), 238.

16. Ibid., 241.

17. Ibid., 330.

18. Ibid., 354.

19. Ibid., 359.

20. Meredith W. Michaels, "Contraception, Freedom and Destiny: A Womb of One's Own," in *The Contraceptive Ethos*, ed. Stuart F. Spicker, William B. Bondeson and H. Tristram Engelhardt, Jr. (Dordrecht and Boston: D. Reidel Company, 1987), 218.

21. Mary O'Brien, *The Politics of Reproduction* (London: Routledge and Kegan Paul, 1981), 21.

22. Germaine Greer, *Sex and Destiny: The Politics of Human Fertility* (London: Secker & Warburg, 1984).

23. See Patricia F. Brown, "In Vitro: Client Rights and the Simple Case," paper presented at the National Conference on Reproductive Technologies, sponsored by the National Feminist Network on Reproductive Technology, Canberra, May 1986.

Questions

1. What is Warren's objection to reproductive research ? What is her objection
   about informed consent? Do you suppose that some women may be irritated
   with Warren when they hear what she thinks about IVF research? Explain.
   How does she defend her position? Do you agree with her position? Explain.
2. What should consent have to do with IVF research? Is informed consent
   adequate protection for women's autonomy in the context of IVF?
3. What is required for a patient to acquire autonomous decision making? Can
   it be that informed consent yields no more than an *appearance* of autonomy?
   How?
4. What is a pre-embryo? Does Warren believe that pre-embryos have moral
   rights? According to Warren, what are moral rights? What does this have to
   do with reproductive rights?
5. What is pronatalism? How does this affect society?
6. What efforts by the medical community should be made to produce autonomy in each medical patient? Do you believe that such autonomy is morally
   necessary?

Part IV
Body and Sexual Images

12

To Be or Not Be a Woman: Anorexia Nervosa, Normative Gender Roles, and Feminism

Mary Briody Mahowald

Introduction

Anorexia nervosa has been called an epidemic in our day.[1] Although historical precedents abound, its apparent prevalence among affluent white teenage girls is a relatively recent phenomenon.[2] Clearly, it is a disease whose causes and treatment are psychosocial as well as psychological.[3] Feminists and nonfeminists alike have recognized its association with an ideal of thinness as essential to feminine beauty.[4] Some have attributed its rising incidence to the impact of the women's movement.[5]

Throughout history, feminine beauty has had different models, some associated with ample body size rather than thinness. Now, however, only slender models, with whom the majority of women can scarcely identify, are presented as ideal. These are the models that sell cars, clothes, perfumes, and various other consumer goods while also selling their image as a stereotypical interpretation of feminine beauty. The term "beauty" is itself gendered: it is rarely associated with what is "masculine" and in fact it may be used derogatorily in that connection. If thinness is an essential component of feminine beauty, it is not typically related to a comparable masculine ideal. The closest parallel for men is an ideal of tallness, musculature, strength, and physical fitness, positive traits that contrast with the unhealthy reality and appearance to which the anorexic aspires. Although the premorbid characteristics, illness features, and prognosis of anorexia nervosa are similar for both sexes, its occurrence in men is relatively rare.[6] Some of the views developed in this article are applicable to men also. In what follows, however, I focus on women without attempting to address the implications of my critique for men who suffer from anorexia nervosa.

In recent years, women have increasingly participated in aerobic and body-building programs in pursuit of their own health and fitness. While such efforts may also be associated with a "fear of fatness" or preference for slenderness, they are not necessarily associated with excessive thinness as an ideal of feminine beauty. Nonetheless, clinical reports and autobiographical statements from anorexics indicate a tendency to exercise with ritualistic intensity. As Brumberg puts it, "How much one runs and how little one eats is the prevailing moral calculus in present-day anorexia nervosa."[7] Ironically, since fitness requires attention to proper nutrition as well as exercise, the anorexic's practice of refusing to eat is incompatible with the goal of fitness.

Because anorexia nervosa occurs mainly in young women who are influenced by a socially induced concept of feminine beauty, it is particularly significant to those concerned about the injustice of gender stereotypes and their impact on women. As "one of those," I propose in this paper to review the salient characteristics of anorexia nervosa, examine its relationship to normative gender roles, and critique those roles on feminist grounds. Much of what I argue is also applicable to bulimia nervosa, another disease associated with "fear of being fat," which occurs even more rarely in men than anorexia nervosa.[8] However, because differences between the two diseases would need to be further explained and explored for their implications, I limit the discussion here to anorexia nervosa.

My critique of normative gender roles rests on their being interpreted stereotypically. I use the term "normative" as a standard against which behaviors are measured. The term "stereotype" refers to so rigid a normative categorization of human behaviors that the possibility of individual variation is ignored, overlooked, or disvalued. At times the categorization leads to the labeling of psychologically healthy individuals as "abnormal."[9] Various versions of feminism condemn these stereotypes as obstructing the development of women's potential as individuals and social beings.

Essential Features of Anorexia Nervosa

According to the diagnostic and statistical manual of mental disorders (*DSM-III-R*), the diagnostic criteria for anorexia nervosa are the following:

A. Refusal to maintain body weight over a minimal normal weight for age and height, e.g., weight loss leading to maintenance of body weight 15% below that expected; or failure to make expected weight gain during period of growth, leading to body weight 15% below that expected.

B. Intense fear of gaining weight or becoming fat, even though underweight.

C. Disturbance in the way in which one's body weight, size, or shape is experienced, e.g., the person claims to "feel fat" even when emaciated, believes that one area of the body is "too fat" even when obviously underweight.

D. In females, absence of at least three consecutive menstrual cycles when otherwise expected to occur (*DSM-III-R*, 1987, p. 67).[10]

Note that these criteria do not allude to the fact that the great majority of anorexics are young women; nor do they suggest that the anorexic's behavior is related to a culturally, temporally defined ideal of feminine beauty. Yet these are circumstances that most diagnosticians recognize as associated with the disease. Whether they ought to be included among the *DSM-III-R's* criteria is a question worth considering. The current formulation indicates no linkage between anorexia nervosa and gender identity disorders. (I will return to this point later.)

Although the term anorexia literally means lack of appetite, in fact anorexics usually crave food but deny themselves because of their unfounded fear of fatness. Because concern about diet and weight gain is so widespread among relatively healthy people, the severity of the disease may be overlooked. Consider, however, this sobering statistic: mortality rates range between 5 percent and 18 percent.[11] Ironically, although anorexics deliberately starve away 20 percent or more of their body weight, the disease prevalently occurs in cultures where food is abundant—in white, affluent, well-educated, hard-driving families, where parents are conscientiously protective of their daughters.[12] Recently, as media images of women reach poorer communities, the incidence of the disease has spread to them as well.

Fully 95 percent of anorexics are women.[13] Ordinarily, its symptoms are first observable in early to late adolescence, when boys and girls alike are concerned about their developing sexuality and gender identity. Predisposing factors include stressful life situations and "perfectionism." The experience of adolescence is stressful for many teenagers (as well as their parents), but those who are perfectionist are driven to conform to unrealistic ideals. For the anorexic, this ideal is construed as essential to personal worthwhileness. As Paul Garfinkel and David Garner put it,

> The feeling of self-worth in anorexic patients is closely bound to external standards for appearance and performance. . . . Pressures on women to be thin and to achieve, and also conflicting role expectations which force women to be paradoxically competitive, yet passive, may partially explain why anorexia nervosa has increased so dramatically. Patients with anorexia nervosa respond to these pressures by equating weight control with self-control and this in turn is equated with beauty and "success."[14]

What is missing in the above quotation is an explanation of the link between self-control and beauty. That link is represented by another equation, namely, that thinness *is* beautiful. The anorexic has clearly been socialized to believe this equation, but unlike equations that represent universally true statements, this one is seldom applied to men. Since the average fat mass of a normal teenage girl is about twice that of her male counterpart[15] the situation should be the opposite. Whether the ideal applies to women or men, however, equating thinness with beauty ignores the actual differences among individuals that make thinness unhealthy or abnormal for many people, male or female. In other words, the extreme thinness that the anorexic seeks is healthy for no one.

Because some anorexics cannot control their appetite to their own satisfaction, they may binge from time to time or have bulimic episodes following by vomiting. Other behavioral characteristics of anorexia nervosa include a tendency to spend considerable time around food, preparing elaborate meals for others, while insuring that one's own intake includes only a narrow selection of low-calorie foods. Anorexics often hoard or conceal food and break it into small pieces before eating or throwing it away.[16] Their preoccupation with food and its preparation is reinforced by an image of women as more nurturant than men. Whether or not this image is supportable by biological or social scientific data, it is often perceived prescriptively as well as descriptively. Its stereotypic imposition belies the fact that some women are not as nurturant as some men.

Cultural expectations have long exerted unhealthy influences on women, presenting them with a forced option between conformity to an ideal of the feminine and physical normality. In prerevolutionary China, for example, the footbinding of women was not only considered beautiful, but a status symbol for their husbands, indicating that their wealth was sufficient for their wives to stay at home. Obviously, this practice limited women's mobility, severely restricting their social involvement.[17] In the nineteenth century, the wearing of tight corsets was a way of promoting the thin appearance expected of women. These not only induced discomfort and interfered with digestion but also sometimes caused serious injury. Even when their harmful effects were recognized, the impetus to wear corsets continued because of their association with beauty and "purity."[18]

Men have also been affected by expectations that impose health risks. Tattooing, scarification, and cranial deformation are historical examples of this.[19] Susan Sontag describes "the tubercular appearance" among upper classes of the last century as an "index of being genteel, delicate and sensitive."[20] Such attributes were mainly esteemed in artists and in women. Note, however, that the characteristics generally attributed to artists conform with feminine rather than masculine stereotypes. The weakness and fragility associated with extreme thinness hardly reflected the strength and robustness attributed to men in general.

Several authors cite consumption as the precursor of anorexia nervosa.[21] Pallor was a fashionable attribute that women used whitening powders to promote. The consumptive appearance pursued by women gave rise to the anorexic look currently glamorized by the media as an ideal of feminine beauty. In a study of dieting behavior among adolescents in Sweden, I. Nylander found that the "feeling of fatness" increased with age among females: 50 percent perceive themselves as fat at 14 years of age, and 70 percent at 18 years. Boys of comparable ages seldom reported feeling fat or dieting. Nylander observed a 10 percent prevalence of "mild cases" of anorexia among girls, and one "serious case" out of every 155 of those considered. Crisp and Toms studied a relatively large school population in London, and found a prevalence rate of 1 in 100 girls aged 16–18 years.[22]

Most anorexics deny or minimize the severity of their illness and are therefore resistant to therapy. They avoid expressions of sexuality, and their psychosexual development is usually delayed. Other types of compulsive behavior, such as excessive handwashing, are often associated with anorexia. Compulsiveness and rigidity reinforce the decision to forgo normal food intake. They also reinforce the tendency to conform to gender stereotypes.

Although the *DSM-III-R* categorizes anorexia nervosa as an eating disorder rather than a gender identity disorder, its definitions of gender identity and gender role suggest that components of this diagnosis are importantly relevant to anorexics. Gender identity, according to the

DSM-III-R, is the private experience of gender role, and gender role is the public expression of gender identity. Gender role can be defined as everything that one says and does to indicate to others or to oneself the degree to which one is male or female.[23] Attempts to reveal one's degree of femininity or masculinity are influenced by one's understanding of societal expectations in that regard. In either of two apparently contradictory ways, anorexia may illustrate a gender role disorder as defined above. First, the anorexic's obsessive pursuit of a feminine ideal of thinness indicates that she is insecure in her gender identity but fiercely wants to fulfill her perceived gender role. Second, the actual look promoted through her refusal of food is more masculine (boylike) than feminine, and amenorrhea is a means of avoiding the monthly reminder of her femininity; in other words, she fiercely wants *not* to fulfill her perceived gender role.

As already remarked, the *DSM-III-R* fails to indicate a linkage between anorexia nervosa and gender identity disorders, despite the fact that the principle symptom of anorexia, obsessive pursuit of extreme thinness, is associated with a *feminine* ideal. The section on gender identity disorders lists four subsets of disorders: (a) those that occur in childhood (302–60); (b) transsexualism (302–50); (c) nontranssexual disorder of adolescence or adulthood (302.85); and (d) "gender identity disorder not otherwise specified (302.85)." Anorexics seldom if ever meet one of the diagnostic criteria included in (c) and (d), viz., cross-dressing in the role of the other sex. But they definitely meet one criterion for gender identity disorder of adolescence or adulthood: "persistent or recurrent discomfort and sense of inappropriateness about one's assigned sex," and usually meet a second criterion: "the person has reached puberty."[24] A third criterion present in (b) but not in other listed gender identity disorders may also be viewed as fulfilled in anorexics, at least if one interprets pursuit of thinness as an attempt to appear masculine rather than feminine: "persistent preoccupation for at least two years with getting rid of one's primary and secondary sex characteristics and acquiring the sex characteristics of the other sex."[25]

Because gender identity issues are so prevalently linked with anorexia nervosa, it seems appropriate to indicate this association among diagnostic criteria for the disease. Alternatively, the disease could be included in the list of gender identity disorders, thus accenting the connection between an obsession with thinness and the obsessive embracing or rejecting of a socially induced stereotype of femininity, both traits that occur in the majority of anorexics. Either revision would also suggest the limitations of the *DSM-III-R's* consideration of gender identity and gender role as normative standards. In the next section, I will discuss the content of these standards and their impact on adolescents.

Normative Gender Roles and Adolescents

While there is general agreement about the content of gender-based behaviors, they have different formulations by different authors. Alfred Heilbrun, for example, begins a discussion of "Sex-role Identity in Adolescent Females" by defining the sex-role identity of the child as "the degree to which his or her behavior and attitudes coincide with cultural stereotypes of masculinity and femininity." He then distinguishes between behaviors:

> Typical of the behavior subsumed under the adult masculine sex-role are: achievement, autonomy, dominance, and endurance; feminine adult sex-role behavior would include deference, abasement, succorance, nurturance, and affiliation.[26]

After thus linking sex-role identity with gender stereotypes, Heilbrun goes on to define adjustment as "the degree to which the individual is capable of maintaining herself interpersonally without seeking professional help for personal problems." He describes the "best adjusted girls" as those who are in "better psychological health" in comparison with others; these need not seek professional help.[27] Some obvious problems arise from identifying health with social adjustment. By such an account, for example, those who adapt to regimes that perpetuate atrocities may be considered healthy, while those who persist in resisting a manifestly evil *status quo,* or seek help in resisting it, are not. Surely, this is not the type of adjustment that Heilbrun had in mind.

Nonetheless, adjustment to one's gender role is often construed as an essential component of healthy maturation. Although maternal identification is sometimes thought to facilitate such adjustment in daughters, research has not borne this out. In fact, when Heilbrun and Donald Fromme studied girls whose parents were atypical with regard to sex roles ("feminine father-masculine mother") they found no relationship between the daughters' parental-identification and their level of adjustment. When their parents represented sex-typical models ("masculine father-feminine mother"), the best-adjusted girls identified more strongly with their fathers than with their mothers. They thus diverged from conformity to gender stereotypes.[28] Supporting this finding, Toby

Sitnick and Jack Katz found that girls with eating disorders had lower ratings of masculine traits than their healthy counterparts. They concluded that "one characteristic of those women vulnerable to developing this syndrome may be a failure to develop adequately those 'masculine' traits that are also necessary for optimal adult female functioning in contemporary society." [29]

Although some clinical studies reflect the widespread practice of measuring adolescent health and psychological maturation by gender specific behavior, [30] this view is troublesome, to say the least. It suggests that the feminine traits that have led to and maintained the oppression of women are crucial to their health, and that the masculine traits that have permitted men to pursue personal power unselfconsciously are healthy for them. To be healthy, therefore, girls should be compliant, while boys should be in charge. The developing capacity for autonomous decision making is thus more likely to be frustrated in girls than in boys. In either case, conformity to normative (stereotypic) gender roles belies the fact that sexuality does not entail a simple division of humanity into two disparate parts, but a continuum for each human trait, various assortments of which are necessary to the health of unique individuals of either sex. On one end of the spectrum are those that epitomize the stereotype of femininity, at the other those that epitomize the stereotype of masculinity. The gender type of individuals is determined by the proportion of masculine or feminine traits that each one embodies. For most, this does not represent conformity to normative gender roles. Accordingly, the health of adolescents should not be defined in terms of adjustment to stereotypically defined gender traits.

Jean Humphrey Block suggests a healthier and more egalitarian approach to adolescent socialization when she writes that

> the ultimate goal in development of sexual identity is *not* [my italics] the achievement of masculinity or femininity as popularly conceived. Rather, sexual identity means, or will mean, the earning of a sense of self in which there is a recognition of gender secure enough to permit the individual to manifest human qualities our society, until now, has labeled as unmanly or unwomanly. [31]

According to this view, a healthy adolescent is one who does not need professional help because she tends to be dominant rather than deferential in her interactions with others, or because affiliation is less important to her than autonomy. Nor would a male adolescent be construed as needing professional help solely because he is more oriented towards nurturance than self-interest, or more compliant than autocratic in his behavior. From a feminist perspective (as well as other perspectives), imposition of normative gender roles on individuals whose natural propensities lie in different directions should be resisted.

Resistance to imposition of normative gender roles is a particular challenge for teenagers because socialization based on gender distinctions reaches a high point during adolescence. Without settling the question of whether observed behavioral differences between boys and girls are triggered more by socialization than by the onset of puberty, many writers support a gender-intensification hypothesis as the explanation for such changes. According to John Hill and Mary Ellen Lynch, adolescence is a period when new domains may become "the object of gender-differential socialization pressure," and increased demands for conformity to such pressure arise.[32] The pressures intensify because of specific developmental tasks faced by teenagers: (a) establishment of a stable sense of self and self-worth, reflecting acceptance of the bodily changes that accompany puberty; (b) achievement of strong friendships, and comfortableness in relating to the opposite sex; (c) transition from physical and emotional dependence on parents to relative independence. Definitions of gender identity relate to each of these tasks, with different implications for boys and girls. The differences, unfortunately, have sexist consequences.

Consider, for example, the fact that early pubertal change tends to be an advantage for boys and a disadvantage for girls. Roberta Simmons and her colleagues suggest that the key difference is

> whether the changes lead one to approximate the cultural ideal or not. For the boy, the physical changes of puberty render him more muscular and athletic and thus more in line with the American physical ideal for males. For the girl, the changes at first lead her to be bigger than all her male and female peers and then on average to be shorter and heavier than the later-developing girls. The result is that she is less likely to approximate the female ideal of beauty than the late-developing tall and slim girl.[33]

When the "cultural ideal" is rigidly imposed on male and female adolescents it thus affects them not only differently but unequally. "Unequally" here refers to the ranking of differences as positive or negative traits.[34] Even if the cultural ideal perfectly reflected the natural propensities of boys and girls as they move towards adulthood, it would entail prejudicial consequences for those of either sex who don't or can't conform to their normative gender role. Moreover, since the role generally relegates women to secondary social status, its overall influence on female adolescents would impede rather than facilitate the development of their full potential.

As already suggested, the reinforcement of gender roles extends beyond physical differences. According to Hill and Lynch, parents are more likely to discourage aggressive behavior in girls than in boys, and this differentiation by parents may increase during adolescence. Standards for achievement become more sex-stereotyped with age, with boys demonstrating better spatial skills and girls better verbal skills during adolescence.[35] In contrast with teenage boys, girls tend to experience decreased self-esteem, increased self-consciousness, and instability of self-concept, but studies have not yet proved that this is related to reinforcement of gender roles.[34] Nonetheless, parents are often more tolerant of independence for their sons; they expect their daughters to be more concerned about their appearance, and most still expect their sons to be the initiators of opposite-sex interaction. The double standard thus evoked tends to become a self-fulfilling promise that has clinical as well as social repercussions. Anorexia nervosa may be a tragic example of these repercussions.

Social Causes of Anorexia

Despite the severity and apparent increase of anorexia nervosa, few authors have argued that normative gender roles should be targeted in pursuit of its cure. For the most part, they simply document the epidemiology of the disease, and some clearly delineate the concurrence of gender socialization and anorexia.[37] From a feminist standpoint, however, preventive treatment is called for, and such treatment clearly requires not only rejection of gender stereotypes but positive efforts to thwart pervasive social tendencies in this regard. Moreover, in treating those who have already contracted the disease, a comparable critique is crucial. So long as girls "buy into" a feminine ideal of thinness that threatens their psychological and physical well being, their low self-esteem is bound to be reinforced, and with that a prolongation or exacerbation of their illness. Insofar as the disease is provoked by gender socialization, they will continue to fall prey to anorexia nervosa until the ideal itself is changed.

Few, however, would argue that anorexia nervosa is caused by gender socialization alone. In *Fasting Girls,* Joan Brumberg describes three types of factors that contribute to its development: biological, psychological, and cultural. Although different theoretical models have emerged for each of these sources, Brumberg maintains that none is adequately explicative of "the current rash of eating disorders and the place of anorexia nervosa in the long history of female food refusal."[38] While she gives most weight to cultural influences, Brumberg clearly views biological vulnerability and psychological predisposition as the villains also. Among biomedical influences, a number of more specific causal candidates emerge: hormonal imbalance, dysfunction of the hypothalamus, lesions in the brain's limbic system, irregular output of vasopressin and gonadotropin, and excess cortisol production. Neither singly nor together do these features adequately explain the distinctive socioeconomic and gender status of anorexic patients, or why its incidence is so great at this time in history.

Psychological explanations interpret anorexia nervosa as "a pathological response to the developmental crisis of adolescence."[39] The teenager's refusal of food is seen as an expression of a struggle for autonomy, individuation and sexuality.[40] Following Freud, psychoanalysts have equated an unwillingness to eat with the desire to suppress one's libido or sexual drive, and resistance to the inexorable progress towards adulthood. Ironically, while repressing that drive, the anorexic nonetheless seeks to control the only thing she feels she can control, her body. Much of her behavior is obsessively compulsive. Family systems theory imputes the behavior traits of anorexics to other family members as well. The "psychosomatic family" is then viewed as "controlling, perfectionistic, and nonconfrontational," descriptives that apply equally to their anorexic daughter.[41]

As with other psychiatric disorders, mothers are targeted as contributing to the disease. The mother of the anorexic is described as frustrated, depressed, perfectionistic, passive, dependent, and unable to see and reflect her daughter as an independent being.[42] Allegedly, preoedipal mother conflict arises from a young girl's identification with her kind, passive father, and her suppressed hostility towards an aggressive castrating mother.[43] The anorexic's intense, unconscious hatred of her mother leads to rejection of feminity in general. The straight-chested appearance and amenorrhea that anorexia involves are further signs of success in her avoidance of feminity.

The same problems found in the biological model of anorexia nervosa are present in the psychological model: incidence, gender, and socioeconomic features of the disease are not thereby explained. Which returns us to the socialization issue, and the cultural model as a limited response to those problems. In general, the incidence of anorexia ner-

298 Mary Briody Mahowald

vosa has increased because society has intensified and extended the perception that thinness is a sign of fitness and attractiveness. Its message, like most new styles, has been "bought" most prevalently by those who have the time, energy and interest to buy it, i.e., affluent or moderately affluent white women.

Susan Bordo describes anorexia nervosa as a crystallization of the psychopathology of contemporary culture. It illustrates "the social manipulation of the female body" that has emerged "as an absolutely central strategy in the maintenance of power relations between the sexes over the last hundred years."[44] The strategy has its roots in the metaphysical dualism that characterizes the writings of Plato, Augustine and Descartes. It is a mind/body dualism that does not simply separate but prioritizes mind over body. To the extent that women are viewed (by themselves as well as men) as sex objects valued solely or primarily for their bodies, sex inequality will inevitably prevail.

To Bordo the patriarchal Graeco-Christian tradition provides a "particularly fertile soil for the development of anorexia."[45] Popular American culture contributes to the development through its vulnerability through physical fitness. Paradoxically and tragically, although the will to conquer and subdue the body sometimes leads to an aesthetic or moral rebellion, "powerlessness is its most outstanding feature."[46]

A sexual double standard is clearly to blame for the fact that anorexia so predominantly afflicts women more than men. According to Hilde Bruch, many anorexics are self-consciously aware of two selves that are in constant conflict: one a dominating male self that represents greater spirituality, intellectuality, and will power; the other a female self that represents uncontrollable appetites and flaws.[47] It is the male self that the anorexic seeks to develop, precisely because it has been so ingrained in her that male is better. Presumably, the adolescent's sense of self-worth is most threatened by the fact that she knows she is female, and therefore a less valued or valuable human being than her male counterpart. Short of changing her social environment, improvement of her sense of self-worth requires helping her to see that worth independently of others' evaluations. This may be cognitively impossible.

Feminist Criticisms

Feminists are particularly prone to blame anorexia on gender socialization, and to propose socially corrective measures as preventative therapy and feminist consciousness raising as individual therapy. For some feminists, however, anorexia nervosa is not only caused by a sexist culture, but constitutes a behavior that is antithetical to that culture. Construed in this way, anorexia nervosa does not involve enslavement to an unhealthy idea of the feminine, nor does it simply mean refusal to accept femininity. It means more than the latter: rebellion against patriarchy through rejection of one's own sexuality. Cases of anorexia nervosa in males may illustrate the same construal.

Liberal feminists[48] are likely to view sexism as a cause of anorexia, and to argue for elimination of the gender stereotyping that imposes so unequal a burden on women. In order to liberate women to develop their full potential as individuals, their options need to be expanded rather than restricted by an ideal of feminine behavior or appearance. Liberal feminism thus supports the right of individual women to pursue this or any ideal, even if it leads to unhealthy consequences for themselves, so long as the pursuit does not impede the liberty or welfare of others. In a capitalist society the means through which to fulfill the ideal of thinness are evident in the huge commercial success of diet, weight loss, and fitness programs that generally attract more women than men. Selling thinness has clearly become a profitable industry. The goal of liberal feminism is to preserve this social structure, but to rectify its sexist flaws. Given the imbeddedness of gender socialization within the structure, it is doubtful that so limited a critique could much reduce the impact of socialization as a cause of anorexia.

Radical feminism would extend its criticism of sexism as a cause of anorexia nervosa to a critique of the patriarchal structure that pervades society as a whole. The critique thus applies to women as a class rather than as individuals. Women become an exploited class in a system wherein men profit by the feminine ideal of thinness. As Susie Orbach put it, "Fat is a feminist issue" because it exemplifies resistance to that ideal. A cult that has enshrined "slimness" as "the new god" is blasphemously anti-feminist and anti-woman.[49] The goal, then, is to recognize the patriarchal nature of the new god, to topple it by substituting a goddess that embodies an ideal of femininity that takes account of the fact that healthy women come in all shapes and sizes, even as men do. In Orbach's words,

> Some of us are short, some of us are tall. We can have short legs, medium-length legs, long legs, big breasts, medium-size breasts, small breasts, . . . large, medium or small hips; we can be pear-shaped, broad or rounded, have flat stomachs, full stomachs, even teeth, crooked teeth, large eyes, dimpled cheeks.[50]

Men of course come in all shapes and sizes also. While tallness remains an advantage to them as well as to some women, society generally accepts a broader range of physical shapes and sizes for men than for women.

A socialist version of feminism would concur with the radical version, particularly targeting the inequality of a social system that creates needs out of desires provoked by a profit motive. Anorexia nervosa exemplifies the dehumanizing effects of such a system. If the feminine ideal were stripped of its debilitating impact on the development of women as individuals, and a masculine ideal were similarly cleansed of its impeding influence on men, then a socialist ideal of equality might be approximated. Socialist feminism would not eschew concern about obesity and health for women, but unlike radical feminism, it would have equal concern about such matters for men. In other words, equality, construed as respect for differences as well as potential among individuals of either gender, would be the criterion governing any ideal of body size or fitness.

Although socialism is in disrepute these days, socialist feminism represents an extension of the radical feminist critique to other social classes, and a critique of the excesses of individualism that liberalism permits. Socialist feminists oppose a free market system that allows affluence in the midst of poverty. Because anorexia nervosa occurs mainly among the affluent, a more equitable distribution of income might reduce its incidence. In other words, anorexia nervosa occurs in part because of the power of a free market system to define a profitable ideal of feminine beauty, and to persuade many women of the necessity of conforming to it. Adolescents, unfortunately, are especially vulnerable to this persuasion. While predisposing biological and psychological factors are also at work, the impact of the social environment fashioned by the marketeers is undeniable.

There is another factor that may contribute to the high incidence of anorexia nervosa among adolescent girls, in contrast with their male counterparts: the ambiguity that many women experience throughout their lives because of conflicts precipitated (in part at least) by gender socialization and social practices. Years ago Simone de Beauvoir defined ambiguity as characteristic of the female sex.[51] Despite the progress of the women's movement, ambiguity remains a common experience of women who struggle to maintain a healthy balance between home and work responsibilities, while their male counterparts are rarely expected or inclined to devote comparable energies to both sets of tasks. When daughters observe the conflicts their mothers confront and the discrepancy between their and their brothers' future prospects, they experience similar ambiguity. To the extent that pressures exerted by normative gender roles are reduced, the ambiguity may be resolved.

For anti-feminists, another means of resolving ambiguity, and thus reducing the incidence of anorexia nervosa among adolescents, is to revert to the days before "women's liberation," when gender stereotypes were generally unchallenged, and little ambiguity or conflict existed with regard to women's options.[52] This position ignores two facts: most women deal successfully and enthusiastically with a broader range of options; and the prevalence of anorexia nervosa in women predates the modern women's movement. Ambiguity is not a problem for most women or men if it simply represents a range of pursuable options. If it involves increased responsibilities with no corresponding increase in opportunities or support for their fulfillment, then the ambiguity has an overall negative impact. According to Carol Gilligan, such ambiguity is greater in girls because of their desire to maintain attachments while establishing their own identity. In *Mapping the Moral Domain,* she writes: "In resisting detachment and critiquing exclusion adolescent girls hold to the view that change can be negotiated through voice, and that voice is the way to sustain attachment across the leavings of adolescence."[53]

Typically, the adolescent's "exit" from childhood leaves a problem of loyalty that she tries to negotiate through use of her own voice. The anorexic's voice is loud at first, but destined to be silenced by weakness, sickness, or even death from the disease. Her desire to be loyal to herself as well as to others inevitably leads to ambiguity. Bruch describes the ambiguity as a conflict between two selves. By dual accounts of anorexic behavior, feminists also suggest a conflict: one between conformity to a socially induced unhealthy stereotype, and refusal to accept the sexist connotations of being female. I believe the anorexic is in fact affirming both messages. Ironically, the messages converge in the reality of the anorexic's behavior, defining the content of her ambiguity: to be or not be a woman.

This returns us to the earlier point about the effect of gender socialization, and the fact that anorexia nervosa is not linked with gender identity disorders in the DSM-III-R. So awful a disease deserves fuller critique of its social as well as biological and psychological causes. Physicians in various specialties have often defined their professional responsibilities as encompassing attempts to correct the social causes of illness—e.g., by lobbying against cigarette advertisements and by organizing other physicians to speak out against the development of

302   *Mary Briody Mahowald*

nuclear weapons. Just as social behaviors need to be modified for therapeutic reasons in these cases, so also with gender socialization as a
cause of anorexia nervosa. Therapeutic effectiveness calls for efforts to
limit the health threatening effects of gender stereotypes.

Notes

1. J. J. Brumberg, *Fasting Girls* (Cambridge: Harvard University, 1988),
31; R. A. Gordon, "A Socio and Cultural Interpretation of the Current Epidemic of Eating Disorders," in B. J. Blinder, B. F. Chaitin, and R. S. Goldstein,
eds., *The Eating Disorders* (New York: PMA Publishing Company, 1988), 151.
2. P. Leichner and A. Gertler, "Prevalence and Incidence Studies of Anorexia Nervosa," in *The Eating Disorders* (New York: PMA Publishing Company, 1988), 131–47.
3. Gordon, 161.
4. Brumberg, 31–38; G. R. Leon and S. Finn, "Sex-role Stereotypes and
the Development of Eating Disorders," in C. S. Widom, ed., *Sex Roles and
Psychopathology* (New York: Plenum, 1984), 326.
5. Brumberg, 38.
6. A. H. Crisp and T. Burns, "Primary Anorexia Nervosa in the Male and
Female: A Comparison of Clinical Features and Prognosis," in A. E. Andersen,
ed., *Males with Eating Disorders* (New York: Brunner/Mazel Publishers, 1990),
92.
7. Brumberg, 255.
8. Although both diseases occur in some individuals, bulimic anorectics,
unlike restrictive anorectics, have been characterized as outgoing, articulate,
socially confident, sexually experienced, and less optimistic before the onset of
their illness. From Casper, Eckert, Helmi et al. 1980, 1030–1040. See also Pyle
and Mitchell, 1988, 267.
9. D. Goleman, "Stereotypes of the Sexes Said to Persist in Therapy," *New
York Times* (April 10, 1990): B1, B7.
10. It is unlikely that the *DSM-IV,* now in preparation, will alter the classification or diagnostic criteria for anorexia nervosa. I base this observation on a
talk on "*DSM-IV*—Work in Progress" by Allen J. Frances, M.D., who heads
the Nomenclature Task Force of the American Psychiatric Association, at the
annual meeting of the American Orthopsychiatric Association in 1990 in Miami
Beach, Florida. In order to align *DSM-IV* classifications as much as possible
with the 10th edition of the International Classification of Diseases, which is
scheduled to appear in 1993, Dr. Frances indicated that controversial revisions
will be avoided, with changes made only on the basis of compelling evidence.
See American Psychatric Association, *Diagnostic and Statistical Manual of
Mental Disorders*, 3rd ed., revised (*DSM-III-R*), (Washington, D.C, 1987), 67.
11. *DSM-III-R,* 66.

12. C. Lawson, "Anorexia: It's Not a New Disease," *New York Times* (December 8, 1985): 93.

13. *DSM-III-R*, 66.

14. Paul Garfinkel and David Garner, *Anorexia Nervosa* (New York: Brunner/Mazel Publishing Company, 1982), 101.

15. Crisp and Burns, 78.

16. *DSM-III-R*, 66.

17. Garfinkel and Garner, 105.

18. Garfinkel and Garner, 105.

19. Garfinkel and Garner, 105.

20. Susan Sontag, *Illness as Metaphor* (New York: Farrar, Straus and Giroux, 1978), 28.

21. See Garfinkel and Garner, 106; Brumberg, 43–44.

22. Crisp, et al., 1976, 549.

23. *DSM-III-R*, 71.

24. *DSM-III-R*, 77.

25. *DSM-III-R*, 77.

26. Alfred Heilbrun, Jr. "Sex-role Identity in Adolescent Females: A Theoretical Paradox," *Adolescence* 3 (1968): 80.

27. Heilbrun, 80–81.

28. Alfred Heilbrun, Jr., and Donald Fromme, "Parental Identification of Late Adolescents and Level of Adjustment: The Importance of Parent-mode Attribute, Ordinal Position and Sex of the Child," *Journal of Genetic Psychology* 107 (1965): 52–54.

29. Toby Sitnick and Jack Katz, "Sex Role Identity and Anorexia Nervosa," *International Journal of Eating Disorders* 3 (1984): 81.

30. Heilbrun cites studies by Emmerich, Bray, Helper Johnson, Mussen, and Distler. In contrast to clear and consistent findings that father-identification in boys is consistent with good subsequent adjustment, Heilbrun considers the findings of studies regarding mother-identification in girls to be equivocal.

31. Jean Humphrey Block, "Conceptions of Sex Role: Some Cross-Cultural and Longitudinal Perspectives," *American Psychologist* 28 (1973): 512.

32. J. P. Hill and M. E. Lynch, "The Intensification of Gender-Related Role Expectations during Early Adolescence," in *Girls at Puberty: Biological and Psychosocial Perspectives,* ed. J. Brooks-Gunn and A. C. Peterson (New York: Plenum), 201–28.

33. R. G. Simmons, D. A. Blyth, and K. L. McKinnery, "The Social and Psychological Effects of Puberty on White Females," in *Girls at Puberty,* 229–72.

34. M. B. Mahowald, "Sex-role Stereotypes in Medicine," *Hypatia* 2: 21–38.

35. Hill and Lynch, 218–19.

36. Hill and Lynch, 218–20.

37. P. E. Garfinkel and D. M. Garner, *Anorexia Nervosa* (New York: Brunner-Mazel).

38. Brumberg, 28.
39. Brumberg, 28.
40. Lawrence, 93.
41. Brumberg, 29.
42. Brumberg, 30.
43. M. Boskind-Lodahl, "Cinderella's Stepsisters: A Feminist Perspective on Anorexia Nervosa and Bulimia," *Signs* 1: 344–45.
44. Bordo, 76–77.
45. Bordo, 97.
46. Bordo, 85.
47. H. Bruch, *The Golden Cage* (New York: Vintage, 1979).
48. Labels for the versions of feminism here described could be debated. My use, however, is consistent with Jaggar's account in *Feminist Politics and Human Nature* (Totowa, N.J.: Rowman and Allanheld, 1983) and with Rosemarie Tong's more recent *Feminist Thought* (Boulder, Co.: Westview, 1989).
49. Susie Orbach, *Fat is a Feminist Issue* (New York, 1982), 27–31.
50. Orbach, 27.
51. Simone de Beauvoir, *The Second Sex,* trans. H. M. Parshley (New York: Alfred A. Knopf, 1972), 133.
52. Brumberg, 38.
53. C. Gilligan, "Exit-Voice Dilemmas in Adolescent Development," in *Mapping the Moral Domain,* ed. C. Gilligan et al. (Cambridge, Mass.: Harvard University Press), 141–57.

Questions

1. What does the anorexic seem to be striving for by controlling her food intake? How does this relate to the statistic that anorexia nervosa is much more prevalent in females than males?
2. How is anorexia nervosa similar to a gender identity disorder? How is it different?
3. Describe the relationship between normative gender roles and normal development. Contrast this with normative gender roles and abnormal development. What part does the influence of culture have to do with these contrasts?
4. How does Mahowald account for the apparent tension between the idea of an anorexic girl simultaneously pursuing the stereotype of the adult woman and rejecting it?
5. Is a girl exhibiting autonomy in being anorexic? Is she behaving responsibly? Compare what she may believe about her own autonomy and responsibility with the possible belief of an objective observer.

13

Women and the Knife: Cosmetic Surgery and the Colonization of Women's Bodies

Kathryn Pauly Morgan

Introduction

Consider the following passages:

> If you want to wear a Maidenform Viking Queen bra like Madonna, be warned: A body like this doesn't just happen. . . . Madonna's kind of fitness training takes time. The rock star *whose muscled body was recently on tour* spends a minimum of three hours a day working out. (italics added)

> A lot of the contestants [in the Miss America Pageant] do not owe their beauty to their Maker but to their Re-Maker. Miss Florida's nose came courtesy of her surgeon. So did Miss Alaska's. And Miss Oregon's breasts came from the manufacturers of silicone.

> Jacobs [a plastic surgeon in Manhattan] constantly answers the call for cleavage. "Women need it for their holiday ball gowns."

> We hadn't seen or heard from each other for 28 years. . . . Then he suggested it would be nice if we could meet. I was very nervous about it. How much had I changed? I wanted a facelift, tummy tuck and liposuction, all in one week. (A woman, age forty-nine, being interviewed for an article on "older couples" falling in love.)

> "It's hard to say why one person will have cosmetic surgery done and another won't consider it, but generally I think people who go for surgery are more aggressive, they are the doers of the world. It's like makeup. You see some women who might be greatly improved by wearing make-up, but

they're, I don't know, granola-heads or something, and they just refuse.''
(Dr. Ronald Levine, director of plastic surgery education at the University
of Toronto and vice-chairman of the plastic surgery section of the Ontario
Medical Association.)

> Another comparable limitation [of the women's liberation movement]
> is a tendency to reject certain good things only in order to punish men. . . .
> There is no reason why a women's liberation activist should not try to
> look pretty and attractive.[1]

Now imagine the needles and knives. Think of them carefully. Look at
them for a long time. *Imagine them cutting into your skin.* Imagine that
you have been given this surgery as a gift from your loved one who
read a persuasive and engaging press release from Drs. John and Jim
Williams that ends by saying, ''The next morning the limo will chauf-
feur your loved one back home again, with a gift of beauty that will last
a lifetime.''[2] Imagine the beauty that you have been promised.

This essay is about women and about the knives that ''sculpt'' our
bodies to make us beautiful forever. I want to explore this topic for five
reasons. First, I am interested in the project of developing a feminist
hermeneutics that tries to understand the words and choices of women
situated in an interface position with various so-called experts in Western culture.

Second, I experience genuine epistemic and political bewilderment
when I, as a feminist woman, think about contemporary practices and
individual choices in the area of elective cosmetic surgery.[3] Is this a
setting of liberation or oppression—or both?

Third, I have come to realize that this is a ''silent'' (if not silenced)
topic both in mainstream bioethics and in recent ground-breaking discussions in feminist medical ethics.[4] Apart from some tangential references, there is virtually no discussion, feminist or otherwise, of the
normative and political issues that might be raised in relation to women
and elective cosmetic surgery. I believe we need a feminist framework
and critique to understand why *breast augmentation,* until recently, was
the most frequently performed kind of cosmetic surgery in North
America[5] and why, according to *Longevity* magazine, 1 in every 225
adult Americans had *elective* cosmetic surgery in 1989. We need a feminist analysis to understand why actual, live women are reduced and
reduce themselves to ''potential women'' and choose to participate in
anatomizing and fetishizing their bodies as they buy ''contoured bodies,'' ''restored youth,'' and ''permanent beauty.'' In the face of grow-

ing market and demand for surgical interventions in women's bodies that can and do result in infection, bleeding, embolisms, pulmonary edema, facial nerve injury, unfavorable scar formation, skin loss, blindness, crippling, and death, our silence becomes a culpable one.

Fourth, I situate this topic in the larger framework of the contemporary existential technologizing of women's bodies in Western culture. We are witnessing a *normalization* of elective cosmetic surgery. As the author of an article targeted to homemakers remarks, "For many women, it's no longer a question of *whether* to undergo cosmetic surgery—but what, when, by whom and how much."[6] Not only is elective cosmetic surgery moving out of the domain of the sleazy, the suspicious, the secretively deviant, or the pathologically narcissistic, *it is becoming the norm*. This shift is leading to a predictable inversion of the domains of the deviant and the pathological, so that women who contemplate *not using* cosmetic surgery will increasingly be stigmatized and seen as deviant. I believe it is crucial that we understand these normative inversions that are catalyzed by the technologizing of women's bodies.

Finally, I am intrigued by the deeper epistemological and metaphysical dynamics of the field of cosmetic surgery. For example, a recent hospital-sponsored *health* conference advertised a special session on "facial regeneration" by asking, "Are you looking in the mirror and, seeing the old you, wishing you could be seeing the you that you used to be?" and then promising that this previous, youthful "you" could be regenerated. As a philosopher, I am shocked at the extent to which patients and cosmetic surgeons participate in committing one of the deepest of original philosophical sins, the choice of the apparent over the real. Cosmetic surgery entails the ultimate envelopment of the lived temporal *reality* of the human subject by technologically created appearances that are then regarded as "the real." Youthful appearance triumphs over aged reality.

"Just the Facts in America, Ma'am"

As of 1990, the most frequently performed kind of cosmetic surgery is liposuction, which involves sucking fat cells out from underneath our skin with a vacuum device. This is viewed as the most suitable procedure for removing specific bulges around the hips, thighs, belly, buttocks, or chin. It is most appropriately done on thin people who want to get rid of certain bulges, and surgeons guarantee that even if there is weight gain, the bulges won't reappear since the fat cells have been permanently removed. At least twelve deaths are known to have resulted from complications such as hemorrhages and embolisms. "All we know is there was a complication and that complication was death," said the partner of Toni Sullivan, age forty-three ("hardworking mother of two teenage children" says the press).[7] Cost $1,000–$7,500.

The second most frequently performed kind of cosmetic surgery is breast augmentation, which involves an implant, usually of silicone. Often the silicone implant hardens over time and must be removed surgically. Over one million women in the United States are known to have had breast augmentation surgery. Two recent studies have shown that breast implants block X-rays and cast a shadow on surrounding tissue, making mammograms difficult to interpret, and that there appears to be a much higher incidence of cancerous lumps in "augmented women."[8] Cost: $1,500–$3,000.

"Facelift" is a kind of umbrella term that covers several sorts of procedures. In a recent Toronto case, Dale Curtis "decided to get a facelift for her fortieth birthday. . . . Bederman used liposuction on the jowls and neck, removed the skin and fat from her upper and lower lids and tightened up the muscles in the neck and cheeks. . . . 'She was supposed to get a forehead lift but she chickened out,' Bederman says."[9] Clients are now being advised to begin their facelifts in their early forties and are also told that they will need subsequent facelifts every five to fifteen years. Cost $2,500–$10,500.

"Nips" and "tucks" are cute, camouflaging labels used to refer to surgical reduction performed on any of the following areas of the body: hips, buttocks, thighs, belly, and breasts. They involve cutting out wedges of skin and fat and sewing up the two sides. These are major surgical procedures that cannot be performed in out-patient clinics because of the need for anaesthesia and the severity of possible postoperative complications. Hence, they require access to costly operating rooms and services in hospitals or clinics. Cost: $3,000–$7,000.

The number of "rhinoplasties," or nose jobs, has risen by 34 percent since 1981. Some clients are coming in for second and third nose jobs. Nose jobs involve either the inserting of a piece of bone taken from elsewhere in the body or the whittling down of the nose. Various styles of noses go in and out of fashion, and various cosmetic surgeons describe the noses they create in terms of their own surnames, such as "the Diamond nose" or "the Goldman nose."[10] Cost: $2,000–$3,000.

More recent types of cosmetic surgery, such as the use of skin-expanders and suction lipectomy, involve inserting tools, probes, and balloons *under* the skin either for purposes of expansion or reduction.[11]

Lest one think that women (who represent between 60 and 70 percent of all cosmetic surgery patients) choose only one of these procedures, heed the words of Dr. Michael Jon Bederman of the Centre for Cosmetic Surgery in Toronto:

> We see working girls, dental technicians, middle-class women who are unhappy with their looks or are aging prematurely. And we see executives—both male and female. . . . Where before someone would have a tummy tuck and not have anything else done for a year, frequently we will do liposuction and tummy tuck and then the next day a facelift, upper and lower lids, rhinoplasty *and other things.* The recovery time is the same whether a person has one procedure or *the works,* generally about two weeks. (italics added)[12]

In principle, there is no area of the body that is not accessible to the interventions and metamorphoses performed by cosmetic surgeons intent on creating twentieth century versions of "femina perfecta."[13]

From Artifice to Artifact: The Creation of Robo Woman?

In his article "Toward a Philosophy of Technology," Hans Jonas distinguishes between premodern and modern technology. Part of what is especially characteristic of modern technology, he suggests, is that the relationship of means and ends is no longer unilinear but circular, so that "new technologies may suggest, create, even impose new ends, never before conceived, simply by offering their feasibility. . . . Technology thus adds to the very objectives of human desires, including objectives for technology itself."[14] In 1979, Jonas only speculated about the final stage of technological creation: "Are we, perhaps, on the verge of a technology, based on biological knowledge and wielding an engineering art which, this time, has man [*sic*] himself for its object? This has become a theoretical possibility . . . and it has been rendered morally possible by the metaphysical neutralizing of man."[15] We now know that the answer to Jonas' question is "yes." We have arrived at the stage of regarding ourselves as both technological subject and object, transformable and literally creatable through biological engineering. The era of biotechnology is clearly upon us and is invading even the most private and formerly sequestered domains of human life, including women's wombs. I interpret the spectacular rise of the technology of cosmetic surgery as a form of biotechnology that fits this dialectical picture of modern technology.

The domain of technology is often set up in oppositional relation to a domain that is designated "the natural." The role assigned to technology is often that of transcendence, transformation, control, exploitation, or destruction, and the technologized object or process is conceptualized as inferior or primitive, in need of perfecting transformation or exploitation through technology in the name of some "higher" purpose or end, or deserving of eradication because it is harmful or evil.

Although there continue to be substantive theoretical challenges to its dominant metaphors, Western scientific medicine views the human body essentially as a machine.[16] The machine model carries with it certain implications, among which is the reduction of spirit, affect, and value to mechanistic processes in the human body. This perspective also facilitates viewing and treating the body in atomistic and mechanical fashion, so that, for example, the increasing mechanization of the body in terms of artificial hearts, kidneys, joints, limbs, and computerized implants is seen as an ordinary progression within the dominant model. Correlative with the rise of the modeling of the human brain as an information-processing machine, we are witnessing the development of genetic engineering; transsexual surgery; the technological transformation of all aspects of human conception, maternity, and birthing; and the artificial prolongation of human life.

What is designated "the natural" functions primarily as a frontier rather than as a barrier. While genetics, human sexuality, reproductive outcome, and death were previously regarded as open to variation primarily in evolutionary terms, they are now seen by biotechnologists as domains of creation and control. Cosmetic surgeons claim a role here too. For them, human bodies are the locus of challenge. As one plastic surgeon remarks, "Patients sometimes misunderstand the nature of cosmetic surgery. It's not a shortcut for diet or exercise. *It's a way to override the genetic code.*"[17] (italics added)

The beauty culture is coming to be dominated by a variety of experts, and consumers of youth and beauty are likely to find themselves dependent not only on cosmetic surgeons but on anaesthetists, nurses, aestheticians, nail technicians, manicurists, dietitians, hairstylists, cosmetologists, masseuses, aroma therapists, trainers, pedicurists, electrolysists, pharmacologists, and dermatologists. All these experts provide services that can be bought; all these experts are perceived as administering and transforming the human body into an increasingly artificial and ever more perfect object. Think of the contestants in the Miss America pageant who undergo cosmetic surgery in preparation for participation. Reflect on the headline of the article in *Newsweek* (May 27, 1985) on cosmetic surgery: "New Bodies for Sale."

How do these general remarks concerning technology and the body apply to women—and to which women—and why? For virtually all women as women, success is defined in terms of interlocking patterns of compulsion: compulsory attractiveness, compulsory motherhood, and compulsory heterosexuality, patterns that determine the legitimate limits of attraction and motherhood.[18] Rather than aspiring to self-determined and woman-centered ideals of health or integrity, women's attractiveness is defined as attractive-to-men; women's eroticism is defined as either nonexistent, pathological, or peripheral when it is not directed to phallic goals; and motherhood is defined in terms of legally sanctioned and constrained reproductive service to particular men and to institutions such as the nation, the race, the owner, and the class—institutions that are, more often than not, male-dominated. Biotechnology is now making beauty, fertility, the appearance of heterosexuality through surgery, and the appearance of youthfulness accessible to virtually all women who can afford that technology—and growing numbers of women are making other sacrifices in their lives in order to buy access to the technical expertise.

In Western industrialized societies, women have also become increasingly socialized into an acceptance of technical knives. We know about knives that can heal: the knife that saves the life of a baby in distress, the knife that cuts out the cancerous growths in our breasts, the knife that straightens our spines, the knife that liberates our arthritic fingers so that we may once again gesture, once again touch, once again hold. But we also know about other knives: the knife that cuts off our toes so that our feet will fit into elegant shoes, the knife that cuts out ribs to fit our bodies into corsets, the knife that slices through our labia in episiotomies and other forms of genital mutilation, the knife that cuts into our abdomens to remove our ovaries to cure our "deviant tendencies,"[19] the knife that removes our breasts in prophylactic or unnecessary radical mastectomies, the knife that cuts out our "useless bag" (the womb) if we're the wrong color and poor or if we've "outlived our fertility," the knife that makes the "bikini cut" across our pregnant bellies to facilitate the cesarean section that will allow the obstetrician to go on holiday. We know these knives well.

And now we are coming to know the knives and needles of the cosmetic surgeons—the knives that promise to sculpt our bodies, to restore our youth, to create beauty out of what was ugly and ordinary. What kind of knives are these? Magic knives. Magic knives in a patriarchal context. Magic knives in a Eurocentric context. Magic knives in a white supremacist context. What do they mean? I am afraid of these knives.

Listening to the Women

In order to give a feminist reading of any ethical situation we must listen to the women's own reasons for their actions.[20] It is only once we have listened to the voices of women who have elected to undergo cosmetic surgery that we can try to assess the extent to which the conditions for genuine choice have been met and look at the consequences of these choices for the position of women. Here are some of those voices:

Voice 1 (a woman looking forward to attending a prestigious charity ball): "There will be a lot of new faces at the Brazilian Ball."[21] [Class/status symbol]

Voice 2: "You can keep yourself trim. . . . But you have no control over the way you wrinkle, or the fat on your hips, or the skin of your lower abdomen. If you are *hereditarily predestined* to stretch out or wrinkle in your face, you will. If your parents had puffy eyelids and saggy jowls, you're going to have puffy eyelids and saggy jowls."[22] [Regaining a sense of control; liberation from parents; transcending hereditary predestination]

Voice 3: "Now we want a nose that makes a statement, with tip definition and a strong bridge line."[23] [Domination; strength]

Voice 4: "I decided to get a facelift for my fortieth birthday after ten years of living and working in the tropics had taken its toll."[24] [Gift to the self; erasure of a decade of hard work and exposure]

Voice 5: "I've gotten my breasts augmented. I can use it as a tax write-off."[25] [Professional advancement; economic benefits]

Voice 6: "I'm a teacher and kids let schoolteachers know how we look and they aren't nice about it. A teacher who looks like an old bat or has a big nose will get a nickname."[26] [Avoidance of cruelty; avoidance of ageist bias]

Voice 7: "I'll admit to a boob job."[27] (Susan Akin, Miss America of 1986.) [Prestige; status; competitive accomplishments in beauty contest]

Voice 8 (forty-five year old grandmother and proprietor of a business): "In my business, the customers expect you to look as good as they do."[28] [Business asset; economic gain; possible denial of grandmother status]

Voice 9: "People in business see something like this as showing an overall aggressiveness and go-forwardness *The trend is to, you know, be all that you can be.*"[29] [Success; personal fulfillment]

Voice 10 (paraphrase): "I do it to fight holiday depression."[30] [Emotional control; happiness]

Voice 11: "I came to see Dr. X for the holiday season. I have important business parties, and the man I'm trying to get to marry me is coming in from Paris."[31] [Economic gain; heterosexual affiliation]

Women have traditionally regarded (and been taught to regard) their bodies, particularly if they are young, beautiful, and fertile, as *a locus of power* to be enhanced through artifice and, now, through artifact. In 1792, in *A Vindication of the Rights of Woman,* Mary Wollstonecraft remarked: "Taught from infancy that beauty is woman's scepter, the mind shapes itself to the body and roaming round its gilt cage, only seeks to adorn its prison." How ironic that the mother of the creator of *Frankenstein* should be the source of that quote. We need to ask ourselves whether today, involved as we are in the modern inversion of "our bodies shaping themselves to our minds," we are creating a new species of woman-monster with new artifactual bodies that function as prisons or whether cosmetic surgery for women does represent a potentially liberating field of choice.[32]

When Snow White's stepmother asks the mirror "Who is fairest of all?" she is not asking simply an empirical question. In wanting to continue to be "the fairest of all," she is striving, in a clearly competitive context, for a prize, for a position, for power. The affirmation of her beauty brings with it privileged heterosexual affiliation, privileged access to forms of power unavailable to the plain, the ugly, the aged, and the barren.

The voices are seductive—they speak the language of gaining access to transcendence, achievement, liberation, and power. And they speak to a kind of reality. First, electing to undergo the surgery necessary to create youth and beauty artificially not only appears to but often actually does give a woman a sense of identity that, to some extent, she has chosen herself. Second, it offers her the potential to raise her status both socially and economically by increasing her opportunities for hetero-sexual affiliation (especially with white men). Third, by committing herself to the pursuit of beauty, a woman integrates her life with a con-sistent set of values and choices that bring her wide-spread approval and a resulting sense of increased self-esteem. Fourth, the pursuit of beauty often gives a woman access to a range of individuals who admin-ister to her body in a caring way, an experience often sadly lacking in the day-to-day lives of many women. As a result, a woman's pursuit of beauty through transformation is often associated with lived experi-ences of self-creation, self-fulfillment, self-transcendence, and being cared for. The power of these experiences must not be underestimated.[33]

While I acknowledge that these choices can confer a kind of integrity on a woman's life, I also believe that they are likely to embroil her in a set of interrelated contradictions. I refer to these as "paradoxes of choice."

Three Paradoxes of Choice

In exploring these paradoxes, I appropriate Foucault's analysis of the diffusion of power in order to understand forms of power that are poten-tially more personally invasive than are more obvious, publicly identi-fiable aspects of power. In the chapter "Docile Bodies" in *Discipline and Punish,* Foucault highlights three features of what he calls disci-plinary power:

(1) The *scale* of the control. In disciplinary power the body is treated individually and in a coercive way because the body itself is the *active* and hence apparently free body that is being controlled through movements, gestures, attitudes, and degrees of rapidity.

(2) The *object* of the control, which involves meticulous control over the efficiency of movements and forces,

(3) the *modality* of the control, which involves constant, uninterrupted coercion.[34]

Foucault argues that the outcome of disciplinary power is the docile body, a body "that may be subjected, used, transformed, and im-proved" (136). Foucault is discussing this model of power in the con-text of prisons and armies, but we can adapt the central insights of this notion to see how women's bodies are entering "a machinery of power that explores it, breaks it down, and rearranges it'' through a recognizably political metamorphosis of embodiment (138).[35] What is important about this notion in relation to cosmetic surgery is the extent to which it makes it possible to speak about the diffusion of power throughout Western industrialized cultures that are increasingly committed to a technological beauty imperative. It also makes it possible to refer to a set of experts—cosmetic surgeons—whose explicit power mandate is to explore, break down, and rearrange women's bodies.

Paradox One: The Choice of Conformity—Understanding the Number 10

While the technology of cosmetic surgery could clearly be used to create and celebrate idiosyncrasy, eccentricity, and uniqueness, it is obvious that this is not how it is presently being used. Cosmetic surgeons report that legions of women appear in their offices demanding "Bo Derek" breasts.[36] Jewish women demand reductions of their noses so as to be able to "pass" as one of their Aryan sisters who form the dominant ethnic group.[37] Adolescent Asian girls who bring in pictures of Elizabeth Taylor and of Japanese movie actresses (whose faces have already been reconstructed) demand the "Westernizing" of their own eyes and the creation of higher noses in hopes of better job and marital prospects.[38] Black women buy toxic bleaching agents in hopes of attaining lighter skin. What is being created in all of these instances is not simply beautiful bodies and faces but white, Western, Anglo-Saxon bodies in a racist, anti-Semitic context.

More often than not, what appear at first glance to be instances of choice turn out to be instances of conformity. The women who undergo cosmetic surgery in order to compete in various beauty pageants are clearly choosing to conform. So is the woman who wanted to undergo a facelift, tummy tuck, and liposuction all in one week, in order to win heterosexual approval *from a man she had not seen in twenty-eight years* and whose individual preferences she could not possibly know. In some ways, it does not matter who the particular judges are. Actual men—brothers, fathers, male lovers, male beauty "experts"—and hypothetical men live in the aesthetic imaginations of women. Whether they are male employers, prospective male spouses, male judges in the beauty pageants, or male-identified women, these modern day Parises are generic and live sometimes ghostly but powerful lives in the reflective awareness of women.[39] A woman's makeup, dress, gestures, voice, degree of cleanliness, degree of muscularity, odors, degree of hirsuteness, vocabulary, hands, feet, skin, hair, and vulva can all be evaluated, regulated, and disciplined in the light of the hypothetical often-white male viewer and the male viewer present in the assessing gaze of other women.[40] Men's appreciation and approval of achieved femininity becomes all the more invasive when it resides in the incisions, stitches, staples, and scar tissue of women's bodies as women choose to conform. And, as various theorists have pointed out, women's public conformity to the norms of beauty often signals a deeper conformity to the norms of compulsory heterosexuality along with an awareness of the violence that can result from violating those norms.[41] Hence the first paradox: that what looks like an optimal situation of reflection, deliberation, and self-creating choice often signals conformity at a deeper level.

Paradox Two: Liberation into Colonization

As argued above, a woman's desire to create a permanently beautiful and youthful appearance that is not vulnerable to the threats of externally applied cosmetic artifice or to the natural aging process of the body must be understood as a deeply significant existential project. It deliberately involves the exploitation and transformation of the most intimately experienced domain of immanence, the body, in the name of transcendence: transcendence of hereditary predestination, of lived time, of one's given "limitations." What I see as particularly alarming in this project is that what comes to have primary significance is not the real given existing woman but her body viewed as a "primitive entity" that is seen only as potential, as a kind of raw material to be exploited in terms of appearance, eroticism, nurturance, and fertility as defined by the colonizing culture.[42]

But for whom is this exploitation and transformation taking place? Who exercises the power here? Sometimes the power is explicit. It is exercised by brothers, fathers, male lovers, male engineering students who taunt and harass their female counterparts, and by male cosmetic surgeons who offer "free advice" in social gatherings to women whose "deformities" and "severe problems" can all be cured through their healing needles and knives.[43] And the colonizing power is transmitted through and by those women whose own bodies and disciplinary practices demonstrate the efficacy of "taking care of herself" in these culturally defined feminine ways.

Sometimes, however, the power may be so diffused as to dominate the consciousness of a given woman with no other subject needing to be present. As Bartky notes, such diffused power also signals the presence of the colonizer:

> Normative femininity is coming more and more to be centered on woman's body. . . . Images of normative femininity . . . have replaced the religious oriented tracts of the past. The woman who checks her makeup half a dozen times a day to see if her foundation has caked or her mascara has run, who worries that the wind or the rain may spoil her hairdo, who looks frequently to see if her stockings have bagged at the ankle, or who, feeling fat, monitors everything she eats, *has become, just as surely as the inmate of the Panopticon, self-policing subject, a self committed to a relentless self-surveillance. This self-surveillance is a form of obedience to patriarchy.*[44] (italics added)

As Foucault and others have noted, practices of coercion and domination are often camouflaged by practical rhetoric and supporting theories that appear to be benevolent, therapeutic, and voluntaristic. Previously, for example, colonizing was often done in the name of bringing "civilization" through culture and morals to "primitive, barbaric people," but contemporary colonizers mask their exploitation of "raw materials and human labor" in the name of "development." Murphy, Piercy, and I have all claimed that similar rhetorical camouflage of colonization takes place in the areas of women's reproductive decision making and women's right to bodily self-determination. In all of these instances of colonization the ideological manipulation of technology can be identified, and, I would argue, in all of these cases this technology has often been used to the particular disadvantage and destruction of some aspect of women's integrity.[45]

In electing to undergo cosmetic surgery, women appear to be protesting against the constraints of the "given" in their embodied lives and seeking liberation from those constraints. But I believe they are in danger of retreating and becoming more vulnerable, at that very level of embodiment, to those colonizing forms of power that may have motivated the protest in the first place. Moreover, in seeking independence, they can become even more dependent on male assessment and on the services of all those experts they initially bought to render them independent.

Here we see a second paradox bound up with choice; that the rhetoric is that of liberation and care, of "making the most of yourself," but the reality is often the transformation of oneself as a woman for the eye, the hand, and the approval of the Other—the lover, the taunting students, the customers, the employers, the social peers. And the Other is almost always affected by the dominant culture, which is male-supremacist, racist, ageist, heterosexist, anti-Semitic, ableist and class-biased.[46]

Paradox Three: Coerced Voluntariness and the Technological Imperative

Where is the coercion? At first glance, women who choose to undergo cosmetic surgery often seem to represent a paradigm case of the rational chooser. Drawn increasingly from wider and wider economic groups, these women clearly make a choice, often at significant economic cost to the rest of their life, to pay the large sums of money demanded by cosmetic surgeons (since American health insurance plans do not cover this elective cosmetic surgery).

Furthermore, they are often highly critical consumers of these services, demanding extensive consultation, information regarding the risks and benefits of various surgical procedures, and professional guarantees of expertise. Generally they are relatively young and in good health. Thus, in some important sense, they epitomize relatively invulnerable free agents making a decision under virtually optimal conditions.

Moreover, on the surface, women who undergo cosmetic surgery choose a set of procedures that are, by definition, "elective." This term is used, quite straightforwardly, to distinguish cosmetic surgery from surgical intervention for reconstructive or health-related reasons (e.g., following massive burns, cancer-related forms of mutilation, etc.). The term also appears to distinguish cosmetic surgery from apparently involuntary and more pathologically transforming forms of intervention in the bodies of young girls in the form of, for example, foot-binding or extensive genital mutilation.[47] But I believe that this does not exhaust the meaning of the term "elective" and that the term performs a seductive role in facilitating the ideological camouflage of the *absence of choice*. Similarly, I believe that the word "cosmetic" serves an ideological function in hiding the fact that the changes are *noncosmetic:* they involve lengthy periods of pain, are permanent, and result in irreversibly alienating metamorphoses such as the appearance of youth on an aging body.

In order to illuminate the paradox of choice involved here, I wish to draw an analogy from the literature on reproductive technology. In the case of reproductive self-determination, technology has been hailed as increasing the range of women's choices in an absolute kind of way. It cannot be denied that due to the advances in various reproductive technologies, especially IVF and embryo freezing, along with various advances in fetology and fetal surgery, there are now women with healthy children who previously would not have had children. Nevertheless, there are two important ideological, choice-diminishing dynamics at work that affect women's choices in the area of the new reproductive technologies. These dynamics are also at work in the area of cosmetic surgery.

The first of these is the *pressure to achieve perfection through technology,* signaled by the rise of new forms of eugenicist thinking. More profoundly than ever before, contemporary eugenicists stigmatize potential and existing disabled babies, children, and adults. More and more frequently, benevolently phrased eugenicist pressures are forcing women to choose to submit to a battery of prenatal diagnostic tests and extensive fetal monitoring in the name of producing "perfect" (white) babies. As more and more reproductive technologies and tests are invented (and "perfected" in and on the bodies of fertile women), partners, parents, family, obstetricians, and other experts on fertility pressure women to submit to this technology in the name of "maximized choice" and "responsible motherhood." As Achilles, Beck-Gernsheim, Rothman, Morgan, and others have argued, women are being subjected to increasingly intense forms of coercion, a fact that is signaled by the intensifying *lack of freedom* felt by women to refuse to use the technology if they are pregnant and the technology is available.[48]

The second important ideological dynamic is *the double-pathologizing of women's bodies.* The history of Western science and Western medical practice is not altogether a positive one for women. As voluminous documentation has shown, cell biologists, endocrinologists, anatomists, sociobiologists, gynecologists, obstetricians, psychiatrists, surgeons, and other scientists have assumed, hypothesized, or "demonstrated" that women's bodies are generally inferior, deformed, imperfect, and/or infantile. Medical practitioners have often treated women accordingly. Until the rise of the new reproductive technologies, however, women's reproductive capacities and processes were regarded as definitional of normal womanhood and normal human reproduction. No longer is that the case. As Corea and others have so amply demonstrated, profoundly misogynist beliefs and attitudes are a central part of the ideological motivation for the technical development of devices for completely extrauterine fetal development.[49] Women's wombs are coming to be seen as "dark prisons." Women are viewed as threatening, irresponsible agents who live in a necessarily antagonistic relationship with the fetus. And women's bodies in general are coming to be viewed as high-risk milieus since fetal development cannot be continuously monitored and controlled in order to guarantee the best possible "fetal outcome" (particularly where middle- and upper-class white babies are concerned).

Increasingly, "fully responsible motherhood" is coming to be defined in technology-dependent terms and, in a larger cultural context of selective obligatory maternity, more and more women are "choosing to act" in accord with technological imperatives prior to conception, through conception, through maternity, and through birthing itself. Whether this is, then, a situation of increased choice is at the very least highly contestable. Moreover, in a larger ideological context of obligatory and "controlled" motherhood, I am reluctant simply to accept the reports of the technologists and fertility experts that their patients "want access" to the technology as a sufficient condition for demonstrating purely voluntary choice.[50]

A similar argument can be made regarding the significance of the pressure to be beautiful in relation to the allegedly voluntary nature of "electing" to undergo cosmetic surgery. It is clear that pressure to use this technology is on the increase. Cosmetic surgeons report on the wide range of clients who buy their services, pitch their advertising to a large audience through the use of the media, and encourage women to think, metaphorically, in terms of the seemingly trivial "nips" and "tucks" that will transform their lives. As cosmetic surgery becomes increasingly normalized through the concept of the female "makeover" that is translated into columns and articles in the print media or made into nationwide television shows directed at female viewers, as the "success stories" are invited on to talk shows along with their "makers," and as surgically transformed women win the Miss America pageants, women who refuse to submit to the knives and to the needles, to the anaesthetics and the bandages, will come to be seen as deviant in one way or another. Women who refuse to use these technologies are already becoming stigmatized as "unliberated," "not caring about their appearance" (a sign of disturbed gender identity and low self-esteem according to various health-care professionals), as "refusing to be all that they could be" or as "granola-heads."

And as more and more success comes to those who do "care about themselves" in this technological fashion, more coercive dimensions enter the scene. In the past, only those women who were perceived to be *naturally* beautiful (or rendered beautiful through relatively conservative superficial artifice) had access to forms of power and economic social mobility closed off to women regarded as plain or ugly or old.

But now womanly beauty is becoming technologically achievable, a commodity for which each and every woman can, in principle, sacrifice if she is to survive and succeed in the world, particularly in industrialized Western countries. Now technology is making obligatory the appearance of youth and the reality of "beauty" for every woman who can afford it. Natural destiny is being supplanted by technologically grounded coercion, and the coercion is camouflaged by the language of choice, fulfillment, and liberation.

Similarly, we find the dynamic of the double-pathologizing of the normal and of the ordinary at work here. In the technical and popular literature on cosmetic surgery, what have previously been described as *normal* variations of female bodily shapes or described in the relatively innocuous language of "problem areas," are increasingly being described as "deformities," "ugly protrusions," "inadequate breasts," and "unsightly concentrations of fat cells"—a litany of descriptions designed to intensify feelings of disgust, shame, and relief at the possibility of recourse for these "deformities." Cosmetic surgery promises virtually all women the creation of beautiful, youthful-appearing bodies. As a consequence, more and more women will be labeled "ugly" and "old" in relation to this more select population of surgically created beautiful faces and bodies that have been contoured and augmented, lifted and tucked into a state of achieved feminine excellence. I suspect that the naturally "given," so to speak, will increasingly come to be seen as the technologically "primitive"; the "ordinary" will come to be perceived and evaluated as the "ugly." Here, then, is the *third paradox:* that the technological beauty imperative and the pathological inversion of the normal are coercing more and more women to "choose" cosmetic surgery.

Are There Any Politically Correct Feminist Responses to Cosmetic Surgery?

Attempting to answer this question is rather like venturing forth into political quicksand. Nevertheless, I will discuss two very different sorts of responses that strike me as having certain plausibility: the response of refusal and the response of appropriation.[51] I regard both of these as utopian in nature.

The Response of Refusal

In her witty and subversive parable, *The Life and Loves of a She-Devil*, Fay Weldon puts the following thoughts into the mind of the cosmetic surgeon whose services have been bought by the protagonist, "Miss Hunter," for her own plans for revenge:

> He was her Pygmalion, but she would not depend upon him, or admire him, or be grateful. He was accustomed to being loved by the women of his own construction. A soft sigh of adoration would follow him down the corridors as he paced them, visiting here, blessing there, promising a future, regretting a past: cushioning his footfall, and his image of himself. But no soft breathings came from Miss Hunter. [He adds, ominously,] . . . he would bring her to it.[52]

But Miss Hunter continues to refuse, and so will many feminist women. The response of refusal can be recognizably feminist at both an individual and a collective level. It results from understanding the nature of the risks involved—those having to do with the surgical procedures and those related to a potential loss of embodied personal integrity in a patriarchal context. And it results from understanding the conceptual shifts involved in the political technologizing of women's bodies and contextualizing them so that their oppressive consequences are evident precisely as they open up more "choices" to women. "Understanding" and "contextualizing" here mean seeing clearly the ideological biases that frame the material and cultural world in which cosmetic surgeons practice, a world that contains racist, anti-Semitic, eugenicist, and ageist dimensions of oppression, forms of oppression to which current practices in cosmetic surgery often contribute.

The response of refusal also speaks to the collective power of women as consumers to affect market conditions. If refusal is practiced on a large scale, cosmetic surgeons who are busy producing new faces for the "holiday season" and new bellies for the "winter trips to the Caribbean" will find few buyers of their services. Cosmetic surgeons who consider themselves body designers and regard women's skin as a kind of magical fabric to be draped, cut, layered, and designer-labeled, may have to forgo the esthetician's ambitions that occasion the remark that "the sculpting of human flesh can never be an exact art."[53] They may, instead, (re)turn their expertise to the victims in the intensive care burn unit and to the crippled limbs and joints of arthritic women. This might well have the consequence of (re)converting those surgeons into healers.

Although it may be relatively easy for some individual women to refuse cosmetic surgery even when they have access to the means, one deep, morally significant facet of the response of refusal is to try to understand and to care about individual women who do choose to undergo cosmetic surgery. It may well be that one explanation for why a woman is willing to subject herself to surgical procedures, anaesthetics, postoperative drugs, predicted and lengthy pain, and possible "side effects" that might include her own death is that her access to other forms of power and empowerment are or appear to be so limited that cosmetic surgery is the primary domain in which she can experience some semblance of self-determination. Lakoff and Scherr comment on this:

> No responsible doctor would advise a drug, or a procedure, whose clearly demonstrated benefits do not considerably out-weigh its risks, so that a health-threatening drug is not prescribed responsibly except to remedy a life-threatening condition. But equally noxious drugs and procedures are medically sanctioned merely to "cure" moderate overweight or flat-chestedness—hardly life-threatening ailments. . . . The only way to understand the situation is to agree that those conditions *are,* in fact, perceived as life-threatening, so dangerous that seriously damaging interventions are justified any risk worth taking, to alleviate them.[54]

Choosing an artificial and technologically designed creation of youthful beauty may not only be necessary to an individual woman's material, economic, and social survival. It may also be the way that she is able to choose, to elect a kind of subjective transcendence against a backdrop of constraint, limitation, and immanence (in Beauvoir's sense of this term).

As a feminist response, individual and collective refusal may not be easy. As Bartky, I, and others have tried to argue, it is crucial to understand the central role that socially sanctioned and socially constructed femininity plays in a male supremacist, heterosexist society. And it is essential not to underestimate the gender-constituting and identity-confirming role that femininity plays in bringing woman-as-subject into existence while simultaneously creating her as patriarchally defined object.[55] In these circumstances, refusal may be akin to a kind of death, to a kind of renunciation of the only kind of life-conferring choices and competencies to which a woman may have access. And, under those circumstances, it may not be possible for her to register her resistance in the form of refusal. The best one can hope for is a heightened sense of the nature of the multiple double-binds and compromises that permeate the lives of virtually all women and are accentuated by the cosmetic surgery culture.

As a final comment, it is worth remarking that although the response

324 Kathryn Pauly Morgan

of refusal has a kind of purity to recommend it, it is unlikely to have much impact in the current ideological and cultural climate. In just one year, the number of breast augmentations has risen 32 percent; eye tucks have increased 31 percent; nose jobs have increased 30 percent; face lifts have increased 39 percent; and liposuction and other forms of "body contouring" have become the most popular form of cosmetic surgery.[56] Cosmetic surgeons are deluged with demands, and research in the field is increasing at such a rapid pace that every area of the human body is seen as open to metamorphosis. Clearly the knives, the needles, the cannulas, and the drugs are exercising a greater and greater allure. Nevertheless, the political significance of the response of refusal should not be underestimated in the lives of individual women since achieved obligatory femininity is a burden borne by virtually all women. And this response is one way of eliminating many of the attendant harms while simultaneously identifying the ways that the technological beauty imperative increasingly pervades our lives.

The Response of Appropriation

In their insightful essay, "The Feminine Body and Feminist Politics," Brown and Adams remark that "since the body is seen as the site of *action*, its investigation appears to combine what are otherwise characterized as discrete sites, the theoretical and the political, in an original unity."[57] Rather than viewing the womanly/technologized body as a site of political refusal, the response of appropriation views it as the site for feminist action through transformation, appropriation, parody, and protest. This response grows out of that historical and often radical feminist tradition that regards deliberate mimicry, alternative valorization, hyperbolic appropriation, street theater, counterguerrilla tactics, destabilization, and redeployment as legitimate feminist politics. Here I am proposing a version of what Judith Butler regards as "Femininity Politics" and what she calls "Gender Performatives." The contemporary feminist guerrilla theater group Ladies Against Women demonstrates the power of this kind of response. In addition to expressing outrage and moral revulsion at the biased dimensions of contemporary cosmetic surgery, the response of appropriation targets them for moral and political purposes.

However, instead of mourning the temporal and carnal alienation resulting from the shame and guilt experienced prior to surgery and from the experience of loss of identity following surgery, the feminist theorist using the response of appropriation points out (like postmodernists) that these emotional experiences simply demonstrate the ubiquitous instability of consciousness itself, that this is simply a more vivid lived instance of the deeper instability that is characteristic of *all* human subjectivity. Along with feeling apprehension about the appropriation of organic processes and bodies by technology, what this feminist theorist might well say is that the technologies are simply revealing what is true for *all* embodied subjects living in cultures, namely, that *all* human bodies are, and always have been, dialectically created artifacts.[58] What the technologies are revealing is that women's bodies, in particular, can be and are read as especially saturated cultural artifacts and signifiers by phenomenologically oriented anthropologists and forensic archaeologists (even if they have never heard about Derrida or postmodernism). Finally, present practices in cosmetic surgery also provide an extremely public and quantified reckoning of the cost of "beauty," thereby demonstrating how both the processes and the final product are part of a larger nexus of women's commodification. Since such lessons are not always taught so easily or in such transparent form, this feminist theorist may well celebrate the critical feminist ideological potential of cosmetic surgery.

Rather than agreeing that participation in cosmetic surgery and its ruling ideology will necessarily result in further colonization and victimization of women, this feminist strategy advocates appropriating the expertise and technology for feminist ends. One advantage of the response of appropriation is that it does not recommend involvement in forms of technology that clearly have disabling and dire outcomes for the deeper feminist project of engaging "in the historical, political, and theoretical process of constituting ourselves as subjects as well as objects of history."[59] Women who are increasingly immobilized bodily through physical weakness, passivity, withdrawal, and domestic sequestration in situations of hysteria, agoraphobia, and anorexia cannot possibly engage in radical gender performatives of an active public sort or in other acts by which the feminist subject is robustly constituted. In contrast, healthy women who have a feminist understanding of cosmetic surgery are in a situation to deploy cosmetic surgery in the name of its feminist potential for parody and protest.

Working within the creative matrix of ideas provided by Foucault, Kristeva, and Douglas, Judith Butler notes, "The construction of stable bodily contours relies upon fixed sites of corporeal permeability and impermeability. . . . The deregulation of such (heterosexual) exchanges accordingly disrupts the very boundaries that determine what it is to be a body at all."[60] As Butler correctly observes, parody "by itself is not

subversive'' (139) since it always runs the risk of becoming ''domesti-
cated and recirculated as instruments of cultural hegemony.'' She then
goes on to ask, in relation to gender identity and sexuality, what words
or performances would ''compel a reconsideration of the *place* and sta-
bility of the masculine and the feminine? And what kind of gender
performance will enact and reveal the performativity of gender itself in
a way that destabilizes the naturalized categories of identity and desire?'' (139). We might, in parallel fashion, ask what sorts of performances would sufficiently destabilize the norms of femininity, what sorts
of performances will sufficiently expose the truth of the slogan ''Beauty
is always made, not born.'' In response I suggest two performance-
oriented forms of revolt.

The first form of revolt involves revalorizing the domain of the
''ugly'' and all that is associated with it. Although one might argue that
the notion of the ''ugly'' is parasitic on that of ''beauty,'' this is not
entirely true since the ugly is also contrasted with the plain and the
ordinary, so that we are not even at the outset constrained by binary
oppositions. The ugly, even in a beauty-oriented culture, has always
held its own fascination, its own particular kind of splendor. Feminists
can use that and explore it in ways that might be integrated with a
revalorization of being old, thus simultaneously attacking the ageist dimension of the reigning ideology. Rather than being the ''culturally
enmired subjects'' of Butler's analysis, women might constitute themselves as culturally liberated subjects through public participation in
Ms. Ugly Canada/America/Universe/Cosmos pageants and *use the technology of cosmetic surgery to do so.*

Contemplating this form of revolt as a kind of imaginary model of
political action is one thing; actually altering our bodies is another matter altogether. And the reader may well share the sentiments of one
reviewer of this paper who asked: ''Having oneself surgically mutilated
in order to prove a point? Isn't this going too far?'' I don't know the
answer to that question. If we cringe from contemplating this alternative, this may, in fact, testify (so to speak) to the hold that the beauty
imperative has on our imagination and our bodies. If we recoil from *this*
lived alteration of the contours of our bodies and regard it as ''mutilation,'' then so, too, ought we to shrink from contemplation of the cosmetic surgeons who de-skin and alter the contours of women's bodies
so that we become more and more like athletic or emaciated (depending
on what's in vogue) mannequins with large breasts in the shop windows
of modern patriarchal culture. In what sense are these not equivalent
mutilations?

What this feminist performative would require would be not only genuine celebration of but *actual* participation in the fleshly mutations needed to produce what the culture constitutes as "ugly" so as to destabilize the "beautiful" and expose its technologically and culturally constitutive origin and its political consequences. Bleaching one's hair white and applying wrinkle-inducing "wrinkle creams," having one's face and breasts surgically pulled down (rather than lifted), and having wrinkles sewn and carved into one's skin might also be seen as destabilizing actions with respect to aging. And analogous actions might be taken to undermine the "lighter is better" aspect of racist norms of feminine appearance as they affect women of color.

A second performative form of revolt could involve exploring the commodification aspect of cosmetic surgery. One might, for example, envision a set of "Beautiful Body Boutique" franchises, responsive to the particular "needs" of a given community. Here one could advertise and sell a whole range of bodily contours; a variety of metric containers of freeze-dried fat cells for fat implantation and transplant; "body configuration" software for computers; sewing kits of needles, knives, and painkillers; and "skin-Velcro" that could be matched to fit and drape the consumer's body; variously sized sets of magnetically attachable breasts complete with discrete nipple pumps; and other inflation devices modulated according to bodily aroma and state of arousal. Parallel to the current marketing strategies for cosmetic breast surgeries,[61] commercial protest booths, complete with "before and after" surgical makeover displays for penises, entitled "The Penis You Were Always Meant to Have" could be set up at various medical conventions and health fairs; demonstrations could take place outside the clinics, hotels, and spas of particularly eminent cosmetic surgeons—the possibilities here are endless. Again, if this ghoulish array offends, angers, or shocks the reader, this may well be an indication of the extent to which the ideology of compulsory beauty has anesthetized our sensibility in the reverse direction, resulting in the domesticating of the procedures and products of the cosmetic surgery industry.

In appropriating these forms of revolt, women might well accomplish the following: acquire expertise (either in fact or in symbolic form) of cosmetic surgery to challenge the coercive norms of youth and beauty, undermine the power dynamic built into the dependence on surgical experts who define themselves as aestheticians of women's bodies, demonstrate the radical malleability of the cultural commodification of women's bodies, and make publicly explicit the political role that technology can play in the construction of the feminine in women's flesh.

Conclusion

I have characterized both these feminist forms of response as utopian in nature. What I mean by "utopian" is that these responses are unlikely to occur on a large scale even though they may have a kind of ideal desirability. In any culture that defines femininity in terms of submission to men, that makes the achievement of femininity (however culturally specific) in appearance, gesture, movement, voice, bodily contours, aspirations, values, and political behavior obligatory of any woman who will be allowed to be loved or hired or promoted or elected or simply allowed to live, and in any culture that increasingly requires women to purchase femininity through submission to cosmetic surgeons and their magic knives, refusal and revolt exact a high price. I live in such a culture.

Notes

1. "Madonna Passionate About Fitness," *Toronto Star*, August 16, 1990. Ellen Goodman, "A Plastic Pageant," *Boston Globe*, September 19, 1989. "Cosmetic Surgery for the Holidays," *Sheboygen Press*, New York Times New Service, 1985. "Falling in Love Again," *Toronto Star*, July 23, 1990. "The Quest to Be a Perfect 10," *Toronto Star*, February 1, 1990. Mihailo Markovic, "Women's liberation and human emancipation," in *Women and Philosophy: Toward a Theory of Liberation*, Carol Gould and Marx Wartofsky, eds. (New York: Capricorn Books, 1976).

2. John Williams, M.D., and Jim Williams, "Say it with liposuction," from a press release; reported in *Harper's* (August, 1990).

3. This paper addresses only the issues generated out of *elective* cosmetic surgery, which is sharply distinguished by practitioners, patients, and insurance plans from reconstructive cosmetic surgery, which is usually performed in relation to some trauma or is viewed as necessary in relation to some pressing health care concern. This is not to say that the distinction is always clear in practice.

4. I regard the *Hastings Center Report* and *Philosophy and Medicine* as the discipline-establishing journals in mainstream bioethics. The feminist literature to which I am referring includes the double special issue of *Hypatia*, 1989 (vol. 4, nos. 2 and 3), the anthology *Healing Technology: Feminist Perspectives*, Hathryn Strother Ratclif, ed. (Ann Arbor: University of Michigan Press, 1989), and the entire journal series *Women and Health* and *Women and Therapy* through 1990. With the exception of a paper by Kathy Davis on this topic that has just appeared ("Remaking the She-Devil: A Critical Look at Feminist

Approaches to Beauty,'' *Hypatia* 6, no. 2 [1991]: 21–43) the only discussions that do exist discuss the case of Quasimodo, the Hunchback of Notre Dame!

5. "New Bodies for Sale," *Newsweek*, May 27, 1985.

6. Nora McCabe, "Cosmetic Solutions," *Homemaker Magazine* (September, 1990): 38–46.

7. "Woman 43 Dies After Cosmetic Surgery," *Toronto Star,* July 7, 1989.

8. "Implants Hide Tumors in Breasts, Study Says," *Toronto Star,* July 29, 1989. Summarized from article in *Journal of the American Medical Association*, July 8, 1988.

9. "Changing Faces," *Toronto Star,* May 25, 1989.

10. "Cosmetic Surgery for the Holidays."

11. Paul Hirschon, "New Wrinkles in Plastic Surgery: An Update on the Search for Perfection," *Boston Globe Sunday Magazine,* May 24, 1987.

12. "Changing Faces."

13. For a thorough account of how anatomical science has conceptualized and depicted the female skeleton and morphology, see Russett's *Sexual Science: The Victorian Construction of Womanhood* (Cambridge, Mass.: Harvard University Press, 1989) and Schiebinger's *The Mind Has No Sex? Women in the Origins of Modern Science* (Cambridge, Mass.: Harvard University Press, 1989), especially the chapter titled "More Than Skin Deep: The Scientific Search for Sexual Difference."

14. Hans Jonas, "Toward a Philosophy of Technology," *Hastings Center Report,* 9 no. 1 (February, 1979): 35.

15. Jonas, 41.

16. Although the particular kind of machine selected as paradigmatic of the human body has shifted from clocks to hydraulics to thermodynamics and now to information-processing models, the Cartesian machine-modeling of the body continues to dominate body, which literally metamorphoses the body into a machine.

17. "Retouching Nature's Way," 1990.

18. I say "virtually all women" because there is now a nascent literature on the subject of fat oppression and body image as it affects lesbians. For a perceptive article on this subject, see Dworkin (1989). I am, of course, not suggesting that compulsory heterosexuality and obligatory maternity affect all women equally. Clearly women who are regarded as "deviant" in some respect or other—because they are lesbian or women with disabilities or "too old" or poor or of the "wrong race"—are under enormous pressure from the dominant culture *not* to bear children, but this, too, is an aspect of patriarchal pronatalism.

19. G. J. Barker-Benfield, *The Horrors of the Half-Known Life* (New York: Harper and Row, 1976.)

20. Susan Sherwin, "A Feminist Approach to Ethics," *Dollhouse Review* 54 no. 4 (1984–85): 704–13 and "Feminist and Medical Ethics: Two Different Approaches to Contextual Ethics," *Hypatia* 4 no. 2 (1989): 57–72.

21. "Changing Faces."

22. "Changing Faces."
23. "Changing Faces."
24. "Changing Faces."
25. "Changing Faces."
26. "Retouching Nature's Way: Is Cosmetic Surgery Worth It?"
27. Goodman, 1986.
28. Hirschon, 1987.
29. "Cosmetic Surgery for the Holidays."
30. "Cosmetic Surgery for the Holidays."
31. "Cosmetic Surgery for the Holidays."
32. The desire to subordinate our bodies to some ideal that involves bringing the body under control is deeply felt by many contemporary women (apart from any religious legacy of asceticism). As Sandra Lee Bartky, "Foucault, Feminity, and the Modernization of Patriarchal Power," in *Feminity and Foucault: Reflections of Resistance,* Irene Diamond and Lee Quinby, eds. (Boston: Notheastern University Press, 1988); Susan R. Bordo, "Anorexia Nervosa: Psychopathology as the Chrystallization of Culture," *The Philosophical Forum* 2 (Winter, 1985): 73–103; "The Body and the Reproduction of Femininity: A Feminist Appropriation of Foucault," in *Gender/body/knowledge: Feminist Reconstructions of Knowledge and Being and Knowing,* Alison Jagger and Susan Bordo, eds. (New Brunswick, N.J.: Rutgers University Press, 1989a) and "Reading the Slender Body," in *Women, Science and the Bosy Politic: Discourses and Representations,* Mary Jacobus, Evelyn Fox Keller, and Sally Shuttleworth, eds. (New York: Methuen, 1989b) have noted, this is an aspect of the disembodying desires of anorexic women and women who "pump iron." In the area of cosmetic surgery, this control is mediated by the technology and expertise of the surgeons, but the theme is continually articulated.

33. A similar point regarding femininity is made by Sandra Bartky (1988) in her discussion of "feminine discipline." She remarks that women will resist the dismantling of the disciplines of femininity because, at a very deep level, it would involve a radical alteration of what she calls our "informal social ontology":

> To have a body felt to be "feminine"—a body socially constructed through the appropriate practices—is in most cases crucial to a woman's sense of herself as female and, since persons currently can *be* only as male or female, to her sense of herself as an existing individual. . . . The radical feminist critique of femininity, then, may pose a threat not only to a woman's sense of her own identity and desirability but to the very structure of her social universe (78)

34. Michel Foucault, *Discipline and Punish: The Birth of the Prison,* Alan Sheridan, trans. (New York: Pantheon, 1979), 136–37.

35. I view this as a recognizably *political* metamorphosis because forensic cosmetic surgeons and social archaeologists will be needed to determine the actual age and earlier appearance of women in cases where identification is

called for on the basic of existing carnal data. See Susan Griffin's ("The Anatomy Lesson," in *Woman and Nature: The Roaring Inside Her* [New York: Harper and Row, 1978]) poignant description in "The Anatomy Lesson" for a reconstruction of the life and circumstances of a dead mother from just such carnal evidence. As we more and more profoundly artifactualize our own bodies, we become more sophisticated archaeological repositories and records that both signify and symbolize our culture.

36. "Cosmetic Surgery for the Holidays."

37. Robin Tolmach Lakoff and Raquel Scherr, *Face Value: The Politics of Beauty* (Boston: Routledge and Kegan Paul: 1984.)

38. "New Bodies for Sale."

39. Berger, 1972.

40. Haug, 1972.

41. For both documentation and analysis of this claim, see Bartky (1988), Bordo (1985, 1989a, 1989b), and Adrienne Rich "Compulsory Heterosexuality and Lesbian Existence," *Signs: Journal of Women in Culture and Society* 5 no. 4 (1980):631–60.

42. I intend to use "given" here in a relative and political sense. I don't believe that the notion that biology is somehow "given" and culture is just "added on" is a tenable one. I believe that we are intimately and inextricably encultured and embodied, so that a reductionist move in either direction is doomed to failure. For a persuasive analysis of this thesis, see Marion Lowe, "The Dialectic of Biology and Culture," in *Biological Woman: The Convenient Myth,* Ruth Hubbard, Mary Sue Henefin, and Barbara Fried, eds. (Cambridge Mass.: Schenkman, 1982) and Donna Haraway, "Animal Sociology and a Natural Economy of the Body Politic," Parts I and II, *Signs: Journal of Woman in Culture and Society* 4 no. 1 (1978): 21–60, and *Primate Visions* (New York: Routledge, 1989). For a variety of political analyses of the "given" as primitive, see Marge Piercy's poem "Right to Life" in *The Moon Is Always Female* (New York: A. Knopf, 1980), Kathryn Pauly Morgan, "Of Woman Born: How Old-fashioned! New Reproductive Technologies and Women's Oppression," in *The Future of Human Reproduction,* Christine Overall, ed. (Toronto: The Women's Press, 1989), and Julie [Julien S.] Murphy, "Egg farming and women's future," in *Test-tube Women: What Future for Motherhood?* Rita Arditti, Renate Duelli-Klein, and Shelley Minden, eds. (Boston: Pandora Press, 1984).

43. Although I am cognizant of the fact that many women are entering medical school, the available literature is preponderantly authored by men most of whom, I would infer, are white, given the general demographics of specializations in medical school. I also stress the whiteness here to emphasize the extent to which white norms of beauty dominate the field. I think of these surgeons as akin to "fairy godfathers" to underscore the role they are asked to play to "correct," "improve," or "render beautiful" what girls and women have inherited from their mothers, who can only make recommendations at the level of artifice, not artifact.

44. Sandra Lee Bartky, "Foucault, Femininity, and the Modernization of Patriarchal Power," in *Feminity and Foucault: Reflections of Resistance,* Irene Diamond and Lee Quinby, eds. (Boston: Northeastern University Press, 1988), 81.

45. Space does not permit development of this theme on an international scale but it is important to note the extent to which pharmaceutical "dumping" is taking place in the so-called "developing countries" under the ideological camouflage of "population control and family planning." See Betsy Hartman, *Reproductive Rights and Wrongs: The Global Politics of Population Control and Contraceptive Choice* (New York: Harper and Row, 1987) for a thorough and persuasive analysis of the exploitative nature of this practice. See also Julie Murphy, op. cit. (1984); Marge Piercy, "Right to Life," in *The Moon Is Always Female* (New York: A. Knopf, 1980); and Kathryn Pauly Morgan, op. cit. (1989).

46. The extent to which ableist bias is at work in this area was brought home to me by two quotations cited by a woman with a disability. She discusses two guests on a television show. One was "a poised, intelligent young woman who'd been rejected as a contestant for the Miss Toronto title. She is a paraplegic. The organizers' lame excuse for disqualifying her: 'We couldn't fit the choreography around you.' Another guest was a former executive of the Miss Universe contest. He declared, 'Her participation in a beauty contest would be like having a blind man compete in a shooting match.' " (Gwyneth Ferguson Matthews, "Mirror, Mirror: Self-Image and Disabled Women," *Women and Disbility: Resources for Feminist Research* 14 no. 1 [1985]:47–50).

47. It is important here to guard against facile and ethnocentric assumptions about beauty rituals and mutilation. See Lakoff and Scherr, op. cit. (1984) for an analysis of the relativity of these labels and for important insights about the fact that use of the term "mutilation" almost always signals a distancing from and reinforcement of a sense of cultural superiority in the speaker who uses it to denounce what other cultures do in contrast to "our culture."

48. Rona Achilles, "What's New About the New Reproductive Technologies? *Discussion Paper: Ontario Advisory Council on the Status of Women* (Toronto: Government of Ontario, 1988); Elisabeth Beck-Gersheim, "From the Pill to Test-tube Babies: New Options, New Pressures in Reproductive Behavior," in *Healing Technology: Feminist Perspectives,* Kathryn Strother Ratcliff, ed. (Ann Arbor: University of Michigan Press, 1989); Barbara Katz Rothman, "The Meanings of Choice in Reproductive Technology," in *Test-tube Women: What Future for Motherhood?* Rita Arditti, Renate Duelli-Klein, and Shelley Minden, eds. (Boston: Pandora Press, 1984); Morgan, op. cit., 1989.

49. Gena Corea, *The Mother Machine* (New York: Harper and Row, 1985).

50. For the most sustained and theoretically sophisticated analysis of pronatalism operating in the context of industrialized capitalism, see Martha Gimenez, "Feminism, Pronatalism, and Motherhood," in *Mothering: Essays in Feminist Theory,* Joyce Trebilcot, ed. (Totowa, N.J.: Rowman and Allenheld,

1984). Gimenez restricts her discussion to working-class women but, unfortunately, doesn't develop a more differentiated grid of pronatalist and antinatalist pressures within that economic and social group. For example, in Quebec there are strong pressures on Francophone working class women to reproduce, while there is selective pressure against Anglophone and immigrant working women bearing children. Nevertheless, Gimenez's account demonstrates the systemic importance of pronatalism in many women's lives.

51. One possible feminist response (that, thankfully, appears to go in *and* out of vogue) is that of feminist fascism, which insists on a certain particular and quite narrow range of embodiment and appearance as the only range that is politically correct for a feminist. Often feminist fascism sanctions the use of informal but very powerful feminist "embodiment police," who feel entitled to identify and denounce various deviations from the normative range. I find this feminist political stance incompatible with any movement that would regard itself as liberatory for women and here I admit that I side with feminist libertists who say that "the presumption must be on the side of freedom" (Mary Anne Warren, *Gendercide: The Implications of Sex Selection* [Totowa, N.J.: Rowman and Allenheld, 1985]) and see that as the lesser of two evils.

52. Fay Weldon, *The Life and Loves of a She-Devil* (London: Coronet Books; New York: Pantheon Books, 1983), 215–16.

53. Harold Silver, "Liposuction Isn't for Everybody," *Toronto Star,* October 20, 1989.

54. Lakoff and Scherr, op. cit., 1984, 165–66.

55. Bartky, 1988; Morgan, 1986.

56. "New Bodies for Sale."

57. Beverley Brown and Parveen Adams, "The Feminine Body and Feminist Politics," *M/F* 3 (1979): 35.

58. Lowe, 1982; Haraway, 1978, 1989.

59. Nancy Hartsock, "Foucault on Power: A Theory for Women?" in *Feminism/postmodernism,* Linda Nicolson, ed. (New York: Routledge, 1990), 170. In recommending various forms of appropriation of the practices and dominant ideology surrounding cosmetic surgery, I think it important to distinguish this set of disciplinary practices from those forms of simultaneous Retreat-and-Protest that Susan Bordo (1989a, 20) so insightfully discusses in "The Body and the Reproduction of Femininity": hysteria, agoraphobia, and anorexia. What cosmetic surgery shares with these gestures is what Bordo remarks upon, namely, the fact that they may be "viewed as a surface on which conventional constructions of femininity are exposed starkly to view, through their inscription in extreme or hyperliteral form." What is different, I suggest, is that although submitting to the procedures of cosmetic surgery involves pain, risks, undesirable side effects, and living with a heightened form of patriarchal anxiety, it is also fairly clear that, most of the time, the pain and risks are relatively short-term. Furthermore, the outcome often appears to be one that generally enhances women's confidence, confers a sense of well-being, contributes to a

greater comfortableness in the public domain, and affirms the individual woman as a self-determining and risk-taking individual. All these outcomes are significantly different from what Bordo describes as the "languages of horrible suffering" (Bordo 1989a, 20) expressed by women experiencing hysteria, agoraphobia, and anorexia.

60. Julia Kristeva, *The Powers of Horror: An Essay on Abjection,* Leon Rudiez, trans. (New York: Columbia University Press, 1982); Mary Douglas, *Purity and Danger* (London: Routledge and Kegan Paul; New York, Praeger, 1966); Judith Butler, *Gender Trouble: Feminism and the Subversion of Identity* (New York: Routledge, 1990), 132–33.

61. A booth of this sort was set up in a prominent location at a large "Today's Woman Fair" at the National Exhibition grounds in Toronto in the summer of 1990. It showed "before" and "after" pictures of women's breasts and advertised itself as "The Breasts *You* Were Always *Meant* to Have." One special feature of the display was a set of photographs showing a woman whose breasts had been "deformed" by nursing but who had finally attained through cosmetic surgery the breasts "she was meant to have had." I am grateful to my colleague June Larkin for the suggestion of the analogous booth.

Questions

1. What does Morgan have to say about the idea that cosmetic surgery can be both liberating and oppressive simultaneously?
2. In what way does Morgan approach the two very different feminist responses of refusal and appropriation?
3. In your opinion, what is beauty? How should beauty be defined? Can beauty be thought of as objective?
4. In what way is success of women connected with female beauty? Can women be empowered by cosmetic surgery? What does this say about women who do not fit the category of "beautiful?"
5. Explain the paradox of the choice of conformity. Do you agree that this is a paradox? How is this related to the second paradox of liberation into colonization and the third paradox, coerced voluntariness and the technological imperative?
6. What is "misogyny?"
7. Does Morgan believe that all cosmetic surgery should be abolished? Explain her position.

14

Beauty's Punishment: How Feminists Look at Pornography

Edward Johnson

Is there anywhere
a man
who
will not punish us
for our beauty?

Diane Wakoski

Whenever a woman is on display, I feel my anger
rising.
She is in danger, her nakedness cause for alarm.
And her beauty is meant as no invitation to me. Rather
it is a punishing lesson to womankind on how to do
it right.

Wendy Chapkis[1]

Simone de Beauvoir's pioneer feminist treatise, *Le deuxième sexe* (1949), was soon joined by "Faut-il brûler Sade?" her study of the patron saint of pornography. The tension between these enterprises expresses a central question of the past four decades of feminism. How could a feminist do both?[2]

The traditional debate about pornography turned on the question of its representation of sex, which was judged inappropriate since it showed what should not be done, or at least what should not be seen, and in doing so affronted, degraded, or corrupted. By the 1960s, the debate seemed to have been largely settled in favor of liberal pro-sex, pro-openness attitudes. But the conservative critique continued, and soon found a surprising ally among feminists, many of whom made the elimination of pornography a central item on their agenda of antisexist social reform. Debate about the issue has revealed some difficult dis-

agreements within feminism—about the nature and (dis)utility of pornography, on the one hand, and about reasonable reactions to it, on the
other.

The antipornography view was articulated, beginning in the mid-
1970s, by feminists such as Kathleen Barry, Susan Brownmiller, Andrea Dworkin, Susan Griffin, Catherine MacKinnon, Robin Morgan,
Diana Russell, and Gloria Steinem, among many others.[3] Part of the
argument, in its early version, is well expressed by a declaration made
in a 1976 study of crimes against women:

> Pornography has been an issue too long neglected by feminists, many of
> whom are still swayed by notions of liberal tolerance. Of course, liberals
> wouldn't tolerate movies of whites beating Blacks, or Christians beating
> Jews, but if it is called pornography and women are the victims, then you
> are a prude to object.[4]

This line of thought suggests that if "liberals" would not tolerate certain kinds of representations of men, but do tolerate analogous representations of women, then this differential toleration reveals unfair discrimination (sexism). Does it?

The liberal may agree that differential toleration is wrong, and decide
that toleration ought to be extended to representations of racial beatings.
After all, the American Civil Liberties Union has been willing to defend
the right of Nazis to march in Skokie—which was arguably more
openly offensive to its Jewish community than a backstreet stalag-film
would have been. Or the liberal may see the situations as different because they involve, not gender, but sexuality. Human sexual preference
is various, and liberals are leery, so to speak, of straightening out people's sexual kinks by declaring what fantasies (which are by definition
exaggerations) should be unacceptable. In short, the liberal is inclined
to give individuals a little leeway when it comes to sex, and for that
reason may be disinclined to see the situations in question as truly analogous. In one sense, the liberal thereby begs the question, since *it is
precisely men's tendency to eroticize contexts involving women that is
at issue.* But the feminist critic must also be wary of begging the question by assuming that a given representation is *not* erotic. As Linda
Williams says, criticizing MacKinnon's analysis of *Deep Throat*:

> MacKinnon invokes a norm—in this case a feminist norm regarding the
> inherently submissive nature of fellatio for women—to condemn the repre-
> sentation and performance of a politically incorrect sexual practice. . . .
> Are feminists to declare themselves against representations of fellatio,

against being on their knees during sex, against anything other than absolutely egalitarian forms of mutual love and affection? Indeed, what forms
of sex *are* egalitarian? . . . One thing is clear: many very different things,
very imperfectly understood, turn both women and men on, including
being dominated and dominating.[5]

The most fundamental problem with the differential-toleration argument is that it cannot do the job the antipornography critic wants done.
Some actions will not in fact reliably elicit the disapproval required,
and for other actions the required comparison will prove too difficult.
Consider the comparatively simple example of fellatio. If a heterosexual male liberal is asked to compare a situation involving a woman and
a situation involving a Black or a Jew, what imaginative act is being
asked for? Is the Black or Jew to be female? If so, the liberal may see
nothing wrong with either situation. If not, then the liberal's imagination may prove an uncertain guide, since he might realize that the fact
that *he* found something intuitively wrong with the racial case (because
it was another man) could hardly show that the act would have been
"wrong" with a woman. I use fellatio as an example, because it is, like
beating, an activity that at least makes some kind of imaginative sense
whatever the sex of the participants. Other examples, even "ordinary"
intercourse, would require more imaginative adjustment.

It is worth noting in passing that "ordinary" intercourse itself has
been problematized by feminist critique. As Williams points out, a
number of antipornography feminists seem to feel that "violence is
inherent in the male role in 'normal' heterosexual relations."[6] Andrea
Dworkin appears to find penetration objectionable. Others have criticized representations of women as sexually passive in "ordinary" intercourse. Tom O'Carroll, whose uneven apology for paedophilia goes
beyond the scope of this paper,[7] plausibly objects against Brownmiller
that

> it does not follow as a matter of logical necessity that because a woman
> may be represented in a passive sexual role that this makes her a "victim."
> Such a view proceeds from a fundamentally anti-sexual (or at least anti-
> heterosexual) outlook, in which it is assumed that a woman could not find
> pleasure in such a role. . . . The mere image of a woman reclining passively
> and nakedly provides no evidence of either the intent or successful effect
> of ridiculing the person depicted, or her sex.[8]

In fact, these issues about "ordinary" intercourse ultimately flow out
of the radical-feminist analogizing of intercourse and rape. Of all the

varieties of sexist oppression feminists opposed, rape seemed the simplest and the worst.[9] So rape came to seem symbolic of sexual oppression. In the process, the concept of rape was transformed, so that it came to be applied to sex itself in a new way. Thus, Robin Morgan could write, in 1974, that

> *rape exists any time sexual intercourse occurs when it has not been initiated by the woman, out of her own genuine affection and desire.* This last qualifier is important, because we . . . know that many women, in responding to this new pressure to be "liberated initiators" have done so *not* out of their own desire but for the same old reasons—fear of losing the guy, fear of being a prude, fear of hurting his fragile feelings, *fear.* . . . Anything short of that is, in a radical feminist definition, rape. Because *the pressure is there* and it need not be a knife-blade against the throat; it's in his body language, his threat of sulking, his clenched or trembling hands, his self-deprecating humor or angry put-down or silent self-pity at being rejected. . . . It must be clear that, under this definition, most of the decently married bedrooms across America are settings for nightly rape.[10]

This kind of persuasive definition, though useful in drawing attention to neglected aspects of social situations, is dangerous because it does so by means of an exaggeration that distorts the utility of the original concept. In effect, Morgan's demand is that sex be separated from "pressure." But even if that is a good idea—and reflection on developments such as the sexual-harassment code at Antioch College reminds us of the complexities here—do we really want to say that if a woman decides to have sex with her husband because she is afraid of "hurting his fragile feelings," or because otherwise he will exhibit a "self-deprecating humor," he has *raped* her? It is a short step from this to simply defining women as victims, which indeed some feminists have in effect done.[11] "No" means *no*, in this view, but "yes" rarely means *yes*. In its more extreme forms, this view calls heterosexuality itself into question.[12]

The differential-toleration argument attempted to refute toleration for pornography with one simple, quick blow. But the antipornography arguments that grew out of the 1970s had other points to make. The most striking of these, of course, was the claim that pornography—either *some* pornography (the "violent" kind) or maybe pornography as an institution—in fact caused harm to women. New research, much of it growing out of the process begun by the 1970 Commission on Pornography, appeared to show that violent pornography, and maybe "degrading" pornography as well, had bad effects on consuming males: it made them more callous in their dealings with women, trivialized rape, etc. Thus, the judgment of the 1970 commission that pornography was relatively benign in its effects was called into question by the 1986 Meese Commission.

The impact the feminist harm argument has had upon the liberal is typified by Joel Feinberg's examination of the subject in his 1985 treatise *Offense to Others*. His position is that "Where pornography is not a nuisance, and (we must now add) not a threat to the safety of women, it can be none of the state's proper business." Thus, Feinberg allows that "if there is a clear enough causal connection to rape, a statute that prohibits violent pornography would be a morally legitimate restriction of liberty." But how clear, and how causal, does the connection between pornography and rape have to be? He says that

> works of pure pornography . . . may yet have an intimate personal value to those who use them, and a social value derived from the importance we attach to the protection of private erotic experience. By virtue of that significance, one person's liberty can be invaded to prevent the harm other parties might cause to *their* victims only when the invaded behavior has a specially direct connection to the harm caused, something perhaps like direct "incitement." . . . Surely, the relation between pornographers and rapists is nowhere near that direct and manipulative. If it were, we would punish the pornographers proportionately more severely, and blame the actual rapist (poor chap; he was "inflamed") proportionately less.[13]

In short, the liberal is quite willing to countenance suitable legal restriction in clear cases of appropriately direct harm, but mindful that the standards of demonstration have to be high because we are dealing with matters that are very important to people. To antipornography feminists such as Dworkin and MacKinnon, this will seem like just another proof that the boys *will* have their porn, whatever it takes. But such an analysis is unresponsive to the questions involved. There are very great differences between the contending parties about a variety of issues. Dworkin and MacKinnon have, for example, made it clear that they "abhor the ACLU's defenses of Klan and Nazi groups."[14] As Donald Alexander Downs observes:

> Historically, liberalism and feminism have gone hand in hand. . . . Yet the feminists who link inequality with pornography believe that it is time to reconsider this association . . . [since] rules associated with civil liberty are not in fact equal or neutral. . . . Liberalism is a form of false consciousness because there is no substantive equality and freedom for women. . . .

> Distrusting free speech, since freedom to speak is inextricably linked with power, MacKinnon essentially advocates a form of "'progressive censorship"—censorship of dominant conservative or reactionary ideas in order that progressive concepts can be heard and acted upon.[15]

From this perspective, expression deserves to be free only if it is sufficiently in tune with what we as a society know to be true about fundamental issues. For MacKinnon, equality is a social goal in tension with liberty, and one that should have greater weight than it does in our social system. And if this is true of expression, and of such pornography as might be able to claim the status of art, how much less will pornographic artifacts with merely private importance matter in the great struggle for egalitarianism!

The first thing to notice about this kind of view is the extent to which it rests upon a kind of moral absolutism. Conservative critics have traditionally argued for the propriety of society's exercising legal control over material that, for example because of its explicitness about sex or violence, offends against prevailing community standards. Often, the argument has had something to do with preserving values, or the power of language, or even the allure of sexuality itself. In her book attacking "right-wing women," Andrea Dworkin showed herself no less an absolutist, arguing that

> the refusal to demand (with no compromise being possible) one absolute standard of human dignity is the greatest triumph of antifeminism over the will to liberation. . . . No liberation movement can accept the degradation of those whom it seeks to liberate by accepting a different definition of dignity for them and stay a movement for their freedom at the same time. (Apologists for pornography: take note.)[16]

The liberal is sympathetic enough, of course, to the rhetoric of dignity and equality. But the sad truth has always been that we only attain broad agreement about such notions by taking them in a relatively formal sense. We can agree about the value of equality, for example, precisely because each person makes the necessary adjustments in understanding. But when we have to decide what equality is to mean substantively, concretely, practically, then we find that folks have quite various conceptions—and persuasion and politics come into play. Nor is this necessarily bad: it is, after all, what makes diplomacy possible. To be sure, substantive agreement about such matters would be nice. But that is something that has to be worked out, worked towards, in particular situations. And no one wins, in the long run, if the means of communication and reflection are tainted for the sake of short-term gain. I cannot discuss here the complex issue of "hate speech," but it seems to me clear that we should strive for as much openness as possible.[17]

Turning back to the issue of pornography, we can observe that objections to antiwoman pornography, which traditionally focused on its explicit sexual content, now often focus instead on its antifemale ideology. Thus, in the same essay in which she offered her transfiguration of the concept of rape, Robin Morgan also characterized pornography as "sexist propaganda," suggested a distinction between pornography (bad) and "genuine erotic art" (good), and articulated her famous slogan: "Pornography is the theory, and rape the practice."[18] Like Morgan, Susan Brownmiller saw pornography as "the undiluted essence of anti-female propaganda."[19] Up to a point, these were useful slogans. But it is important to remember that, to the extent that pornography, or some of it, *is* antifemale ideology, it has some right to be. If Nazis think that the world would be better without Jews in it, then by all means let them say so. Let them say so because, in the first place, people have a right to say what they actually think about how things should be. To suppose otherwise is to hold that not only people's *behavior*, but their very political *thought*, must comply with what the rest of us find acceptable.

The problem here, of course, is to try to delineate the line between general pronouncement and individual threat. In effect, the radical feminist construes all ("violent") pornography as constituting one giant threat, and sees this threat as leading to a harm (rape), or constituting a harm (intimidation, defamation).[20] By allowing pornography to flourish openly, society is seen as endorsing the threatening warning: This is what we do to little girls who don't behave! It is important to recognize the state of mind from which this interpretation comes. It is, as Morgan suggested, one of fear. That women in our society often live in fear is not to be forgotten. But fear-inspiring messages are not the only ones society sends. And while many of the more positive messages can be faulted, as in varying degrees stereotyped, that too is changing, in part as a result of feminism.

Still, *if* pornography is ideology, a kind of grafitti politics, then let us grant it the right to be open about its preferences, however nasty we may find them, because—and this is the second reason—we are all better off that way. If people hate us, then perhaps it is better to know that.

Some philosophers disagree, however, with the idea that pornography represents an ideology—that it states ideas that could be understood to threaten or defame.[21] And of course some feminists have thought that, whatever pornography's prejudices, what it provides, or sometimes can provide, is of value to women. Thus, Angela Carter holds that "Sade . . . put pornography in the service of women, or, perhaps, allowed it to be invaded by an ideology not inimical to women."[22] And Erica Jong holds that "Henry Miller's writing, with its open expression and final transcendence of male rage and its ability to recognize female creativity, is a good place to begin searching for the honesty both sexes must find. Shall we burn Miller? Better to emulate him."[23] Anthropologist and psychoanalyst Muriel Dimen argues as follows:

> Given the ongoing patriarchal construction of desire, it is likely that private fantasy and public pornography will continue to portray men as Subjects and women as Objects who need Subjects to complete and elevate them. But people can identify, and empathize, across the boundaries of gender. . . . Pornography is private fantasy made public. Its images may be misogynist, but that is all they are—make-believe images. To equate images with actions is to misunderstand the function of fantasy in personal experience in general and sexual desire in particular. . . . The capacity for make-believe, play, and fantasy means that women, like men, see more in pornography, or any image, than what is on the surface. When women get aroused by lewd stories or pictures, they are finding their own desire. . . . They become the female Subject.[24]

Now, listen to Dworkin and MacKinnon:

> Feminists say [to us] shut up because if you speak we will have other women here calling themselves feminists to defend this exploitation of women. In this way, we will wipe out what you have said. We don't do this to anyone else who stands up for the rights of women, but we will do this to you because we want you to shut up. You make us feel bad. We can't stand up to the pornographers. They are too mean, too real, and too powerful. . . . So we are having these women in here who say they are feminists but enjoy calling themselves "girls," and they want us to have fun having sex now, and they say pornography is just part of liberated sex, and if they say so it must be true for them so you aren't even right when you say pornography hurts women because it doesn't hurt all women (it doesn't hurt these "girl"-women), and if we listen to them we don't have to listen to you, which means, shut up.[25]

What do we hear in this passage? Sarcasm and complaint: complaint that other feminists don't agree with them; complaint that disagreeing with them is trying to "wipe out" what they have said, trying to make them "shut up"; sarcasm that suggests those who don't agree with them are "girls," have been intimidated by pornographers, are only "calling themselves feminists." What we hear is simple intolerance for the voices of those who disagree.

It is possible to argue, as I think Dworkin and MacKinnon would, that some restriction of voice is necessary in order to encourage variety. Essentially, the argument would suggest that we do not live in a society where diverse points of view really receive expression. Instead, the uniformity of the messages we receive might be emphasized. This is the sort of argument Noam Chomsky and others have frequently made with regard to American politics and the information media.[26] Where diverse views do not have equal social voice, one might try to remedy the situation either by encouraging underrepresented views or by restricting dominant views. Those who do not feel that their message is being heard (sc., being accepted) may be tempted to wish that those who disagree with them could be shut up.

Conservative theories offer us a vision of what is "truly" beautiful, in an exclusive and absolute sense, and claim the right to restrict those forms of representation that are seen as inimical to its proper appreciation. The procensorship feminism of Dworkin and MacKinnon offers its own theory of true beauty: since we know that egalitarianism is the true ideal, we need worry less about freedom of expression for views incompatible with that ideal. Liberals, who recognize a diversity of ideals of beauty, seek to provide as much space for their private celebration as is compatible with the functioning of society.

Some feminists have thought that what is needed is a proliferation of erotic images rather than a restriction of pornographic ones. Thus, Linda Williams indicts "the central fallacy of all the anti-porn feminist positions: that a single, whole sexuality exists opposed to the supposed deviations and abnormalities of somebody else's fragmentation." The anticensorship feminists she prefers to call " 'social construction' feminists, given their emphasis on social and historical factors in the construction of sexuality and their work to defend the expression of diverse sexualities and to oppose the notion of any kind of 'politically correct,' ideal sexuality."[27] For such feminists, images have for different individuals a multiplicity of meanings about which no simple story is to be told. Williams herself says that

> while I would agree with antipornography feminists that pornography . . . offers exemplary symbolic representations of patriarchal power in heterosexual pleasure, and while I believe that a feminist critique of this power is crucial, I side with the anti-censorship feminists who hold that censor-

ship of these pleasures offers no real solution to patriarchal violence and abuse. . . . In attacking the penis rather than the phallus, antipornography feminism evades the real sources of masculine power. . . . As Edward Donnerstein's research shows . . . nonexplicit sexual representations can be more hierarchical and violent than explicit, X-rated ones; moreover, they appear to be just as effective at "teaching" callous attitudes toward sexual violence against women as explicit violent pornography.[28]

Since images have very different meanings to different individuals, and those meanings have very individualized relationships to how someone experiences desire and fulfillment, we need to be cautious in supposing that we know pornography when we see it. It is important to remember that, as feminism helped us appreciate, the sexual *is* the political.[29] It is also important to remember that the effective defense of a way of life usually involves its presentation: the reader, the viewer, must come to see life from a new perspective in order to understand what is at stake. Accordingly, we must grant the right to such explicitness as is necessary to give us some idea about what is attractive in this alien way of life. Each form of beauty is a form of truth, though of course not all of truth: it is the truth about the valorization of reality from a particular point of view. Each ideal presses upon us its own claims. But as Donnerstein says, "The problem is that these messages are all over the place, not just in pornography."[30] Erica Jong speaks in similar terms:

Distressing as it is to be surrounded by images of abused women, it is equally disturbing to be surrounded by the pretty young females who dominate our visual media. . . . A distressing conformity is imposed upon us all. Pornography is only part of the problem. Advertising, movies, television, and romance novels also overwhelmingly present only one face of woman. . . . These things are just as damaging as pornography.[31]

If the goal is diversity in the images that surround us, in our ideals of what is sexy, what is beautiful, then it is important to remember that no form of censorship can provide that. Even with an edge provided by censorship, alternative ideals cannot move us if they are not articulated; if they are, then perhaps they can be effective without censorship's risky aid. Wendy Chapkis, in her social-constructionist study of women and the politics of appearance, says:

Creating our own erotic images is an important step in reclaiming our bodies and our sexuality. What would such a woman-empowering porno look like? . . . It would visually acknowledge the lustiness and attraction of women of different body types—a radical challenge to existing imagery which reinforces the feeling that sex is for a physical elite. Helen Gurley Brown has commented, "*Playboy* doesn't denigrate women, only women who are not beautiful." Much the same could be said of the images found in the pages of *Cosmopolitan*. New erotic images full of the diversity of female beauty could help dissolve the commercial monopoly on sex appeal and break down the division between the supposedly sexually desirable and the undeserving.[32]

This imposed uniformity has been seen as damaging also to men who are, as Harry Brod puts it, "dominated by desires not authentically their own."[33] This has helped lead to a movement of men confronting pornography's impact on their lives. Particularly striking is Keith Mc-Walter's confession:

By a certain age, most modern men have been so surfeited with images of unattainably beautiful women in preposterous contexts that we risk losing the capacity to respond to the ordinarily beautiful women we love in our bedrooms. There have been too many times when I have guiltily resorted to impersonal fantasy because the genuine love I felt for a woman wasn't enough to convert feeling into performance. And in those sorry, secret moments, I have resented deeply my lifelong indoctrination into the esthetic of the centerfold.[34]

And, of course, the door swings both ways. As Chapkis says: "Feeling unworthy of admiration, undeserving of the desire of another is partly a consequence of the Larger than Life culture promoted in film, novels, television and advertisements."[35] Sociologist Edwin Schur has suggested that

the link between pornography and the objectified uses of female sexuality in ordinary "respectable" advertising may be very close indeed. It could be that until women's bodies no longer are used *to sell* commodities, the treatment and sale of women's bodies *as* commodities, through pornography, will be bound to persist.[36]

Beauty's punishment is twofold. On the one hand, a woman who strives not to stimulate unwanted male desire is stigmatized as unwomanly, unfeminine, and punished for her lack of beauty.[37] On the other hand, a woman who responds to society's demand that she be beautiful finds that her efforts stimulate male desire beyond her ability or willingness to satisfy, and so she is punished for her beauty. As Michael Kimmel says:

> If men can see women's beauty and sexuality as so injurious that they can fantasize about rape as a retaliation for harm already committed by women, is it also possible that pornographic fantasies draw from this same reservoir of men's anger? If so, it would seem that men's rage at women, and not its pornographic outlet, ought to be our chief concern. . . . For men to "confront" pornography means . . . exploring the mechanisms that will allow us to . . . create images that arouse us without depicting the punishment of others as the basis for that arousal.[38]

But do we lack such images now? And is there any reason to be confident that such images would, should, or could suffice for the expression of male desire? Linda Williams sees antipornography feminism as suggesting, erroneously, "that if female sexuality were ever to get free of its patriarchal contaminations it would express no violence, would have no relations of power, and would produce no transgressive sexual fantasies."[39] The assumption is, to say the least, equally questionable for male sexuality. Some theorists have suggested that violent fantasy may be a central element in (especially male) sexual desire.[40]

Our understanding the role of violence in sexuality is not aided by the fact that we have little comprehension of the role violent representations play in human lives generally.[41] Certainly, we must keep in mind the difference between violence and "the show of violence." And we must recognize that social-constructionist accounts have to operate within whatever constraints biology may in fact impose on us.

Just as male animals may compete, sexually and otherwise, in ways that emphasize threat and posturing, but stop short of serious injury, so humans may do the same, only in a culturally mediated way. There is a ritualization of violence. James Twitchell claims that "aggressive fantasies are central to the maturation of males regardless of cultural context" and suggests that rather than attempting to exorcise aggression, "we should make sure to ritualize it in the least disruptive and most socially advantageous ways." Modern fables of aggression—slasher movies and the rest—are simply "what happens when a relatively free mass media allow an adolescent audience with disposable time and money to play out aggressive fantasies."[42] The function of these, Twitchell argues, is to protect society, both by letting us come to understand where the boundaries of transgression are, and by allowing us to let off steam through vicarious experience. He says that one of the more popular social science approaches to rituals of preposterous violence . . . is to argue that watching violence makes us more prone to violence. Possibily, for some consumers, this is true in the very short run, but it inhibits the desire for violence in the majority over time. . . . We may condemn our appetites for pornography or violent entertainment . . . but when we look at the tribes and cultures which have squabbled themselves out of existence we may be thankful that such aggression has been sublimated. The question is . . . to what degree sex and violence, if not repressed [by means of ritualized violence], will result in destructive forms.[43]

If an account such as Twitchell's should be correct, violence in pornography might often play a role quite different from that of expressing hostility toward objects of sexual choice; the victim, female or otherwise, might be merely a technicality needed to make narrative sense out of a sequence of violent gestures, much as an object of sexual fantasy is sometimes merely a figurehead useful in orchestrating a sequence of masturbatory gestures.

Feminists sometimes sound much like conservatives, arguing pornography is somehow diminishing people's ability to relate to each other sexually. Kathleen Barry, for example, says that

when sexual experience with another is determined by fantasy, the social-sexual reality of the other person is replaced by the fantasy. . . . One of the effects of widespread pornography has been to introduce movies, books, or pictures as the erotic stimulant between two people, thereby reducing the need for people to relate to *each other*.[44]

The second point here, though perhaps true, is to a considerable extent simply the effect, in the area of sexual relationships, of the general transformation of modern life by electronic media: one might complain in a similar vein about their effect on family meals, or on the art of conversation. To say this is not necessarily to deny that the loss is real, but merely to emphasize that it is not unique to sex, and so not a problem specific to pornography. It remains an open question whether the effects of mass electronic media in this area of human life are more to be lamented than elsewhere. We look back on the great uproar about horror comics with amusement: the new pornography, indeed! But I suppose it remains debatable whether we have learned that comics were all right after all, or have just become more jaded.[45]

Barry's first point, about fantasy obstructing the reality of the other person, is harder to evaluate. Though it has elements of truth, it comes too close to familiar conservative arguments against fantasy/masturbation, such as those offered by Roger Scruton.[46] A common complaint about both fantasy and masturbation is that men turn to it because they do not wish to deal with "real" women.[47] I remain unconvinced that this is a problem. Sometimes you feel like a knot; sometimes you don't. We ought to resist the temptation to invalidate masturbatory sexuality as somehow immature, incomplete, or inadequate.[48] Downs, in his policy recommendations about pornography, partly inspired by feminist criticisms, though he recognizes that "sexual desire and arousal inescapably involve objectification as well as personalization," takes Scruton's inadequate view of masturbation much too seriously.[49]

"It is difficult to be an enemy of pornography," Kenneth Tynan once said in praising hardcore, "without also disapproving of masturbation."[50] Some feminist thinkers over the past two decades have, in effect, tried to do exactly that. In order to achieve this, they have usually been obliged to distinguish between the good pornography ("erotica") that is a natural adjunct to masturbation and the bad pornography that is seen as dangerous and defamatory. But such a distinction ultimately requires a normative theory of sexuality which cannot be uncontroversial, despite absolutist appeals, whether conservative or radical-feminist.

Given the unavoidable controversy, anything resembling censorship seems a bad idea in principle. One of the fundamental points of freedom of expression, after all, is precisely not to foreclose debate on matters about which there is moral, social, or political controversy. The fact that not even feminists can agree on this issue constitutes, I think, decisive evidence that *censorship* of pornography, at least on present evidence, cannot be justified. Many feminists would agree with that conclusion, whatever their personal reactions to pornography. Erica Jong articulates one of the most fundamental reasons:

> Even though we must raise society's consciousness about the many ways in which images of female abuse pervade our culture, there is a greater danger in legally equating such images—or words, for that matter—with acts. . . . Imagine a society in which novelists and poets could only write nice things about women. How would we show the very real suffering of women in our culture? Suppose we could never write about sadomasochistic relationships? How would we show that sadomasochistic relationships are often the rule, not the exception? How could we change society if we could not chronicle it honestly?[51]

Another compelling practical consideration is the fact that censorship, when available, has been used against women's interests in the past and can be counted on to be so used again—even by some feminists against other women who are only "calling themselves feminists."[52] Elizabeth Fox-Genovese, a critic of those forms of feminism she sees as excessively individualistic, opposes pornography because "it offers us an unacceptable mirror of ourselves as a people," and because "the public degradation of women undermines all sense of community." She says:

> MacKinnon and those who share her perspective find it irrelevant to distinguish between the pornographic imagination and the pornographic commodity. In contrast, I should argue that the pornographic imagination is a private matter and, like humor, from which it is sometimes difficult to separate it, is very much a matter of individual perception. But if we agree that it is not the business of the state to reform imaginations, we may nonetheless recognize that the forms in which imaginations are expressed is indeed a matter for public concern.[53]

We can make such a distinction between the imagination and a commodity in which it is expressed, perhaps, but only with a risk about which I cannot be as sanguine as Fox-Genovese. She is confident that "neither flag burning nor pornography has anything to do with free speech," and that we can simply rely on "the sober good sense of the American people" (as opposed, presumably, to the drunken bad sense of those who are appointed to the Supreme Court by representatives elected by the American people).[54] But her own example of flagburning suggests how difficult it is to separate image from artifact, and so imagination from commodity. Nor is the distinction likely to become any easier in a world increasingly defined by electronic media of communication. In such a world, discovering the difference between one's own fantasy and the fantasy one has bought from society is difficult, when it is not meaningless.[55]

No doubt, the "male flood" of pornographic images complicates the enterprise of determining one's authentic sexuality (or, alternatively, the choice of a sexual life project). But surely Muriel Dimen is right in observing that "people can identify, and empathize, across the boundaries of gender," and that "women, like men, see more in pornography, or any image, than what is on the surface." And Joanna Russ is right to suggest: "If female sex fantasies can't be taken at face value, maybe male fantasies can't either."[56] And Erica Jong is right to declare that "we must grant each sex its honest expression of feeling."[57] But an honest expression of feeling is not necessarily easy to achieve or to

comprehend. As Jungian theorist Andrew Samuels says, "it is clarification of the *image* that is needed in relation to aggressive imagery:
biting is not tearing, nor smearing, nor cutting, nor punching, nor shooting, nor beating."[58] No matter where we think society should end up,
we must start from where we are; we have little hope of figuring out
where we are if we are not free to think and speak and write openly.

After Paul Tillich's death, his widow revealed the theologian to have
been a devotee of pornography. She described lurid fantasy images involving the flagellation of crucified girls.[59] But what these images may
have meant to Tillich is hard to judge. They were sexual, of course. But
are we able to say what sort of beauty he might have seen in them?
What image is more violent than a crucifix?[60] Yet what believer sup-
poses herself to carry violence between her breasts? The crucifix, despite its literal meaning to an eye unmoved by passion, does not seem
violent to Christians, who see beauty in the place of beauty's punishment.

Notes

1. Diane Wakoski, "Beauty," in *The Magellanic Clouds* (Los Angeles:
Black Sparrow Press, 1971), 127; Wendy Chapkis, *Beauty Secrets: Women and
the Politics of Appearance* (Boston: South End Press, 1986), 146.

2. Beauvoir indicates clearly in her autobiography (*La Force des choses*
[Paris: Gallimard, 1963], Ch. 5; *Force of Circumstance* [Penguin, 1968], 255)
that "circumstances and my own pleasure led me to write about Sade. . . .
Justine's epic extravagance was a revelation. . . . Often Sade's narratives were
as lifeless as the engravings; then suddenly a cry, a light would spring from the
page and redeem everything." Her essay on Sade appeared in two issues of *Les
Temps Modernes* (December 1951 and January 1952) and subsequently, along
with two other essays, in her book *Privilèges*. Deirdre Bair, in *Simone de Beauvoir: A Biography* ([New York: Summit Books, 1990], 663), reports with obvious annoyance: "In 1982, when she was asked about the development of her
feminist philosophy . . . she insisted that these three [essays in *Privilèges*]
offered the most appropriate place to start and were examples of her most significant philosophical and sociopolitical commentary."

3. Cf. Kate Millett, *Sexual Politics* (New York: Doubleday, 1970); Andrea
Dworkin, *Woman Hating* (New York: Dutton, 1974); Susan Brownmiller,
Against Our Will: Men, Women and Rape (New York: Simon and Schuster,
1975); Robin Morgan, *Going Too Far: The Personal Chronicle of a Feminist*
(New York: Random House, 1977); Ann Garry, "Pornography and Respect for
Women," *Social Theory and Practice* 4, no. 4 (Spring 1978): 395–421; Kath-
leen Barry, *Female Sexual Slavery* (New York: New York University Press,

1979); Laura Lederer, ed., *Take Back the Night: Women on Pornography* (New York: Morrow, 1980); Andrea Dworkin, *Pornography: Men Possessing Women* (New York: Perigee/Putnam, 1981); Susan Griffin, *Pornography and Silence* (New York: Harper and Row, 1981); Gloria Steinem, *Outrageous Acts and Everyday Rebellions* (New York: Holt, Rinehart and Winston, 1983); Andrea Dworkin, *Right-wing Women* (New York: Perigee/Putnam, 1983); Susanne Kappeler, *The Pornography of Representation* (Minneapolis: University of Minnesota, 1986); J. M. Masson, *A Dark Science* (New York: Farrar, Straus and Giroux, 1986); Dworkin, *Intercourse* (New York: Free Press, 1987); Catharine A. MacKinnon, *Feminism Unmodified* (Cambridge, MA: Harvard University Press, 1987); Andrea Dworkin, *Letters from a War Zone* (London: Secker and Warburg, 1988); Andrea Dworkin and Catherine A. MacKinnon, *Pornography and Civil Rights* (Minneapolis: Organizing Against Pornography, 1988); Catherine A. MacKinnon, *Toward a Feminist Theory of the State* (Cambridge, MA: Harvard University Press, 1989); Elizabeth Fox-Genovese, *Feminism Without Illusions* (Chapel Hill: University of North Carolina, 1991); Marilyn French, *The War Against Women* (New York: Summit, 1992); Catherine Itzin, ed., *Pornography: Women, Violence and Civil Liberties, A Radical View* (Oxford: Oxford University Press, 1992); Catherine A. MacKinnon, *Only Words* (Cambridge, MA: Harvard University Press, 1993); Diana E. H. Russell, ed., *Making Violence Sexy: Feminist Views on Pornography* (New York: Teachers College Press, 1993).

4. Diana E. H. Russell and Nicole Van de Ven, eds., *Crimes Against Women: Proceedings of the International Tribunal* (Millbrae, CA: Les Femmes, 1976), 181.

5. Linda Williams, *Hard Core: Power, Pleasure, and the "Frenzy of the Visible"* (Berkeley: University of California Press, 1989), 24–25, 27.

6. Ibid., 17.

7. I am not discussing harms to those involved in the production of pornography. If the harms were not consented to, then legal remedies already exist; if they were consented to, then perhaps they are not unjustifiable harms. In the case of adult sex workers, one can ask, with Rosemarie Tong, "if women are incapable of consent, what entitles them to be treated less paternalistically than children?" (*Feminist Thought* [Boulder, CO: Westview, 1989], 119; cf. also her "Feminism, Pornography and Censorship," *Social Theory and Practice* 8 [1982]: 1–17; "Women, Pornography, and the Law," *Academe* 73, no. 5 [September/October 1987]: 14–22). Antipornography critics usually cite Linda Lovelace's *Ordeal* (Secaucus, NJ: Citadel, 1980) as a paradigm of how women are intimidated into sex work. But one must weigh against this such testimony as that provided in Frédérique Delacoste and Priscilla Alexander, eds., *Sex Work: Writings by Women in the Sex Industry* (Pittsburgh, PA: Cleis Press, 1987). Do consumers have an obligation to know, or at least to make an effort to know, under what circumstances a pornographic commodity was produced?

Whatever view one takes of this, it is clear that a somewhat different treat-

ment is needed for cases of "kiddie porn," since the nature of the harms involved, the legal status of "consent," and the acceptable limits of state paternalism, may diverge from any model that involves only adults. Tom O'Carroll,
in *Paedophilia: The Radical Case* (Boston, MA: Alyson, 1982), 187, acknowledges that "undoubtedly the strongest arguments against child erotica relate to
the effects on the children involved in its production." His attempts to minimize
these seem rather naive, though space does not permit a full exploration here.
But if one accepts that children are not sexless creatures, then the issues are
complex, and shade into difficult questions about the morality of sex between
individuals possessing different degrees of power. (It is worth noting that the
word "incest" has in recent years acquired a meaning in which consanguinity
is less important than power.) Legislation against child pornography, though
well-intentioned, requires care in its application. No doubt, parents sometimes
exploit their children in ways we want to discourage. On the other hand, it is
also obvious that parents may have views about nudity, or sex education, or sex
itself that are not fashionable, and it is not clear at what point we should interfere in such matters. It is easy to understand why Erica Jong worries: "I do not
think we can afford to have any sexually repressive laws on the books at all,
however benign or protective they may at first seem. I can easily foresee a day
when parents who have taken nude pictures of their adorable babies will be
arrested for child pornography." (*The Devil at Large* [New York: Turtle Bay/
Random House, 1993], 208)

   8. O'Carroll, *Paedophilia*, 195, 196. But the story may be more complicated. John Berger claims in *Ways of Seeing* (New York: Penguin, 1972),
54–55: "In the average European oil painting of the nude the principal protagonist is never painted. He is the spectator in front of the picture and he is presumed to be a man. Everything is addressed to him. Everything must appear to
be the result of his being there. It is for him that the figures have assumed their
nudity. . . . Women are there to feed an appetite, not to have any of their own."
Cf. Gill Saunders, *The Nude: A New Perspective* (New York: Harper and Row,
1989); Lynda Nead, *The Female Nude: Art, Obscenity and Sexuality* (London:
Routledge, 1992).

   9. H. E. Baber argues, in "How Bad Is Rape?" *Hypatia* 2, no. 2 (Summer
1987): 125-38, that "while rape is very bad indeed, the work that most women
employed outside the home are compelled to do is more seriously harmful,"
and "to consider it the most serious of all harms is no less sexist than to consider it no harm at all."

   10. Morgan, *Going Too Far*, 165–66.

   11. For criticism of the victim mentality, cf. Katie Roiphe, *The Morning
After: Sex, Fear, and Feminism on Campus* (Boston: Little, Brown, 1993);
Christina Hoff Sommers, *Who Stole Feminism?* (New York: Simon and Schus-
ter, 1994).

   12. For some of the ambiguities, see, e.g., Ruth Colker, "Feminism, Sexuality and Authenticity," in *At the Boundaries of Law: Feminism and Legal The-*

ory, ed. M. A. Fineman and N. S. Thomadsen (London: Routledge, 1991), 135–47; Christine Overall, "Heterosexuality and Feminist Theory," *Canadian Journal of Philosophy* 20, no. 1 (March 1990): 1–17; Sheila Jeffreys, *Anticlimax* (London: Women's Press, 1990); Sue Cartledge and Joanna Ryan, eds., *Sex and Love: New Thoughts on Old Contradictions* (London: Women's Press, 1983).

13. Joel Feinberg, *The Moral Limits of the Criminal Law*, Vol. 3, *Offense to Others* (Oxford: Oxford University Press, 1985), 189, 154, 157. See also Irene Diamond, "Pornography and Repression," in *Women: Sex and Sexuality*, ed. C. R. Stimpson and E. S. Person (Chicago: University of Chicago Press, 1980), 129–44; David Copp and Susan Wendell, eds., *Pornography and Censorship* (Buffalo, NY: Prometheus, 1983); Judith Wagner DeCew, "Violent Pornography: Censorship, Morality and Social Alternatives," *Journal of Applied Philosophy* 1, no. 1 (1984): 79–94; Fred Berger, "Pornography, Feminism, and Censorship," in *Philosophy and Sex*, ed. R. Baker and F. Elliston (Buffalo, NY: Prometheus, 1984), 327–51; J. M. Davies, "Pornographic Harms," in *Feminist Perspectives*, ed. L. Code, S. Mullett, and C. Overall (Toronto: University of Toronto Press, 1988), 127–45; Alan Soble, "Pornography and the Social Sciences," *Social Epistemology* 2, no. 2 (1988): 135–44; Susan Gubar and Joan Hoff, eds., *For Adult Users Only: The Dilemma of Violent Pornography* (Bloomington: University of Indiana, 1989); Garry Wills, *Under God: Religion and American Politics* (New York: Simon and Schuster, 1990), Part 6.

14. Dworkin and MacKinnon, in *Making Violence Sexy*, 92; cf. MacKinnon, *Only Words*, 109.

15. D. A. Downs, *The New Politics of Pornography* (Chicago: University of Chicago, 1989), 30. Downs points out a resemblance with Herbert Marcuse's well-known critique of "repressive tolerance."

16. Andrea Dworkin, *Right-wing Women*, 219–20.

17. There is danger in reconceptualizing free speech so much that we end up believing that "men telling sexist jokes together in a locker room must . . . be understood as harming not only women, but also themselves through such practices (and thus, as not speaking freely)." Cf. Lisa Heldke, "Do You Mind if I Speak Freely? Reconceptualizing Freedom of Speech," *Social Theory and Practice* 17, no. 3 (Fall 1991): 349–68; 367.

18. Morgan, *Going Too Far*, 169.

19. Brownmiller, *Against Our Will*, 394.

20. Cf. MacKinnon, *Only Words*, 13: "A sign *saying* 'White Only' is only words, but it is not legally seen as expressing the viewpoint 'we do not want Black people in this store,' or as dissenting from the policy view that both Blacks and whites must be served, or even as hate speech, the restriction of which would need to be debated in first Amendment terms. It is seen as the act of segregation that it is, like 'Juden nicht erwünscht!' "

21. Cf. Alan Soble, "Pornography: Defamation and the Endorsement of Degradation," *Social Theory and Practice* 11, no. 1 (Spring 1985): 61–87; 67:

Pornographic fantasies go beyond the merely factually false to the grossly unrealistic, and things in this category are not usefully seen as propositional. . . . Men consume pornography because they find that entering its fantasy world is enjoyable, not because it is sexually arousing to perpetrate discredited theories about the nature of women. Similarly, the massive consumption of romance novels by women is motivated by the enjoyment of contemplating a fantasy world in which everlasting loves are more plentiful that they happen to be; these novels hardly depict men as they are, yet they are not defamatory. The key here is that to engage in pretense is not to disseminate lies.

See also Soble's *Pornography: Marxism, Feminism, and the Future of Sexuality* (New Haven, CT: Yale University Press, 1986).

22. Angela Carter, *The Sadeian Woman and the Ideology of Pornography* (New York: Pantheon, 1978), 37; cf. 19–20:

A moral pornographer might use pornography as a critique of current relations between the sexes. His business would be the total demystification of the flesh and the subsequent revelation, through the infinite modulations of the sexual act, of the real relations of man and his kind. Such a pornographer would not be the enemy of women, perhaps because he might begin to penetrate to the heart of the contempt for women that distorts our culture even as he entered the realms of true obscenity as he describes it.

23. Jong, *The Devil at Large*, 212.

24. Muriel Dimen, *Surviving Sexual Contradictions* (New York: Macmillan, 1986), 187f.

25. Dworkin and MacKinnon, in *Making Violence Sexy*, 88.

26. Cf., e.g., Herbert I. Schiller, *Culture, Inc.: The Corporate Takeover of Public Expression* (Oxford: Oxford University Press, 1989).

27. Williams, *Hard Core*, 23. Cf. Ann Snitow et al., eds., *Powers of Desire: The Politics of Sexuality* (New York: Monthly Review Press, 1983); Carole Vance, ed., *Pleasure and Danger: Exploring Female Sexuality* (London: Routledge, 1984); Varda Burstyn, ed., *Women Against Censorship* (Vancouver: Douglas and McIntyre, 1985); Joanna Russ, *Magic Mommas, Trembling Sisters, Puritans and Perverts: Feminist Essays* (Trumansburg, NY: Crossing Press, 1985); Mariana Valverde, *Sex, Power, and Pleasure* (Toronto: Women's Press, 1985); Kate Ellis et al., eds., *Caught Looking: Feminism, Pornography, and Censorship* (New York: Caught Looking, 1986); Barbara Ehrenreich, et al., *Re-Making Love: The Feminization of Sex* (New York: Anchor/Doubleday, 1986); Jessica Benjamin, *The Bonds of Love: Psychoanalysis, Feminism, and the Problem of Domination* (New York: Pantheon, 1988); Zillah Eisenstein, *The Female Body and the Law* (Berkeley: University of California Press, 1988), 162–73; Avis Lewallen, "Lace: Pornography for Women?" in *The Female Gaze: Women as Viewers of Popular Culture*, ed. L. Gamman and M. Marshment (Seattle, WA: Real Comet Press, 1989), 86–101; Sallie Tisdale, "Talk Dirty to Me: A Woman's Taste for Pornography," *Harper's*, February 1992, 37–46; Lynne Segal and Mary McIntosh, eds., *Sex Exposed: Sexuality and the Pornography Debate* (New Brunswick, NJ: Rutgers University Press, 1993); Pamela

Church Gibson and Roma Gibson, eds., *Dirty Looks: Women, Pornography, Power* (Bloomington: Indiana University Press, 1993); Marcia Pally, *Sex and Sensibility: Reflections on Forbidden Mirrors and the Will to Censor* (Hopewell, NJ: Ecco, 1994).

28. Williams, *Hard Core*, 22, 267. Anthony Storr points out in *Human Destructiveness* ([New York: Basic Books, 1972], 58) that "Freud always seems to have treated the penis as an irreducible reality for which many other things might stand, never seeming to realize that the penis itself might signify something other than sexuality." On Donnerstein's research, see, e.g., E. Donnerstein, D. Linz, and S. Penrod, *The Question of Pornography: Research Findings and Policy Implications* (New York: Free Press, 1987). Diana Russell criticizes Donnerstein's changes of tune in "The Experts Cop Out," in her anthology *Making Violence Sexy*, 151–66.

29. John Rechy, *The Sexual Outlaw* (New York: Grove Press, 1977), 71: "When gay people fuck and suck in the streets, that too is a revolutionary act." Though sexually explicit, Rechy's book is plainly a political statement. The life of gay street-sex Rechy describes and defends has been muted by AIDS, but his picture of what it is like to live as a member of a proscribed erotic minority serves as a vivid reminder that the personal is the political. Individuals whose sexuality is not consistent with the norm may find their politics dismissed as pornography; early feminists had this experience with their birth-control literature. Sade's work, and its influence on the surrealists, ought to remind us that a position does not have to be realistic—or even coherent—to be political. As Daniel Cottom says, in *Abyss of Reason* ([Oxford: Oxford University Press, 1991], 21), "a confrontation with the monsters and abysses of reason may lead us to discover other, more satisfying worlds in that which we call the world." Cf. Helena Lewis, *The Politics of Surrealism* (New York: Paragon House, 1988); Amos Vogel, *Film as a Subversive Art* (New York: Random House, 1974).

30. Downs, *The New Politics of Pornography*, 189–90.

31. Jong, *The Devil at Large*, 209.

32. Chapkis, *Beauty Secrets*, 146. Cf. Alan Soble, "Physical Unattractiveness and Unfair Discrimination," *International Journal of Applied Philosophy* 1, no. 1 (1982): 37–64.

33. Harry Brod, "Pornography and the Alienation of Male Sexuality," *Social Theory and Practice* 14, no. 3 (Fall 1988): 265–84.

34. Ibid., 272.

35. Chapkis, *Beauty Secrets*, 140.

36. Edwin M. Schur, *Labeling Women Deviant: Gender, Stigma, and Social Control* (Philadelphia, PA: Temple University Press, 1984), 179.

37. Cf. N. S. Kinzer, *Put Down and Ripped Off: The American Woman and the Beauty Cult* (New York: Crowell, 1977); R. T. Lakoff and R. L. Scherr, *Face Value: The Politics of Beauty* (London: Routledge, 1984); Susan Brownmiller, *Femininity* (New York: Simon and Schuster, 1984); Rosalind Coward, *Female*

Desires: How They Are Sought, Bought and Packaged (New York: Grove Press, 1985); Naomi Wolf, *The Beauty Myth: How Images of Beauty Are Used Against Women* (New York: Morrow, 1991).

38. Michael Kimmel, ed., *Men Confront Pornography* (New York: Crown, 1990), 310, 318–19. For other attempts at a new male understanding, see T. Beneke, *Men on Rape* (New York: St. Martin's Press, 1982); Anthony Wilden, *Man and Woman, War and Peace* (London: Routledge, 1987); John Stoltenberg, *Refusing to Be a Man: Essays on Sex and Justice* (New York: Meridian/ Penguin, 1990); Ron Thorne-Finch, *Ending the Silence: The Origins and Treatment of Male Violence against Women* (Toronto: University of Toronto, 1992). Cf. Klaus Theweleit, *Männerphantasien*, Vol. 1 (N.p.: Verlag Roter Stern, 1977); L. Hudson and B. Jacot, *The Way Men Think: Intellect, Intimacy and the Erotic Imagination* (New Haven, CT: Yale University Press, 1991).

39. Williams, *Hard Core*, 20.

40. Cf. Dorothy Dinnerstein, *The Mermaid and the Minotaur: Sexual Arrangements and Human Malaise* (New York: Harper and Row, 1976), and various books by Robert Stoller—*Perversion: The Erotic Form of Hatred* (New York: Delta, 1976); *Sexual Excitement: Dynamics of Erotic Life* (New York: Pantheon, 1979); *Observing the Erotic Imagination* (New Haven, CT: Yale University Press, 1985); *Porn: Myths for the Twentieth Century* (New Haven, CT: Yale University Press, 1991); *Pain and Passion: A Psychoanalyst Explores the World of S & M* (New York: Plenum, 1991); (with I. S. Levine) *Coming Attractions: The Making of an X-Rated Video* (New Haven, CT: Yale University Press, 1993). Cf. Susanne Schad-Somers, *Sadomasochism: Etiology and Treatment* (New York: Human Sciences Press, 1982), 87–88:

> If one accepts the fact—and I believe one must—that childhood is never without trauma, that men raised in the nuclear family never completely lose their awe, fear and envy of women, then it would follow that a certain and minute element of perversion . . . and sadomasochism are present in the relationship between all men and women. . . . It appears that the most likely place for the manifestation of these fears and fantasies would be pornography.

41. Camille Paglia, *Sexual Personae* (New Haven, CT: Yale University Press, 1990), 24: "The imagination cannot and must not be policed. Pornography shows us nature's daemonic heart, those eternal forces at work beneath and beyond social convention. Pornography cannot be separated from art; the two interpenetrate each other, far more than humanistic criticism has admitted." Cf. also Paglia, *Sex, Art, and American Culture* (New York: Vintage, 1992). Jong, *The Devil at Large*, 206: "Since sex is indeed a violent pagan force, we cannot blame the artist who attempts to mirror this force. Similarly, women who write about female sexuality, female rage, female vulnerability to rape, ought not to be attacked for mirroring life accurately." Discussions of antipornographic rage range from T. Baxter and N. Craft, "There Are Better Ways of Taking Care of Bret Easton Ellis Than Just Censoring Him," in *Making Violence Sexy*, 245–

53, to Martha Nussbaum, "Equity and Mercy," *Philosophy and Public Affairs* 22, no. 2 (Spring 1993): 83–125. On sadomasochistic sex-play, see, e.g., William Carney, *The Real Thing* (New York: Putnam, 1968); Gerald and Caroline Greene, *S-M The Last Taboo* (New York: Grove Press, 1974); S. Janus et al., *A Sexual Profile of Men in Power* (Englewood Cliffs, NJ: Prentice-Hall, 1977); Ian Young et al., "Forum on Sado-Masochism," in *Lavender Culture*, ed. Karla Jay and Allen Young (New York: Jove/HBJ, 1979), 85–117; Pat Califia, "Feminism and Sadomasochism," *Heresies*, no. 12 (1981), reprinted in *CoEvolution Quarterly* (Spring 1982): 33–40; R. Linden et al., eds., *Against Sadomasochism: A Radical Feminist Analysis* (East Palo Alto, CA: Frog in the Well, 1982); Gini G. Scott, *Dominant Women Submissive Men* (New York: Praeger, 1983); T. Weinberg and G. W. Levi Kamel, eds., *S and M* (Buffalo, NY: Prometheus, 1983); Geoff Mains, *Urban Aboriginals: A Celebration of Leathersexuality* (San Francisco: Gay Sunshine Press, 1984); Claudia Card, "Sadomasochism and Sexual Preference," *Journal of Social Philosophy* 15, no. 2 (Summer 1984): 42–52; Irene Reti, *Remember the Fire: Lesbian Sadomasochism in a Post Nazi-Holocaust World* (Santa Cruz, CA: HerBooks, 1986); Patrick D. Hopkins, "Rethinking Sadomasochism: Feminism, Interpretation, and Simulation," *Hypatia* 9, no. 1 (Winter 1994): 116–41.

42. James B. Twitchell, *Preposterous Violence: Fables of Aggression in Modern Culture* (Oxford: Oxford University Press, 1989), 37.

43. Ibid., 46, 36. In recent years there has been much feminist comment on traditional associations of women with death. Beth Ann Bassein, *Women and Death: Linkages in Western Thought and Literature* ([Westport, CT: Greenwood, 1984], 42), comments:

> The common strand running through all this evidence of the need to take into the hands objects that arouse is the inseparable triad: woman, sex, death. While crematoriums and relatively guarded burial sites now keep us from excessive fondling of skulls, we have substitutes in pornography and the arts. Given our lengthened life span compared to that during the Middle Ages and, it is hoped, our greater capacity to think clearly, we ought to be able to exorcise death from our psyches, and possibly even the tendency to handle its tangible images and symbols. Most pressing of all is the need to pry apart the unreasonable link between women and death.

It seems naive to think that our relatively greater lifespan could help us exorcise death from our psyches. If our culture separates us more from the details of death, that might rather increase our concern with its representation; cf. Walter Kendrick, *The Thrill of Fear: 250 Years of Scary Entertainment* (New York: Grove Weidenfeld, 1991). As more cultural representations are created by heterosexual women and by homosexual men, it may be that the link between women and death will be joined by an analogous link between men and death. But that would not necessarily sever eros from thanatos. Cf. Georges Bataille, *L'érotisme* (Paris: Minuit, 1957); *Les larmes d'Eros* (Paris: Jean-Jacques Pauvert, 1961).

44. Barry, *Female Sexual Slavery*, 213.
45. Kendrick, *The Thrill of Fear*, 240ff; cf. Twitchell, *Preposterous Violence*, Ch. 4. Schur notes, in *Labeling Women Deviant*, 179:

The potential impact of softcore and borderline depictions that objectify and degrade women may be heightened by the very fact of their quasi-respectability. Current trends in the market for pornography suggest a pro-liferation-escalation-legitimation cycle. Once a form of pornography be-comes quite common, it loses its forbidden quality and may no longer excite in the same degree as before. Escalation, in terms of new or more extreme forms, may then be needed to satisfy the growing market. Once those forms have become widespread, the earlier ones—by contrast—may appear "tame," even inoffensive. Softcore materials, then, give rise to hardcore ones; and are in return to some extent "legitimated" by them.

46. Roger Scruton, *Sexual Desire: A Moral Philosophy of the Erotic* (New York: Free Press, 1986); for criticism, see E. Johnson, "Inscrutable Desires," *Philosophy of the Social Sciences* 20, no. 2 (June 1990): 208–21.
47. Schur, *Labeling Women Deviant*, 181: "Students of pornography . . . have noted that imagined sex with fantasized females does not pose for the man the complications that are involved in dealing with 'real world' women." Cf. Kimmel, *Men Confront Pornography*, 52.
48. Cf., e.g., Suzanne and Irving Sarnoff, *Sexual Excitement, Sexual Peace: The Place of Masturbation in Adult Relationships* (New York: M. Evans, 1979); Alan Soble, "Masturbation," *Pacific Philosophical Quarterly* 61 (1980): 233–44; revised in "Masturbation and Sexual Philosophy," in Soble, *The Philosophy of Sex*, 2d ed. (Lanham, MD: Rowman and Littlefield, 1991), 133–57; Nancy Friday, *Women on Top: How Real Life Has Changed Women's Sexual Fantasies* (New York: Simon and Schuster, 1991), Part 2.
49. Downs, *The New Politics of Pornography*, 179–80.
50. Kenneth Tynan, *The Sound of Two Hands Clapping* (New York: Holt, Rinehart and Winston, 1975).
51. Jong, *The Devil at Large*, 210.
52. For example, Marjorie Heins, in *Sex, Sin, and Blasphemy: A Guide to America's Censorship Wars* (New York: New Press, 1993), 163–64, describes how artist Carol Jacobsen's show at the University of Michigan was censored because of its inclusion of a video involving sex-worker Veronica Vero. Ronald Dworkin, in replying to MacKinnon in the *New York Review*, 3 March 1994, 49, points out that "a Canadian censorship law . . . as many had warned, has been used by conservative moralists to ban gay and lesbian literature by well-known authors, a book on racial injustice by the black feminist scholar Bell Hooks, and, for a time, Andrea Dworkin's own feminist writing as well." (For Ronald Dworkin's own views, see, e.g., "Do We Have a Right to Pornography?" in *A Matter of Principle* [Cambridge, MA: Harvard University Press, 1985]; "Women and Pornography," *New York Review*, 21 October 1993, 36–42; for criticism, see Rae Langton, "Whose Right? Ronald Dworkin, Women,

and Pornographers,'' *Philosophy and Public Affairs* 19, no. 4 [Fall 1990]: 311–59; "Speech Acts and Unspeakable Acts,'' *Philosophy and Public Affairs* 22, no. 4 [Fall 1993]: 293–330.) Thelma McCormack, in "If Pornography Is the Theory, Is Inequality the Practice?'' *Philosophy of the Social Sciences* 23, no. 3 (September 1993): 298–326, examines the Canadian situation and argues that women have nothing to gain from censorship.

53. Fox-Genovese, *Feminism Without Illusions*, 110.

54. Ibid., 111.

55. The 1970s saw an explosion in the public sharing of sexual fantasies. Since this literature was seen as valuable in aiding women to discover their authentic sexuality and overcome patriarchal definitions of female desire and pleasure, feminists welcomed it. Nancy Friday's *My Secret Garden: Women's Sexual Fantasies* (New York: Trident, 1973) began a small industry; also influential was Lonnie Barbach's brief for masturbation, *For Yourself: The Fulfillment of Female Sexuality* (New York: Doubleday, 1975). On "romance'' novels, see Beatrice Faust, *Women, Sex, and Pornography* (New York: Macmillan, 1980); Helen Hazen, *Endless Rapture: Rape, Romance, and the Female Imagination* (New York: Scribner, 1983); Carol Thurston, *The Romance Revolution: Erotic Novels for Women and the Quest for a New Sexual Identity* (Urbana: University of Illinois Press, 1987). Pornography, feminists like Steinem said, is about dominance and violence, while erotica is about equality and mutuality. But what does this mean? If a couple takes turns tying each other up, is that equality and mutuality, or dominance and violence? Or is it domination when he does it, and equality when she returns the favor? Is Anne Rice reasonable in considering her equal-opportunity sadomasochistic fantasies "a real moral cause'' in behalf of women? (Cf. Edward de Grazia, *Girls Lean Back Everywhere: The Law of Obscenity and the Assault on Genius* [New York: Random House, 1992], 617.) For Rice's pseudonymous erotica/pornography, see A. N. Roquelaure, *The Claiming of Sleeping Beauty* (New York: Dutton, 1983), *Beauty's Punishment* (New York: Dutton, 1984), *Beauty's Release* (New York: Dutton, 1985); Anne Rampling, *Exit to Eden* (New York: Arbor House, 1985).

56. Russ, *Magic Mommas*, 91. She goes on to suggest that "such fantasies may be a kind of half-way house *out of* violence rather than into it,'' that they are "attempts to partly undo the violence in the 'respectable' part of the culture, where violence has been *substituted for* sexual enjoyment.'' Cf. Jong on Henry Miller. For other meditations on the relation between pornography and knowledge see, e.g., Murray Davis, *Smut* (Chicago: University of Chicago Press, 1983); Peter Michelson, *Speaking the Unspeakable* (Albany: State University of New York Press, 1993).

57. Jong, *The Devil at Large*, 212.

58. Andrew Samuels, *The Plural Psyche: Personality, Morality, and the Father* (London: Routledge, 1989), 209; Ch. 11 speculates about the relation between aggressive fantasy and moral imagination.

59. Hannah Tillich, *From Time to Time* (New York: Stein and Day, 1973),

189 (discovery of her husband's interest), 14 (cross fantasy). Robin Morgan's suggestion that, through Tillich's work, pornography has "influenced all of twentieth-century theology" is, indeed, going too far.

60. Cf. Twitchell, *Preposterous Violence*, 23ff; Caroline W. Bynum et al., eds., *Gender and Religion: On the Complexity of Symbols* (Boston, MA: Beacon Press, 1986), 15:

> While sympathetic to the intention of those who would reshape the palpable inequities in society by providing new images, we find the meaning of symbols, myths, and rituals too multilayered, too complex in its relationship to social structure and social values, to feel confident either that new rituals are easily created or that radical excisions of traditional symbols will have predictable results.

Questions

1. What tension exists between the interpretations of sex offered by social-construction feminists and biology-based accounts like Twitchell's? Can these be reconciled?
2. In what ways can pornography be viewed as inflicting harm, direct or indirect, on women? Is Johnson's treatment sufficiently responsive to these harms? How are these harms to be balanced against other harms with which the liberal feminist is concerned?
3. How is the pornography industry related to the beauty industry in modern society? Can the connections be severed? Do both need to be transformed?
4. Does the fact that feminists disagree about censorship constitute, as Johnson claims, decisive evidence against censorship?
5. Is the fact that pornography is a commodity important in evaluating it? What role does the fact of profit play in evaluating pornography?
6. Suppose censorship is unacceptable. What reactions to pornography are acceptable? Protest? Publicity? Boycott? Destruction? Violence?
7. How important a problem is pornography for feminist theory and practice? Does it distract from deeper issues? Or is it central?
8. Do you distinguish between pornography and erotica? How?

15

Feminine Masochism and the Politics of Personal Transformation

Sandra Lee Bartky

To be at once a sexual being and a moral agent can be troublesome indeed: no wonder philosophers have wished that we could be rid of sexuality altogether. What to do, for example, when the structure of desire is at war with one's principles? This is a difficult question for any person of conscience, but it has a particular poignancy for feminists. A prime theoretical contribution of the contemporary feminist analysis of women's oppression can be captured in the slogan "the personal is political." What this means is that the subordination of women by men is pervasive, that it orders the relationship of the sexes in every area of life, that a sexual politics of domination is as much in evidence in the private spheres of the family, ordinary social life, and sexuality as in the traditionally public spheres of government and the economy. The belief that the things we do in the bosom of the family or in bed are either "natural" or else a function of the personal idiosyncracies of private individuals is held to be an "ideological curtain that conceals the reality of women's systematic oppression."[1] For the feminist, two things follow upon the discovery that sexuality too belongs to the sphere of the political. The first is that whatever pertains to sexuality—not only actual sexual behavior, but sexual desire and sexual fantasy as well—will have to be understood in relation to a larger system of subordination; the second, that the deformed sexuality of patriarchical culture must be moved from the hidden domain of "private life" into an arena for struggle, where a "politically correct" sexuality of mutual respect will contend with an "incorrect" sexuality of domination and submission.

A number of questions present themselves at once. What is a politically correct sexuality, anyhow? What forms would the struggle for

361

such a sexuality assume? Is it possible for individuals to prefigure more liberated forms of sexuality in their own lives now, in a society still marked by the subordination of women in every domain? Finally, the question with which we began, the moral worry about what to do when conscience and sexual desire come into conflict, will look like this when seen through the lens of feminism: What to do when one's own sexuality is "politically incorrect," when desire is wildly at variance with feminist principles? I turn to this question first.

The Story Of P.

If any form of sexuality has a prima facie claim to be regarded as politically incorrect, it would surely be sadomasochism. I define sadomasochism as any sexual practice that involves the eroticization of relations of domination and submission. Consider the case of P., a feminist, who has masochistic fantasies. If P. were prepared to share her secret life with us, this is what she might say, "For as long as I can remember (from around age six . . .), my sexual fantasies have involved painful exposure, embarrassment, humiliation, mutilation, domination by Gestapo-like characters."[2] P. regarded her fantasies as unnatural and perverse until she discovered that of all women who have sexual fantasies, 25 percent have fantasies of rape.[3] Indeed, much material that is often arousing to women, material not normally regarded as perverse, is thematically similar to P.'s fantasies. Many women of her mother's generation were thrilled when the masterful Rhett Butler overpowered the struggling Scarlett O'Hara and swept her triumphantly upstairs in an act of marital rape: "treating 'em rough" has enhanced the sex appeal of many a male film star ever since.[4]

The feminine taste for fantasies of victimization is assumed on virtually every page of the large pulp literature produced specifically for women. Confession magazines, Harlequin romances, and the genre of historical romance known in the publishing trade as the "bodice-ripper" have sales now numbering in the billions, and they can be bought in most drugstores and supermarkets across the land. The heroes of these tales turn out to be nice guys in the end, but only in the end; before that they dominate and humiliate the heroines in small "Gestapo-like" ways. In the Harlequin romance *Moth to the Flame* (she the moth, he the flame), the hero, Santino, "whose mouth, despite its sensual curve looked as if it had never uttered the word 'compromise' in its life," insults the heroine, Juliet, mocks her, kidnaps her, steals her clothes,

imprisons her in his seaside mansion in Sicily, and threatens repeatedly
to rape her.[5] Ginny, the heroine of *Sweet Savage Love* is "almost raped,
then almost seduced, then deflowered—half by rape and half by seduc-
tion, then alternately raped and seduced"—all this by Steve, who is by
turns her assailant and lover.[6] The purity and constancy of women like
Juliet and Ginny finally restrain the brutality of their lovers and all ends
happily in marriage, but one cannot escape the suspicion that the ruth-
lessness of these men constitutes a good part of their sex appeal. When
at last brutality recedes and the couple is reconciled, the fantasy ends;
the story is over.[7]

It might be ventured that standard heterosexual desire in women has
often a masochistic dimension, though such desire would fall out far
lower on a continuum of masochistic desire than P.'s fantasies or the
average Harlequin romance. Essential to masochism is the eroticization
of domination. Now women are regularly attracted by power, its possession and exercise. Male power manifests itself variously as physical
prowess, muscular strength, intellectual brilliance, worldly position, or
the kind of money that buys respect. One or another of these kinds of
power may become erotically charged for a woman depending on her
values, her history, or her personal idiosyncracies. In a sexually inegalitarian society, these manifestations of male power are precisely the instruments by which men are able to accomplish the subordination of
women. Hence, insofar as male power is eroticized, male dominance
itself becomes erotically charged.

One might object that there is nothing masochistic in the female attraction to power at all, that because the possession of power is a source
of status for men, a woman who can attach herself to a powerful man
will thereby enhance her own status. But this implies that the woman
attracted by the athlete is aware only that his muscular prowess can
protect her or gain him the esteem of his fellows, not that he can use it
to restrain her if he wants, or that the student who idolizes her professor
is unaware that he can use his stinging wit as much to put her down as
to overawe his classes. I suggest instead that there is contained in the
very apprehension of power the recognition that it can overwhelm and
subdue as well as protect and impress. Power can raise me from my
lowly status and exalt me; it is also that *before which I tremble.*

P. is deeply ashamed of her fantasies. Shame, according to John
Deigh, is typically expressed in acts of concealment; it is a reaction to
the threat of demeaning treatment one would invite in appearing to be
a person of lesser worth.[8] P. would be mortified if her fantasies were
somehow to be made public. But she suffers a continuing loss of esteem

in her own eyes as well. While one of Schlafly's lieutenants might be embarrassed by such fantasies, too, P.'s psychic distress is palpable, for she feels obliged to play out in the theater of her mind acts of brutality which are not only abhorrent to her but which, as a political activist, she is absolutely committed to eradicating. She experiences her own sexuality as doubly humiliating; not only does the content of her fantasies concern humiliation but the very having of such fantasies, given her politics, is humiliating as well. Two courses of action seem open to someone in P.'s predicament; she can either get rid of her shame and keep her desire, or else get rid of her desire. I shall discuss each of these alternatives in turn.

Sadomasochism and Sexual Freedom

Sadomasochism has been roundly denounced in feminist writing, in particular the sadism increasingly evident in much male-oriented pornography.[9] Feminists have argued that sadomasochism is one inevitable expression of a women-hating culture. It powerfully reinforces male dominance and female subordination because, by linking these phenomena to our deepest sexual desires—desires defined by an ideologically tainted psychology as instinctual—it makes them appear natural. To participate willingly in this mode of sexuality is thus to collude in women's subordination. No wonder, then, that the emergence of Samois has shocked and offended many in the feminist community. Samois is an organization of and for sadomasochistic women which describes itself both as "lesbian" and "feminist."

In several recent publications, members of Samois have tried to justify their sexual tastes against the standard feminist condemnation. Women like P. are urged to set aside shame, to accept their fantasies fully, to welcome the sexual satisfaction such fantasies provide and even, in controlled situations, to act them out. Most manifestations of sexuality are warped anyhow, they argue, so why the particular scorn heaped upon sadomasochism? Why are the acts of sadomasochistic women—"negotiated mutual pleasure"—in which no one is really hurt worse than, e.g., conventional heterosexuality where the structure of desire in effect ties a woman erotically to her oppressor?[10] The critics of sadomasochism conflate fantasy and reality: Representations of violent acts should not be regarded with the same loathing as the acts themselves. Sadomasochism is ritual or theater in which the goings-on are entirely under the control of the actors; the participants are no more

likely to want to engage in real acts of domination or submission than
are the less sexually adventurous. Further, sadomasochism is liberatory,
say its defenders, in that it challenges the sexual norms of the bourgeois
family, norms still rooted to a degree in an older, more repressive sexual
ethic that saw sexual acts as legitimate only if they were performed in
the service of reproduction. Sadomasochism is the "quintessence of
nonreproductive sex": its devotees have a "passion for making use of
the entire body, every nerve fiber and every wayward thought."[11] Some
members of Samois claim that there are moral values inherent in the
sadomasochistic encounter itself, for example in the heightened trust
the submissive member of a pair practicing bondage must have in the
dominant member. An unusual attentiveness and sensitivity to the partner are required of one who has permission to inflict pain ("Good tops
are the most compassionate and sensitive beings on earth"), while overt
physical aggression "can function to keep a relationship clean," i.e.,
free of festering guilt and psychological manipulation.[12]

Finally, sadomasochism is defended on general grounds of sexual
freedom. Here, three arguments are brought forward. First, since sex is
a basic human need and the right to seek sexual satisfaction is a basic
human right, it follows that sexual freedom, in and of itself, is an intrinsic good, provided of course that the sexual activity in question is consensual. Second, the feminist condemnation of sadomasochism is said
to be sexually repressive, perpetuating shame and secrecy in sexual
matters and discouraging sexual experimentation and the exploration of
unfamiliar terrain. Third, anything less than a total commitment to sexual freedom is said to endanger the future of the women's movement
by giving ground to the newly militant Right. In the wake of its crusade
against pornography, so say the women of Samois, the contemporary
women's movement has abandoned its earlier commitment to sexual
freedom and taken up positions that are clearly reactionary.

Gayle Rubin, feminist anthropologist and leading Samois theorist, is
highly critical of a recent resolution of the National Organization for
Women that denies that sadomasochism, cross-generational sex, pornography, and public sex—unlike gay and lesbian sexuality—are issues
of sexual or affectional preference that merit its support. For Rubin, this
puts NOW on record as opposing sexual freedom and the civil rights of
sexual nonconformists. Sexual freedom, she argues, is inextricable from
political freedom. The rejection of persecuted and stigmatized erotic
minorities plays into the hands of the conservative Right, which has
been extraordinarily successful of late in tapping "pools of erotophobia
in its accession to state power," power it uses, in turn, to consolidate
its hold over many other kinds of erotic activity.[13]

How convincing is Samois's defense of sadomasochism? There is, first of all, some question whether the arguments they adduce are mutually consistent. It seems odd to insist that sadomasochistic practices are isolated in compartmentalized rituals that do not resonate with the rest of one's life activity and at the same time to claim that they can enhance the quality of ongoing real relationships, e.g., in the development of trust or the "clean" acting out of aggression. The claim that sadomasochism creates unique opportunities for the building of trust, while true in some sense, strikes me as peculiar. If someone—the "bottom"— allows herself to be tied helplessly to the bedpost, she must of course trust the one doing the tying up—the "top"—not to ignore whatever limits have been agreed upon in advance. If the bottom already knows her top and has reason to believe in her trustworthiness, how can this trust have come about except in the ordinary ways in which we all develop trust in intimate relationships? But if top and bottom are not well acquainted and the activity in question caps a chance meeting in a bar, the awarding of trust in such circumstances is an act of utter foolhardiness. Further, there is little consolation in the observation that sadomasochistic sexuality is no worse than the usual forms of sexuality under patriarchy. If true, this claim does not establish the allowability of sadomasochism at all but only highlights once more the thoroughgoing corruption of much of what we do and the urgent need for a radical revision of erotic life. Nor can sadomasochistic sexuality be justified solely on the grounds that it is frequently nonprocreative or that it violates the norms of the bourgeois family, for there are morally reprehensible practices, e.g., necrophilia, which shock respectable people too and are nonprocreative into the bargain.[14]

I agree entirely with Gayle Rubin's demand that feminists defend sexual freedom, most tested in the case of sexual minorities, against a newly militant Right. But a political movement may defend some type of erotic activity against prudery or political conservatism without implying in any way that the activity in question is mandated by or even consistent with its own principles. Prostitution is a case in point. There are reasons, in my view, why feminists ought to support the decriminalization of prostitution. If prostitution were legalized, prostitutes would no longer be subject to police or Mafia shakedowns or to the harassment of fines and imprisonment, nor would they need the protection of pimps who often brutalize them. However, none of this implies approval of prostitution as an institution or an abandonment of the feminist vision of a society without prostitutes.

The most convincing defense of sadomasochism, no doubt, is the claim that since sexual satisfaction is an intrinsic good, we are free to engage in any sexual activities whatsoever, provided of course that these activities involve neither force nor fraud. But this is essentially a *liberal* response to a *radical* critique of sexuality and, as such, it fails entirely to engage this critique. As noted earlier, one of the major achievements of contemporary feminist theory is the recognition that male supremacy is perpetuated not only openly, through male domination of the major societal institutions, but more covertly, through the manipulation of desire. Moreover, desires may be produced and managed in ways which involve neither force nor fraud nor the violation of anyone's legal rights. Elsewhere, none other than Gayle Rubin herself has described the "sex-gender system," that complex process whereby bi-sexual infants are transformed into male and female gender personalities, the one destined to command, the other to obey:

> While particular socio-sexual systems vary, each one is specific and individuals within it will have to conform to a finite set of possibilities. Each new generation must learn and become its sexual destiny, each person must be encoded with its appropriate status within the system.[15]

From this perspective, the imposition of masculinity and femininity may be regarded as a process of organizing and shaping desire. The truly "feminine" woman, then, will have "appropriate" sexual desires for men, but she will wish to shape herself, physically and in other ways, into a woman men will desire. Thus, she will aspire to a life-plan proper for a member of her sex, to a certain ideal configuration of the body and to an appropriate style of self-presentation. The idea that sexual desire is a kind of bondage is very ancient; the notion takes on new meaning in the context of a radical feminist critique of male supremacy.

The "perverse" behavior defended by Rubin and the other members of Samois is clearly not identical to "ordinary" feminine masochism, to that masochism so characteristic of women that it has been regarded by all psychoanalysts and many feminists as one of the typical marks of femininity in this culture.[16] But it is not so very different either. The "normal" and the "perverse" have in common the sexualization of domination and submission, albeit to different degrees. Feminine masochism, like femininity in general, is an economical way of embedding women in patriarchy through the mechanism of desire, and while the eroticization of relations of domination may not lie at the heart of the system of male supremacy, it surely perpetuates it. The precise mechanisms at work in the sexualization of domination are unclear, and it

would be difficult to show in every case a connection between a particular sexual act or sexual fantasy and the oppression of women in general.
While it would be absurd to claim that women accept less pay than men
because it is sexually exciting to earn sixty-two cents for every dollar a
man earns, it would be equally naive to insist that there is no relationship whatever between erotic domination and sexual subordination.
Surely women's acceptance of domination by men cannot be entirely
independent of the fact that for many women, *dominance in men is
exciting.*

The right, staunchly defended by liberals, to desire what and whom
we please and, under certain circumstances, to act on our desire, is not
an issue here; the point is that women would be better off if we learned
when to refrain from the exercise of this right. A thorough overhaul of
desire is clearly on the feminist agenda: the fantasy that we are overwhelmed by Rhett Butler should be traded in for one in which we seize
state power and reeducate him. P. has no choice, then, except to reject
the counsel of Samois that, unashamed, she make space in her psyche
for the free and full enjoyment of every desire. Samois in effect advises
P. to ignore in her own life a general principle to which, as a feminist,
she is committed and which she is therefore bound to represent to all
other women: the principle that we struggle to decolonize our sexuality
by removing from our minds the internalized forms of oppression that
make us easier to control.

In their enthusiasm for sexual variation, liberals ignore the extent to
which a person may experience her own sexuality as arbitrary, hateful,
and alien to the rest of her personality. Each of us is in pursuit of an
inner integration and unity, a sense that the various aspects of the self
form a harmonious whole. But when the parts of the self are at war with
one another, a person may be said to suffer from self-estrangement.
That part of P. that is compelled to produce sexually charged scenarios
of humiliation is radically at odds with the P. who devotes much of
her life to the struggle against oppression. Now perfect consistency is
demanded of no one, and our little inconsistencies may even lend us
charm. But it is no small thing when the form of desire is disavowed by
the personality as a whole. The liberal is right to defend the value of
sexual satisfaction, but the struggle to achieve an integrated personality
has value too and the liberal position does not speak to those situations
in which the price of sexual satisfaction is the perpetuation of self-
estrangement.

Phenomenologists have argued that affectivity has a cognitive dimension, that emotions offer a certain access to the world. P.'s shame, then,

is the reflection in affectivity of a recognition that there are within her deep and real divisions. Insofar as these divisions cannot be reconciled—the one representing stubborn desire, the other a passionate political commitment—there is a sense in which P. is entitled to her shame. Now this is *not* to say that P. *ought* to feel shame: Profound existential contradictions are not uncommon and our response to them may vary. But it seems equally mistaken to claim that P. ought not to feel what she feels. Her desires are not worthy of her, after all, nor is it clear that she is a mere helpless victim of patriarchal conditioning, unable to take any responsibility at all for her wishes and fantasies.

It is often the case that the less unwanted desires are acknowledged as belonging to the self and the more they are isolated and compartmentalized, the more psychic distress is minimized. The more extreme the self-estrangement, in other words, the less intense the psychic discomfort. P.'s shame and distress may well be a sign that she is *not* reconciled to her lack of inner harmony and integration and that she clings to the hope that the warring factions within her personality will still somehow be reconciled.

The Strangest Alchemy: Pain into Pleasure

If P. is not well advised just to keep her desires, getting rid of them seems to be the obvious alternative. Now it seems reasonable to assume that an unwelcome thought, e.g., an obsession, might be banished more easily from the mind if one could learn how it got there in the first place. What, then, are the causes of masochism? Two difficulties present themselves at the outset.

First, writers in the psychoanalytic tradition have used the term *masochism* to refer to anything from the self-chosen martyrdom of Simone Weil to the bizarre rituals of the leather fetishist, from the hysteric who uses an illness to manipulate those around her to the cabinet minister who pays a prostitute to whip him. Second, even a cursory review of the psychological literature turns up a bewildering array of theories. For the sake of simplicity, let us restrict our investigation to theories of masochism that focus on feminine masochism in particular.

Freud and the early psychoanalysts never doubted that the female nature was inherently masochistic.[17] They believed masochism in women to be largely instinctual in origin, i.e., the consequence of a certain channeling of libido away from its earlier "active-sadistic" clitoral "cathexis" to a "passive-masochistic" investment in the vagina.

What does this mean? A "narcissistic wound" is suffered by the girl when she discovers the "inferiority" of her own organ; this causes her to turn away in disappointment from her "immature" clitoral invest-ment and from active self-stimulation of her own body. She then begins to anticipate fulfillment first from the father, then, much later, from his representative. Since the potential of the vagina for sexual pleasure is awakened only by penetration, the psychosexually mature women, fit for heterosexual intercourse and hence for the reproduction of the spe-cies, must wait to be chosen and then "taken" by the male. The repres-sion of clitoral sexuality is necessary if this is to happen.[18]

The eminent Freudian Helene Deutsch believed that since menstrua-tion, defloration, and childbirth—the principal events in the sexual lives of women—are painful, feminine masochism is functionally necessary for the preservation of the species.[19] Marie Bonaparte believed that the idea of intercourse causes the girl to fear attack to the inside of her body; only the transformation from the active-sadistic to the passive-masochistic libido can allow a woman to accept the "continual lacera-tion of sexual intercourse."[20] Sandor Rado, another Freudian, believed that the extreme mental pain suffered by the girl when she discovers her "castration" excites her sexually; hereafter she can only attain sexual satisfaction through suffering.[21] This seems counterintuitive: Why should the trauma of an imagined castration be sexually exciting? In a later and more convincing attempt to account for the eroticization of suffering, Rado tries to show how some pains can become pleasures: The pain the masochist seeks is expiation, the pleasure the license pur-chased by pain to gratify forbidden desires.[22] The idea that sexual guilt is the key to an understanding of masochism is a common thread that connects a variety of theories of masochism and appears to be favored by the very few feminists who have had something to say on the topic. Women are taught to be more inhibited and guilty about their sexual desires than are men; hence the greater proneness of women to masoch-ism. Rape and bondage fantasies, in particular, are said to allow a woman to imagine herself engaged in wicked but intensely pleasurable activities without any connivance on her part whatsoever; pleasure, so to speak, must be inflicted upon her.[23]

Adolf Grunberger believes that women have a guilty fantasy of steal-ing the penis: "Women pretend to offer themselves entirely, in place of the stolen penis proposing that the partner do to her body, to her ego, to herself, what she had in fantasy done to his penis."[24] Here the principal mechanism at work seems not so much the need to expiate the sin of sexual desire, but the displacement of aggression: Hostility aimed at first outward toward another, gets turned round upon the self. Social constraints, fear of punishment, or else guilt in the face of one's own anger (especially when the parents are its object) make it unsafe to vent aggressive feelings against anyone but oneself. Theodore Reik, in particular, is associated with the view that masochism in both sexes is frustrated sadism. Since our system of social conventions allows men more freedom to vent their anger, it is no wonder that the masochistic disposition is observed more frequently in the female.[25]

The same phenomenon—feminine masochism—is ascribed by Melanie Klein to infantile hatred for the mother and by Helle Thorning, a contemporary feminist psychologist, to desire to merge with the mother. According to Klein, when the little girl finds that the mother cannot satisfy all her desires, she turns away from the "bad" maternal breast—the symbol of libidinal frustration—and seeks a "good object"—the father—who will furnish her with the "object-oriented and narcissistic satisfactions she lacks."[26] Her second object, the father, will be idealized in proportion to the child's disappointment in her first object—the mother. Because of this, the girl will have to repress and, in psychoanalytic jargon, "countercathect" the aggression which exists in her relation to the father: The anal-sadistic desire for the penis is thus changed into the typical passive-masochistic posture of the "feminine" woman. A number of themes are brought together in this account: penis envy, incestuous fantasy, the helplessness and dependency of the child, and the inhibition of infantile aggression.

Thorning starts from the same premise, i.e., the child's total dependency upon the maternal caregiver. But for her, feminine masochism, female passivity, and the fear of independent action in general represent an incomplete individuation from the mother, the failure to achieve an independent identity. The fantasy of total powerlessness is really an attempt to achieve oneness once more with the omnipotent caretaker of early childhood.[27] This sampling of psychoanalytic theories of masochism should not obscure the fact that there are nonpsychoanalytic theories as well. George Bataille has produced a neo-Hegelian theory of erotic violation, while Sartre and Simone de Beauvoir believe that masochism is a self-deceived hence futile effort to turn oneself into an object for another in order to escape the "anguish" of freedom and the frightening evanescence of consciousness.[28]

What is P. to make of this chaos of theories? Indeed, what are *we* to make of it? Which account best explains that perverse alchemy at the heart of masochism—the transformation of pain into pleasure? Is it possible that the variety of things that go by the name of masochism are really multiple effects of multiple causes and that each theory captures something of what went on sometime, somewhere, in the psychosexual development of someone? To whom ought P. to turn for advice? What Sartre tells us in regard to the choice of a moral authority is true of the choice of a psychotherapeutic "expert" as well, namely, that the decision to whom to turn for advice is already a decision about what sort of advice we are prepared to take.

Let us suppose that P., determined to bring her desires into line with her ideology, embarks upon a course of traditional psychotherapy, and let us further suppose that her psychotherapy is unsuccessful. As part of her political education P. is now exposed to a radical critique of psychotherapy: Psychotherapy is sexist; it is authoritarian and hierarchical; it is mired in the values of bourgeois society. P. now resolves to consult a "politically correct" therapist, indeed, a feminist therapist. In order to bring our discussion forward, let us suppose that this second attempt is unsuccessful too, for in spite of its popularity there is evidence that therapy fails as often as it succeeds, whatever the theoretical orientation of the therapist.[29] P. is finding it no simple thing to change her desires. Ought she to try again? In a society with little cohesiveness and less confidence in its own survival, an obsessional preoccupation with self has come to replace more social needs and interests. For many people, there is no higher obligation than to the self—to get it "centered," to realize its "potentialities," to clear out its "hangups"—and little to life apart from a self-absorbed trek through the fads, cults, and therapies of our time. But how compatible is such a surrender to the "new narcissism" (the old "bourgeois individualism") with a serious commitment to radical reform? Few but the relatively privileged can afford psychotherapy anyhow, and the search for what may well be an unrealizable ideal of mental health can absorb much of a person's time, energy, and money. It is not at all clear that the politically correct course of action for P. is to continue in this way whatever the cost; perhaps she is better advised to direct her resources back toward the women's movement. She is, after all, not psychologically disabled; within the oppressive realities of the contemporary world, her life is richer and more effective than the lives of many other people, and she is reconciled to her life—in every respect but one.

Paradise Lost and Not Regained: The Failure of a Politics of Personal Transformation

The view is widespread among radical feminists, especially among certain lesbian separatists, that female sexuality is malleable and diffuse and that a woman can, if she chooses, alter the structure of her desire. Here then is a new source of moral instruction for P., a source at the opposite pole from Samois. Without the help of any paid professional— for no such help is really needed—P. is now to pull herself up by her own psychological bootstraps.

The idea that we can alter our entire range of sexual feelings I shall call "sexual voluntarism." Sexual voluntarism has two sources: first, the fact that for many women, thoroughgoing and unforeseen personal changes, including the rejection of heterosexuality for lesbian sexuality, have often accompanied the development of a feminist politics; second, a theory of sexuality that relies heavily on Skinnerian-style behaviorism. While it is a fact that many women (and even some men) have been able to effect profound personal transformations under the influence of feminist ideas, a theory of sexuality I believe to be both false and politically divisive has taken this fact as evidence for the practicability of a willed transformation of self.

For the sexual voluntarist, individuals are thought to be blank tablets on which the culture inscribes certain patterns of behavior. Sexual norms are embedded in a variety of cultural forms, among them "common sense," religion, the family, books, magazines, television, films, and popular music. Individuals are "positively reinforced," i.e., rewarded, when they model their behavior on images and activities held out to them as normal and desirable, "negatively reinforced," i.e., punished, when their modeling behavior is done incorrectly or not done at all.

> If we come to view male-dominated heterosexuality as the only healthy form of sex, it is because we are bombarded with that model for our sexual fantasies long before we experience sex itself. Sexual images of conquest and submission pervade our imagination from an early age and determine how we will later look upon and experience sex.[30]

The masters of patriarchal society make sure that the models set before us incorporate their needs and preferences: All other possibilities become unspeakable or obscene. Thus, the pervasiveness of propaganda for heterosexuality, for female passivity, and male sexual aggressivity are responsible not only for ordinary heterosexuality but for sadomasochism as well. Sadomasochists reveal to the world, albeit in an exaggerated form, the inner nature of heterosexuality and they are stigmatized by the larger society precisely because they tear the veil from what patriarchal respectability would like to hide.[31] Sadomasochism is a conditioned response to the sexual imagery that barrages women in this society . . . . It is not surprising that women respond physically and emotionally to sadomasochistic images. Whether a woman identifies with the dominant or submissive figure in the fantasy, she is still responding to a model of sexual interaction that has been drummed into us throughout our lives.[32]

The language of these passages is graphic and leaves little doubt as to the theory of sexuality that is being put forward. Models of sexual relationship bombard us: they are drummed into our heads: the ideological apparatus of patriarchal society is said to condition the very structure of desire itself.

What is valuable in this view is the idea that sexuality is socially constructed. But are the voluntarists right about the mode of its construction? And those patterns of desire that may have been present in a person's psyche from the virtual dawn of consciousness: Are voluntarists perhaps too sanguine about the prospects of radically altering these patterns in adult life? Writing in *Signs*, Ethel Spector Person denies the ability of theories like this to account for sexual deviance; why it is, for example, that fully 10 percent of the American population is said to be exclusively homosexual, in spite of incessant bombardment by propaganda for heterosexuality?[33] Quite early in life, many people discover unusual sexual predilections which have been "modeled" for them by no one. "I thought I was the only one," such people say, when they "come out," enter psychoanalysis, or write their memoirs. Furthermore, deviance rarely goes unpunished: Punishments may range from a purely private embarrassment before the spectacle of one's own fantasy life to electric shock, the stake, or the concentration camp. Indeed, the history of sexual deviance, insofar as this history is known at all, is the history of the failure of massive negative reinforcement to establish an absolute hegemony of the "normal."

One can deviate from a feminist standard of sexual behavior as well as from the obligatory heterosexuality of the larger society. Given their theoretical commitments, feminist sexual voluntarists are unable to regard departure from feminist sexual norms as due to anything but a low level of political understanding on the one hand, or to weakness of will on the other or, of course, to a little of both.[34] They reason that if our sexuality is in fact a product of social conditioning, then we can become ourselves our own social conditioners and programmers, substituting a feminist input for a patriarchal one. Failure to do this is made out to fear, or insufficient determination, or not trying hard enough, i.e., to some form of *akrasia* or else to an inability to comprehend the extent to which certain patterns of sexual behavior—for example, sadomasochism or heterosexuality—support the patriarchal order. The feminist analysis of sexuality has, quite correctly, been a major theoretical achievement of the Second Wave; crucial to this analysis is an understanding of the extent to which our sexuality has been colonized. Hence, the refusal or inability of a woman to bring her sexuality into conformity is a serious matter indeed and may tend, in the eyes of many, to diminish her other contributions to the women's movement, whatever they may be. This kind of thinking has led to painful divisions within the radical women's movement. The accused, guilt-ridden heterosexuals or closeted masochists, stand charged with lack of resolve, inconsistency, or even collusion with the enemy, while their accusers adopt postures of condescension or self-righteousness.

"Any woman can"—such is the motto of voluntarism. Armed with an adequate feminist critique of sexuality and sufficient will power, any woman should be able to alter the pattern of her desires. While the feminist theory needed for this venture is known to be the product of collective effort, and while groups of women—even, in the case of lesbian separatism, organized communities of women—may be waiting to welcome the reformed pervert, the process of transformation is seen, nonetheless, as something a woman must accomplish alone. How can it be otherwise, given the fact that no tendency within the contemporary women's liberation movement has developed a genuinely collective *praxis* that would make it possible for women like P. to bring their desires into line with their principles? A pervasive and characteristic feature of bourgeois ideology has here been introduced into feminist theory, namely, the idea that the victims, the colonized, are responsible for their own colonization and that they can change the circumstances of their lives by altering their consciousness. Of course, no larger social transformation can occur unless individuals change as well, but the tendency I am criticizing places the burden for effecting change squarely upon the individual, an idea quite at variance with radical feminist thinking generally.

One final point, before I turn to another mode of theorizing about sexuality—one not as subject to moralism and divisiveness. Those who claim that any woman can reprogram her consciousness if only she is sufficiently determined hold a shallow view of the nature of patriarchal oppression. Anything done can be undone, it is implied; nothing has been permanently damaged, nothing irretrievably lost. But this is tragically false. One of the evils of a system of oppression is that it may damage people in ways that cannot always be undone. Patriarchy invades the intimate recesses of personality where it may maim and cripple the spirit forever. No political movement, even a movement with a highly developed analysis of sexual oppression, can promise an end to sexual alienation or a cure for sexual dysfunction. Many human beings, P. among them, may have to live with a degree of psychic damage that can never be fully healed.

Sex-Print, Microdots and the Stubborn Persistence of the Perverse

The difficulties individuals experience in trying to propel themselves, through "will power" or various therapies into more acceptable modes of sexual desire may be due to a connection between sexuality and personal identity too complex and obscure to be contained within the simple schemas of determinism. Ethel Spector Person has suggested that the relationship between sexuality and identity is mediated not only by gender, but by what she calls the "sex-print." The sex-print is "an individualized script that elicits erotic desire," an "individual's erotic signature."[35] Because it is experienced not as chosen but as revealed, an individual script is normally felt to be deeply rooted, "deriving from one's nature," unchanging and unique, somewhat like a fingerprint. Person does not claim that one's sex-print is absolutely irreversible, only relatively so, in part because the learning of a sex-print is so connected to the process of identity formation. "To the degree that an individual utilizes sexuality (for pleasure, for adaptation, as the resolution of unconscious conflict) . . . one's sexual 'nature' will be experienced as more or less central to personality."[36] In other words, what I take to be my "self" is constituted in large measure by certain patterns of response—to the events that befall me, to other people, even to inanimate nature. Thus, if someone asks me what I am like and I describe myself as aggressive, or ambitious, or fun-loving, I am naming certain modes of adaptation that capture who I am. Since sexuality is a major mode of response—a way of inhabiting the body as well as entering into relationships with others—patterns of sexual response may well be central to the structure of a person's identity.

Person suspects some factors that may be involved in psychosexual development. Following Chodorow, she grants that the larger observed differences between male and female sex-prints may be due to the differing outcomes of virtually universal female mothering for boy and girl children. Repression and fixation play a role too, as does the general structure of the family in modern patriarchal society and one's own family romance in particular. "Direct cultural proscriptions" have some influence too, though "such strictures are not usually decisive in psychological life."[37] The fact that sexual excitement is so often tied to ideas of domination and submission may be due to the fact that sensual feelings develop in the helpless child, dependent not only for gratification but for its very survival on powerful adults.[38]

The psychoanalyst Robert Stoller characterizes the individualized sexual script not as a "sex-print" but as a "microdot," a highly compressed and encoded system of information out of which can be read—by one who knows how to read it—the history of a person's psychic life. Stoller regards as central to a person's sexual scenario the history of her infantile sexual traumas and her concomitant feelings of rage and hatred. Of the various modes of adaptation and response that get inscribed in the sex-print or microdot,

> it is hostility—the desire, overt or hidden, to harm another person—that generates and enhances sexual excitement. . . . The exact details of the script underlying the excitement are meant to reproduce and repair the precise traumas and frustrations—debasements—of childhood.[39]

Theories of the microdot and sex-print provide an alternative to the Skinnerian-style behaviorism of some radical feminists. While they remain within the psychoanalytic mode, these formulations nonetheless avoid the arbitrariness and excessive speculation so characteristic of earlier psychoanalytic theories. More general than the earlier theories, they are, in a sense, less informative, but their weakness in this regard may turn out to be an advantage. One suspects that many classical psychoanalytic theories (including some I examined earlier) are based on little more than an extrapolation from the analysis of a very few patients. Theories of this sort may well be subsumable under the more general formulations put forward by Person and Stoller, for the tales of psychosexual development told by these older theories may represent nothing more than the analyst's reading of the microdots of a limited range of patients.

There exists a substantial theoretical literature on the subject of human psychosexual development. Taken as a whole, this literature is confusing and often contradictory. While highly provocative and at times extraordinarily illuminating, much of it is methodologically suspect, lacks an adequate empirical foundation, and is often grounded in systems of ideas, e.g., Freudian psychology, that continue to generate enormous controversy. While some factors involved in the genesis of a sexual script have surely been identified, albeit in a very general way, Ethel Spector Person can still judge, correctly, I think, that "the mechanism of sex-printing is obscure" and that the connection between the learning of sexual scenario and the process of identity formation remains mysterious.[40]

Whatever the precise mechanisms involved in the formation of a sexprint, it seems clear to me that each of us has one and that feminist theorists have focused far too much on the larger and more general features of a scenario such as a person's sexual orientation and too little on its "details." Does a person favor promiscuity or monogamy, for example, sex with "irrelevant" fantasies or sex without them, sex with partners of her own or of another race? People with the "wrong" kind of sexual orientation suffer a special victimization in our society; nevertheless, less dramatic features of the sex-print may be quite as saturated with meaning and just as revelatory of the basic outlines of a personality; the fact, for example, that Portnoy desires only gentile women is not less important in understanding *who he is* than the fact that he desires women.

Stoller has written that the history of a person's psychic life lies hidden in her or his sexual script. This history and the meanings which compose it can sometimes be read out of someone's scenario but often as not, it is shrouded in mystery—as P., to her sorrow, has already learned. Is Portnoy's attraction to gentile women a manifestation of Jewish self-hatred? Or a feeble attempt to deceive the superego about the real object of desire, his mother—a Jewish woman? Or, by picking women with whom he has little in common, is Portnoy acting on a masochistic need to be forever unhappy in love? The pattern of Portnoy's desire may reflect a mode of adaptation to the conflict and pain of early life, to a buried suffering Portnoy can neither recover nor surmount.

Sexual desire may seize and hold the mind with the force of an obsession, even while we remain ignorant of its origin and meaning. Arbitrary and imperious, desire repels not only rational attempts to explain it but all too often the efforts of rational individuals to resist it. At the level of theory the lack of an adequate account of the mechanisms involved in sex-printing (and hence of sadomasochism) is a failure of *science;* at the level of personal experience, the opacity of human sexual desire represents a failure of *self-knowledge.*

Instead of a Conclusion

P. will search the foregoing discussion in vain for practical moral advice. The way out of her predicament seemed to be the abandonment either of her shame or of her desire. But I have suggested that there is a sense in which she is "entitled" to her shame, insofar as shame is a wholly understandable response to behavior that is seriously at variance with principles. In addition, I have argued that not every kind of sexual behavior, even behavior that involves consenting adults or is played out in the private theater of the imagination, is compatible with feminist principles, a feminist analysis of sexuality, or a feminist vision of social transformation. To this extent, I declare the incompatibility of a classical liberal position on sexual freedom with my own understanding of feminism.

P.'s other alternative, getting rid of her desire, is a good and sensible project if she can manage it, but it turns out to be so difficult in the doing that to preach to her a feminist code of sexual correctness in the confident anticipation that she will succeed would be a futility—and a cruelty. Since many women (perhaps even most women) are in P.'s shoes, such a code would divide women within the movement and alienate those outside of it. "Twix't the conception and creation," writes the poet, "falls the shadow." Between the conception of a sexuality in harmony with feminism and the creation of a feminist standard of political correctness in sexual matters, fall not one but two shadows: first, the lack of an adequate theory of sexuality; the second the lack of an effective political practice around issues of personal transformation. The second shadow need not wait upon the emergence of the first, for to take seriously the principle of the inseparability of theory and practice is to see that a better theoretical understanding of the nature of sexual desire might well begin to emerge in the course of a serious and sustained attempt to alter it.

I am not suggesting that human sexuality is entirely enigmatic. Quite the contrary. There have been revolutionary advances in our knowledge of human sexual psychology over the last ninety years, and the work of feminist theorists such as Nancy Chodorow, Esther Person, and Dorothy Dinnerstein promises to extend our understanding still further. Nor do I want to substitute a sexual determinism for sexual voluntarism. Some people try to reorganize their erotic lives and they succeed. Others, caught up in the excitement of a movement that calls for the radical transformation of every human institution, find that they have changed without even trying. But more often than not, sexuality is mysterious and opaque, seemingly unalterable because its meaning is impenetrable. The significance of a particular form of desire as well as its persistence may lie in a developmental history only half-remembered or even repressed altogether. However embarrassing from a feminist perspective, a tabooed desire may well play a crucial and necessary role in a person's psychic economy.

The order of the psyche, here and now, in a world of pain and oppression, is not identical to the ideal order of a feminist political vision. We can teach a woman how to plan a demonstration, how to set up a phone bank, or how to lobby. We can share what we have learned about starting up a women's studies program or a battered women's shelter. But we cannot teach P. or the women of Samois or even ourselves how to decolonize the imagination: This is what I meant earlier by the claim that the women's movement has an insufficiently developed practice around issues of sexuality. The difficulties that stand in the way of the emergence of such a practice are legion; another paper would be required to identify them and also to examine the circumstances in which many women and some men have been able to effect dramatic changes in their lives. But in my view, the prevalence in some feminist circles of the kind of thinking I call "sexual voluntarism," with its simplistic formulas, moralism, intolerance, and refusal to acknowledge the obsessional dimension of sexual desire, is itself an obstacle to the emergence of an adequate practice.

Those who find themselves in the unfortunate situation of P. are living out, in the form of existential unease, contradictions that are present in the larger society. I refer to the contradiction between our formal commitment to justice and equality on the one hand—a commitment that the women's movement is determined to force the larger society to honor—and the profoundly authoritarian character of our various systems of social relationships on the other. Those who have followed my "Story of P." will have to decide whether P. is in fact caught in a historical moment that we have not as yet surpassed or whether I have merely written a new apology for a very old hypocrisy.

Notes

1. Alison Jaggar, *Feminist Politics and Human Nature* (Totowa, N.J.: Rowman & Allanheld, 1983), 122.
2. *Ms.,* July–August 1982, 35.
3. Maria Marcus, *A Taste for Pain: On Masochism and Female Sexuality*

(New York: St. Martin's Press, 1981), 46. Needless to say, the having of a fantasy, every detail of which the woman orchestrates herself, is not like a desire for actual rape. The pervasive fear of rape hangs like a blight over the lives of women, where it may severely restrict spontaneity and freedom of movement. Even if a woman escapes impregnation, venereal disease, or grave bodily injury during a rape, the psychological consequences to her may be devastating. The aftermath of rape, only recently documented by feminist scholars, may include nightmares, excessive fearfulness, phobic behavior, loss of sexual desire, and the erosion of intimate relationships. None of this is part of the typical rape fantasy.

4. A recent history of women in Hollywood film sets out at some length the increasingly brutal treatment of women in the movies, movies made by men to be sure, but patronized and enjoyed by large numbers of women. See Molly Haskell, *From Reverence to Rape* (New York: Penguin Books, 1974).

5. Sara Craven, *Moth to the Flame* (Toronto: Harlequin Books, 1979).

6. Beatrice Faust, *Women, Sex and Pornography* (New York: Macmillan, 1980), 147. "Sweet Savagery girls cede a great deal of the responsibility to the heroes, saying 'no' until virile and sometimes vicious men force them to say 'yes.' Much of the time the relationship between heroines and heroes is that of master and slave, teacher and pupil, leader and the led. The heroines achieve autonomy only to relinquish it in marriage" (ibid., 156).

7. For a penetrating analysis of the Harlequin-type romance, see Ann Barr Snitow, "Mass Market Romance: Pornography for Women Is Different," *Radical History Review* vol. 20 (Spring–Summer 1979): 141–161.

8. John Deigh, "Shame and Self-Esteem: A Critique," *Ethics* vol. 93 (January 1983): 225–245.

9. Laura Lederer, ed., *Take Back the Night: Women on Pornography* (New York: William Morrow, 1980).

10. Janet Schrim, "A Proud and Emotional Statement," in *What Color Is Your Handkerchief?* ed. Samois, (Berkeley, Calif.: Samois, 1981).

11. Pat Califia, "Feminism and Sadomasochism," *Heresies* vol. 12: 32.

12. Martha Equinox, "If I Ask You to Tie Me Up, Will You Still Want to Love Me?" in *Coming to Power,* ed. Samois (Berkeley, Calif.: Samois, 1981), 36; also Susan Farr, "The Art of Discipline: Creating Erotic Dramas of Play and Power" (ibid., 187).

13. Gayle Rubin, "The Leather Menace: Comments on Politics and S/M," in *Coming to Power,* 211 and 193.

14. For another analysis of Samois's position and an attack on lesbian sadomasochism, see Bat-Ami Bar-On, "Feminism and Sadomasochism: Self-Critical Notes," in *Against Sadomasochism: A Radical Feminist Analysis,* ed. Linden et al. (Palo Alto, Calif.: Frog-in-the-Well Press, 1982); also, in the same volume, Sarah Lucia Hoagland, "Sadism, Masochism and Lesbian-Feminism."

15. Gayle Rubin, "The Traffic in Women," in *Toward an Anthropology of Women,* ed. Rayna Reiter (New York: Monthly Review Press, 1975), 161.

16. "I believe that freedom for women must begin in the repudiation of our own masochism . . . . I believe that ridding ourselves of our own deeply entrenched masochism, which takes so many tortured forms, is the first priority: it is the first deadly blow that we can strike against systematized male dominance." Andrea Dworkin, *Our Blood: Prophecies and Discourses on Sexual Politics* (New York: Perigee Books, 1976), 111.

17. This receives confirmation from a contemporary feminist psychologist: "Masochistic and hysterical behavior is so similar to the concept of 'femininity' that the three are not clearly distinguishable." Betsy Belote, "Masochistic Syndrome, Hysterical Personality and the Illusion of a Healthy Woman," in *Female Psychology: The Emerging Self,* ed. Sue Cox (Chicago: Science Research Associates, 1976), 347.

18. Sigmund Freud, "The Psychology of Women," chapter 23 of *New Introductory Lectures on Psychoanalysis* (London: Hogarth Press, 1933).

19. Helene Deutsch, "Significance of Masochism in the Mental Life of Women," *Int. J. Psychoanalysis* 11 (1930): 48–60; also, *Psychology of Women* (New York: Grune and Stratton, 1944).

20. Cited in Janine Chasseguet-Smirgel, *Female Sexuality: New Psychoanalytic Views* (London: Virago Press, 1981), 29.

21. Belote, op. cit., 337.

22. Sandor Rado, *Psychoanalysis of Behavior* (New York: Grune and Stratton, 1956).

23. See, for example, Marcus, op. cit.

24. Cited in Chasseguet-Smirgel, op. cit., 13.

25. Theodore Reik, *Masochism in Sex and Society* (New York: Grove Press, 1962), 217. Freud makes a similar observation (see Chasseguet-Smirgel, 131).

26. Cited in Chasseguet-Smirgel, op. cit., 97.

27. Helle Thorning, "The Mother-Daughter Relationship and Sexual Ambivalence," *Heresies* vol. 12 (1981): 23–26. For a more complex development of a similar theory, see Jessica Benjamin, "The Bonds of Love: Rational Violence and Erotic Domination," *Feminist Studies* 6, no. 1: 144–174. Thorning and Benjamin make use of accounts within object-relations theory of pre-Oedipal development, especially of the genesis of male and female gender-personality in relation to the maternal caregiver; for the most influential such account within feminist theory, see Nancy Chodorow, *The Reproduction of Mothering: Psychoanalysis and the Sociology of Gender* (Berkeley, Calif.: University of California Press, 1978).

28. See George Bataille, *Death and Sensuality* (New York: Walker and Co., 1962); also Jean-Paul Sartre, *Being and Nothingness* (New York: Philosophical Library, 1956), esp. part 3, chapter 3, "Concrete Relations with Others," 361–430.

29. See H. J. Eysenck, "The Effects of Psychotherapy: An Evaluation," *Journal of Consulting Psychology* 16 (1952): 319–324. For further discussion of this topic, see A. J. Fix and E. Haffke, *Basic Psychological Therapies: Comparative Effectiveness* (New York: Human Sciences Press, 1976).

30. Linda Phelps, "Female Sexual Alienation," in *Women: A Feminist Perspective,* 2d ed., ed. Jo Freeman (Palo Alto, Calif.: Mayfield, 1979).
31. See Sarah Lucia Hoagland, "Sadism, Masochism and Lesbian-Feminism," in *Against Sadomasochism.*
32. Jeannette Nichols, Darlene Pagano, and Margaret Rossoff, "Is Sadomasochism Feminist?" in *Against Sadomasochism.* Many feminists, especially those in the antipornography movement, believe that men in particular will want to imitate the images of sexual behavior with which they are now being bombarded; this accounts for the urgency of these feminists' attack on male-oriented violent pornography. See Laura Lederer, ed., *Take Back the Night,* esp. Ann Jones, "A Little Knowledge," 179 and 183, and Diana E.H. Russell, "Pornography and Violence: What Does the New Research Say?" 236.
33. Ethel Spector Person, "Sexuality as the Mainstay of Identity: Psychoanalytic Perspectives," *Signs* 5, no. 4 (Summer 1980): 605–630.
34. The literature of lesbian separatism, in particular, is replete with examples of sexual voluntarism: " 'Do what feels good. Sex is groovy. Gay is just as good as straight. I don't care what you do in bed, so you shouldn't care what I do in bed.' This argument assumes that Lesbians have the same lifestyle and sexuality as straight women. But we don't—straight women choose to love and fuck men. Lesbians have commitments to women. Lesbians are not born. We have made a conscious choice to be Lesbians. We have rejected all that is traditional and accepted, and committed ourselves to a lifestyle that everybody . . . criticizes." Barbara Solomon, "Taking the Bullshit by the Horns," in *Lesbianism and the Women's Movement,* ed. Nancy Myron and Charlotte Bunch (Baltimore: Diana Press, 1975), 40. For similar statements, see in the same volume, pp. 18, 36, and 70.
35. Ethel Spector Person, op. cit., 620.
36. Ibid., 620.
37. Ibid., 625.
38. Ibid., 627.
39. Robert Stoller, *Sexual Excitement* (New York: Simon and Schuster, 1979), 6 and 13.
40. Person, op. cit., 621.

Questions

1. What is masochism? Explain why feminists might argue that if a woman is masochistic, she is not feminist?
2. What does Bartky mean by "politically correct sexuality"? How does she account for the idea of a feminist masochist? Are these concepts inconsistent? What does Bartky suggest and explain how she defends her position? Do you agree?
3. How does Bartky use romantic fiction to illustrate her point that many

women are attracted to brutality? Does this mean that women want to be beaten? Is there any connection in Bartky's paper with Wendell's notion of the responsible agent perspective?
4. What does Bartky mean by the ''new narcissism''? How does it relate to P's predicament?
5. Describe ''sexual voluntarism.'' What is the sexual voluntanist's view of sadomasochism? What is the problem with this argument?

Index

ableist bias, 318, 332n46
abortion, 9, 86, 197; arguments
against, 153–54; vs contract
pregnancy, 190n29; decision
making, 204–5; government
constraints on, 220–21; new
technologies, 147; parental consent
and notification requirements,
224–25; for privacy, 200–203;
privacy arguments for, 206–7;
right-wing opposition to, 85;
secular moral opposition to, 203;
selective, 166n17; sex-selective,
276; spousal notification and
consent requirements, 223–24;
state laws prohibiting, 202, 222
*Abortion and the Politics of
Motherhood* (Luker), 81–82, 197
Abortion Control Act (PA), 202
abortion rights: effects on birth
control, 197; equality perspective
on, 212
abuse: alcohol and drug, 256, 264n56;
child, 252–53; sexual, 140
abusiveness, perception of, 113–15
accutane, 264n56
ACLU. *See* American Civil Liberties
Union
acquiescent employee, sexual
harassment and, 108–9
acquired immunodeficiency syndrome
(AIDS), 264n58
activists: pro-choice, 204; pro-life,
204

adolescents: Asian girls, 315;
constitutional rights of, 224–25;
dieting behavior among, 291;
normative gender roles and,
293–96; sex-role identity of
females, 293; socialization of, 294,
295
adoption, 178, 197
advertisements, singles,' 178
agency picture problem, 42–43,
68–69
AID. *See* artificial insemination by
donor
AIDS. *See* acquired
immunodeficiency syndrome
Akin, Susan, 312
akrasia, 375
alchemy, of pain into pleasure,
369–72
alcohol abuse, 256; birth defects and,
264n56
AMA. *See* American Medical
Association
ambiguity, to be or not to be woman,
300–301
American Civil Liberties Union
(ACLU), 254, 336
American College of Obstetrics and
Gynecology, 247
American Cyanamid, 84
American Medical Association
(AMA), 247
Anderson, Elizabeth, 176, 179
animal experimentation, 167n28
animus harassment, 112–15

385

394   *Index*

liberal neutrality, 186–87
liberalism, 172, 205; democratic, 216;
  and feminism, 339–40; traditional,
  31
liberation: into colonization, 316–18;
  rhetoric of, 317–18; theory of
  constitutional liberty, 214
libertarians, 216
liberty: constitutional, 214; equal
  protection vs, 211–14; negative,
  209; positive, 209; vs privacy,
  208–11; reproductive, 193–239,
  231–32; reproductive technology
  and, 8–10, 145–284. *See also*
  freedom
The Life and Loves of a She-Devil
  (Weldon), 321–22
lifestyles: right-wing, 88; traditional,
  81, 86
lipectomy, suction, 308
liposuction, 307–8
literature: bioethic, IVF in, 150–55;
  censorship of, 358n52; of lesbian
  separatism, 383n34; pulp, 362–63
logic of identity, 29
Longevity, 306
love: familial, 196; maternal, 178;
  personal, 67, 120
Luker, Kristin, 81–84, 86, 197
Lynch, Mary Ellen, 295

MacKinnon, Catherine, 212, 213, 336,
  340, 342
Madonna, 305
magazines: beauty, 100n53;
  confession, 362; singles'
  advertisements in, 178
Maidenform Viking Queen bra, 305
males: anorexia nervosa in, 299; birth
  control pills for, 248. *See also* men
manipulation, wrongful, 275
Mapping the Moral Domain
  (Gilligan), 301
market theory, 171–72, 186

markets: for pornography, 358n45; in
  women's reproductive labor,
  169–92
marriage, as protection from men, 85,
  87
Marshall, Thurgood, 126–27
masculine beauty, 287
masochism, 12; alchemy of pain into
  pleasure, 369–72; definition of, 12;
  feminine, 361–62, 367–68; P's
  fantasies, 362–64; theories of,
  369–72
masochistic feminists, 12
masturbation, 348
maternal love, 178
McCorvey, Norma, 200
McWalter, Keith, 345
medical autonomy, 268
1986 Meese Commission, 339
men: anorexia nervosa in, 299; birth
  control pills for, 248; rage at
  women, 346; responsibility for
  ending women's oppression, 72n6
Meritor Savings Bank v Vinson, 106,
  108–12, 115, 119n25
Mertus, Julie, 254
Michaels, Meredith, 276
microdots, 377
midwifery, 226
military: discipline in, 133; equality
  in, 123–24
military, women in, 8, 123–24;
  current debate on, 138–40;
  performance record of, 132; proper
  role for, 128; restrictions, 141n17
military combat. *See* combat
military draft. *See* draft
Military Selective Service Act, 124
Mill, J. S., 244
Miller, Alice, 50, 51
Millet, Kate, 31
minor women, constitutional rights of,
  224–25
Minow, Martha, 135–36

pregnancy: contract, 9, 148, 169–70, 173–74, 178–87, 190n29; as control over men, 85; as reason women cannot serve effectively in combat, 132–33; self-determination respecting, 215; teen, 230–31
pregnancy contracts, 187, 187n2; brokerage of, 186; first reported in U.S., 181; markets in, 169; mechanisms to ensure compliance, 184; potential caveats, 185–86
prenatal screening, 148, 149
Presidential Commission on Women in the Military, 138
principle of fair opportunity, 195
privacy, 9, 193; aborting for, 200–203; arguments for abortion, 206–7; of birth, 225–28; consistency with motherhood, 194–96; decisional, 201–2, 207–23, 225–31; equal protection vs, 211–14; family, 193–207, 210, 228–31; at home, 194–96, 202, 238n77; implications of childrearing for, 232n10; informational, 202, 223, 231–32; liberty vs, 208–11; physical, 231–32; planning for, 196–98; and reproductive liberty, 193–239; right to, 208, 210, 234n33, 243, 244, 260n11; tiers of, 202
Privacy and Freedom (Westin), 229
privacy doctrine, rejection of, 213
privacy law, 212
private morality, 218
problems of responsibility, 68–72
procensorship feminism, 343
pro-choice activists, 204, 206
pro-life activists, 204, 206
pro-life women, 79; profile, 81–82. *See also* anti-choice women
pronatalism, 273, 275, 278
propaganda: anti-female, 341; sexist, 341

prostitution, 91, 366; objection to, 174; women who engage in, 79, 88
protectionism, justification for combat exclusion, 131
provocative speech or dress, 111, 115
Proxmire, William, 134
psychiatric disorders, anorexia nervosa as, 297
psychological differences, justification for combat exclusion, 132
psychology, sexual, 379–80
psychosexual development: factors in, 376–77; theoretical literature on, 377–78
psychosomatic family, 297
psychotherapy, 372
public policy, 147
Puerto Rican women, pill testing on, 248
pulp literature, 362–63

Quakers, 243
quid pro quo harassment, 105, 106; unwelcomeness requirement, 109–12

racial discrimination, 248
racial eugenic planning, 148
radical feminism, 41, 299, 341
Radin, Margaret, 175
Rado, Sandor, 370
Ramsey, Paul, 151, 152
rape, 78, 338, 352n9; definition of, 338; on the job, 85
Ratcliff, Kathryn, 148
Rational Relationship test, 245, 252–53, 255
Ratner, Herbert, 247
Rawls, John, 195
reasoning, objective, 26
Reed v Reed, 125
Rehnquist, William, 123–28, 136
Reik, Theodore, 371

About the Contributors

Anita L. Allen is Professor of Law at Georgetown University Law Center.

Sandra Lee Bartky is Professor of Philosophy at University of Illinois, Chicago.

Dana E. Bushnell is Assistant Professor of Philosophy at Edinboro University of Pennsylvania.

John Christman is Associate Professor of Philosophy at Virginia Polytechnic Institute and State University.

Judith Wagner DeCew is Associate Professor of Philosophy at Clark University.

Edward Johnson is Professor of Philosophy and Chair of the Philosophy Department at University of New Orleans.

Lenore Kuo is Professor of Philosophy and Coordinator of the Women's Studies Program at University of Nebraska at Omaha.

Mary Briody Mahowald is Professor of Obstetrics and Gynecology in the College and Center for Clinical Medical Ethics, University of Chicago.

Kathryn Pauly Morgan is Professor of Philosophy at University of Toronto.

Melinda Roberts is Assistant Professor of Philosophy at Trenton State College.

Debra Satz is Assistant Professor of Philosophy at Stanford University.

Susan Sherwin is Professor of Philosophy at Dalhousie University, Halifax, Nova Scotia.

Anita M. Superson is Assistant Professor of Philosophy at University of Kentucky.

Mary Anne Warren is Associate Professor of Philosophy at San Francisco State University.

Susan Wendell is Associate Professor of Women's Studies at Simon Fraser University in British Columbia.